The Editor

MICHAEL NEILL is Emeritus Professor of English at the
University of Auckland and Professor of Early Modern Lit-
erature at the University of Kent. He is the author of *Issues
of Death: Mortality and Identity in English Renaissance
Tragedy* (1997) and *Putting History to the Question* (2000).
His editions include *Anthony and Cleopatra* (1994) and
Othello (2006) for the Oxford Shakespeare, Thomas Mid-
dleton's *The Changeling* for New Mermaids (2006), and
Massinger's *The Renegado* for Arden Early Modern Drama
(2010).

W. W. NORTON & COMPANY, INC.
Also Publishes

ENGLISH RENAISSANCE DRAMA: A NORTON ANTHOLOGY
edited by David Bevington et al.

THE NORTON ANTHOLOGY OF AFRICAN AMERICAN LITERATURE
edited by Henry Louis Gates Jr. and Nellie Y. McKay et al.

THE NORTON ANTHOLOGY OF AMERICAN LITERATURE
edited by Nina Baym and Robert Levine et al.

THE NORTON ANTHOLOGY OF CHILDREN'S LITERATURE
edited by Jack Zipes et al.

THE NORTON ANTHOLOGY OF DRAMA
edited by J. Ellen Gainor, Stanton B. Garner Jr., and Martin Puchner

THE NORTON ANTHOLOGY OF ENGLISH LITERATURE
edited by Stephen Greenblatt et al.

THE NORTON ANTHOLOGY OF LATINO LITERATURE
edited by Ilan Stavans et al.

THE NORTON ANTHOLOGY OF LITERATURE BY WOMEN
edited by Sandra M. Gilbert and Susan Gubar

THE NORTON ANTHOLOGY OF MODERN AND CONTEMPORARY POETRY
edited by Jahan Ramazani, Richard Ellmann, and Robert O'Clair

THE NORTON ANTHOLOGY OF POETRY
edited by Margaret Ferguson, Mary Jo Salter, and Jon Stallworthy

THE NORTON ANTHOLOGY OF SHORT FICTION
edited by R. V. Cassill and Richard Bausch

THE NORTON ANTHOLOGY OF THEORY AND CRITICISM
edited by Vincent B. Leitch et al.

THE NORTON ANTHOLOGY OF WORLD LITERATURE
edited by Martin Puchner et al.

THE NORTON FACSIMILE OF THE FIRST FOLIO OF SHAKESPEARE
prepared by Charlton Hinman

THE NORTON INTRODUCTION TO LITERATURE
edited by Kelly J. Mays

THE NORTON READER
edited by Linda H. Peterson and John C. Brereton et al.

THE NORTON SAMPLER
edited by Thomas Cooley

THE NORTON SHAKESPEARE, BASED ON THE OXFORD EDITION
edited by Stephen Greenblatt et al.

For a complete list of Norton Critical Editions, visit
wwnorton.com/college/English/nce

A NORTON CRITICAL EDITION

Thomas Kyd

THE SPANISH TRAGEDY

AUTHORITATIVE TEXT
SOURCES AND CONTEXTS
CRITICISM

Edited by

MICHAEL NEILL
UNIVERSITY OF KENT

W · W · NORTON & COMPANY · *New York* · *London*

W. W. Norton & Company has been independent since its founding in 1923, when William Warder Norton and Mary D. Herter Norton first published lectures delivered at the People's Institute, the adult education division of New York City's Cooper Union. The firm soon expanded its program beyond the Institute, publishing books by celebrated academics from America and abroad. By midcentury, the two major pillars of Norton's publishing program—trade books and college texts—were firmly established. In the 1950s, the Norton family transferred control of the company to its employees, and today—with a staff of four hundred and a comparable number of trade, college, and professional titles published each year—W. W. Norton & Company stands as the largest and oldest publishing house owned wholly by its employees.

Manufacturing by Courier
Production manager: Sean Mintus

Library of Congress Cataloging-in-Publication Data

Kyd, Thomas, 1558–1594.
 The Spanish tragedy : authoritative text, sources and contexts, criticism /
Thomas Kyd; edited by Michael Neill, University of Kent.
     pages cm. — (A Norton critical edition)
 Includes bibliographical references.
 ISBN 978-0-393-93400-7 (pbk.)
 1. Kyd, Thomas, 1558–1594. Spanish tragedy. I. Neill, Michael, 1942–editor
of compilation. II. Title.

 PR2654.S6 2013
 822'.3—dc23
                                                              2013015039

W. W. Norton & Company, Inc., 500 Fifth Avenue, New York, NY 10110
wwnorton.com

W. W. Norton & Company Ltd., Castle House, 75/76 Wells Street, London
W1T 3QT

1 2 3 4 5 6 7 8 9 0

Contents

CONTENTS

Illustrations

Abbreviations

Texts

Dates refer to the various editions published between 1592 and 1633.

Editions

Boas	F. S. Boas, *The Works of Thomas Kyd* (Oxford, 1901)
Cairncross	Andrew S. Cairncross, *The First Part of Hieronimo* and *The Spanish Tragedy* (London: Edward Arnold, 1967)
Collier	J. P. Collier, *Dodsley's Old Plays* (London, 1825), Vol. III
Dodsley	Robert Dodsley, *Select Collection of Old Plays* (London, 1744), Vol. II
Edwards	Philip Edwards, *The Spanish Tragedy* (London: Methuen, 1969)
Hawkins	Thomas Hawkins, *Origins of the English Drama* (London, 1773), Vol. II
Hazlitt	W. C. Hazlitt, *Dodsley's Old Plays* (London, 1874), Vol. V
Lamb	Charles Lamb, *Specimens of English Dramatic Writers* (1808)
Manly	J. M. Manly, *Specimens of the Pre-Shakespearean Drama* (Boston, 1897), Vol. II
Schick	J. Schick, *The Spanish Tragedy* (London, 1898)

Abbreviations Used in Notes and Collations

ca.	circa
conj.	conjectured
OED	*Oxford English Dictionary*
SD	stage direction

sig.	signature
SP	speech prefix
subs.	substantially
this edn.	this edition
Tilley	M. P. Tilley, *A Dictionary of the Proverbs in England in the Sixteenth and Seventeenth Centuries* (Ann Arbor, Michigan, 1950)

Acknowledgments

It is impossible to complete an edition of this sort without the help of numerous individuals and institutions. I am particularly indebted to Sally Hoare and Elizabeth Welsh for bibliographic assistance; to Carol Bemis and Rivka Genesen at Norton for their meticulous editorial attention; to staff of the Auckland University Library, Folger Shakespeare Library, Cambridge University Library, and the library of Trinity College, Cambridge; to colleagues in the English Department at the University of Auckland (especially Tom Bishop, and Mac Jackson); and to John Kerrigan. It goes without saying that I have profited enormously from the work of previous editors—especially Philip Edwards, J. R. Mulryne, and Andrew Gurr.

Introduction

The Dramatist

The Spanish Tragedy enjoys a double distinction: as the first revenge tragedy in English, written in about 1587,[1] it exercised a formative influence on later examples of the genre, including its most widely celebrated exemplar, Shakespeare's *Hamlet*; but it is also a formidable work in its own right and one that enjoyed almost unparalleled popularity in its own time. Despite the scantiness of contemporary records, we know of at least twenty-nine performances in the five years after its first publication in 1592, and in the final decade of Elizabeth's reign alone it seems to have been staged by at least four different companies (including Shakespeare's own Lord Chamberlain's Men). The canny entrepreneur Philip Henslowe thought it worthwhile paying Ben Jonson to refurbish it with new material in 1602—and the play was probably updated more than once, since the additions that appeared in print for the first time in that same year do not strongly resemble Jonson's other work.[2] *The Spanish Tragedy* seems to have been regularly revived until the closure of the theaters in 1642, and its extraordinary success on the stage was matched by unusually heavy demand for printed texts, leading to at least nine reprintings before 1633. More than a hundred allusions to Kyd's tragedy have been traced in other texts, and its surefire success with audiences is further evidenced by Francis Beaumont's affectionate parody in *The Knight of the Burning Pestle* (1607),[3] and by Ben

---

1. The exact date of first performance is unknown. The imitation of Sonnet 47 from Thomas Watson's 1582 collection, *Hekatompathia*, at 2.1.3–10 means that it can hardly be earlier than that year; the style of the play suggests a date closer to its date of publication (1592), while the absence of any reference to the Armada in the roll call of English triumphs over the Spanish that accompanies Hieronimo's dumb show at 1.4.137–67 suggests that it is probably earlier than 1588.
2. Anne Barton, however, has made a case for Ben Jonson by connecting the powerful rendering of paternal grief, especially in Addition 4, with Jonson's poem mourning the loss of his eldest son in 1603. See her *Ben Jonson, Dramatist* (Cambridge: Cambridge University Press, 1984), pp. 21–27.
3. "When I was mortal, this my costive corpse / Did lap up figs and raisins in the strand" (5.1.303–4ff.); cf.I.I.1–2.

Jonson's backhanded compliments in his induction to *Bartholomew Fair* (1614).[4]

For all the celebrity attracted by *The Spanish Tragedy*, details of its author's life are somewhat scanty. None of the surviving sixteenth- and seventeenth-century editions troubled to include his name on the title page, and we know of his identity only through a casual reference in Thomas Heywood's *An Apology for Actors* (1612), which cites three lines from the play (4.1.86–88) attributing them to "M. *Kid* in the *Spanish Tragedy*" (E3v–E4). Thomas Kyd was born in 1558, the son of a prominent London scrivener, Francis Kyd, and his wife, Anna. He was educated at the recently founded Merchant Taylors' School, run by the well-known humanist Richard Mulcaster, where fellow students included the dramatist Thomas Lodge and the poet Edmund Spenser as well as the divine and biblical scholar Lancelot Andrewes. A gibe by Kyd's contemporary Thomas Nashe, mocking the playwright as an undereducated pretender to wit, who once engaged in "the trade of Noverint",[5] suggests that he was initially apprenticed to his father's trade, but by 1587 he had entered the service of a nobleman, probably either the Earl of Sussex or Lord Strange. Each of these courtiers presided over his own company of players, and it seems likely that Kyd's engagement was a form of patronage intended to support his career as a writer. In May 1593, however, disaster struck: Kyd had been rooming with the turbulent Christopher Marlowe, who was wrongly suspected to be the author of a printed libel stirring up resentment against London's immigrant population. A raid on the writers' lodgings unearthed a number of "atheistical" papers, containing "vile hereticall Conceiptes denyinge the deity of Jhesus Christe":[6] though Kyd was quick to attribute these to his fellow playwright, whom he denounced, he was nevertheless interrogated under torture, an experience from which his health seems never to have recovered; little more than a year later he died, leaving a train of debts, and was buried at St. Mary Colechurch on August 15, 1594.

A scattering of references in contemporary texts indicate that during this relatively short career Thomas Kyd established a substantial reputation as a playwright, but frustratingly little of his work has come down to us. Nashe's characterization of him as an "English

4. "He that will swear *Jeronimo* [i.e., *The Spanish Tragedy*] or [Shakespeare's *Titus*] *Andronicus* are the best plays yet shall pass unexcepted at here as a man whose judgement shows it is constant, and hath stood still these five and twenty or thirty years" (Induction, lines 113–17). For a detailed discussion of the numerous satiric allusions to *The Spanish Tragedy*—none of which troubles to name the play's author—see Emma Smith, "Author Versus Character in Early Modern Dramatic Authorship: The Example of Thomas Kyd and *The Spanish Tragedy*," *MRDE* 11 (1999): 129–42.
5. Preface to Robert Greene's *Menaphon* in *The Works of Thomas Nashe*, ed. R. B. McKerrow (London, 1904–10), pp. 315–16.
6. British Library, Harley ms. 6848, fols. 187–89.

Seneca [capable of] whole Hamlets, I should say handfuls of Tragicall speeches"[7] suggests that he was probably the author of the so-called *ur-Hamlet*, an early dramatization of the Hamlet story, staged in the late 1580s, but unless it contributed to the notorious peculiarities that mar the First Quarto of Shakespeare's tragedy, no trace of this version survives. Apart from *The Spanish Tragedy*, the only works that can be attributed to Kyd with any certainty are a pair of translations, renderings of Torquato Tasso's domestic handbook, *The Householder's Philosophy* (published 1588) and of Robert Garnier's tragedy *Cornelia* (published 1594). There are enough stylistic similarities to suggest that Kyd may also have been responsible for the anonymous tragedy *Soliman and Perseda* (ca. 1589–92), which makes use of the same source material as Hieronimo's playlet in the final scene of *The Spanish Tragedy*. He has sometimes been credited with *The First Part of Hieronimo* (otherwise known as *The Spanish Comedy*), a "prequel" to *The Spanish Tragedy*, probably written to capitalize on its success and published anonymously in 1605. But the style of this play bears so little resemblance to the dramatist's other work that, in its existing form at least, it can hardly be his. Were it not for *The Spanish Tragedy*, then, Kyd's name would long ago have faded into the obscurity to which Jonson was tempted to consign it.

The Play

1. *The Languages of* The Spanish Tragedy

By the time that Jonson and Beaumont satirized their audiences' continuing fondness for *The Spanish Tragedy*, Kyd's play had already come to appear old-fashioned, and to modern readers, their tastes schooled by the relatively naturalistic dramaturgy of Shakespeare's maturity, it is likely to seem stiffly archaic both in its elaborately ornamented language and in its highly stylized visual effects. Whether his characters are engaged in big public speeches, private soliloquies, formal debate, or intimate conversation, much of Kyd's dramatic verse is marked by conspicuous rhetorical and rhythmic patterning: drawing on the figurative repertoire developed in classical rhetoric and taught in Elizabethan grammar schools, it aims not at naturalistic imitation but at emotional and intellectual persuasion. Dialogue between characters makes frequent use of stichomythia, its to-and-fro patterns of repetition and antithesis often pointed up by the use of rhyme—as in the wooing of Horatio and Bel-Imperia:

7. Ibid.

HORATIO
Hark, madam, how the birds record by night,
For joy that Bel-Imperia sits in sight.
BEL-IMPERIA
No, Cupid counterfeits the nightingale,
To frame sweet music to Horatio's tale.
HORATIO
If Cupid sing, then Venus is not far:
Ay, thou art Venus or some fairer star.
BEL-IMPERIA
If I be Venus, thou must needs be Mars,
And where Mars reigneth there must needs be wars.
HORATIO
Then thus begin our wars: put forth thy hand
That it may combat with my ruder hand.

2.4.28–37

Many of the play's monologues and soliloquies employ a similarly dialectical structure. When Balthazar contemplates his chances of winning Bel-Imperia's love, for example, it is as though he were quite literally engaged in a debate with himself:

Yet might she love me for my valiancy—
Ay, but that's slandered by captivity.
Yet might she love me to content her sire—
Ay, but her reason masters his desire.
Yet might she love me as her brother's friend—
Ay, but her hopes aim at some other end.
Yet might she love me to uprear her state—
Ay, but perhaps she hopes some nobler mate.
Yet might she love me as her beauty's thrall
Ay, but I fear she cannot love at all.

2.1.19–28

Kyd, however, seldom uses such language in an inert or mechanical fashion; indeed the play has several ways of foregrounding the self-consciously constructed nature of language, drawing attention to what Patricia Parker has described as "the mutually reflective relation between particular tropes and the orders they exemplify."[8] So the carefully balanced figures of antithesis and chiasmus that characterize the language of the Spanish court work as a kind of rhetorical equivalent of the scales of justice: even the wrangling between Lorenzo and Horatio over the capture of Balthazar is marked by a rhetorical symmetry that seems to anticipate the even-handed equity

---

8. Patricia Parker, "Motivated Rhetorics: Gender, Order, Rule," in *Literary Fat Ladies* (London: Methuen, 1984), p. 99.

with which the King resolves their quarrel, in a speech whose concluding rhyme mimics the harmonious agreement on which he insists:

LORENZO
This hand first took his courser by the reins.
HORATIO
But first my lance did put him from his horse.
LORENZO
I seized his weapon and enjoyed it first.
HORATIO
But first I forced him lay his weapons down.
KING
Let go his arm, upon our privilege!
                    [LORENZO *and* BALTHAZAR] *let him go.*
Say, worthy prince, to whether didst thou yield?
BALTHAZAR
To him in courtesy, to this perforce:
He spake me fair, this other gave me strokes;
He promised life, this other threatened death;
He won my love, this other conquered me;
And, truth to say, I yield myself to both.

                    *   *   *

KING
Then by my judgment thus your strife shall end:
You both deserve and both shall have reward.
Nephew, thou tookst his weapon and his horse,
His weapons and his horse are thy reward.
Horatio, thou didst force him first to yield,
His ransom therefore is thy valor's fee.
Appoint the sum as you shall both agree.
                                        1.2.155–84

In a similar fashion, when the General describes the confrontation of the opposing Spanish and Portuguese forces, his elaborate parallel contructions evoke a world in which warfare is imagined as a species of chivalric ritual:

Where Spain and Portingale do jointly knit
Their frontiers, leaning on each other's bound,
There met our armies in their proud array,
Both furnished well, both full of hope and fear:
Both menacing alike with daring shows,
Both vaunting sundry colors of device,
Both cheerly sounding trumpets, drums and fifes
Both raising dreadful clamors to the sky

> That valleys, hills, and rivers made rebound,
> And heaven itself was frighted with the sound.
>
> 1.2.22–31

Moreover there are a number of ways in which the ceremonious style that predominates in Kyd's court world is placed under strain. Sometimes the dramatist exploits a deliberate tension between the emotion that drives a given speech and the language in which it is couched: so in the third scene we are introduced to the Portuguese Viceroy, grieving for the loss of his son in battle; he rails against the arbitrary cruelty of Fortune, yet the very structure of his monologue, built on the figures of antithesis and *gradatio*, suggests a world governed not by chance but by ineluctable chains of consequence that lead him to a final acknowledgment of his own responsibility:

> My late ambition hath distained my faith,
> My breach of faith occasioned bloody wars,
> Those bloody wars have spent my treasure,
> And with my treasure my people's blood,
> And with their blood, my joy and best beloved,
> My best beloved, my sweet and only son.
> O wherefore went I not to war myself?
> The cause was mine, I might have died for both.
>
> 1.3.33–40

At other times, striking dramatic effects are produced by violent disruption of the play's stately rhetorical norms. The first of Hieronimo's great soliloquies on revenge, for example, begins like a piece of artfully crafted oratory, with its poised antitheses and heavily end-stopped lines. But as the old man's distress grows, the patterning becomes less conspicuous and the iambic rhythms more agitated while the rush of Hieronimo's emotion begins to push across the line endings, until it is checked by the imposition of a rhymed couplet. Though even here the four extra syllables of line 11, suggest the fragility of this formal restraint:[9]

> O eyes, no eyes, but fountains fraught with tears;
> O life, no life, but lively form of death;
> O world, no world, but mass of public wrongs,
> Confused and filled with murder and misdeeds!
> O sacred heavens, if this unhallowed deed,
> If this inhuman and barbarous attempt,
> If this incomparable murder thus
> Of mine—but now no more my son—

9. Compare the way in which the rhetorical control reimposed by a second couplet at lines 22–23 is compromised by its jagged punctuation, incomplete syntax, and the missing syllable in line 22.

Shall unrevealed and unrevengèd pass,
How should we term your dealings to be just,
If you unjustly deal with those that in your justice trust?
                                                    3.2.1–11

Here the stylistic shifts are a device used by the dramatist to mimic the struggle in Hieronimo's psyche between passion and rational self-control. Elsewhere, however, Kyd makes his characters themselves conscious of style and its implications. Particularly striking are Lorenzo's exhibitions of contempt for the ceremonious modes of address that ostensibly regulate social exchange in the court world. Cutting through the stilted conceits of Balthazar's wooing with an impatient "Tush, tush," he urges the prince to "let go these ambages, / And in plain terms acquaint her with your love" (1.4.90–1). For Lorenzo, the first true Machiavel on the English stage, courtly speech, unless employed as a form of guise, amounts to no more than empty circumlocution, an expression of those foolish "ecstasies" for which he reproves the Portuguese prince in their next scene together (2.1.29, 134). Indeed language itself means little to him compared with the more effective instruments of policy through which he suborns Pedringano's betrayal of Bel-Imperia: "Where words prevail not, violence prevails— / But gold doth more than either of them both" (lines 108–09).

In a world that placed a high value on the ordering capacity of speech, Lorenzo's cynicism has dangerous political implications. It was language, Aristotle had taught, that distinguished men from beasts, for it was language alone that made possible the formation of civil society and the establishment of a *polis*. More than that, in the Christian understanding, it was the human counterpart to the divine word, that expression of divine wisdom on which the order of the universe itself was founded. Thus in his *Arte of Rhetorique* (1553), Thomas Wilson wrote that, after the Fall,

> when man was thus paste all hope of amendemente, God * * * stirred vp his faithefull and elect, to perswade with reason, all men to societye. And gaue his appoynted ministers knowledge * * * and also graunted them the gifte of vtteraunce, that they myghte with ease, wynne folke at their will, and frame them by reason to all good order.
> And therefore, where as men liued brutishly in open feldes * * * these appointed of God called them together by vtteraunce of speache.[1]

In *The Spanish Tragedy*—as in Shakespeare's early tragedy *Titus Andronicus*—social and political disintegration is figured precisely

---

1. Thomas Wilson, *The Arte of Rhetorique* (1553), Preface, sig. A3v.

as linguistic breakdown. The anarchic energy expressed in the Machiavel's contempt for mere words finds its counterpart in the berserk gestures with which the revenger answers his own sense of linguistic impotence. Both repudiate Wilson's "gift of utterance" in favor of the brutish language of violence. In the soliloquy with which he begins Act 3, Scene 7, Hieronimo at first attributes an Orphic power to speech, imagining that "The blust'ring winds, conspiring with my words, / At my lament have moved the leafless trees * * * And broken through the brazen gates of hell" (lines 5–9); by the end, however, the supernatural powers prove immune to his pleas: "I find the place impregnable, and they / Resist my woes, and give my words no way" (lines 17–18). Resolving to waste no more "unfruitful words, / When naught but blood will satisfy my woes," he turns to the fount of earthly justice, determining to "cry aloud for justice through the court" (lines 67–70)—only to be met with the King's uncomprehending bafflement. Hieronimo's response is a show of histrionic violence that mimics the vengeance he cannot yet exact:

> Away! I'll rip the bowels of the earth,
>> *He diggeth with his dagger.*
> And ferry over to th'Elysian plains,
> And bring my son to show his deadly wounds.
>>>>> 3.12.71–73

Although it remains opaque to the King ("What means this outrage?," line 79), the wordless eloquence of Hieronimo's gesture is surpassed only by an even more bizarre episode in the following scene: here, in his role of Knight Marshal, Hieronimo is confronted by a set of petitioners seeking legal redress; they include Bazulto, whose grief for a murdered son mirrors his own. Hieronimo first calls on the old man to "be my Orpheus" (3.13.117), imagining that if the bereaved father can only "sound the burden of [his] sore heart's grief" (3.13.119), the power of his utterance will gain them access to the underworld and to the prospect of revenge from Proserpine. But then, in a sudden outburst of savagery that symbolically renounces both law and language, Hieronimo destroys the petitioners' depositions:

> Then will I rend and tear them thus and thus,
> Shivering their limbs in pieces with my teeth.
>> *He tears their papers with his teeth.*
>>>>> lines 122–23

The failure of language marked by these wild gestures is elsewhere suggested by the pattern of biblical allusions that provides a mythic underpinning for the action. These involve the Genesis story of the Tower of Babel: imagined as a second fall of mankind, it accounts for humanity's woeful history of internecine strife in terms of the curse of linguistic division, and Kyd's play highlights the existence of this division in a number of ways. At the simplest level, the convenient pretense of linguistic transparency that allows all the characters, whether Spanish or Portuguese, to speak English is destabilized by the insertion of passages in a variety of foreign tongues: they include numerous Latin tags, substantial chunks of Latin verse (1.2.12–14, 2.5.67–80), several lines of Italian (2.1.41, 3.4.83–84), and even an exclamation in Spanish (3.14.118). Such interpolations were a standard ornament of Renaissance rhetoric, but for the uneducated majority of Kyd's audience they must have seemed as opaque as the mixture of "unknown languages"—Latin, Greek, Italian, and French—in which the perplexed cast of Hieronimo's climactic play-within-the-play are instructed to speak their parts before an equally puzzled court (4.1.171–76). When Balthazar protests that this performance will be "a mere confusion" (line 178), he uses a word whose scriptural resonance Hieronimo himself will confirm at the end of the scene, when he identifies his production with the originating moment of linguistic division, the "confusion of tongues" that ensued from God's destruction of Babel (Genesis 11.1–9): "Now shall I see the fall of Babylon / Wrought by the heavens in this confusion" (lines192–93).[2]

The self-consciousness with which Hieronimo's brief soliloquy hints at the hidden significance of his entertainment picks up his earlier promise to Batlthazar:

> And I myself in an oration—
> And with a strange and wondrous show besides,
> That I will have there behind a curtain—
> Assure yourself shall make the matter known;
>
> lines 182–85

Communication, as the revelatory power of his "strange and wondrous show" reminds us, can be visual as well as verbal. The gestural vocabulary of the dumb show with which Revenge instructs Andrea's Ghost on the "mystery" of delayed retribution (3.15.26–36) is the most obvious case in point, but the main action of *The Spanish Tragedy* is full of stylized visual devices, many of them consciously

2. All three translations of the Bible available to Kyd treat *Babel* and *Babylon* as interchangeable names, and each speaks of "confusion" as God's punishment for the presumption embodied in the Tower of Babel: in the Geneva Bible (1560) the key passage in verse 7 reads: "Come on, let vs goe downe, and there *confound* their language, that euery one perceiue not anothers speache"; and the translators supply a marginal gloss: "By this great plague of the *confusion of tongues*, appeareth Gods horrible iudgement against mans pride and vaine glorie" (emphasis added). The same phrase is repeated in the summary at the head of chapter 11 in the Bishops' Bible (1568), while the Great Bible (1539) annotates the passage with the note "Confusyon." For a more extensive account of the Babel/Babylon motif in the play, see S. F. Johnson, "*The Spanish Tragedy* or Babylon Revisited," in *Essays on Shakespeare and Elizabethan Drama. In Honour of Hardin Craig,* ed. Richard Hosley (London: Routledge, 1963), pp. 23–36.

devised by the characters themselves, which the audience (like the courtly onlookers at Hieronimo's play) must strive to interpret. In Act 1, Scene 3, for example, the Portuguese Viceroy accompanies his formal lament over the apparent death of Balthazar with a gesture that may at first seem extravagantly melodramatic

> But wherefore sit I in a regal throne?
> This better fits a wretch's endless moan;
> *Falls to the ground.*
> Yet this is higher than my fortune's reach,
> And therefore better than my state deserves.
> Ay, ay, this earth, image of melancholy,
> Seeks him whom fates adjudge to misery:
> Here let me lie, now am I at the lowest.
>
> lines 8–14

However, the extravagance makes dramatic sense once we realize that the Viceroy is engaged in a deliberately contrived performance, designed (as his reference to fortune suggests) to milk the pathos of his situation by linking it to the iconography of the goddess Fortuna, to whose capricious interventions so much human misery could be attributed: traditionally represented as a blindfold woman, Fortune sometimes stands on a rolling stone, blown about by the haphazard violence of the winds, or she is shown turning her wheel, at the apex of which sits a king on his throne, who then tumbles downward, until (like the Viceroy) he lies prostrate on the earth, with his crown fallen from his head (Fig. 1):

> Yes, Fortune may bereave me of my crown:
> Here take it now; let Fortune do her worst,
>
>   *   *   *
>
> Fortune is blind and sees not my deserts,
>
>   *   *   *
>
> Suppose that she could pity me, what then?
> What help can be expected at her hands,
> Whose foot standing on a rolling stone
> And mind more mutable then fickle winds?
>
> lines 18–30

Hieronimo makes use of a similarly well-scripted gesture at the beginning of 3.12, when he delivers his soliloquy clutching "*a poniard in one hand, and a rope in the other*" (SD)—stock emblems that identify him as an embodiment of suicidal Despair. Such demonstrations belong on a continuum of histrionic display that ranges from the court entertainments organized by the protagonist in 1.4 and 4.4 and Revenge's allegorical dumb show in 3.15, to the improvised spectacle

The Goddess Fortuna Casts a King from his Throne.

The Spanish Tragedie:

OR,

Hieronimo is mad againe.

Containing the lamentable end of *Don Horatio*, and
Belimperia; with the pittifull death of *Hieronimo*.

Newly corrected, amended, and enlarged with new
Additions of the *Painters* part, and others, as
it hath of late been diuers times acted.

LONDON,
Printed by W. White, for I. White and T. Langley,
and are to be sold at their Shop ouer against the
Sarazens head without New-gate. 1615.

Hieronimo Discovering Horatio's Body: 1615 Title-Page Woodcut.
© British Library.

through which Lorenzo transforms Horatio's murder into a tableau titled "the fruits of love." Unlike the "show" or "spectacle" (4.4.89, 113) with which Hieronimo's confronts the court in the final scene, this one lacks an accompanying "oration * * * [to] make the matter known" (4.1.182–85); instead the audience is meant to read it through the visual suggestiveness of the arbor—the stylized garden whose dramatic importance is foregrounded by the title page woodcut of the 1615 edition (Fig. 2). Hieronimo's description of the arbor as "this sacred bower" (2.5.27), together with Isabella's denunciation of "this [accursed] garden plot" (4.2.12–13), implicitly identifies it with the gardens of scripture, both the violated earthly paradise of Eden, the scene of Satan's seductive plot, and its New Testament counterpart Gethsemane, which emblematic practice assimilated with Golgotha, the place of crucifixion (Fig. 3). Lorenzo's sarcastic gibe transforms the young man's body, as it hangs *in the arbor* (2.4.53 SD), into a vicious parody of Christ's crucifixion, as it was represented in the emblem tradition, by which the Cross became a tree festooned with fruits of divine love for humankind (Fig. 4).

The parallel is reinforced in the final scene where Hieronimo concludes his revenge play with an epilogue whose punning reference to a "garden plot * * * Where hanging on a tree I found my son" (4.4.104–11) echoes descriptions of Christ's betrayal in the garden of Gethsemane and his execution on the Cross/"tree" (2 Peter 2.24).[3] The significance of this spectacle is complicated by its political suggestiveness, for the garden was also a familiar emblem for the state itself, as it is in *Richard II*, in whose garden scene the "blessed plot" (2.1.50) of England must have been represented by an arbor like that in Kyd's play. In *Richard II*, the gardener's role as "old Adam's likeness" (3.4.74), mirrors that of the ruler in a kingdom figured as "this other Eden" (2.1.0). By the end of Shakespeare's play, however, England's "demi-paradise" has been reduced to "the field of Golgotha and dead men's skulls" (4.1.0), and much the same transformation occurs in *The Spanish Tragedy* as Hieronimo's "sacred bower," having become a place of death, is symbolically laid waste by the frantic Isabella:

---

3. Biblical commentary habitually identified the crucifixion tree as the redemptive counterpart of the fatal Tree of Knowledge in Genesis. The suggestion of parodic sacrifice is underlined by the author of Addition 4, which adds lines in which the distraught Hieronimo is made to echo Lorenzo's blasphemous gibe about "the fruits of love":

> At last it grew, and grew, and bore and bore,
> Till at the length
> It grew a gallows, and did bear our son:
> It bore thy fruit and mine.
>
> 3.12a.[68–71]

Hieronimo then instructs the Painter to "paint me a youth *** hanging upon this tree *** [surrounded by "notorious villains" with] beards *** of Judas his own color" (lines [124–30]).

The Gardens of Eden and Gethsemane/Golgotha: The Typology of Original Sin, Death, and Redemption. By permission of the Folger Shakespeare Library.

> I will revenge myself upon this place,
> Where thus they murdered my belovèd son.
>   *She cuts down the arbor.*
> Down with these branches and these loathsome boughs
> Of this unfortunate and fatal pine;
> Down with them, Isabella, rend them up,
> And burn the roots from whence the rest is sprung:

The Fruits of Love. After an engraving dated 1512.

I will not leave a root, a stalk, a tree,
A bough, a branch, a blossom, nor a leaf,
No, not an herb within this garden plot,
Accursed complot of my misery.
Fruitless for ever may this garden be,
Barren the earth, and blissless whosoever
Imagines not to keep it unmanured!
An eastern wind commixed with noisome airs
Shall blast the plants and the young saplings;
The earth with serpents shall be pesterèd,

> And passengers for fear to be infect,
> Shall stand aloof, and, looking at it, tell:
> "There, murdered, died the son of Isabel.
>
> 4.2.4–22

The apocalyptic language of this speech—following, as it imme-diately does, Hieronimo's promise to stage "the fall of Babylon"—echoes the biblical prophecy in which that ancient city, famous for its hanging gardens, is reduced to the condition of wilderness by the wrath of God: "Babylon shall become an heape of stones, a dwellyng place for dragons, a fearefulnesse and wonderyng, and no man shall dwell there" (Jeremiah 51.37).[4] The parallel explains why Kyd chose to call his Portuguese prince by the fateful name of Balthazar; for, in the two officially sanctioned translations available to Elizabethans, this (rather than the now more familiar form, Belshazzar) was the name of the last king of Babylon. Thus, even as the confusion of tongues in Hieronimo's play recalls the original fall of Babel, its assimilation with Babylon transforms the revels at the Spanish court into a reenactment of the dreadful feast at which Balthasar/Belshaz-zar was warned "God hath numbred thy kingdome, and brought it to an ende" (Daniel 5.26). For Kyd's audience this recollection of divine retribution against the enemy of God's chosen people will have had powerful political resonances, for the destruction of Babylon, "the mother of whoredome," described in three books of the Old Testa-ment and made central to the apocalyptic vision of Revelation (14.8, 15.19, 17.5), was taken by Protestants to foreshadow the destruction of that scourge of true religion, papal Rome—"the whore of Babylon"—herself. In this context Kyd's title takes on additional meaning: it transforms *The Spanish Tragedy* from a drama of personal revenge into an exercise in theatrical prophecy, announcing the apocalyptic destruction of a self-proclaimed Catholic monarchy that, to Protes-tant English eyes at least, represented as the militant arm of the papa-cy.[5] From this perspective, Soliman, the Oriental tyrant and scourge of Christians in Hieronimo's play, provides a perfect mirror for that enemy of true religion, the papal Antichrist.

---

4. Quotation from the Bishops' Bible (from which, unless otherwise specified, all biblical texts are quoted). Cf. Isaiah 13.19–22, Revelation 18.2.
5. Although we do not know the exact date on which *The Spanish Tragedy* was first per-formed, it was evidently written at the height of the conflict between England and its most powerful Catholic adversary. See above, p. xi, n.1.

2. The Tragedy of Revenge

Viewed from this point of view, Kyd's play might easily be dismissed as a patriotic display of sectarian tub thumping—the Elizabethan theater's contribution to the war effort, as it were. But that would leave unexplained its continuing popularity until well into the 1630s, long after the main crisis of relations with Spain had passed. More important, it would make it difficult to account for its powerful influence on later playwrights, especially its shaping role in the evolution of one of the most distinctive forms of early modern drama: revenge tragedy. It is in this context that Kyd's once intimate relationship with the iconoclastic Christopher Marlowe becomes significant, for, in its own way, *The Spanish Tragedy* is as subversive as anything that Marlowe wrote, and its heterodoxy has everything to do with its skeptical attitude toward the operation of justice and the law and toward the forms of social order that they were supposed to guarantee. It is a play, that is to say, which, while ostensibly imagining the overthrow of those forces that threatened England from without, actually contrives to speak to the unvoiced (and largely unvoiceable) resentments that threatened it from within.[6]

In Ben Jonson's induction to *Bartholomew Fair,* the Scrivener mocks the reactionary opinions of a "commission of wit * * * that sits on the bench [to] indict and arraign plays daily * * * swear[ing] that *Jeronimo* or *Andronicus* are the best plays yet" (lines 101–09). Jonson's legal metaphors are carefully chosen, for the point of his gibe is that *The Spanish Tragedy* and Shakespeare's *Titus Andronicus* are linked by more than mere chronology: both plays are preoccupied with judgment of another kind and with the radical issues of justice and injustice raised by the controversial ethics of revenge.[7]

Revenge plots, as Hollywood long ago discovered, have an abiding fascination for audiences everywhere: deeply engrained in the human psyche is the desire for payback famously exemplified in the Old Testament insistence on sanguinary reciprocity: "he shall geue life for life, Eye for eye, tothe for tothe, hande for hande, foote

6. C. L. Barber's spirited essay "Unbroken Passion: Social Piety and Outrage in *The Spanish Tragedy,*" in his *Creating Elizabethan Tragedy: The Theater of Marlowe and Kyd* (Chicago: University of Chicago Press, 1988), pp. 131–63, sees *The Spanish Tragedy* as "an heroic-nihilistic play. . . . Heroic insofar as it is a play of protest, grounded in a demonstration of the ruthless forces latent beneath the ideal of benevolent royalty sustaining a sanctified society—forces ready to destroy at need the new high middle-class servants of the state. . . . when their rising fortunes challenged case interests" (p. 159). A more nuanced and historically detailed approach to the treatment of rank in the play, with a strong emphasis on issues of gender, is Frank Whigham's "Forcing Divorce in *The Spanish Tragedy,*" in *Seizures of the Will in Early Modern English Drama* (Cambridge: Cambridge University Press, 1996), pp. 22–62.
7. For the knowing, the joke is given further spice by putting it in the mouth of a man who shares Kyd's old profession of scrivener—a trade that (as the Scrivener's formal covenant with the audience reminds us) had close connections with the law.

for foote, Burnyng for burnyng, wounde for wounde, strype for strype' (Exodus 21: 23–5).[8] But the particular form of revenge narratives is determined by the circumstances of their production. So, for example, the most popular of all Japanese revenge stories, *Chūshingura*—the story of forty-seven samurai who exact a long delayed revenge on the powerful *daimyo* responsible for their own lord's death—has some marked structural resemblances to *The Spanish Tragedy* as well as to *Hamlet*: where Hieronimo and Hamlet veil their intentions with a show of madness, "Dissembling quiet in unquietness" as Kyd's hero puts it (3.13.30), the samurai leader conceals his vindictive design by debauching himself in the merchant quarter of the capital while awaiting his opportunity; in each case the demands of honor are pitched against rules of society and the might of authority, and in each case too, these contradictory imperatives drive the protagonists to self-destruction. But while the emphasis of the Japanese story is upon the *bushido* ethos of group loyalty, English revenge tragedies concentrate on the predicament of a single protagonist who is forced to bear the burden of revenge alone.

Although the term *revenge tragedy* was not in use in his own time, Kyd can fairly claim to have established the set of conventions that identify a distinct subgenre within the fairly permissive definitions of early modern tragedy. It is often assumed that he simply adapted these practices from the classical past, especially from the dramatist with whom Nashe associated him, Lucius Annaeus Seneca (3 B.C.E.–65 C.E.), whose style he frequently imitates and from whose plays he quotes almost as often as he does from scripture.[9] But for Seneca the fascination of revenge lay in its murderous chains of cause and effect, the mechanisms of fatality by which a whole house could be brought to destruction; by contrast, the imaginative focus of Kyd's play, though its plot involves the destruction of a Spanish dynasty, is almost entirely fixed on the emotional suffering of an isolated individual, one who finds himself caught between his official function as the agent of royal justice and his overwhelming need to exact private retribution for a murder that lies beyond legal redress. The great originality of *The Spanish Tragedy* lies here: it was the first play on the English stage to dramatize the conflict between the appetite for extra-judicial vengeance and the demands of the law. In this it spoke directly to the stresses and anxieties of its own time.[1]

8. For a brilliant account of the long history of revenge as a literary motif, see John Kerrigan, *Revenge Tragedy: Aeschylus to Armageddon* (Oxford: Clarendon, 1996).
9. For a through analysis of Kyd's generic debts to Seneca, see Gordon Braden, *Renaissance Tragedy and the Seneca Tradition* (New Haven, CT: Yale University Press, 1985), esp. pp. 201–15.
1. See Gregory Colòn Semenza, "*The Spanish Tragedy* and Metatheatre," in *English Revenge Tragedy*, ed. Emma Smith and Garrett Sullivan (Cambridge: Cambridge University Press, 2010), pp. 153–62; Michael Neill, "English Revenge Tragedy," in *A Companion*

The bloody internecine wars that had divided England in the fifteenth century, followed by the complicated history of betrayal and counterbetrayal attendant on the religious upheavals of the Reformation, left a legacy of grudges and feuds, which the Tudors sought to control by insisting on the absolute authority of the law to address all grievances. Indeed it was the ruler's claim (as the divinely mandated "fountainhead of justice") to guarantee equal redress to every subject under the law which helped establish the legitimacy of what had originally been an usurping dynasty. The essayist Francis Bacon—himself a prominent lawyer, who was later to become attorney General and ultimately lord chancellor—echoed the official Tudor position when he wrote of revenge as savage manifestation of man's fallen nature: a kind of "wild justice, which the more man's nature runs to, the more ought law to root it out."[2] The appetite for vengeance, Bacon insists, is a symptom of humankind's fallen condition and one that threatens to undermine the very institution on which the social order depends, for, whereas the initial offense "doth but offend the law, revenge of that wrong putteth the law out of office."[3]

Yet, as *The Spanish Tragedy* repeatedly implies, the administration of law, in the obsessively litigious society to which he belonged, was often haphazard and sometimes corrupt. While the determination of private lawsuits could be maddeningly slow, fueling the vindictive impulses of plaintiffs,[4] criminal punishments could be brutally swift and were subject to the unscrupulous machinations of power and wealth. Kyd seems to have remembered a particularly scandalous episode in which Elizabeth's favorite, the Earl of Leicester, ensured the execution of an inconvenient accomplice, while pretending to work for his release—"a piece of gentlemanlike knavery" mirrored in the trick by which Lorenzo consigns the gullible Pedringano to his death (3.5.7–8).[5] Leicester was in a position to exploit the privilege of royal patronage, but often enough in this world, even the most powerful families could find themselves cheated of justice—as witness a bizarre painting that commemorates the murder of Lord Darnley, husband of Mary Queen of Scots, by her lover, the Earl of Bothwell (Fig. 5). Commissioned by the victim's parents, the Darnley memorial includes a portrait of Mary's heir, the infant James, with a speech bubble bearing the legend "Arise, O Lord, and

to Tragedy ed. Rebecca Bushnell (Oxford: Blackwell, 2005), pp. 328–50; and Katherine Maus's excellent introduction to her edition of *Four Revenge Tragedies* (Oxford: Oxford University Press, 1995).

2. "Of Revenge" in *Francis Bacon's Essays*, intro. Oliphant Smeaton (London: Dent, 1906), p. 13. A full text of Bacon's essay is printed on pp. 150–51.

3. ibid.

4. The numbers of private suits multiplied so rapidly between 1550 and 1625 that the courts became jammed with cases, extending the average decision time to five years, while enforcement of the verdict might be an even more protracted business.

5. Philip Edwards (ed.), *The Spanish Tragedy* (London; Methuen, 1959), p. xlix.

Revenge Painting: The Darnley Memorial. © Leeds Museums and Art Galleries (Temple Newsam House). UK/The Bridgeman Art Library.

avenge the innocent blood of the king my father, and I beseech thee defend me with thy right hand."[6] Vividly illustrating the degree to which the duty of revenge was ingrained in early modern culture, the image was a token designed to goad the conscience of Darnley's kin: a more sophisticated counterpart of Hieronimo's grisly memento— the "handkerchief besmeared with blood" that he plucks from Horatio's corpse, (2.5.51–52)[7]—it has an even more direct equivalent in the most powerful of the later additions to Kyd's play, where the embittered Knight Marshal is made to commission an elaborately detailed picture from the Painter that identifiably belongs to the same genre as the Scottish revenge painting (3.12a.[110–58]).

6. An inset in the painting shows the defeat of Mary and Bothwell's forces by a confederation of Scottish lords at the battle of Carberry in 1567. In an odd anticipation of Kyd's garden murder, the rebels' banner features the corpse of Darnley lying under a tree, with the motto "Judge and Revenge my cause, O Lord."

7. This cloth probably embodies the play's whole sequence of revenges because as Mulryne points out, it is almost certainly to be identified with the scarf given to Andrea as a chivalric "favor" by Bel-Imperia, taken from his corpse by Horatio "in remembrance of my friend" and subsequently awarded by the princess to Horatio himself (1.4.42–49). Andrew Sofer's essay "Absorbing Interests: Kyd's Bloody Handkerchief as Political Palimpsest," *CompD* 34 (2000), 127–54, traces the descent of the handkerchiefs in *The Spanish Tragedy* and *Othello*, from the blood-stained cloths of medieval sacred drama, suggesting that Hieronimo's "is no demystified idol, but a fetish endowed with new and appalling life" (p. 147). Such tokens have their equivalents in later revenge plays, notably the skull of his wronged mistress treasured by Vindice in Thomas Middleton's *Revenger's Tragedy*, which the hero turns into the actual instrument of his revenge against her lecherous persecutor. For further discussion of remembrance and revenge, see Neill, "English Revenge Tragedy."

In its appeal to the vengeful hand of divine anger, the Darnley memorial appears to make God the patron of revenge. But it was precisely the exhortations of established religion that the Tudors enlisted in their efforts to displace the ethics of private vengeance: sermons and homilies stressed the quietism of St. Matthew's gospel: "Ye haue hearde, that it is sayde, an eye for an eye, and a tooth for a tooth. But, I say vnto you, that ye resist not euyll. But, whosoeuer geueth thee a blowe on thy right cheeke, turne to him the other also" (5:38–39); and this was reinforced with St. Paul's insistence that retribution belongs to God alone—and hence, of course, to his anointed deputy, the monarch: "Dearely beloued, auenge not your selues, but rather geue place vnto wrath. For it is written: Uengeaunce is myne, I wyll repay sayth the Lorde" (Romans 12:19). In Kyd's play, it is St. Paul whom Hieronimo quotes to announce the crisis of conscience that produces his most famous soliloquy:

> *Vindicta mihi!*
> Ay, heaven will be revenged of every ill,
> Nor will they suffer murder unrepaid:
> Then stay, Hieronimo, attend their will,
> For mortal men may not appoint their time.
> 3.13.1–5

But the irony of Hieronimo's position, emphasized by the events of the preceding scene, is that God's vicegerent and prime instrument of heavenly justice, the king, remains coldly indifferent to his plight; so the old man brushes St. Paul aside with a motto from the archpriest of pagan revenge, Seneca: "*Per scelus semper tutum est sceleribus iter* [The safest path for crime is always through further crime]. / Strike and strike home, where wrong is offered thee" (lines 6–7). Later in the scene, Hieronimo orders the supposed ghost of Horatio to return to the underworld, declaring the impossibility of legitimate redress: "Go back, my son, complain to Aeacus, / For here's no justice; gentle boy be gone, / For Justice is exilèd from the earth" (lines 137–39). His reference is to the myth of Astraea, the classical goddess of justice, who, with onset of the bloody Iron Age, became the last of the immortals to leave the earth, abandoning it to the murderous savagery that Bacon characterized as "wild justice." It is precisely such anarchy that is implied by the Portuguese Viceroy's declaration that "They reck no laws that meditate revenge" (1.3.48). It is his own Spanish enemies whom the Viceroy has in mind, imagining that his son has fallen victim to their vindictive spite, but his aphorism serves as a motto for the entire play. Kyd presents a world in which the passion for retribution can find relief only in actions that threaten to undo the entire fabric of law and order, and Hieronimo's position—as

both the agent of revenge and the officer responsible for the administration of law within the purlieus of the court—highlights the
paradox.

The play's preoccupation with issues of justice is highlighted from
the very beginning through its sequence of Chorus scenes. In the
first of them, the ghost of the young warrior Andrea relates the story
of his death in battle and his subsequent journey through the underworld to face the three judges of classical Hades; Minos, Aeacus, and
Rhadamanthus. They are expected to pass judgment on his life, but
unable to agree on a verdict, they have referred his case to Pluto's
Court. Before the infernal king can respond, however, he is fore-
stalled by his wife, Proserpina, who begs "that only she might give
[the] doom" (1.1.79). Her enigmatic sentence returns Andrea's ghost
to the mortal world, where he will be instructed in the "mystery" of
her decision. By a suitable paradox, however, his tutor in the the
secrets of divine justice will be no Astraea but the incarnate figure of
Revenge, and the spectacle Andrea is compelled to witness turns
out to be one of justice denied and retribution repeatedly deferred.
Despite the promise that he is about to "see the author of [his] death.
* * * Deprived of life by Bel-Imperia" (1.1.87–89), Andrea is first confronted with "Nothing but league, and love, and banqueting" (1.5.4),
then with the killing of his friend Horatio and the abuse of Bel-
Imperia (2.6.1–6), and finally with the seeming reconciliation between
Hieronimo and his son's killers, which leads to a final outburst of
frustration and the cries of "Awake Erichtho. * * * Revenge, awake.
* * * Awake, Revenge" (3.15.1–15) that usher in the last act. Echoing
the revenger's own vow to "rest me in unrest, / Dissembling quiet in
unquietness" (3.13.29–30), his guide seeks to reassure him: "Nor dies
Revenge, although he sleep a while, / For in unquiet, quietness is
feigned" (3.15.23–24); and then presents him a dumb show in which
a scene of nuptial celebration, anticipating the wedding feast of
Balthazar and Bel-Imperia is quenched in the blood that marks the
triumph of "wild justice."

The drama that is framed by these scenes is itself structured
around a sequence of trials. It begins in a scene in which the Spanish King salutes the heavenly "justice" that has ensured Spanish
triumph over the rebellious Portuguese (1.2.10–11): "*recti soror est
victoria juris*," proclaims his brother, Castile, "victory is the sister of
true justice" (1.2.14). The King is then called on to adjudicate between
Castile's son, Lorenzo, and the young knight, Horatio, both of whom
lay claim to the glory of having captured the Portuguese Prince.
The perfect equity of the king's "judgment"—"You both deserve and
both shall have reward" (line 179)—appears to confirm the estimate
of his "just and wise" character expressed by Hieronimo, who sees
it as conforming to the dispensations of both "nature and the law of

arms" (lines 166–68). But the ensuing action will rapidly undo this verdict. In Act 2 Lorenzo organizes the hanging of Horatio, overruling his protests with a vicious pun: "O sir, forbear, your valor is already tried" (2.4.52). Two scenes later the Portuguese courtier, Alexandro, almost shares Horatio's fate, when the Viceroy arbitrarily condemns this virtuous subject for the supposed murder of Balthazar—a sentence that is subsequently transferred with equal abruptness to Alexandro's traducer, Villuppo. In the next act Hieronimo presides over the formal trial of Lorenzo's tool villain, Pedringano, condemning him to be hanged for the silencing of his accomplice Serberine and declaring (with a slightly disquieting echo of the biblical rhetoric of revenge) that "blood with blood shall, while I sit as judge, / Be satisfied, and the law discharged" (3.6.35–36). This is as far as state justice can reach in Horatio's case, however. Hieronimo may be the official principally charged with administration of law; yet, as he bitterly reflects before the sentencing of Pedringano, he is powerless to indict either of the princes whom he knows to be responsible for his own son's death:

> Thus must we toil in other men's extremes,
> That know not how to remedy our own,
> And do them justice, when unjustly we,
> For all our wrongs, can compass no redress.
>
>   *   *   *
>
> This toils my body, this consumeth age,
> That only I to all men just must be,
> And neither gods nor men be just to me.
>   3.6.1–10

The old man's frantic appeals to the King for justice in 3.12 are easily brushed aside by Lorenzo as symptoms of lunatic grief, and the irony of his position is pointed up with cruel insistence in the following scene, by the swarm of petitioners seeking legal redress for their own grievances. In the end Hieronimo's longing for justice can be satisfied only by surrender to the thirst for vengeance that has possessed him since he learned the truth of his son's murder: the result is that it is the Knight Marshal himself who faces interrogation and judgment in the play's closing sequence. Judicial process does not end with his suicide, however, for the final chorus returns us to the scene of infernal judgment, where Revenge installs Andrea's delighted ghost as the arbiter of punishment, accepting his claim to the right of sentence: "Then, sweet Revenge, do this at my request: / Let me be judge and doom them to unrest" (4.5.29–30).

That the punishments that Andrea duly pronounces are so self-consciously modeled on the vicious torments of the classical underworld appears to signal the triumph of pagan revenge over both Christian precept and the law, and this suggestion is underlined by the striking anomaly of Castile's fate. The Duke is the last victim of the murderous frenzy in which Hieronimo's life ends and the first to be condemned by Andrea: he is to take the place of the legendary rapist Tityus, whose liver was to be devoured for all eternity by a pair of monstrous vultures (4.5.31). But it is difficult to see what offense Castile has committed, beyond his understandable hostility to Bel-Imperia's liaison with a socially inferior lover (2.1.45–48). However, the savage disproportion of his punishment makes sense once it is recognized that it answers only to the "endless tragedy" announced by Revenge (4.5.48), whose "wild justice" indeed appears to have "put the law out of office" for all eternity. On the face of things, Andrea's dispensation may seem to return us to the orderly world of heavenly justice celebrated by the Spanish King in 1.2, but more narrowly inspected, it offers no answer to the question articulated by Hieronimo in the depths of his despair: "How should we term your dealings to be just, / If you unjustly deal with those that in your justice trust?" (3.2.10–11).

The ending of *The Spanish Tragedy*, then, is fraught with contradiction: on the one hand Hieronimo invites us to see the killing of Balthazar and Lorenzo as an act of properly symmetrical retribution that, by rendering loss for loss and grief for grief, restores a proper balance to the world:

> Speak Portuguese, whose loss resembles mine:
> If thou canst weep upon thy Balthazar,
> 'Tis like I wailed for my Horatio.
>
>   4.4.114–16

On the other hand, the old man's gloating over the savage wit that transforms the mere theater of "our play's catastrophe" (line 121) into an apocalyptic cataclysm identifies the scene as a triumph of wild justice. It is the same antinomy that marks the final exchange between Andrea and Revenge, which sets the rhetoric of judicial process ("Let me be judge," 4.5.30), against the private satisfaction of "sharp revenge" (line 16).

The effect of such unresolved oppositions is to undermine the sense of closure toward which Kyd's tragic narrative has seemed to drive. Revenge plots, as Proserpine's enigmatically suspended sentence in the opening Chorus reminds us, are all about putting an end to unfinished business: to "find relief" for the "endless woe" of Horatio's murder (2.5.39–41), Hieronimo must contrive to write *finis* to his own story, and he does so through the murderous artifice of a play-within-the-play whose epilogue announces the consummation of his vindictive ends in the climactic revelation of Horatio's hanging corpse:

Behold the reason urging me to this: *Shows his dead son.*
See here my show, look on this spectacle:
Here lay my hope, and here my hope hath *end*;

*   *   *

And, princes, now behold Hieronimo,
Author and actor in this tragedy,
Bearing his *latest* fortune in his fist,
And will as resolute *conclude* his part
As any of the actors gone before.
And, gentles, thus I *end* my play—
Urge no more words, I have no more to say.
                    4.4.88–152 (emphasis added)

In his repeated stress on the accomplishment of "ends" (cf. also lines 85, 121, 130, and 143), it is if Hieronimo were being made to rehearse the motto pronounced by Revenge: "The end is crown of every work well done" (2.6.8), and the absolute termination of his own "story" (4.4.141) is marked by the biting out of his tongue—a berserk repudiation of speech through which the old man seeks, in the words of Addition 5, "to express the rupture of my part" (line [48])

Pleased with their deaths, and eased with their revenge,
First take my tongue, and afterwards my heart.
                    4.4.190–91

His enemies, in their turn, seek to impose their own formal closure on the action through the funeral obsequies they command for their murdered kin:

The trumpets sound a dead march, the KING *of Spain mourning after his brother's body, and the* VICEROY *of Portingale bearing the body of his son.*
                    5.4.217

As the mourners file from the stage, in this conventional sign of tragic ending,[8] Andrea proclaims his satisfaction at the seeming finality of the performance: "Ay, now my hopes have *end* in their effects, / When blood and sorrow *finish* my desires" (4.5.1–2; emphasis added). Barely are these words out of the Ghost's mouth, however, than the wished for consummation is rendered chimerical: for so far are his vindictive hopes and desires from being fully satisfied that he now insists on an afterlife of "endless" punishment for his enemies: "For here," he declares, "though death hath end their misery, / I'll there

---

8. For an extended account of the problematics of ending, especially in revenge tragedy, see Michael Neill, "Making an End: Death's Arrest and the Shaping of Tragic Narrative," in *Issues of Death: Mortality and Identity in English Renaissance Tragedy* (Oxford: Oxford University Press, 1997), pp. 201–61.

begin their endless tragedy" (lines 47–48). No wonder that the author of Addition 4 has the demented Hieronimo warn of the impossibility of ending, even within the frame of a work of art: "is this the end?" the Painter demands, after the old man has outlined his programme for a memorial masterpiece; "O no," Hieronimo replies, "there is no end: the end is death and madness" (3.12a.[153]).

3. Kyd's English Tragedy

The mere accomplishment of revenge, then, proves powerless to halt its compulsive repetitions. By pitting the nightmare of no end against the formal closure of its catastrophe, The Spanish Tragedy deliberately unsettles the consolations of tragic design, and the effect is to question the framework of cosmic and human order as Kyd's contemporaries were taught to understand it. The play's deliberate attempt to upset contemporary preconceptions is initiated in the opening Chorus: here we learn how Revenge has ushered Andrea's ghost onto the stage "through the gates of horn, / Where dreams have passage in the silent night" (1.1.82–83), making it seem as if the whole ensuing action constituted a kind of waking man's dream, playing out the truth of the audience's own dark fantasies. These have to do not merely with the rights of vengeful subjects to defy the law but with the transgressions against social hierarchy that are variously exemplified in the ambitious careers of Andrea and Horatio, in Bel-Imperia's rebellious determination "to spite the prince * * * Balthazar," her designated husband (1.4.68–69) and, above all, in Hieronimo's treasonable decision to turn against his master, the King.

What ultimately is at issue in Hieronimo's decision to take the law into his own hands is the fundamental right of kings to govern if they cannot supply the justice on which their claim to legitimacy is founded. But the subversive implications of Kyd's design are given a further twist by the nationalistic implications of the pageant with which Hieronimo entertains the court in the latter part of 1.4. Here three English knights are shown overcoming three Iberian kings before "tak[ing] their crowns and them captive" (line 137 SD). The parallel between the knights' martial "service" (line 156) and the young knight Horatio's capture of Prince Balthazar is plain enough, so the performance must be intended by Hieronimo to remind the king of his son's merit—even as its display of Spanish and Portuguese defeats tactfully allows the royal audience to interpret it as a parable of national humility (1.4.147–49, 158–60, 168–71). The parade of English victories will have had a rather different effect on Kyd's own audience, however: by associating the spectacle of defeated kings and triumphant knights with a fantasy of Iberian pride humbled by English arms, the dramatist establishes an emotive link between England's resistance to the might of Catholic Spain and the social dissidence that pits the play's underdogs against the overweening power of royalty.

The way in which the plot of *The Spanish Tragedy* focuses on the dilemma of an isolated, powerless individual makes it, like other English revenge plays, a natural vehicle for the resentments nourished by the abuse of hierarchical order, but Kyd goes out of his way to make the ruthless arrogance of rank explicit. Gazing contemptuously at Horatio's hanged body, Lorenzo comments sarcastically

> Although his life were still ambitious proud,
> Yet is he at the highest now he is dead.
>   2.4.60–61

and he nourishes an even more brutal disdain for his lowly accomplices in murder:

> And better 'tis that base companions die,
> Than by their life to hazard our good haps.
> For die they shall—slaves are ordained to no other end.
>   3.2.116–20

No wonder that the Page should take vicarious delight in the "gentlemanlike knavery" by which his master accomplishes the deaths of both Serberine and Pedringano (3.5.9) or that the Hangman should be made to gloat over the prospect of Pedringano's hanging with an echo of Lorenzo's own vicious wordplay: "I hope you will never grow so high while I am in the office" (3.6.63).

In Horatio's case, it is his courtship of Bel-Imperia that—like Andrea's earlier affair with the princess—becomes the principle vehicle of the ambitious pride that so offends Lorenzo, and Kyd underlines the subversive potential of the affair by his handling of the well-established conventions of courtly love. Deriving from the medieval chivalric code, courtly love typically involved a liaison between a highborn lady and a less exalted member of her husband's or father's household. Far from disguising his social inferiority, the lover was expected to exaggerate it by wooing his mistress in the abject language of domestic service (1.4.6, 54). As Kyd's Princess reminds Horatio (line 49), to "deserve" a mistress's favor, he must "serve" her with all the unquestioning deference of a feudal retainer.[9] But *The Spanish Tragedy* uses this vocabulary of subservience only to

---

9. For discussion of the now extensive literature on early modern ideas of service (both literal and erotic), see "Shakespeare and the Bonds of Service," in *The Shakespearean International Yearbook* 5 (2005), pp. 3–146; Michael Neill, "Servant Obedience and Master Sins: Shakespeare and the Bonds of Service," in *Putting History to the Question: Power, Politics, and Society in English Renaissance Drama* (New York: Columbia University Press, 2000), pp. 13–48; and David Schalkwyk, *Shakespeare, Love and Service* (Cambridge: Cambridge University Press, 2008).

emphasize the challenge to established hierarchy that emerges as soon as the courtly lover's desire comes into conflict with the realities of aristocratic power and (in this case) with the proverbial pride of Spain. Thus Kyd's design ensures that the audience's natural sympathy for the plight of young lovers becomes entangled both with the play's questioning attitude to the prerogatives of rank and with the nationalistic attitudes that are made to bolster that subversion. Looked at from this perspective, *The Spanish Tragedy*, despite its title, becomes a profoundly English play, and when, with the death of his brother "and the whole succeeding hope / That Spain expected after my decease," the King announces the end of his dynasty—"I am the next, the nearest, last of all" (4.4.203–08)—he articulates something more than a comforting fantasy of Spanish humiliation: however circumspect Kyd's approach to this dangerous matter, it is difficult to avoid the conclusion that in this play it is monarchy itself that, like Balthazar's Babylon, has been "wayed in the balau[n]ce, and . . . founde wanting" (Daniel 5.27).

Sources

No source has been discovered for the main plot of *The Spanish Tragedy*, which appears to be of Kyd's own invention. Nevertheless Kyd was an inveterate borrower: as the commentary notes to this edition will show, he made extensive use of both Seneca and Virgil, partly no doubt to exhibit his own learning and thereby elevate himself above the status of mere popular entertainer. From Seneca he derived not only the idea of revenge as a fit subject for tragedy but some of his plot machinery, notably the presence of a vindictive ghost; and the play is, of course, littered with quotations from the Roman tragedian. Other Latin tags are adapted from Virgil, whose great epic the *Aeneid* supplied much of the detail that fleshes out Andrea's account of the underworld (see pp. 123–29). Among the work of his contemporaries, Kyd seems to have particularly admired the French Senecan dramatist Robert Garnier, while he adapted the plot of Hieronimo's inset revenge play from the story of Soiman and Perseda in Sir Henry Wotton's translation of Jacques Yver's *A Courtly Contorversy of Cupid's Cautels* (1578) (see pp. 129–39). He also made use of less literary material, including a scandalous pamphlet detailing the villainies of Queen Elizabeth's favorite, the Earl of Leicester, whose Machiavellian betrayal of one of his own followers apparently provided the inspiration for the witty ruthlessness with which Lorenzo manages Pedringano's undoing (see pp. 139–40).

The ballad version of Hieronimo's story, published in 1620, is clearly based on Kyd's play, whose popularity it seeks to exploit by using the same title. It is reprinted here (pp. 153–58) to illustrate which details of *The Spanish Tragedy* most struck the imagination of an interested contemporary.

Textual Note

The only surviving text of *The Spanish Tragedy* with any claim to authority is the Quarto-form octavo, published by Edward White in 1592, on which all subsequent editions were based. But there is evidence that an earlier edition existed; for in that same year, according to the Stationers' Register, White was fined for a breach of copyright in "print[ing] the spanishe tragedie belong to Abell Jeffes," and White's title page, with an insolent dig at Jeffes, announces that it offers a version of the play "Newly corrected and amended of such grosse faults as passed in the first impression." It is generally recognized that White's printers worked from what was, for the most part at least, reliable copy—perhaps Kyd's own manuscript. But there are reasons for thinking, as Philip Edwards first suggested, that the second half of the play, may have been subjected to tampering. There is evidence of some corruption here, especially in the Chorus scene at the end of Act 3 and in the opening scene of Act 4, where there are strange hiatuses in speeches by Andrea and Bel-Imperia (3.15.4–5 and 4.1.9). The division of the play into four acts is peculiar, given that the classical tradition, with which Kyd was familiar, insisted on five, and the arrangement looks even more suspicious, given that Act 3 is more than twice as long as any of the other acts. It seems likely that some cutting has occurred and that Kyd's original text included an additional Chorus scene—perhaps after Hieronimo's soliloquy at the end of 3.7, which concludes the Pedringano subplot, marking a break between Act 3 and what was intended to make up Act 4.

As we have seen, the 1602 edition of the play, though still based on the original octavo, introduced some fresh material: describing its text as "enlarged with new additions of the Painters part, and others," the title page claimed to offer readers a version of the play "as it hath of late been diuers times acted." This boast needs to be treated with caution, however, because the additions have been rather inexpertly grafted into the 1592 text, with no regard for the duplication that results—most conspicuously in the case of Addition 4, which is made to precede the episode with Bazulto that it was clearly designed to replace. Thus it is highly unlikely that the 1602 edition and the subsequent editions based on it represent a version that was ever played on the stage. Nevertheless it has seemed sensible to print these additions as they were placed in the 1602 edition, rather than (as most modern editions choose to do) in the form of appendices, not just because their dramatic function is more readily appreciated when they appear in situ but because their presence there is a reminder of the fluid nature of early modern playscripts. As recent scholarship has made us increasingly aware, popular plays might be cut, expanded, or significantly rewritten several times in their theatrical lives; and because copyright, in so far as it existed, belonged to acting companies (or to publishers) rather than to authors, these alterations were often carried out by the players themselves or (in the case of more elaborate revisions) entrusted to other playwrights. Thus, from the point of view of a contemporary playgoer, neither the play as it appeared in the 1602 edition nor the presumably different version augmented by Jonson would have been regarded as any less authentic than Kyd's original, let alone the less than perfect copy of it that appeared in 1592.

With the exception of the additions, the text of the present edition is based on the 1592 octavo held in British Library, carefully collated with the library's copy of the 1602 edition, but it is also necessarily influenced by a number of modern editions, including those of Boas (1901), Mulryne (1970/1989), Gurr (2009), and especially Edwards (1959). Spelling is modernized, and punctuation lightly altered in broad conformity with modern practice. Significant departures from the 1592 text are recorded in the textual notes.

The Text of
THE SPANISH TRAGEDY

List of Characters

The Chorus
Ghost of ANDREA
REVENGE

The Spanish
KING OF SPAIN
Cyprian, DUKE OF CASTILE, his brother
LORENZO, the Duke's son
CHRISTOPHIL, Lorenzo's servant
[Jerome], Page to Lorenzo
BEL-IMPERIA, the Duke's daughter
PEDRINGANO, servant to Bel-Imperia
GENERAL of the Spanish army
HIERONIMO, Knight Marshal of Spain
ISABELLA, his wife
HORATIO, their son
Deputy to the Knight Marshal
Maid to Isabella
Servant
BAZULTO, an old man
Hangman
Three Watchmen
Three Citizens
Messenger

The Portuguese
VICEROY OF PORTUGAL
PEDRO, his brother
BALTHAZAR, the Viceroy's son
SERBERINE, servant to Balthazar
ALEXANDRO ⎫ Portuguese noblemen
VILLUPPO ⎭
AMBASSADOR of Portugal
Two Noblemen
Two Portuguese
Nobles, Soldiers, Officers, Attendants, Halberdiers

Balthazar: the usual form of Belshazzar in the two versions of the Bible—the Great Bible (1539) and the Bishops' Bible (1568)—most commonly used by the Church of England in Kyd's day. One of a number of details linking the action to the legend of Babylon (see pp. xviii–xix and 4.1.192, 4.2.5 SD).

In the First Dumb Show
Three Knights, Three Kings, a Drummer

In the Second Dumb Show
Hymen, Two Torch-bearers

In Hieronimo's Play
SULEIMAN, Sultan of Turkey (Balthazar)
ERASTO, Knight of Rhodes (Lorenzo)
PASHA (Hieronimo)
PERSEDA, Erasto's beloved (Bel-Imperia)

In the 1602 Additions
BAZARDO, a painter
PEDRO
JACQUES } Hieronimo's servants

Actus Primus

[1.1]

[*Chorus*]
Enter the Ghost of ANDREA, *and with him* REVENGE.

ANDREA

When this eternal substance of my soul
Did live imprisoned in my wanton flesh,
Each in their function serving other's need,
I was a courtier in the Spanish court;
My name was Don Andrea, my descent—   5
Though not ignoble—yet inferior far
To gracious fortunes of my tender youth:
For there, in prime and pride of all my years,
By duteous service and deserving love,

1.1. SD. **Andrea . . . Revenge:** Since they come from the underworld, they are probably meant to enter through a trapdoor, though "*Enter*" in the 1592 text usually refers to entries through the stage doors. They are evidently intended to remain on stage throughout the first three acts, and although a stage direction requires them to exit at the end of Act 3 and to reenter for the final chorus (4.5) this must be due to textual corruption because it is clearly contradicted by the Ghost's "I will sit to see the rest" (3.15.37) and his subsequent gratification at the "spectacles to please my soul" (4.5.12) that form the play's catastrophe.

1–4. When . . . court: among the most frequently parodied lines in the period. E.g., see Beaumont's *Knight of the Burning Pestle*: "When I was mortal, this my costive corpse / Did lap up figs and raisins in the Strand" (5.1.304).

6. not ignoble . . . inferior: the social gap between Andrea and Bel-Imperia, which will be mirrored in her relationship with Horatio, is emphasized from the beginning.

8. pride: self-esteem, magnificence, sexual desire.

9. duteous service: associates Andrea's affair with the Spanish princess (like Horatio's later) with the tradition of courtly love in which a knightly lover played the role of servant to a mistress of higher rank.

In secret I possessed a worthy dame,   10
Which hight sweet Bel-Imperia by name.
But in the harvest of my summer joys,
Death's winter nipped the blossoms of my bliss,
Forcing divorce betwixt my love and me;
For in the late conflict with Portingale,   15
My valor drew me into danger's mouth,
Till life to death made passage through my wounds.
When I was slain, my soul descended straight,
To pass the flowing stream of Acheron;
But churlish Charon, only boatman there,   20
Said that, my rites of burial not performed,
I might not sit amongst his passengers.
Ere Sol had slept three nights in Thetis' lap
And slaked his smoking chariot in her flood,
By Don Horatio our Knight Marshal's son,   25
My funerals and obsequies were done.
Then was the ferryman of hell content
To pass me over to the slimy strand,
That leads to fell Avernus' ugly waves:
There pleasing Cerberus with honeyed speech,   30
I passed the perils of the foremost porch.
Not far from hence, amidst ten thousand souls,
Sat Minos, Aeacus, and Rhadamanth,
To whom no sooner 'gan I make approach
To crave a passport for my wandering ghost,   35
But Minos, in graven leaves of lottery,
Drew forth the manner of my life and death:
"This knight," quoth he, "both lived and died in love,
And for his love tried fortune of the wars,
And by war's fortune lost both love and life."   40
"Why then," said Aeacus, "convey him hence

---

10. **secret:** The secrecy of Andrea's affair (again like Horatio's) is several times referred to in the play; see 2.1.45–48, 3.10.54–55, 3.14.111–12.

15. **late conflict:** For Kyd's audience, this will have recalled the recent Spanish conquest and annexation of Portugal (1580–82). **Portingale:** Portugal.

18–84. **When . . . here:** self-consciously modeled on the hero's descent into the underworld in Virgil's *Aeneid*, Book 6.

19. **Acheron:** one of the rivers of the classical underworld.

20. **Charon:** the ferryman who carried the souls of the dead across the river Styx (here conflated with Acheron).

23. **Sol:** the sun. **Thetis:** Greek nymph, daughter of the sea god Nereus; here the sea.

25. **Knight Marshal:** in England the legal officer responsible for justice within twelve miles of the royal court.

29. **Avernus:** lake in southern Italy thought to be an entrance to the underworld.

30. **Cerberus:** three-headed canine monster who guarded the underworld.

33. **Minos . . . Rhadamanth:** judges of the classical underworld.

35. **passport:** safe conduct.

36. **graven . . . lottery:** i.e., the slips on which Andrea's fate (or lot) was inscribed.

To walk with lovers in our fields of love,
And spend the course of everlasting time
Under green myrtle trees and cypress shades."
"No, no," said Rhadamanth, "it were not well,   45
With loving souls to place a martialist:
He died in war, and must to martial fields
Where wounded Hector lives in lasting pain,
And Achilles' Myrmidons do scour the plain."
Then Minos, mildest censor of the three,   50
Made this device to end the difference:
"Send him," quoth he, "to our infernal king
To doom him as best seems his majesty."
To this effect my passport straight was drawn.
In keeping on my way to Pluto's Court   55
Through dreadful shades of ever-glooming night,
I saw more sights than thousand tongues can tell,
Or pens can write, or mortal hearts can think.
Three ways there were: that on the right-hand side,
Was ready way unto the foresaid fields,   60
Where lovers live and bloody martialists—
But either sort contained within his bounds.
The left hand path, declining fearfully,
Was ready downfall to the deepest hell,
Where bloody Furies shakes their whips of steel,   65
And poor Ixion turns an endless wheel,
Where usurers are choked with melting gold,
And wantons are embraced with ugly snakes,
And murderers groan with never-killing wounds,
And perjured wights scalded in boiling lead,   70
And all foul sins with torments overwhelmed.
'Twixt these two ways, I trod the middle path,
Which brought me to the fair Elysian green,
In midst whereof there stands a stately tower,
The walls of brass, the gates of adamant.   75

---

46. **martialist:** warrior.
48–49. **Hector . . . Achilles':** In Homer's *Iliad*, the Trojan hero, Hector, is overwhelmed and killed by the followers of his Greek rival, Achilles.
50. **censor:** judge.
53. **doom:** pass judgment on.
55. **Pluto:** ruler of the underworld.
65. **Furies:** spirits of revenge in classical myth. **shakes:** Singular verb forms with plural subjects were not uncommon in the period.
66. **Ixion:** king of the Lapiths in Greek myth, bound to a fiery wheel for adultery with Hera, wife of Zeus, ruler of the gods.
73. **Elysian green:** the Elysian Fields, home of the blessed in the Virgilian underworld.
75. **adamant:** diamond.

Here finding Pluto with his Proserpine,
I showed my passport, humbled on my knee—
Whereat fair Proserpine began to smile,
And begged that only she might give my doom.
Pluto was pleased and sealed it with a kiss.   80
Forthwith, Revenge, she rounded thee in th'ear, ~secret~
And bade thee lead me through the gates of horn,
Where dreams have passage in the silent night.
No sooner had she spoke but we were here,
I wot not how, in twinkling of an eye.   85

REVENGE
Then know, Andrea, that thou art arrived
Where thou shalt see the author of thy death,
Don Balthazar, the Prince of Portingale,
Deprived of life by Bel-Imperia.
Here sit we down to see the mystery,   90
And serve for Chorus in this tragedy.

[1.2]

Enter KING OF SPAIN, GENERAL, DUKE OF CASTILE, HIERONIMO.

KING
Now say, Lord General, how fares our camp?
GENERAL
All well, my sovereign liege, except some few
That are deceased by fortune of the war.
KING
But what portends thy cheerful countenance,
And posting to our presence thus in haste?   5
Speak man, hath fortune given us victory?
GENERAL
Victory, my liege—and that with little loss.
KING
Our Portingales will pay us tribute then?

---

76. **Proserpine:** or Persephone, queen of the underworld, to whom Aeneas presents his golden bough in the *Aeneid*.
81. **rounded:** whispered.
82. **gates of horn:** in Virgil the gates from which true dreams and visions emerge (as opposed to the false ones issuing from the gates of ivory).
85. **wot:** know. **twinkling . . . eye:** The phrase echoes St. Paul's description of the Last Judgment (1 Corinthians 15:52).
90. **mystery:** something yet to be revealed, events with a secret meaning.
1. **Now . . . camp:** parodied in Jonson's *The Alchemist* (3.3.33). **camp:** army in the field.
5. **posting:** hurrying.
8. **Our:** royal plural, claiming the defeated enemy as his subjects. **Portingales:** Portuguese.

GENERAL
Tribute and wonted homage therewithal.

KING
Then blest be heaven, and guider of the heavens,   10
From whose fair influence such justice flows.

CASTILE
O multum dilecte Deo, tibi militat aether,
Et conjuratae curvato poplito gentes
Succumbunt: recti soror est victoria juris.

KING
Thanks to my loving brother of Castile.   15
But, general, unfold in brief discourse
Your form of battle and your war's success,
That, adding all the pleasure of thy news
Unto the height of former happiness,
With deeper wage and greater dignity   20
We may reward thy blissful chivalry.

GENERAL
Where Spain and Portingale do jointly knit
Their frontiers, leaning on each other's bound,
There met our armies in their proud array,
Both furnished well, both full of hope and fear: 25
Both menacing alike with daring shows,
Both vaunting sundry colors of device,
Both cheerly sounding trumpets, drums and fifes
Both raising dreadful clamors to the sky
That valleys, hills, and rivers made rebound,   30
And heaven itself was frighted with the sound.
Our battles both were pitched in squadron form,
Each corner strongly fenced with wings of shot,
But, ere we joined and came to push of pike,
I brought a squadron of our readiest shot   35
From out our rearward to begin the fight:
They brought another wing to encounter us.
Meanwhile our ordnance played on either side,
And captains strove to have their valors tried.

12–14. O multum . . . juris: O beloved of God, the heavens fight for you, and the united
  peoples fall on bended knee: victory is the sister of true justice. Adapted from Claudian,
  De Tertio Consulatu Honorii, lines 96–98.
21. chivalry: feats of arms.
23. bound: boundary.
25. furnished: equipped.
27. vaunting: proudly displaying. colors of device: heraldic banners.
32. battles: troops in battle array. squadron form: square formation.
33. shot: troops equipped with firearms.
34. push of pike: hand-to-hand fighting.

Don Pedro, their chief horsemen's colonel,   40
Did, with his cornet, bravely make attempt
To break the order of our battle ranks;
But Don Rogero, worthy man of war,
Marched forth against him with our musketeers,
And stopped the malice of his fell approach.   45
While they maintain hot skirmish to and fro,
Both battles join and fall to handy blows,
Their violent shot resembling th'oceans rage,
When, roaring loud and with a swelling tide,
It beats upon the rampiers of huge rocks,   50
And gapes to swallow neighbor-bounding lands.
Now, while Bellona rageth here and there,
Thick storms of bullets rain like winter's hail,
And shivered lances dark the troubled air.
   Pede pes et cuspide cuspis,   55
  Arma sonant armis, vir petiturque viro.
On every side drop captains to the ground
And soldiers—some ill-maimed, some slain outright;
Here falls a body sundered from his head,
There legs and arms lie bleeding on the grass,   60
Mingled with weapons and unboweled steeds
That scattering overspread the purple plain.
In all this turmoil, three long hours and more,
The victory to neither part inclined,
Till Don Andrea with his brave lanciers,   65
In their main battle made so great a breach
That, half dismayed, the multitude retired;
But Balthazar, the Portingales' young prince,
Brought rescue and encouraged them to stay.
Here-hence the fight was eagerly renewed,   70
And in that conflict was Andrea slain—
Brave man-at-arms, but weak to Balthazar.
Yet, while the Prince, insulting over him,
Breathed out proud vaunts, sounding to our reproach,

---

40. colonel: pronounced with three syllables.
41. cornet: troop of cavalry led by an ensign, or cornet.
45. fell: fierce, terrible.
47. handy: hand-to-hand.
50. rampiers: ramparts.
52. Bellona: Roman goddess of war.
55–56. Pede . . . viro: Foot against foot and lance against lance, arms resound on arms, and man is assailed by man. Loosely adapted from Claudian, *Thebais*, viii.399.
62. purple: dyed with royal blood.
65. lanciers: lancers.
70. Here-hence: as a result.
72. man-at-arms: heavily armed soldier on horseback.

Friendship and hardy valor joined in one,   75
Pricked forth Horatio, our Knight Marshal's son,
To challenge forth that prince in single fight.
Not long between these twain the fight endured;
But straight the Prince was beaten from his horse,
And forced to yield him prisoner to his foe.   80
When he was taken, all the rest they fled,
And our carbines pursued them to the death,
Till, Phoebus waning to the western deep,
Our trumpeters were charged to sound retreat.

KING

Thanks, good Lord General, for these good news;   85
And—for some argument of more to come—
Take this and wear it for thy sovereign's sake.
        Gives him his [own] chain.
But tell me now, hast thou confirmed a peace?

GENERAL

No peace, my liege, but peace conditional
That if, with homage, tribute be well paid,
The fury of your forces will be stayed;   90
And to this peace their Viceroy hath subscribed.
        Gives the KING *a paper.*
And made a solemn vow that during life
His tribute shall be truly paid to Spain.

KING

These words, these deeds, become thy person well.   95
But now, Knight Marshal, frolic with thy king,
For 'tis thy son that wins this battle's prize.

HIERONIMO

Long may he live to serve my sovereign liege,
And soon decay unless he serve my liege.

KING

Nor thou, nor he shall die without reward.   100
        A tucket afar off.
What means this warning of the trumpet sound?

GENERAL

This tells me that your grace's men-of-war,
Such as war's fortune hath reserved from death,
Come marching on toward your royal seat,

---

76. **Pricked**: spurred.
82. **carbines**: musketeers.
83. **Phoebus**: the sun.
86. **argument**: token.
92. **subscribed**: signed his name.
100. SD. *tucket*: cavalry trumpet call.

To show themselves before your majesty,
For so I gave in charge at my depart;
Whereby by demonstration shall appear,
That all—except three hundred or few more—
Are safe returned and by their foes enriched.

KING

A gladsome sight! I long to see them here.   110

The army enters, BALTHAZAR *between* LORENZO *and*
HORATIO *captive.*
They enter and pass by.

Was that the warlike Prince of Portingale
That by our nephew was in triumph led?

GENERAL

It was, my liege, the Prince of Portingale.

KING

But what was he that on the other side
Held him by th'arm as partner of the prize?   115

HIERONIMO

That was my son, my gracious sovereign,
Of whom though from his tender infancy
My loving thoughts did never hope but well,
He never pleased his father's eyes till now,
Nor filled my heart with over-cloying joys.   120

KING

Go let them march once more about these walls,
That staying them we may confer and talk
With our brave prisoner and his double guard.
Hieronimo, it greatly pleaseth us,
That in our victory thou have a share,   125
By virtue of thy worthy son's exploit.

Enter [*the army*] *again.*

Bring hither the young Prince of Portingale—
The rest march on, but, ere they be dismissed,
We will bestow on every soldier
Two ducats, and on every leader ten,   130
That they may know our largesse welcomes them.

Exeunt all [*the army*] *but* BALTHAZAR, LORENZO,
[*and*] HORATIO.

Welcome, Don Balthazar, welcome nephew,
And thou, Horatio, thou art welcome too:
Young prince, although thy father's hard misdeeds

---

110. SD. *The army . . . captive*: after line 109 in the 1592 edition. *pass by*: i.e., they march
  across the stage from one stage door to the other, passing in review before the King.
122. **staying**: stopping.

.n keeping back the tribute that he owes   135
Deserve but evil measure at our hands,
Yet shalt thou know that Spain is honorable.
BALTHAZAR
The trespass that my father made in peace
Is now controlled by fortune of the wars;
And, cards once dealt, it boots not ask why so: 140
His men are slain, a weakening to his realm,
His colors seized, a blot unto his name,
His son distressed, a corsive to his heart—
These punishments may clear his late offence.
KING
Ay, Balthazar, if he observe this truce,   145
Our peace will grow the stronger for these wars.
Meanwhile live thou, though not in liberty,
Yet free from bearing any servile yoke;
For in our hearing thy deserts were great,
And in our sight thyself art gracious.   150
BALTHAZAR
And I shall study to deserve this grace.
KING
But tell me—for their holding makes me doubt—
To which of these twain art thou prisoner?
LORENZO
To me, my liege.
HORATIO   To me, my sovereign.
LORENZO
This hand first took his courser by the reins.   155
HORATIO
But first my lance did put him from his horse.
LORENZO
I seized his weapon and enjoyed it first.
HORATIO
But first I forced him lay his weapons down.
KING
Let go his arm, upon our privilege!
        [LORENZO *and* BALTHAZAR] *let him go.*
Say, worthy prince, to whether didst thou yield?   160

---

139. **controlled:** overpowered (and therefore canceled out).
140. **boots:** profits.
143. **corsive:** corrosive poison.
152. **their holding:** the way they are both holding you.
155. **courser:** warhorse.
159. **our privilege:** my royal authority.
160. **whether:** which of the two.

BALTHAZAR
   To him in courtesy, to this perforce:
   He spake me fair, this other gave me strokes;
   He promised life, this other threatened death;
   He won my love, this other conquered me;
   And, truth to say, I yield myself to both.   165

HIERONIMO
   But that I know your grace for just and wise,
   And might seem partial in this difference,
   Enforced by nature and by law of arms,
   My tongue should plead for young Horatio's right.
   He hunted well that was a lion's death,   170
   Not he that in a garment wore his skin—
   So hares may pull dead lions by the beard.

KING
   Content thee, Marshal, thou shalt have no wrong,
   And for thy sake thy son shall want no right.
   Will both abide the censure of my doom?   175

LORENZO
   I crave no better than your grace awards.

HORATIO
   Nor I, although I sit beside my right.

KING
   Then by my judgment thus your strife shall end:
   You both deserve and both shall have reward.
   Nephew, thou tookst his weapon and his horse,   180
   His weapons and his horse are thy reward.
   Horatio, thou didst force him first to yield,
   His ransom therefore is thy valor's fee.
   Appoint the sum as you shall both agree;
   But, nephew, thou shalt have the prince in guard,   185
   For thine estate best fitteth such a guest.
   Horatio's house were small for all his train;
   Yet, in regard thy substance passeth his,
   And that just guerdon may befall desert,
   To him we yield the armor of the prince.   190
   How likes Don Balthazar of this device?

170–72. He . . . beard: proverbial, see Tilley H165.
174. want: lack.
175. censure . . . doom: sentence of my judgment.
177. sit . . . right: stand on my just claim.
186. estate: rank.
188. substance: wealth.
189. guerdon: reward.

BALTHAZAR

   Right well, my liege, if this proviso were,
   That Don Horatio bear us company,
   Whom I admire and love for chivalry.

KING

   Horatio, leave him not that loves thee so.   195
   Now let us hence to see our soldiers paid,
   And feast our prisoner as our friendly guest.

                                  Exeunt.

[1.3]

    Enter VICEROY, ALEXANDRO, VILLUPPO, [*and Attendants*]

VICEROY

   Is our ambassador despatched for Spain?

ALEXANDRO

   Two days, my liege, are past since his depart.

VICEROY

   And tribute payment gone along with him?

ALEXANDRO

   Ay, my good lord.

VICEROY

   Then rest we here a while in our unrest,   5
   And feed our sorrows with some inward sighs,
   For deepest cares break never into tears.
   But wherefore sit I in a regal throne?
   This better fits a wretch's endless moan;   *Falls to the ground.*
   Yet this is higher than my fortune's reach,   10
   And therefore better than my state deserves.
   Ay, ay, this earth, image of melancholy,
   Seeks him whom fates adjudge to misery:
   Here let me lie, now am I at the lowest.
     Qui jacet in terra non habet unde cadat.   15
     In me consumpsit vires fortuna nocendo,
     Nil superest ut jam possit obesse magis.
   Yes, Fortune may bereave me of my crown:

---

7. deepest . . . tears: proverbial, see Tilley S664 and W130.

9. SD. Falls . . . ground: the Viceroy enacts the familiar emblem of the Wheel of Fortune, in which the enthroned king from the top of the wheel lies prostrate at its base (see p. xx and Fig. 1).

12. earth . . . melancholy: In geohumoral theory, the four humors (blood, melancholy, choler, and phlegm) were supposed to correspond to the four elements of creation (air, earth, fire, and water).

15–17. Qui . . . magis: Someone who throws himself to the ground has no farther to fall. In my case, Fortune has no power to hurt me; there is nothing more that can harm me now. The first line is from Alanus de Insulis, *Liber de Parabolis* 2.19; and the second, adapted from Seneca's *Agamemnon* l.698.

Here take it now; let Fortune do her worst,
She will not rob me of this sable weed—   20
O no, she envies none but pleasant things,
Such is the folly of despiteful chance!
Fortune is blind and sees not my deserts,
So is she deaf and hears not my laments;
And could she hear, yet is she wilful mad,   25
And therefore will not pity my distress.
Suppose that she could pity me, what then?
What help can be expected at her hands,
Whose foot is standing on a rolling stone
And mind more mutable then fickle winds?   30
Why wail I, then, where's hope of no redress?
O yes, complaining makes my grief seem less.
My late ambition hath distained my faith,
My breach of faith occasioned bloody wars,
Those bloody wars have spent my treasure,   35
And with my treasure my people's blood,
And with their blood, my joy and best beloved,
My best beloved, my sweet and only son.
O wherefore went I not to war myself?
The cause was mine, I might have died for both: 40
My years were mellow, his but young and green,
My death were natural, but his was forced.

ALEXANDRO
No doubt, my liege, but still the prince survives.

VICEROY
Survives? Ay, where?

ALEXANDRO
In Spain, a prisoner by mischance of war.   45

VICEROY
Then they have slain him for his father's fault.

ALEXANDRO
That were a breach to common law of arms.

VICEROY
They reck no laws that meditate revenge.

---

20. **sable weed:** black mourning dress.
22. **despiteful:** malignant, spiteful.
23–30. **Fortune . . . winds:** In emblem books Fortune was depicted as a blind (or some-
    times blindfolded) woman, standing on a rolling sphere, to symbolize her arbitrary and
    capricious nature. See also Tilley F164.
33. **distained:** sullied, dishonored.
35, 36. **treasure:** pronounced with three syllables here (though not elsewhere).
42, 47. **were:** would have been (subjunctive mode).
46. **fault:** i.e., his breach of faith.
48. **reck:** heed.

ALEXANDRO
His ransom's worth will stay from foul revenge.
VICEROY
No, if he lived the news would soon be here.   50
ALEXANDRO
Nay, evil news fly faster still than good.
VICEROY
Tell me no more of news, for he is dead.
VILLUPPO
My sovereign, pardon the author of ill news,
And I'll bewray the fortune of thy son.
VICEROY
Speak on—I'll guerdon thee whate'er it be: 55
Mine ear is ready to receive ill news,
My heart grown hard 'gainst mischief's battery;
Stand up, I say, and tell thy tale at large.
VILLUPPO
Then hear that truth which these mine eyes have seen:
When both the armies were in battle joined,   60
Don Balthazar, amidst the thickest troops,
To win renown did wondrous feats of arms;
Amongst the rest I saw him hand to hand
In single fight with their Lord General,
Till Alexandro—that here counterfeits   65
Under the color of a duteous friend—
Discharged his pistol at the prince's back,
As though he would have slain their general;
But therewithal Don Balthazar fell down,
And when he fell, then we began to fly;   70
But had he lived the day had sure been ours.
ALEXANDRO
O wicked forgery! O traitorous miscreant!
VICEROY
Hold thou thy peace! But now, Villuppo, say
Where then became the carcass of my son?
VILLUPPO
I saw them drag it to the Spanish tents.   75
VICEROY
Ay, ay, my nightly dreams have told me this.
Thou false, unkind, unthankful, traitorous beast,

---

49. **stay:** hold [them] back.
51. **evil . . . good:** proverbial, see Tilley N147.
54. **bewray:** reveal.
77. **unkind:** unnatural, ungrateful, wicked.

Wherein had Balthazar offended thee
That thou shouldst thus betray him to our foes?
Was't Spanish gold that blearèd so thine eyes   80
That thou couldst see no part of our deserts?
Perchance because thou art Terceira's lord,
Thou hadst some hope to wear this diadem,
If first my son and then myself were slain;
But thy ambitious thought shall break thy neck.   85
Ay, this was it that made thee spill his blood,
    Take[s] the crown and put[s] it on again.
But I'll now wear it till thy blood be spilt.

ALEXANDRO

Vouchsafe, dread sovereign, to hear me speak.

VICEROY

Away with him, his sight is second hell!
Keep him till we determine of his death: 90
If Balthazar be dead, he shall not live.
    [*Exeunt Attendants with* ALEXANDRO]
Villuppo, follow us for thy reward.   *Exit* VICEROY

VILLUPPO

Thus have I with an envious forged tale
Deceived the king, betrayed mine enemy,
And hope for guerdon of my villainy.   *Exit.* 95

[1.4]

    Enter HORATIO *and* BEL-IMPERIA.

BEL-IMPERIA

Signior Horatio, this is the place and hour
Wherein I must entreat thee to relate
The circumstance of Don Andrea's death,
Who living was my garland's sweetest flower,
And in his death hath buried my delights.   5

HORATIO

For love of him and service to yourself,
I nill refuse this heavy doleful charge;
Yet tears and sighs, I fear, will hinder me.

---

82. Terceira: one of the larger islands and site of the historic capital of the Azores, where opposition to the Spanish conquest of Portugal was strongest.
2. thee: the singular pronoun is used either to social inferiors (as here, because Bel-Imperia is a princess and Horatio merely the son of a court official), to children, or to intimates. In line 6 Horatio uses the more respectful plural form. See also 2.4.18, 3.12.33.
6. service: see note to 1.1.9.
7. nill: will not.

When both our armies were enjoined in fight,
Your worthy chevalier amidst the thick'st,   10
For glorious cause still aiming at the fair'st,
Was at the last by young Don Balthazar
Encountered hand to hand: their fight was long,
Their hearts were great, their clamours menacing,
Their strength alike, their strokes both dangerous;   15
But wrathful Nemesis, that wicked power,
Envying at Andrea's praise and worth,
Cut short his life to end his praise and worth.
She, she herself, disguised in armor's mask,
As Pallas was before proud Pergamus,   20
Brought in a fresh supply of halberdiers,
Which paunched his horse and dinged him to the ground;
Then young Don Balthazar with ruthless rage,
Taking advantage of his foe's distress,
Did finish what his halberdiers begun,   25
And left not till Andrea's life was done.
Then, though too late, incensed with just remorse,
I with my band set forth against the prince,
And brought him prisoner from his halberdiers.

BEL-IMPERIA

Would thou hadst slain him that so slew my love.   30
But then was Don Andrea's carcass lost?

HORATIO

No, that was it for which I chiefly strove,
Nor stepped I back till I recovered him:
I took him up and wound him in mine arms,
And wielding him unto my private tent,   35
There laid him down and dewed him with my tears,
And sighed and sorrowed as became a friend.
But neither friendly sorrow, sighs nor tears
Could win pale death from his usurpèd right.
Yet this I did, and less I could not do: 40
I saw him honored with due funeral;

---

16. **Nemesis:** classical spirit of divine vengeance.
20. **Pallas:** or Pallas Athena, patron goddess of Troy ("Pergamus"), who nevertheless took
the side of the Greeks in the Trojan War.
21. **halberdiers:** infantry armed with halberds (a combination of spear and battle-ax).
22. **paunched:** disemboweled. **dinged:** hammered.
23–26. **Then . . . done:** Of the several accounts of the battle, this is the only one that
exposes Balthazar's unchivalrous killing of Andrea, which recalls the ruthless slaughter
of Hector at the hands of Achilles's Myrmidons.
27. **remorse:** pity (but perhaps including regret for his own failure to rescue his
friend).
35. **wielding:** carrying. In the 1592 edition "welding" is an obsolete variant spelling.

This scarf I plucked from off his lifeless arm,
And wear it in remembrance of my friend.

BEL-IMPERIA
I know the scarf—would he had kept it still,
For had he lived he would have kept it still,   45
And worn it for his Bel-Imperia's sake,
For 'twas my favor at his last depart;
But now wear thou it both for him and me,
For after him thou hast deserved it best.
But for thy kindness in his life and death,   50
Be sure while Bel-Imperia's life endures,
She will be Don Horatio's thankful friend.

HORATIO
And, madam, Don Horatio will not slack
Humbly to serve fair Bel-Imperia.
But now, if your good liking stand thereto,   55
I'll crave your pardon to go seek the prince,
For so the duke your father gave me charge.   *Exit.*

BEL-IMPERIA
Ay, go Horatio, leave me here alone,
For solitude best fits my cheerless mood;
Yet what avails to wail Andrea's death,   60
From whence Horatio proves my second love?
Had he not loved Andrea as he did,
He could not sit in Bel-Imperia's thoughts.
But how can love find harbor in my breast,
Till I revenge the death of my beloved?   65
Yes, second love shall further my revenge:
I'll love Horatio, my Andrea's friend,
The more to spite the prince that wrought his end;
And where Don Balthazar, that slew my love,
Himself now pleads for favor at my hands,   70
He shall in rigor of my just disdain,
Reap long repentance for his murderous deed—
For what was't else but murderous cowardice
So many to oppress one valiant knight,
Without respect of honor in the fight?   75
And here he comes that murdered my delight.
         Enter LORENZO *and* BALTHAZAR.

---

42. **this scarf:** a favor granted to Andrea by his mistress and now passed on to Horatio, as Bel-Imperia's reply makes clear. Presumably the same bloody handkerchief (2.5.51) or napkin (3.13.85) that Hieronimo will take from the murdered body of his son and keep as a token of his intended revenge.
54. **serve:** see notes to line 6 and 1.1.9.
71. **in . . . disdain:** in the harshness of my righteous indignation.

LORENZO
Sister, what means this melancholy walk?
BEL-IMPERIA
That for a while I wish no company.
LORENZO
But here the prince is come to visit you.
BEL-IMPERIA
That argues that he lives in liberty.   80
BALTHAZAR
No, madam, but in pleasing servitude.
BEL-IMPERIA
Your prison then belike is your conceit.
BALTHAZAR
Ay, by conceit my freedom is enthralled.
BEL-IMPERIA
Then with conceit enlarge yourself again.
BALTHAZAR
What if conceit have laid my heart to gage?   85
BEL-IMPERIA
Pay that you borrowed and recover it.
BALTHAZAR
I die if it return from whence it lies.
BEL-IMPERIA
A heartless man and live? A miracle!
BALTHAZAR
Ay, lady, love can work such miracles.
LORENZO
Tush, tush, my lord, let go these ambages,   90
And in plain terms acquaint her with your love.
BEL-IMPERIA
What boots complaint, when there's no remedy?
BALTHAZAR
Yes, to your gracious self must I complain,
In whose fair answer lies my remedy,
On whose perfection all my thoughts attend,   95

77–92 **Sister . . . remedy:** This verbal fencing of this line-by-line repartee imitates Senecan *stichomythia*.
81. **pleasing servitude:** Balthazar plays on the conceit of his literal captivity as constituting a kind of courtly service to Bel-Imperia.
82. **conceit:** witty figure of speech (*OED* n. 8). Wittily enough, the play on various meanings of the word in lines 82–85 itself constitutes such a conceit.
83. **conceit:** morbid affection or seizure of the mind (*OED* n. 11). **enthralled:** enslaved.
84. **conceit:** imagination (*OED* n. 7b). **enlarge:** set free.
85. **conceit:** fanciful notion, whim (*OED* n. 7), perhaps with an ironic suggestion of "self-conceit, vanity" (*OED* n. 5b). **to gage:** as a pledge.
90. **ambages:** roundabout ways of speaking; equivocations or quibbles, wordplay.

On whose aspect mine eyes find beauty's bower,
In whose translucent breast my heart is lodged.

BEL-IMPERIA

Alas, my lord, these are but words of course,
And but device to drive me from this place.

> *She, in going in, lets fall her glove, which* HORATIO,
> *coming out, takes up.*

HORATIO

Madam, your glove.   100

BEL-IMPERIA

Thanks, good Horatio, take it for thy pains.

BALTHAZAR

Signior Horatio stooped in happy time.

HORATIO

I reaped more grace than I deserved or hoped.

LORENZO

My lord, be not dismayed for what is past:
You know that women oft are humorous;   105
These clouds will overblow with little wind.
Let me alone, I'll scatter them myself.
Meanwhile let us devise to spend the time
In some delightful sports and reveling.

HORATIO

The king, my lords, is coming hither straight   110
To feast the Portingale ambassador:
Things were in readiness before I came.

BALTHAZAR

Then here it fits us to attend the king,
To welcome hither our ambassador,
And learn my father and my country's health.   115

> *Enter the banquet, trumpets, the* KING *and* AMBASSADOR.

KING

See, lord ambassador, how Spain entreats
Their prisoner, Balthazar, thy viceroy's son:
We pleasure more in kindness than in wars.

---

96. **aspect:** look, face, appearance.
98. **words of course:** conventional phrases.
99. **but device:** merely a device. **SD.** *lets fall her glove*: presumably a deliberate gesture, enabling her to grant Horatio a second favor in front of his rival.
102. **happy:** lucky.
103. **grace:** Horatio makes use of the religious vocabulary of courtly love in which a lady's grant of favor is described as "grace" or "mercy".
105. **humorous:** capricious; i.e, at the mercy of their erratic humors (see note to 1.3.12).
109. **sports and reveling:** pastimes and festivities.
113. **fits:** befits.
115. **SD.** *Enter the banquet:* "carried onstage as a table laden with dishes; stools or benches would have been brought on too" [Gurr's note]. See lines 127–29.

AMBASSADOR

Sad is our King, and Portingale laments,

Supposing that Don Balthazar is slain.   120

BALTHAZAR

[*Aside*] So am I slain by beauty's tyranny.

[*Aloud*] You see, my lord, how Balthazar is slain:

I frolic with the Duke of Castile's son,

Wrapped every hour in pleasures of the court,

And graced with favors of his majesty.   125

KING

Put off your greetings till our feast be done,

Now come and sit with us and taste our cheer.

    Sit[s]to the banquet.

Sit down, young prince, you are our second guest;

Brother, sit down, and nephew, take your place;

Signior Horatio, wait thou upon our cup,   130

For well thou hast deservèd to be honored.

Now, lordings, fall to: Spain is Portugal,

And Portugal is Spain, we both are friends,

Tribute is paid, and we enjoy our right.

But where is old Hieronimo, our Marshal?   135

He promised us, in honor of our guest,

To grace our banquet with some pompous jest.

    Enter HIERONIMO *with a drum, [and] three Knights, each*

    [with] his scutcheon; then he fetches three Kings;

    [the Knights] take their crowns and them captive.

Hieronimo, this masque contents mine eye,

Although I sound not well the mystery.

HIERONIMO

The first armed knight that hung his scutcheon up,   140

    He takes the scutcheon and gives it to the KING

Was English Robert, Earl of Gloucester,

Who, when King Stephen bore sway in Albion,

130–31. wait . . . honored: The office of royal cupbearer was a prestigious one in European courts, but neither Horatio nor his father is among those "lordings" (line 132) invited to sit at the royal banquet.

132. fall to: begin eating.

132–33. Spain . . . friends: Spain and Portugal stand for their rulers as well as for the countries themselves, some public gesture of bonding with Balthazar may be implied here.

137. pompous jest: stately entertainment. SD. Enter . . . captive: In addition to its obvious flattery of Kyd's English audience, Hieronimo's dumb show is designed to serve the interests of his family because it shows three princes being overcome and taken captive by three warriors of lesser rank. The narratives belong to popular legend rather than history. scutcheon: heraldic shield; here, they bear the arms of Gloucester, Kent/York, and Lancaster, respectively.

139. sound . . . mystery: fathom the hidden meaning; see note to 1.1.90.

142. Albion: England.

Arrived with five-and-twenty thousand men
In Portingale, and by success of war
Enforced the king, then but a Saracen,   145
To bear the yoke of the English monarchy.

KING

My lord of Portingale, by this you see
That which may comfort both your king and you,
And make your late discomfort seem the less.
But say, Hieronimo, what was the next?   150

HIERONIMO

The second knight that hung his scutcheon up,
    He doth as he did before.
Was Edmund, Earl of Kent in Albion,
When English Richard wore the diadem.
He came likewise and razèd Lisbon walls,
And took the King of Portingale in fight—   155
For which, and other such like service done,
He after was created Duke of York.

KING

This is another special argument
That Portingale may deign to bear our yoke,
When it by little England hath been yoked.   160
But now, Hieronimo, what were the last?

HIERONIMO

The third and last, not least in our account,
    Doing as before.
Was as the rest a valiant Englishman,
Brave John of Gaunt, the Duke of Lancaster,
As by his scutcheon plainly may appear.   165
He with a puissant army came to Spain,
And took our King of Castile prisoner.

AMBASSADOR

This is an argument for our viceroy
That Spain may not insult for her success,
Since English warriors likewise conquered Spain,   170
And made them bow their knees to Albion.

KING

Hieronimo, I drink to thee for this device,
Which hath pleased both the ambassador and me.
Pledge me, Hieronimo, if thou love the king.
    Takes the cup of Horatio.

---

158. **argument:** proof, demonstration.
166. **puissant:** powerful.
169. **insult:** brag, exult contemptuously.

My lord, I fear we sit but over-long,   175
Unless our dainties were more delicate;
But welcome are you to the best we have.
Now let us in, that you may be despatched;
I think our council is already set.

> *Exeunt omnes.*

[1.5]

[*Chorus*]

why are we watching this?

ANDREA

Come we for this from depth of underground,
To see him feast that gave me my death's wound?
These pleasant sights are sorrow to my soul—
Nothing but league, and love, and banqueting!

REVENGE

Be still, Andrea: ere we go from hence,   5
I'll turn their friendship into fell despite,
Their love to mortal hate, their day to night,
Their hope into despair, their peace to war,
Their joys to pain, their bliss to misery.

Actus Secundus.

[2.1]

Enter LORENZO *and* BALTHAZAR.

LORENZO

My lord, though Bel-Imperia seem thus coy,
Let reason hold you in your wonted joy:
In time the savage bull sustains the yoke,
In time all haggard hawks will stoop to lure,
In time small wedges cleave the hardest oak,   5
In time the flint is pierced with softest shower;
And she in time will fall from her disdain,
And rue the sufferance of your friendly pain.

---

176. **more delicate:** i.e., than they actually are.
178. **that . . . despatched:** so that we can settle your business and send you quickly on
   your way.
6. **fell despite:** deadly contempt and malice.
3–6, 9–10. **In time . . . shower; No, she . . . wall:** closely adapted from Sonnet 47 (lines
   1–6) in Thomas Watson's *Hekatompathia* (1582).
3. **sustains:** submits to.
4. **haggard:** wild, untrained. **stoop to lure:** swoop down to take the falconer's bait.
8. **sufferance:** patient endurance, suffering.

BALTHAZAR

No, she is wilder and more hard withal,
Then beast, or bird, or tree, or stony wall.   10
But wherefore blot I Bel-Imperia's name?
It is my fault, not she that merits blame:
My feature is not to content her sight;
My words are rude and work her no delight;
The lines I send her are but harsh and ill,   15
Such as do drop from Pan and Marsyas' quill;
My presents are not of sufficient cost,
And, being worthless, all my labor's lost.
Yet might she love me for my valiancy—
Ay, but that's slandered by captivity.   20
Yet might she love me to content her sire—
Ay, but her reason masters his desire.
Yet might she love me as her brother's friend—
Ay, but her hopes aim at some other end.
Yet might she love me to uprear her state—   25
Ay, but perhaps she hopes some nobler mate.
Yet might she love me as her beauty's thrall—
Ay, but I fear she cannot love at all.

LORENZO

My Lord, for my sake leave these ecstasies,
And doubt not but we'll find some remedy.   30
Some cause there is that lets you not be loved:
First that must needs be known and then removed.
What if my sister love some other knight?

BALTHAZAR

My summer's day will turn to winter's night.

LORENZO

I have already found a stratagem   35
To sound the bottom of this doubtful theme.
My lord, for once you shall be ruled by me:
Hinder me not whate'er you hear or see.
By force or fair means will I cast about
To find the truth of all this question out.   40

11–28. But . . . at all: A famous, frequently parodied speech; e.g., Nathan Field, *A Woman is a Weathercock* (1609), 1.2.345–46.
13. feature: bodily proportions, shape, appearance. **to:** such as to.
14. rude: lacking in polish, unmusical.
16. Pan and Marsyas: gods who foolishly challenged Apollo at the flute. **quill:** (1) quill pen; (2) musical pipe.
20. slandered: brought into disrepute.
25. uprear her state: raise her social station.
29. ecstasies: extravagant displays of passion

Ho, Pedringano!
PEDRINGANO [*within*]   Signior?
LORENZO   *Vien qui presto!*
        Enter PEDRINGANO
PEDRINGANO
  Hath your lordship any service to command me?
LORENZO
  Ay, Pedringano, service of import;
  And, not to spend the time in trifling words,
  Thus stands the case: it is not long, thou know'st,   45
  Since I did shield thee from my father's wrath
  For thy conveyance in Andrea's love,
  For which thou wert adjudg'd to banishment;
  I stood betwixt thee and thy punishment,
  And since, thou know'st how I have favored thee.   50
  Now to these favors will I add reward,
  Not with fair words, but store of golden coin,
  And lands and living joined with dignities,
  If thou but satisfy my just demand.
  Tell truth and have me for thy lasting friend.   55
PEDRINGANO
  Whate'er it be your lordship shall demand,
  My bounden duty bids me tell the truth—
  If case it lie in me to tell the truth.
LORENZO
  Then, Pedringano, this is my demand:
  Whom loves my sister Bel-Imperia?   60
  For she reposeth all her trust in thee—
  Speak man, and gain both friendship and reward—
  I mean, whom loves she in Andrea's place?
PEDRINGANO
  Alas, my lord, since Don Andrea's death,
  I have no credit with her as before,   65
  And therefore know not if she love or no.
LORENZO
  Nay, if thou dally then I am thy foe,   [*Draws his sword.*]
  And fear shall force what friendship cannot win:
  Thy death shall bury what thy life conceals.
  Thou diest for more esteeming her than me.   70

---

41. *Vien qui presto*: Come here at once (Italian). Gurr suggests that Lorenzo's fondness
  for Italian phrases is meant to mark him as a disciple of Machiavelli.
43. import: importance.
47. conveyance: underhand dealing (*OED* n. 11b).
52. store: abundance.
58. if . . . me: provided that I am able.

PEDRINGANO
   O stay, my lord!
LORENZO
   Yet speak the truth and I will guerdon thee,
   And shield thee from what ever can ensue,
   And will conceal whate'er proceeds from thee;
   But if thou dally once again, thou diest.   75
PEDRINGANO
   If madam Bel-Imperia be in love—
LORENZO
   What, villain, ifs and ands?   [*Offer[s] to kill him.*]
PEDRINGANO
   O stay, my lord, she loves Horatio!   BALTHAZAR *starts back.*
LORENZO
   What, Don Horatio, our Knight Marshal's son?
PEDRINGANO
   Even him, my lord.   80
LORENZO
   Now say but how know'st thou he is her love,
   And thou shalt find me kind and liberal—
   Stand up, I say, and fearless tell the truth.
PEDRINGANO
   She sent him letters which myself perused,
   Full fraught with lines and arguments of love,   85
   Preferring him before Prince Balthazar.
LORENZO
   Swear on this cross that what thou say'st is true,
   And that thou wilt conceal what thou hast told.
PEDRINGANO
   I swear to both, by him that made us all.
LORENZO
   In hope thine oath is true, here's thy reward—   90
   But if I prove thee perjured and unjust,
   This very sword whereon thou tookst thine oath
   Shall be the worker of thy tragedy.
PEDRINGANO
   What I have said is true, and shall for me
   Be still concealed from Bel-Imperia—   95
   Besides, your honor's liberality
   Deserves my duteous service, even till death.

---

77. **ands:** ifs.
87. **this cross:** i.e., his sword hilt.
91. **unjust:** faithless, dishonest.

LORENZO

Let this be all that thou shalt do for me:
Be watchful when and where these lovers meet,
And give me notice in some secret sort.   100

PEDRINGANO

I will, my lord.

LORENZO

Then shalt thou find that I am liberal:
Thou know'st that I can more advance thy state
Than she, be therefore wise and fail me not.
Go and attend her as thy custom is,   105
Lest absence make her think thou dost amiss.

                                        Exit PEDRINGANO.

Why so: *tam armis quam ingenio*:
Where words prevail not, violence prevails—
But gold doth more than either of them both.
How likes Prince Balthazar this stratagem?   110

BALTHAZAR

Both well and ill: it makes me glad and sad—
Glad, that I know the hinderer of my love,
Sad, that I fear she hates me whom I love;
Glad that I know on whom to be reveng'd,
Sad, that she'll fly me if I take revenge.   115
Yet must I take revenge or die myself,
For love resisted grows impatient.
I think Horatio be my destined plague:
First in his hand he brandishèd a sword,
And with that sword he fiercely wagèd war,   120
And in that war he gave me dangerous wounds,
And by those wounds he forcèd me to yield,
And by my yielding I became his slave.
Now in his mouth he carries pleasing words,
Which pleasing words do harbor sweet conceits,   125
Which sweet conceits are limed with sly deceits,
Which sly deceits smooth Bel-Imperia's ears,
And through her ears dive down into her heart,
And in her heart set him where I should stand.
Thus hath he ta'en my body by his force,   130
And now by sleight would captivate my soul;

---

100. **give . . . sort:** inform me by some secret means.
103. **state:** social and material condition.
107. *tam . . . ingenio:* as much by force of arms as by clever device.
125. **sweet conceits:** (1) beautiful thoughts; (2) attractive figures of speech.
126. **limed:** made into traps (as sticky birdlime was smeared on branches to entrap birds).
127. **smooth:** flatter, soothe.

But in his fall I'll tempt the destinies,
And either lose my life, or win my love.
LORENZO
Let's go, my lord—your staying stays revenge.
Do you but follow me and gain your love: 135
Her favor must be won by his remove.

Exeunt.

[2.2]

Enter HORATIO *and* BEL-IMPERIA.
HORATIO
Now madam, since by favor of your love
Our hidden smoke is turned to open flame,
And that with looks and words we feed our thoughts—
Two chief contents, where more cannot be had—
Thus in the midst of love's fair blandishments,   5
Why show you sign of inward languishments.
       PEDRINGANO *showeth all to the Prince* [BALTHAZAR]
       and LORENZO, *placing them in secret* [*above*].
BEL-IMPERIA
My heart, sweet friend, is like a ship at sea:
She wisheth port, where riding all at ease
She may repair what stormy times have worn,
And, leaning on the shore, may sing with joy   10
That pleasure follows pain, and bliss annoy.
Possession of thy love is th'only port
Wherein my heart, with fears and hopes long tossed,
Each hour doth wish and long to make resort,
There to repair the joys that it hath lost,   15
And, sitting safe, to sing in Cupid's choir
That sweetest bliss is crown of love's desire.
BALTHAZAR [*above*]
O sleep, mine eyes, see not my love profaned;
Be deaf my ears, hear not my discontent;
Die heart, another joys what thou deserv'st.   20

---

134. **staying:** dwelling on the topic. **stays:** delays.
4. **contents:** sources of contentment.
6. SD. *above:* i.e., on the tarras, or gallery above the main stage. In the 1592 edition, "Balthazar *and* Lorenzo *aboue*" (line 17 SD) indicates that their dialogue is not meant to be heard by the characters below.
7. **friend:** lover.
11. **pleasure . . . annoy:** proverbial; see Tilley P408. Cf. S908 "after a storm comes a calm"; the sentiment is reversed in Sonnet 58 of Thomas Watson's posthumously printed *Teares of Fancie* (1593): "pleasure doubleth paine and blisse annoy" (line 10). **bliss annoy:** happiness [follows] trouble.
20. **joys:** enjoys.

LORENZO [*above*]
  Watch still mine eyes, to see this love disjoined;
  Hear still mine ears, to hear them both lament;
  Live heart, to joy at fond Horatio's fall.
BEL-IMPERIA
  Why stands Horatio speechless all this while?
HORATIO
  The less I speak, the more I meditate.   25
BEL-IMPERIA
  But whereon dost thou chiefly meditate?
HORATIO
  On dangers past, and pleasures to ensue.
BALTHAZAR [*above*]
  On pleasures past, and dangers to ensue.
BEL-IMPERIA
  What dangers, and what pleasures dost thou mean?
HORATIO
  Dangers of war, and pleasures of our love.   30
LORENZO [*above*]
  Dangers of death, but pleasures none at all.
BEL-IMPERIA
  Let dangers go, thy war shall be with me—
  But such a war as breaks no bond of peace:
  Speak thou fair words, I'll cross them with fair words;
  Send thou sweet looks, I'll meet them with sweet looks;   35
  Write loving lines, I'll answer loving lines;
  Give me a kiss, I'll countercheck thy kiss:
  Be this our warring peace, or peaceful war.
HORATIO
  But gracious madam, then appoint the field
  Where trial of this war shall first be made.   40
BALTHAZAR [*above*]
  Ambitious villain, how his boldness grows!
BEL-IMPERIA
  Then be thy father's pleasant bower the field,
  Where first we vowed a mutual amity:
  The court were dangerous, that place is safe;
  Our hour shall be when Vesper 'gins to rise,   45

23. **fond:** foolish.
34. **cross:** counter.
35. **meet:** oppose in battle.
36. **answer:** meet in combat.
42. **bower:** arbor, garden seat covered with branches.
44. **were:** would be (subjunctive mode).
45. **Vesper:** the evening star, Venus.

That summons home distressful travelers.
There none shall hear us but the harmless birds.
Happily the gentle nightingale
Shall carol us asleep ere we be ware,
And, singing with the prickle at her breast,   50
Tell our delight and mirthful dalliance.
Till then each hour, will seem a year and more.

HORATIO
But, honey-sweet and honorable love,
Return we now into your father's sight:
Dangerous suspicion waits on our delight.   55

LORENZO [above]
Ay, danger mixed with jealous despite
Shall send thy soul into eternal night.

                                                              Exeunt.

[2.3]

Enter KING OF SPAIN, PORTINGALE AMBASSADOR, *Don Cyprian*
[*Duke of* CASTILE], [*Nobles and Attendants*]

KING
Brother of Castile, to the prince's love
What says your daughter Bel-Imperia?

CASTILE
Although she coy it as becomes her kind,
And yet dissemble that she loves the prince:
I doubt not, I, but she will stoop in time;   5
And were she froward—which she will not be—
Yet herein shall she follow my advice,
Which is to love him or forgo my love.

KING
Then, Lord Ambassador of Portingale,
Advise thy King to make this marriage up,   10
For strengthening of our late confirmèd league:
I know no better means to make us friends.
Her dowry shall be large and liberal:

---

46. distressful travelers: either weary travelers or exhausted laborers (travailers).
48. Happily: perhaps.
49. ware: aware.
50. singing . . . breast: according to a popular legend (debunked by Sir Thomas Browne in *Pseudodoxia Epidemica*), the nightingale, whose song echoed the pains of lovers, sang with a thorn pressed to its breast.
56. jealous: the old spelling is needed to preserve the meter.
3. coy it: pretend shyness. **as . . . kind:** as womenkind naturally do.
4. yet: still. **dissemble that:** closes her eyes to the fact that.
5. stoop: see note to 2.1.4.
6. froward: perverse, ungovernable.

Besides that she is daughter and half heir
Unto our brother here, Don Cyprian,   15
And shall enjoy the moiety of his land,
I'll grace her marriage with an uncle's gift;
And this it is: in case the match go forward,
The tribute which you pay shall be released;
And if by Balthazar she have a son,   20
He shall enjoy the kingdom after us.

AMBASSADOR

I'll make the motion to my sovereign liege,
And work it if my counsel may prevail.

KING

Do so, my lord, and if he give consent,
I hope his presence here will honor us   25
In celebration of the nuptial day,
And let himself determine of the time.

AMBASSADOR

Wilt please your grace command me aught beside?

KING

Commend me to the king, and so farewell.
But where's Prince Balthazar to take his leave?   30

AMBASSADOR

That is performed already, my good lord.

KING

Amongst the rest of what you have in charge,
The prince's ransom must not be forgot:
That's none of mine, but his that took him prisoner,
And well his forwardness deserves reward—   35
It was Horatio, our Knight Marshal's son.

AMBASSADOR

Between us there's a price already pitched,
And shall be sent with all convenient speed.

KING

Then once again farewell, my lord.

AMBASSADOR

Farewell, my lord of Castile and the rest.   *Exit.* 40

KING

Now, brother, you must take some little pains
To win fair Bel-Imperia from her will:
Young virgins must be rulèd by their friends;

---

16. **moiety:** half share.
37. **pitched:** settled.
42. **will:** wilfulness; but perhaps also including sexual appetite.

The prince is amiable and loves her well;
If she neglect him and forgo his love,   45
She both will wrong her own estate and ours.
Therefore, whiles I do entertain the prince
With greatest pleasure that our court affords,
Endeavour you to win your daughter's thought—
If she give back, all this will come to naught.   *Exeunt.* 50

[2.4]

Enter HORATIO, BEL-IMPERIA, *and* PEDRINGANO.

HORATIO
  Now that the night begins with sable wings
  To over-cloud the brightness of the sun,
  And that in darkness pleasures may be done,
  Come, Bel-Imperia, let us to the bower,
  And there in safety pass a pleasant hour.   5
BEL-IMPERIA
  I follow thee, my love, and will not back,
  Although my fainting heart controls my soul.
HORATIO
  Why, make you doubt of Pedringano's faith?
BEL-IMPERIA
  No, he is as trusty as my second self.
  Go, Pedringano, watch without the gate,   10
  And let us know if any make approach.
PEDRINGANO [*aside*]
  Instead of watching, I'll deserve more gold
  By fetching Don Lorenzo to this match.   *Exit* PEDRINGANO.
HORATIO
  What means my love?
BEL-IMPERIA   I know not what myself;
  And yet my heart foretells me some mischance.   15
HORATIO
  Sweet, say not so: fair fortune is our friend,
  And heavens have shut up day to pleasure us;

[handwritten margin notes: "your characterization of Lorenzo's prose", "erotic + trag"]

---

46. estate: exalted rank.
50. give back: either turn her back on us (Edwards, citing *OED, back,* n.¹, 24d) or retreat, run away (24c).
1–2. night . . . sun: ironically Horatio reverses the usual associations of night and the sun.
7. controls: overmasters (i.e., the fearful emotion of her heart is stronger than the reason that guides her soul).
10. without: outside.

The stars, thou seest, hold back their twinkling shine,
And Luna hides herself to pleasure us.

BEL-IMPERIA

Thou hast prevailed, I'll conquer my misdoubt,   20
And in thy love and counsel drown my fear:
I fear no more, love now is all my thoughts.
Why sit we not? for pleasure asketh ease.

HORATIO

The more thou sit'st within these leafy bowers,
The more will Flora deck it with her flowers.   25

BEL-IMPERIA

Ay, but if Flora spy Horatio here,
Her jealous eye will think I sit too near.

HORATIO

Hark, madam, how the birds record by night,
For joy that Bel-Imperia sits in sight.

BEL-IMPERIA

No, Cupid counterfeits the nightingale,   30
To frame sweet music to Horatio's tale.

HORATIO

If Cupid sing, then Venus is not far:
Ay, thou art Venus or some fairer star.

BEL-IMPERIA

If I be Venus, thou must needs be Mars,
And where Mars reigneth there must needs be wars.   35

HORATIO

Then thus begin our wars: put forth thy hand
That it may combat with my ruder hand.

BEL-IMPERIA

Set forth thy foot to try the push of mine.

HORATIO

But first my looks shall combat against thine.

BEL-IMPERIA

Then ward thyself: I dart this kiss at thee.   40

HORATIO

Thus I retort the dart thou threw'st at me.

---

18. **thou:** Horatio's switch to the singular pronoun marks the new intimacy of their relationship; see note to 1.4.2.
19. **Luna:** the moon.
25. **Flora:** Roman goddess of flowering plants, associated with sex and fertility.
32. **Cupid:** Venus's son in classical mythology.
34. **Venus . . . Mars** Bel-Imperia invokes the famously illicit liaison between the deities of love and war.
40. **ward:** guard, protect.

BEL-IMPERIA
Nay then, to gain the glory of the field,
My twining arms shall yoke and make thee yield.
HORATIO
Nay then, my arms are large and strong withal:
Thus elms by vines are compassed till they fall.   45
BEL-IMPERIA
O let me go, for in my troubled eyes
Now may'st thou read that life in passion dies.
HORATIO
O stay a while, and I will die with thee:
So shalt thou yield, and yet have conquered me.
BEL-IMPERIA
Who's there? Pedringano? We are betrayed!   50

> Enter LORENZO, BALTHAZAR, SERBERINE, [and]
> PEDRINGANO, disguised.

LORENZO
[To BALTHAZAR] My lord, away with her! Take her aside.
[To HORATIO] O sir, forbear: your valor is already tried.
[To PEDRINGANO and SERBERINE] Quickly—despatch,
    my masters!
> They hang him in the arbor.
HORATIO
What, will you murder me?
LORENZO
Ay, thus, and thus: these are the fruits of love!   55
> They stab him.
BEL-IMPERIA
O save his life and let me die for him!
O save him, brother! Save him, Balthazar!
I loved Horatio, but he loved not me.
BALTHAZAR
But Balthazar loves Bel-Imperia.

---

45. **elms . . . fall:** Wittily transforms a familiar emblem of Venus: usually the vine supports the elm, even after the latter's death, as a sign of undying love; here the vine (Horatio), pulls down the elm (Bel-Imperia) to achieve sexual death (lines 47–48).
48. **die:** experience orgasm.
52. **tried:** tested.
55. **fruits of love:** Lorenzo plays blasphemously with a familiar image of Christ's sacrifice, in which the fruit of love (hanging on the tree of crucifixion) cancels out the sinful legacy of Genesis's forbidden fruit. See Figure 4 (p. xxv) and 4.4.111–12. There may also be an ironic recollection of Catullus, Poem 55, lines 18–19: "*Si linguam clause tenes in ore / fructus proicies amoris omnes*" (If you keep your tongue shut within your mouth, you will waste all the fruits of love).

LORENZO

    Although his life were still ambitious proud,   60

    Yet is he at the highest now he is dead. *hung up*

BEL-IMPERIA

    Murder! murder! Help, Hieronimo, help!

LORENZO

    Come, stop her mouth! away with her!

                              Exeunt [, leaving Horatio's body].

[2.5]

      Enter HIERONIMO *in his shirt [, carrying a sword and torch]*

HIERONIMO

    What outcries pluck me from my naked bed,

    And chill my throbbing heart with trembling fear,

    Which never danger yet could daunt before?

    Who calls Hieronimo? Speak!—here I am.

    I did not slumber, therefore 'twas no dream;   5

    No, no, it was some woman cried for help,

    And here within this garden did she cry,

    And in this garden must I rescue her.

    But stay, what murd'rous spectacle is this?

    A man hanged up and all the murderers gone,   10

    And in my bower, to lay the guilt on me:

    This place was made for pleasure not for death.

      He cuts him down.

    Those garments that he wears I oft have seen—

    Alas, it is Horatio my sweet son!

    O no, but he that whilom was my son.   15

    O was it thou that calledst me from my bed?

    O speak, if any spark of life remain:

    I am thy father. Who hath slain my son?

    What savage monster not of human kind

    Hath here been glutted with thy harmless blood,   20

    And left thy bloody corpse dishonored here

    For me, amidst this dark and deathful shades,

    To drown thee with an ocean of my tears?

    O heavens, why made you night to cover sin?

[handwritten margin note: visual emblem intended to have a theatrical effect]

2.5 SD. *shirt:* nightshirt. *sword and torch:* In the 1592 edition the "&c." almost certainly refers to the properties that Hieronimo describes in his instructions to the Painter in Addition 4 (lines 137–38), and which he is shown carrying in the 1615 title page wood-cut of this scene. The sword is required to cut down Horatio's body at line 12, while torches were the usual device for indicating nighttime in the daylight theater of Kyd's day.

15. whilom: formerly.

21. dishonored: hanging was considered a dishonorable form of death.

22. this: allowable as a plural in Kyd's time.

By day this deed of darkness had not been.   25
O earth, why didst thou not in time devour
The vile profaner of this sacred bower?
O poor Horatio, what hadst thou misdone,
To leese thy life ere life was new begun?
O wicked butcher, whatsoe'er thou wert,   30
How could thou strangle virtue and desert?
Ay me most wretched, that have lost my joy,
In leesing my Horatio, my sweet boy!

     Enter ISABELLA

ISABELLA

My husband's absence makes my heart to throb.
Hieronimo!   35

HIERONIMO

Here Isabella, help me to lament,
For sighs are stopped, and all my tears are spent.

ISABELLA

What world of grief—my son Horatio!
O where's the author of this endless woe?

HIERONIMO

To know the author were some ease of grief,   40
For in revenge my heart would find relief.

ISABELLA

Then is he gone? and is my son gone too?
O gush out tears, fountains and floods of tears,
Blow sighs and raise an everlasting storm!
For outrage fits our cursed wretchedness.   45

Addition 1

    Ay me, Hieronimo, sweet husband, speak!

HIERONIMO

He supped with us tonight, frolic and merry.
And said he would go visit Balthazar
At the Duke's palace—there the prince doth lodge.
He had no custom to stay out so late: [5]
He may be in his chamber—some go and see.
Roderigo, ho!

     Enter PEDRO *and* JACQUES.

---

29. **leese:** lose.
37. **stopped:** choked.
45. **outrage:** violent clamor; passionate behavior.
[7]. **Roderigo:** no character of this name appears, but because Jacques is unnamed in the
    dialogue, the audience will not have noticed the anomaly.

ISABELLA
> Ay me, he raves! Sweet Hieronimo!

HIERONIMO
> True, all Spain takes note of it;
> Besides, he is so generally beloved—   [10]
> His majesty the other day did grace him
> With waiting on his cup: these be favors
> Which do assure he cannot be short lived.

ISABELLA
> Sweet Hieronimo!

HIERONIMO
> I wonder how this fellow got his clothes.   [15]
> Sirrah, sirrah, I'll know the truth of all:
> Jacques, run to the Duke of Castile's presently,
> And bid my son Horatio to come home—
> I and his mother have had strange dreams tonight.
> Do ye hear me, sir?

JACQUES   Ay, sir.

HIERONIMO   Well sir, begone!   [20]
> Pedro, come hither: know'st thou who this is?

PEDRO
> Too well, sir.

HIERONIMO
> Too well? Who? Who is it? Peace, Isabella!
> Nay, blush not, man.

PEDRO   It is my lord Horatio.

HIERONIMO
> Ha, ha!, Saint James, but this doth make me laugh   [25]
> That there are more deluded than myself.

PEDRO
> Deluded?

HIERONIMO   Ay.
> I would have sworn myself within this hour
> That this had been my son Horatio,
> His garments are so like.   [30]
> Ha! are they not great persuasions?

ISABELLA
> O would to God it were not so!

HIERONIMO
> Were not, Isabella? dost thou dream it is?
> Can thy soft bosom entertain a thought

[9]. **True . . . it:** Hieronimo appears to be answering some imaginary interlocutor.
[15]. **I . . . clothes:** Hieronimo persuades himself that the corpse is that of some low-ranked man dressed up as his son ("fellow" is contemptuous here).
[17]. **presently:** at once.

That such a black deed of mischief should be done   [35]
On one so pure and spotless as our son?
Away! I am ashamed.

ISABELLA   Dear Hieronimo,
Cast a more serious eye upon thy grief:
Weak apprehension gives but weak belief.

HIERONIMO
It was a man, sure, that was hanged up here—   [40]
A youth, as I remember: I cut him down.
If it should prove my son now after all—
Say you? say you? Light! lend me a taper;
Let me look again. O God!
Confusion, mischief, torment, death and hell   [45]
Drop all your stings at once in my cold bosom
That now is stiff with horror. Kill me quickly:
Be gracious to me, thou infective night,
And drop this deed of murder down on me;
Gird in my waste of grief with thy large darkness,   [50]
And let me not survive to see the light
May put me in the the mind I had a son.

ISABELLA
O sweet Horatio! O my dearest son!

HIERONIMO
How strangely had I lost my way to grief.
Sweet lovely rose, ill plucked before thy time,
Fair worthy son, not conquered but betrayed,
I'll kiss thee now, for words with tears are stayed.

ISABELLA
And I'll close up the glasses of his sight,
For once these eyes were only my delight,   50

HIERONIMO
Seest thou this handkerchief besmeared with blood?
It shall not from me till I take revenge.
Seest thou those wounds that yet are bleeding fresh?
I'll not entomb them till I have revenged:
Then will I joy amidst my discontent;   55
Till then my sorrow never shall be spent.

---

[48]. infective: carrying infection.
[50]. Gird in: confine. waste: desert, devastated territory (with a play on *waist* suggested
by "gird").
46. sweet lovely rose: perhaps echoing the identification of Christ in biblical typology as
the rose of Sharon from Song of Solomon 2.1.
48. stayed: stopped.
49. glasses . . . sight: his eyes.
51. handkerchief: kerchief; presumably the same scarf once given to Andrea as a favor by
Bel-Imperia and taken by Horatio as a memento from his dead friend (see 1.4.42).

ISABELLA

The heavens are just, murder cannot be hid:
Time is the author both of truth and right,
And time will bring this treachery to light.

HIERONIMO

Meanwhile, good Isabella, cease thy plaints,   60
Or at the least dissemble them a while;
So shall we sooner find the practice out,
And learn by whom all this was brought about.
Come Isabel, now let us take him up,   *They take him up.*
And bear him in from out this cursèd place.   65
I'll say his dirge, singing fits not this case.
O aliquis mihi quas pulchrum ver educet herbas
          HIERONIMO *sets his breast unto his sword.*
Misceat et nostro detur medicina dolori;
Aut, si qui faciunt animis oblivia, succos
Prebeat; ipse metam magnam quaecunque per orbem   70
Gramina Sol pulchras effert in luminis oras;
Ipse bibam quicquid meditatur saga veneni,
Quicquid et herbarum vi caeca nenia nectit:
Omnia perpetiar, lethum quoque, dum semel omnis
Noster in extincto moriatur pectore sensus.   75
Ergo tuos oculos nunquam, mea vita, videbo,
Et tua perpetuus sepelivit lumina somnus?
Emoriar tecum: sic, sic juvat ire sub umbras.
At tamen absistam properato cedere letho,
Ne mortem vindicta tuam tum nulla sequatur.   80
     Here he throws [the sword] *from him and bears the body away.*

---

57. murder . . . hid: proverbial, see Tilley M1315.
58. Truth and right: proverbial, see Tilley T324.
62. practice: conspiracy, treacherous plot.
67–80. O aliquis . . . sequatur: Let someone mix me the herbs that beautiful spring produces, and let a medicine be given for our suffering; or let him apply juices, if there are any that can bring oblivion to minds; I myself will collect anywhere in the great world whatever herbs the sun brings forth into the lovely regions of light; I myself shall drink whatever poison the wise woman concocts, and whatever herbs she mixes together with the secret power of spells. I shall face everything, even death until all feeling is extinct in my dead breast. Shall I never again, my life, look into your two eyes, and has perpetual slumber buried the light of your life? I shall die with you—thus, thus will I go rejoicing to the shades beneath. Nonetheless, I shall hold myself back from a hasty death, for fear that no revenge follow your death. "A *pastiche*, in Kyd's singular fashion, of tags from classical poetry, and lines of his own composition" [Boas's note].

[2.6]

[*Chorus*]

ANDREA

Brought'st thou me hither to increase my pain?
I looked that Balthazar should have been slain,
But 'tis my friend Horatio that is slain;
And they abuse fair Bel-Imperia
On whom I doted more than all the world   5
Because she loved me more than all the world.

REVENGE

Thou talk'st of harvest when the corn is green:
The end is crown of every work well done;
The sickle comes not till the corn be ripe.
Be still, and ere I lead thee from this place,   10
I'll show thee Balthazar in heavy case.

Actus Tertius.

[3.1]

Enter VICEROY *of Portingale, Nobles,* [*and*] VILLUPPO.

VICEROY

Infortunate condition of kings,
Seated amidst so many helpless doubts!
First we are placed upon extremest height,
And oft supplanted with exceeding heat,
But ever subject to the wheel of chance;   5
And at our highest never joy we so
As we both doubt and dread our overthrow.
So striveth not the waves with sundry winds
As fortune toileth in the affairs of kings,
That would be feared, yet fear to be beloved,   10
Sith fear or love to kings is flattery:
For instance, lordings, look upon your king,
By hate deprivèd of his dearest son,
The only hope of our successive line.

---

8. The end . . . done: proverbial, see Tilley E116. Often cited as a Latin tag, *Finis coronat opus*.
1–11. Infortunate . . . flattery: adapted from Seneca, *Agamemnon* 57–73.
4. heat: passion, rage.
5. wheel of chance: see note to 1.3.9.
11. Sith: since.
14. successive line: line of succession.

1 NOBLE

I had not thought that Alexandro's heart   15
Had been envenomed with such extreme hate:
But now I see that words have several works,
And there's no credit in the countenance.

VILLUPPO

No—for, my lord, had you beheld the train
That feignèd love had colored in his looks,   20
When he in camp consorted Balthazar,
Far more inconstant had you thought the sun
That hourly coasts the center of the earth
Than Alexandro's purpose to the Prince.

VICEROY

No more, Villuppo! thou hast said enough,   25
And with thy words thou slay'st our wounded thoughts;
Nor shall I longer dally with the world,
Procrastinating Alexandro's death:
Go some of you and fetch the traitor forth,
That as he is condemnèd he may die.   30
          Enter ALEXANDRO *with a Nobleman and Halberdiers.*

2 NOBLE

In such extremes, will nought but patience serve.

ALEXANDRO

But in extremes, what patience shall I use?
Nor discontents it me to leave the world,
With whom there nothing can prevail but wrong.

2 NOBLE

Yet hope the best.

ALEXANDRO   'Tis Heaven is my hope.   35
As for the earth, it is too much infect
To yield me hope of any of her mold.

VICEROY

Why linger ye? Bring forth that daring fiend,
And let him die for his accursèd deed.

ALEXANDRO

Not that I fear the extremity of death—   40
For nobles cannot stoop to servile fear—

---

17. **several works:** various outcomes.
19. **train:** guile, treacherous deceit (*OED* n.² 1).
20. **colored:** disguised (*OED* v. 3).
21. **consorted:** accompanied.
22–23 **the sun . . . earth:** the sun that circles this earth, center of the universe, with the regular movement that marks the hours; a familiar figure for constancy. Kyd invokes the traditional cosmology, according to which all heavenly bodies revolved around the earth.
36. **infect:** infected.
37. **any . . . mold:** anyone fashioned from the earth; i.e., any mere mortal.

Do I, O king, thus discontented live;
But this, O this torments my laboring soul,
That thus I die suspected of a sin,
Whereof, as heavens have known my secret thoughts,   45
So am I free from this suggestion.

VICEROY

No more I say! To the tortures! When?
Bind him, and burn his body in those flames
        They bind him to the stake.
That shall prefigure those unquenchèd fires,
Of Phlegethon prepared for his soul.   50

ALEXANDRO

My guiltless death will be avenged on thee—
On thee, Villuppo, that hath maliced thus,
Or for thy meed, hast falsely me accused.

VILLUPPO

Nay, Alexandro, if thou menace me,
I'll lend a hand to send thee to the lake   55
Where those thy words shall perish with thy works—
Injurious traitor, monstrous homicide!
        Enter AMBASSADOR.

AMBASSADOR

Stay! hold a while,
And here, with pardon of his majesty,
Lay hands upon Villuppo.

VICEROY   Ambassador,   60
What news hath urged this sudden entrance?

AMBASSADOR

Know, sovereign lord, that Balthazar doth live.

VICEROY

What say'st thou? liveth Balthazar our son?

AMBASSADOR

Your highness' son, Lord Balthazar, doth live,
And, well entreated in the court of Spain,   65
Humbly commends him to your majesty.
These eyes beheld, and these my followers;
With these, the letters of the king's commends
        Gives him letters.

---

50. **Phlegethon:** literally, "flaming"; a stream of fire that constituted one of the five rivers of the classical underworld.
52. **maliced:** sought to injure [me] (*OED* v. 1).
53. **meed:** reward.
55. **lake:** the Acherusian lake into which the rivers Phlegethon and Acheron reputedly flowed.
61. **entrance:** pronounced with three syllables (enteránce).
68. **commends:** greetings.

Are happy witnesses of his highness' health.
The VICEROY *looks on the letter and proceeds.*

VICEROY

"Thy son doth live, your tribute is received,   70
Thy peace is made, and we are satisfied.
The rest resolve upon as things proposed
For both our honors and thy benefit."

AMBASSADOR

These are his highness' further articles.
He gives him more letters.

VICEROY

Accursèd wretch to intimate these ills   75
Against the life and reputation
Of noble Alexandro. [*To* VILLUPPO] Come, my lord,
     unbind him.
[*To* ALEXANDRO] Let him unbind thee that is bound to death,
To make a quital for thy discontent.
     They unbind him.

ALEXANDRO

Dread Lord, in kindness you could do no less   80
Upon report of such a damnèd fact;
But thus we see our innocence hath saved
The hopeless life which thou, Villuppo, sought
By thy suggestions to have massacred.

VICEROY

Say, false Villuppo, wherefore didst thou thus   85
Falsely betray Lord Alexandro's life—
Him whom thou know'st, that no unkindness else,
But even the slaughter of our dearest son,
Could once have moved us to have misconceived?

ALEXANDRO

Say, treacherous Villuppo, tell the king   90
Wherein hath Alexandro used thee ill?

VILLUPPO

Rent with remembrance of so foul a deed,
My guilty soul submits me to thy doom;
For not for Alexandro's injuries,

---

75. **intimate these ills:** promulgate these falsehoods.
78. **bound to:** (1) tied to; (2) headed for.
79. **quital:** recompense.
80. **in kindness:** according to your (kingly) nature.
87. **unkindness:** vicious and unnatural deed.
89. **misconceived:** falsely suspected.
93. **doom:** judgment.

But for reward and hope to be preferred,   95
Thus have I shameless hazarded his life.

VICEROY
Which, villain, shall be ransomed with thy death—
And not so mean a torment as we here
Devised for him who thou said'st slew our son,
But with the bitterest torments and extremes   100
That may be yet invented for thine end.

ALEXANDRO *seems to entreat.*

Entreat me not—go, take the traitor hence!

Exit VILLUPPO

And, Alexandro, let us honor thee
With public notice of thy loyalty.
To end those things articulated here   105
By our great lord, the mighty king of Spain,
We with our council will deliberate.
Come, Alexandro, keep us company.

Exeunt.

[3.2]

Enter HIERONIMO.

HIERONIMO
O eyes, no eyes, but fountains fraught with tears;
O life, no life, but lively form of death;
O world, no world, but mass of public wrongs,
Confused and filled with murder and misdeeds!
O sacred heavens, if this unhallowed deed,   5
If this inhuman and barbarous attempt,
If this incomparable murder thus
Of mine—but now no more my son—
Shall unrevealed and unrevengèd pass,
How should we term your dealings to be just,   10
If you unjustly deal with those that in your justice trust?
The night, sad secretary to my moans,
With direful visions wakes my vexèd soul,
And with the wounds of my distressful son
Solicits me for notice of his death.   15

95. **preferred:** promoted.
98. **mean:** inconsiderable (*OED* a.² 3b).
105. **articulated here:** set forth in these articles (i.e., of the treaty with Spain).
1. **O eyes . . . tears:** translating a much-imitated line from Petrarch's sonnet 161: "*Oi occhi miei, occhi no gia, ma fonti!*" The transposition of a line from a love sonnet to a revenger's soliloquy creates an irony that Kyd must have expected literate members of his audience to recognize. **fraught:** filled.
12. **sad:** (1) sorrowful; (2) dark; (3) grave, serious (*OED* a. 5, 8, 4). **secretary:** confidant.
15. **notice of:** information about.

The ugly fiends do sally forth of hell,
And frame my steps to unfrequented paths,
And fear my heart with fierce inflamèd thoughts.
The cloudy day my discontents records,
Early begins to register my dreams,   20
And drive me forth to seek the murderer.
Eyes, life, world, heavens, hell, night and day,
See, search, show, send, some man, some mean, that may—
    A letter [in red ink] falleth.
What's here? a letter? tush, it is not so!
A letter written to Hieronimo!   25
"For want of ink, receive this bloody writ.
Me hath my hapless brother hid from thee:
Revenge thy self on Balthazar and him,
For these were they that murderèd thy son.
Hieronimo, revenge Horatio's death,   30
And better fare then Bel-Imperia doth."
What means this unexpected miracle?
My son slain by Lorenzo and the prince!
What cause had they Horatio to malign?
Or what might move thee, Bel-Imperia,   35
To accuse thy brother, had he been the mean?
Hieronimo beware, thou art betrayed,
And to entrap thy life this train is laid.
Advise thee therefore, be not credulous:
This is devisèd to endanger thee,   40
That thou by this Lorenzo shouldst accuse,
And he, for thy dishonor done, should draw
Thy life in question and thy name in hate.
Dear was the life of my beloved son,
And of his death behoves me be revenged: 45
Then hazard not thine own, Hieronimo,
But live t'effect thy resolution.
I therefore will by circumstances try
What I can gather to confirm this writ,
And, hark'ning near the Duke of Castile's house,   50

---

18. **fear:** frighten.
23. **mean:** means. SD. **Red ink:** The 1592 edition's "Red incke" after line 25 is probably a
    surviving authorial note indicating that Bel-Imperia's "bloody writ" is to be taken
    literally.
27. **hapless:** unlucky (i.e., bringing ill-fortune to me).
34. **malign:** plot against; hate, resent (*OED* v. 3, 4).
38. **train:** plot.
47. **t'effect thy resolution:** bring about what you have decided to do.
48. **circumstances:** circumstantial evidence (*OED* n. 3).
49. **writ:** letter (*OED* n. 1d).

Close if I can with Bel-Imperia
To listen more, but nothing to bewray.
      Enter PEDRINGANO.
Now, Pedringano!
PEDRINGANO   Now, Hieronimo!
HIERONIMO
Where's thy lady?
PEDRINGANO   I know not. Here's my lord.
      Enter LORENZO.
LORENZO
How now, who's this? Hieronimo?
HIERONIMO   My lord.   55
PEDRINGANO
He asketh for my lady Bel-Imperia.
LORENZO
What to do, Hieronimo? The duke my father hath
Upon some disgrace a while removed her hence;
But if it be aught I may inform her of,
Tell me Hieronimo, and I'll let her know it.   60
HIERONIMO
Nay, nay, my lord, I thank you, it shall not need:
I had a suit unto her, but too late,
And her disgrace makes me unfortunate.
LORENZO
Why so, Hieronimo? use me.
HIERONIMO
O no, my lord, I dare not, it must not be.   65
I humbly thank your lordship.

Addition 2

HIERONIMO   Who, you, my lord?
I reserve your favor for a greater honor—
This is a very toy, my lord, a toy.
LORENZO
All's one, Hieronimo: acquaint me with it.
HIERONIMO
I'faith, my lord, it is an idle thing,   [5]

---

52. bewray: divulge (*OED* v. 3).
58. disgrace: stress on the first syllable.
61. it . . . need: that's unnecessary.
Addition 2: *replaces Hieronimo's speech at* 3.2.65–6 *in the* 1602 *edition.*
[3]. toy: trivial thing.
[5]. idle: insignificant (*OED* a. 2a).

I must confess. I ha' been too slack, too tardy,
Too remiss unto your honor.

LORENZO   How now, Hieronimo?

HIERONIMO

In troth, my lord, it is a thing of nothing,
The murder of a son, or so—
A thing of nothing, my lord.   [10]

LORENZO   Why then, farewell.

HIERONIMO

My grief no heart, my thoughts no tongue can tell.   *Exit.*

LORENZO

Come hither, Pedringano: seest thou this?

PEDRINGANO

My lord, I see it, and suspect it too.

LORENZO

This is that damnèd villain Serberine,   70
That hath, I fear, revealed Horatio's death.

PEDRINGANO

My Lord, he could not, 'twas so lately done—
And since, he hath not left my company.

LORENZO

Admit he have not, his condition's such
As fear or flattering words may make him false.   75
I know his humor, and therewith repent
That e'er I used him in this enterprise.
But, Pedringano, to prevent the worst
(And 'cause I know thee secret as my soul)
Here, for thy further satisfaction, take thou this.   80
     Gives him more gold.
And hearken to me—thus it is devised:
This night thou must (and prithee so resolve)
Meet Serberine at Saint Luigi's Park—
Thou knowest 'tis here hard by behind the house—
There take thy stand; and see thou strike him sure,   85
For die he must, if we do mean to live.

PEDRINGANO

But how shall Serberine be there my lord?

LORENZO

Let me alone, I'll send to him to meet
The prince and me where thou must do this deed.

---

74. **condition:** nature, character; circumstances, social position (*OED* n. 11; 10).
76. **humor:** disposition, character (*OED* n. 4).
88. **Let me alone:** leave it to me.

PEDRINGANO

It shall be done, my lord, it shall be done;   90
And I'll go arm myself to meet him there.

LORENZO

When things shall alter, as I hope they will,
Then shalt thou mount for this: thou know'st my mind.

Exit PEDRINGANO

Che le Jerome!
   Enter Page.

PAGE   My lord?

LORENZO   Go, sirrah, go to Serberine,   95
And bid him forthwith meet the prince and me
At Saint Luigi's Park, behind the house,
This evening, boy.

PAGE   I go, my lord.

LORENZO

But, sirrah, let the hour be eight o'clock—
Bid him not fail.

PAGE   I fly, my lord.   *Exit.* 100

LORENZO

Now to confirm the complot thou hast cast
Of all these practices, I'll spread the watch,
Upon precise commandment from the king,
Strongly to guard the place where Pedringano
This night shall murder hapless Serberine.   105
Thus must we work that will avoid distrust;
Thus must we practice to prevent mishap;
And thus one ill, another must expulse.
This sly enquiry of Hieronimo
For Bel-Imperia breeds suspicion,   110
And this suspicion bodes a further ill.
As for myself, I know my secret fault—
And so do they, but I have dealt for them.
They that for coin their souls endangered
To save my life, for coin shall venture theirs;   115
And better 'tis that base companions die,

---

93. mount: (1) climb socially; (2) mount the scaffold. Cf. Lorenzo's similar jest when Horatio is hanged (2.4.61).
94. *Che le Jerome*: If the 1592 edition's "Ieron" looks as if it may be a proper name, perhaps it's a misprint for *Ierom* (i.e., Jerome). Thus the phrase would be rough Spanish for "Hey there, Jerome."
101–02. complot . . . practices: conspiracy you have contrived from all these cunning stratagems.
102. spread: position.
107. practice: scheme.
108. expulse: expel.
116. base companions: low fellows.

Than by their life to hazard our good haps.
Nor shall they live for me to fear their faith:
I'll trust myself, myself shall be my friend,
For die they shall—slaves are ordainèd to no other end.   120

                                                              Exit.

[3.3]

Enter PEDRINGANO *with a pistol.*

PEDRINGANO

Now, Pedringano, bid thy pistol hold;
And hold on, Fortune! once more favor me:
Give but success to mine attempting spirit,
And let me shift for taking of mine aim.
Here is the gold, this is the gold proposed—   5
It is no dream that I adventure for,
But Pedringano is possessed thereof;
And he that would not strain his conscience
For him that thus his liberal purse hath stretched,
Unworthy such a favor may he fail,   10
And wishing, want, when such as I prevail.
As for the fear of apprehension,
I know, if need should be, my noble lord
Will stand between me and ensuing harms;
Besides, this place is free from all suspect: 15
Here, therefore, will I stay and take my stand.

          Enter the Watch.

1 WATCHMAN

I wonder much to what intent it is,
That we are thus expressly charged to watch?

2 WATCHMAN

'Tis by commandment in the king's own name.

3 WATCHMAN

But we were never wont to watch and ward   20
So near the duke his brother's house before.

2 WATCHMAN

Content yourself—stand close, there's somewhat in't.

          Enter SERBERINE.

---

117. **our:** the royal plural, normally used only by a monarch, emphasises Lorenzo's arrogance. **haps:** fortune.
118. **fear their faith:** worry about their keeping faith.
1. **hold:** continue to function (*OED* v. 16).
4. **let me shift:** leave it to me.
12. **apprehension:** being arrested.
15. **suspect:** suspicion.
20. **watch and ward:** patrol and guard (legally defined duties of watchmen).
22. **somewhat in't:** something going on.

SERBERINE
  Here, Serberine, attend and stay thy pace,
  For here did Don Lorenzo's page appoint,
  That thou by his command shouldst meet with him.   25
  How fit a place, if one were so disposed,
  Methinks this corner is to close with one.

PEDRINGANO
  Here comes the bird that I must seize upon:
  Now, Pedringano, or never, play the man!

SERBERINE
  I wonder that his lordship stays so long;   30
  Or wherefore should he send for me so late?

PEDRINGANO
  For this, Serberine, and thou shalt ha't.   *Shoots the dag.*
  So, there he lies—my promise is performed.
      The Watch [*come forward*].

1 WATCHMAN
  Hark, gentlemen, this is a pistol shot.

2 WATCHMAN
  And here's one slain. Stay the murderer!   35

PEDRINGANO
  Now, by the sorrows of the souls in hell,
      He strives with the Watch.
  Who first lays hand on me, I'll be his priest.

3 WATCHMAN
  Sirrah, confess, and therein play the priest:
  Why hast thou thus unkindly killed the man?

PEDRINGANO
  Why? because he walked abroad so late.   40

3 WATCHMAN
  Come, sir, you had been better kept your bed
  Than have committed this misdeed so late.

2 WATCHMAN
  Come, to the marshal's with the murderer!

1 WATCHMAN
  On to Hieronimo's! Help me here
  To bring the murdered body with us too.   45

PEDRINGANO
  Hieronimo? carry me before whom you will—

---

23. attend . . . pace: stop and wait.
27. close: grapple (*OED* v. 13).
32. SD. *dag*: heavy pistol.
35. stay: take prisoner (*OED* v. 20d).
37. I'll . . . priest: help him to the next world (i.e., kill him).
39. unkindly: unnaturally.

Whate'er he be I'll answer him and you;
And do your worst, for I defy you all!

Exeunt.

[3.4]

Enter LORENZO *and* BALTHAZAR.

BALTHAZAR
How now, my lord, what makes you rise so soon?
LORENZO
Fear of preventing our mishaps too late.
BALTHAZAR
What mischief is it that we not mistrust?
LORENZO
Our greatest ills we least mistrust, my lord,
And inexpected harms do hurt us most.   5
BALTHAZAR
Why tell me, Don Lorenzo, tell me man,
If aught concerns our honor and your own?
LORENZO
Nor you, nor me, my lord, but both in one.
For I suspect—and the presumption's great—
That by those base confederates in our fault   10
Touching the death of Don Horatio,
We are betrayed to old Hieronimo.
BALTHAZAR
Betrayed, Lorenzo? tush, it cannot be!
LORENZO
A guilty conscience, urgèd with the thought
Of former evils, easily cannot err: 15
I am persuaded, and dissuade me not,
That all's revealèd to Hieronimo;
And therefore know that I have cast it thus—
     [*Enter Page*]
But here's the page: how now, what news with thee?
PAGE
My lord, Serberine is slain.
BALTHAZAR   Who? Serberine, my man?   20
PAGE
Your highness' man, my lord.
LORENZO   Speak, page: who murdered him?

3. **mistrust:** anticipate.
10. **fault:** crime.
18. **cast it:** made plans.
20. **Serberine:** The meter requires that this name be elided as *Serb'rine* in the first half of
     the line.

PAGE
　He that is apprehended for the fact.
LORENZO
　Who?
PAGE　Pedringano.
BALTHAZAR
　Is Serberine slain that loved his lord so well?
　Injurious villain, murderer of his friend!   25
LORENZO
　Hath Pedringano murdered Serberine?
　My lord, let me entreat you to take the pains
　To exasperate and hasten his revenge
　With your complaints unto my lord the king.
　This their dissension breeds a greater doubt.   30
BALTHAZAR
　Assure thee, Don Lorenzo, he shall die,
　Or else his highness hardly shall deny.
　Meanwhile, I'll haste the marshal-sessions,
　For die he shall for this his damnèd deed.   *Exit* BALTHAZAR
LORENZO
　Why so, this fits our former policy,   35
　And thus experience bids the wise to deal.
　I lay the plot, he prosecutes the point;
　I set the trap, he breaks the worthless twigs,
　And sees not that wherewith the bird was limed.
　Thus hopeful men that mean to hold their own   40
　Must look like fowlers to their dearest friends.
　He runs to kill whom I have holp to catch,
　And no man knows it was my reaching fatch.
　'Tis hard to trust unto a multitude—
　Or anyone, in mine opinion—   45
　When men themselves their secrets will reveal.
　　　Enter a Messenger with a letter.
LORENZO
　Boy!
PAGE　My lord?
LORENZO　　What's he?

---

28. **exasperate:** make more harsh. **his revenge:** revenge upon him.
30. **doubt:** danger, risk (*OED* n. 4b).
32. **Or else . . . deny:** unless the king is harsh enough to refuse me [justice in the matter].
33. **marshal-sessions:** legal hearings presided over by the Knight Marshal.
35. **policy:** Machiavellian plotting (see note to 2.1.41).
37. **prosecutes the point:** follows it thorough to its desired conclusion.
39. **limed:** see note to 2.1.126.
43. **reaching:** far-reaching, designing. **fatch:** obsolete form of *fetch* (stratagem, device).

MESSENGER   I have a letter to your lordship.

LORENZO
  From whence?

MESSENGER   From Pedringano that's imprisoned.

LORENZO
  So, he is in prison then?

MESSENGER   Ay, my good lord.

LORENZO
  What would he with us? He writes us here   50
  To stand good lord and help him in distress.
  Tell him I have his letters, know his mind,
  And what we may, let him assure him of.
  Fellow, begone! my boy shall follow thee.

                           Exit Messenger.

  This works like wax; yet once more try thy wits,   55
  Boy, go convey this purse to Pedringano—
  Thou know'st the prison, closely give it him;
  And be advised that none be there about.
  Bid him be merry still, but secret;
  And, though the marshal-sessions be today,   60
  Bid him not doubt of his delivery.
  Tell him his pardon is already signed,
  And thereon bid him boldly be resolved;
  For, were he ready to be turnèd off—
  As 'tis my will the uttermost be tried—   65
  Thou with his pardon shalt attend him still:
  Show him this box, tell him his pardon's in't,
  But open't not, and if thou lov'st thy life;
  But let him wisely keep his hopes unknown:
  He shall not want while Don Lorenzo lives.   70
  Away!

PAGE   I go my lord, I run.

LORENZO
  But, sirrah, see that this be cleanly done.   *Exit Page.*
  Now stands our fortune on a tickle point,
  And now or never ends Lorenzo's doubts.
  One only thing is uneffected yet,   75

---

51. **stand**: act as.
55. **This . . . wax**: i.e., the situation is easily molded to his designs.
57. **closely**: secretly.
58. **advised**: careful.
64. **turnèd off**: hanged.
68. **and if**: if.
72. **sirrah**: contemptuous or condescending form of *sir,* used to social inferiors and children.
73. **tickle**: precarious.
74. **doubts**: fears.

And that's to fee the executioner—
But to what end? I list not trust the air
With utterance of our pretence therein,
For fear the privy whisp'ring of the wind
Convey our words amongst unfriendly ears   80
That lie too open to advantages.
    E quel che voglio io, nessun-le sa,
    Intendo io: quel mi basterà.

                                                                    Exit.

                                    [3.5]

    Enter PAGE *with the box.*

PAGE   My master hath forbidden me to look in this box; and by
my troth 'tis likely, if he had not warned me, I should not have
had so much idle time, for we men's-kind in our minority are
like women in their uncertainty: that they are most forbidden,
they will soonest attempt—so I now. [*Opens the box*] By my bare   5
honesty, here's nothing but the bare empty box! Were it not sin
against secrecy, I would say it were a piece of gentlemanlike
knavery. I must go to Pedringano, and tell him his pardon is in
this box—nay, I would have sworn it, had I not seen the
contrary. I cannot choose but smile to think how the villain   10
will flout the gallows, scorn the audience, and descant on the
hangman—and all presuming of his pardon from hence. Will't
not be an odd jest for me to stand and grace every jest he
makes, pointing my fingers at this box, as who would say,
"Mock on, here's thy warrant"? Is't not a scurvy jest, that a man   15
should jest himself to death? Alas, poor Pedringano! I am in a
sort sorry for thee; but if I should be hanged with thee, I
cannot weep.

                                                                    Exit.

77. list not: have no wish to.
82–83. *E quel . . . basterà*: And what I want, no one knows; I understand it, and that is
enough for me (Italian; see note to 2.1.41).
3. idle time: time to engage in idle behavior.
4. uncertainty: capriciousness (*OED uncertain* a. 5b).
6. empty box: probably remembering the box given to Pandora (the first woman on earth
in Greek myth), which after she inquisitively opened it was emptied of everything but
hope. An allusion to the Silenus box, which Plato's *Symposium* uses to represent the disparity between illusion and reality, is also possible.
8. knavery: trickery, but also playing on the sense of *knave* as "one of low degree" (*OED*
n. 2).
11. flout: jeer at. descant: comment (satirically) on.
13. grace: embellish (*OED* v.41).
15. scurvy: sorry, shabby.

[3.6]

Enter HIERONIMO *and the* DEPUTY.

HIERONIMO

Thus must we toil in other men's extremes,
That know not how to remedy our own,
And do them justice, when unjustly we,
For all our wrongs, can compass no redress.
But shall I never live to see the day   5
That I may come, by justice of the heavens,
To know the cause that may my cares allay?
This toils my body, this consumeth age,
That only I to all men just must be,
And neither gods nor men be just to me.   10

DEPUTY

Worthy Hieronimo, your office asks
A care to punish such as do transgress.

HIERONIMO

So is't my duty to regard his death
Who, when he lived, deserved my dearest blood.
But come, for that we came for, let's begin;   15
For here lies that which bids me to be gone.

> *Enter [Hangman], Officers, Page [with the box], and*
> PEDRINGANO, *with a letter in his hand, bound. [The Page*
> *stands apart, pointing at the box.]*

DEPUTY

Bring forth the prisoner, for the court is set.

PEDRINGANO [*aside to the Page*]

Gramercy boy, but it was time to come,
For I had written to my lord anew
A nearer matter that concerneth him,   20
For fear his Lordship had forgotten me;
But sith he hath remembered me so well—
[*Aloud*] Come, come, come on, when shall we to this gear?

HIERONIMO

Stand forth, thou monster, murderer of men,
And here for satisfaction of the world,   25

3.6. SD. **Deputy**: official title of the Knight Marshal's assistant.
1. **extremes**: extremities, hardships (*OED* n. 4b).
4. **compass**: achieve.
7. **cause**: legal process, suit (*OED* n. 8).
11. **asks**: requires.
13. **regard**: pay heed to, take care of.
18. **Gramercy**: thank you (from French *grand merci*).
20. **nearer**: more closely affecting him.
23. **gear**: business.

Confess thy folly and repent thy fault,
For there's thy place of execution.

PEDRINGANO
This is short work! well, to your marshalship
First I confess—nor fear I death therefore—
I am the man, 'twas I slew Serberine.   30
But sir, then you think this shall be the place
Where we shall satisfy you for this gear?

DEPUTY
Ay, Pedringano.

PEDRINGANO   Now I think not so.

HIERONIMO
Peace, impudent! for thou shalt find it so.
For blood with blood shall, while I sit as judge,   35
Be satisfied, and the law discharged.
And though myself cannot receive the like,
Yet will I see that others have their right.
Despatch! the fault's approvèd and confessed,
And by our law he is condemned to die.   40

HANGMAN
Come on, sir, are you ready?

PEDRINGANO   To do what,
My fine officious knave?

HANGMAN   To go to this gear.

PEDRINGANO   O sir, you are too forward: thou wouldst fain furnish me with a halter to disfurnish me of my habit; so I should
go out of this gear, my raiment, into that gear, the rope. But,   45
hangman, now I spy your knavery, I'll not change without
boot, that's flat.

HANGMAN   Come, sir.

PEDRINGANO   So then, I must up?

HANGMAN   No remedy.   50

PEDRINGANO   Yes, but there shall be for my coming down.

HANGMAN   Indeed, here's a remedy for that.

PEDRINGANO   How? be turned off?

HANGMAN   Ay, truly—come, are you ready? I pray, sir, despatch:
the day goes away.   55

PEDRINGANO   What do you hang by the hour? If you do, I may
chance to break your old custom.

HANGMAN   Faith, you have reason, for I am like to break your
young neck.

44–45. disfurnish . . . habit: The hangman was entitled to take the clothes of his victim.
47. boot: compensation, remedy (with a pun on footwear).
53. turned off: see note to 3.4.64.

PEDRINGANO   Dost thou mock me hangman? Pray God I be not   60
preserved to break your knave's pate for this!

HANGMAN   Alas, sir, you are a foot too low to reach it; and I hope
you will never grow so high while I am in the office.

PEDRINGANO   Sirrah, dost see yonder boy with the box in his
hand?   65

HANGMAN   What, he that points to it with his finger?

PEDRINGANO   Ay, that companion.

HANGMAN   I know him not, but what of him?

PEDRINGANO   Dost thou think to live till his old doublet will make
thee a new truss?   70

HANGMAN   Ay, and many a fair year after, to truss up many an
honester man than either thou or he.

PEDRINGANO   What hath he in his box, as thou think'st?

HANGMAN   Faith, I cannot tell, nor I care not greatly. Methinks
you should rather hearken to your soul's health.   75

PEDRINGANO   Why, sirrah hangman, I take it that that is good
for the body is likewise good for the soul; and it may be, in that
box is balm for both.

HANGMAN   Well, thou art even the merriest piece of man's flesh
that e'er groaned at my office door!   80

PEDRINGANO   Is your roguery become an 'office' with a knave's
name?

HANGMAN   Ay, and that shall all they witness that see you seal it
with a thief's name.

PEDRINGANO   I prithee, request this good company to pray with   85
me.

HANGMAN   Ay marry sir, this is a good motion: my masters, you
see here's a good fellow.

PEDRINGANO   Nay, nay, now I remember me, let them alone till
some other time, for now I have no great need.   90

HIERONIMO
I have not seen a wretch so impudent!
O monstrous times, where murder's set so light,
And where the soul, that should be shrined in heaven,
Solely delights in interdicted things,
Still wand'ring in the thorny passages,   95
That intercepts itself of happiness!
Murder, O bloody monster—God forbid,

---

67. **companion:** fellow.
70. **truss:** close-fitting jacket or breeches (*OED* n. 3a–b).
71. **truss up:** fasten on a gallows, hang (*OED* v. 7).
75. **hearken:** have regard (*OED* v. 3).
87. **motion:** proposal.
96. **That . . . of:** which cut off the soul from.

A fault so foul should 'scape unpunished!
Despatch and see this execution done—
This makes me to remember thee, my son.   *Exit* HIERONIMO. 100
PEDRINGANO   Nay soft, no haste!
DEPUTY
    Why, wherefore stay you? have you hope of life?
PEDRINGANO   Why, ay.
HANGMAN   As how?
PEDRINGANO
    Why, rascal, by my pardon from the king   105
HANGMAN
    Stand you on that? then you shall off with this.
        He turns him off.
DEPUTY
    So, executioner, convey him hence,
    But let his body be unburied:
    Let not the earth be chokèd or infect
    With that which heavens contemns and men neglect.   110
                                                    Exeunt.

[3.7]

        Enter HIERONIMO.
HIERONIMO
    Where shall I run to breathe abroad my woes,
    My woes whose weight hath wearièd the earth,
    Or mine exclaims that have surcharged the air,
    With ceaseless plaints for my deceasèd son?
    The blust'ring winds, conspiring with my words,   5
    At my lament have moved the leafless trees,
    Disrobed the meadows of their flowered green,
    Made mountains marsh with springtides of my tears,
    And broken through the brazen gates of hell;
    Yet still tormented is my tortured soul   10
    With broken sighs and restless passions
    That wingèd mount, and, hovering in the air,

---

101. **soft:** hold on.
102. **stay:** delay.
106. **stand:** depend. **SD.** *turns him off:* It was the hangman's task to push the condemned man off the bench that supported his feet. The spectacle of Pedringano's hanging body mirrors the hanging of Horatio in the arbor (2.4), and editors have suggested that the same property (stripped of its leaves) may have been used to represent the gallows.
110. **heavens:** here treated as a collective. Such uses of plural nouns with singular verbs are not uncommon in the period. **contemns:** despises.
1. **breathe abroad:** express.
5. **conspiring:** plays on the literal sense "breathing together with."
11. **passions:** passionate speeches or outbursts (*OED* n. 6d).

Beat at the windows of the brightest heavens,
Soliciting for justice and revenge;
But they are placed in those empyreal heights   15
Where, countermured with walls of diamond,
I find the place impregnable, and they
Resist my woes, and give my words no way.
        Enter HANGMAN *with a letter.*
HANGMAN   O Lord, sir, God bless you, sir! the man, sir, Petergade,
   sir, he that was so full of merry conceits—   20
HIERONIMO   Well, what of him?
HANGMAN   O Lord, sir, he went the wrong way: the fellow had
   a fair commission to the contrary. Sir, here is his passport, I
   pray you sir, we have done him wrong!
HIERONIMO   I warrant thee, give it me.   25
HANGMAN   You will stand between the gallows and me?
HIERONIMO   Ay, ay.
HANGMAN   I thank your lord worship.   *Exit* HANGMAN.
HIERONIMO
   And yet, though somewhat nearer me concerns,
   I will, to ease the grief that I sustain,   30
   Take truce with sorrow while I read on this:
   "My Lord, I write as mine extremes required,
   That you would labor my delivery;
   If you neglect, my life is desperate,
   And in my death I shall reveal the truth.   35
   You know, my lord, I slew him for your sake,
   And was confederate with the prince and you;
   Won by rewards and hopeful promises,
   I holp to murder Don Horatio too."
   Holp he to murder mine Horatio?   40
   And actors in th'accursèd tragedy
   Wast thou, Lorenzo, Balthazar and thou,
   Of whom my son, my son deserved so well?
   What have I heard, what have mine eyes beheld?
   O sacred heavens, may it come to pass   45

---

15. **empyreal** of the highest heaven (pronounced like *imperial*).
16. **countermured**: defensively walled.
20. **conceits**: see note to 1.4.82.
23. **fair commission** proper written authority. **passport**: letter of authorization.
25. **I warrant thee**: I will protect you.
29. **somewhat . . . concerns**: I have more pressing matters to deal with.
34. **my . . . desperate**: I despair of my life.
42. **thou** Hieronimo's shifts from *you* (the polite form of address to social superiors) to
   thou (the form used to inferiors).

That such a monstrous and detested deed,
So closely smothered, and so long concealed,
Shall thus by this be vengèd or revealed?
Now see I what I durst not then suspect,
That Bel-Imperia's letter was not feigned,   50
Nor feigned she, though falsely they have wronged
Both her, myself, Horatio, and themselves.
Now may I make compare, 'twixt hers and this,
Of every accident. I ne'er could find
Till now—and now I feelingly perceive—   55
They did what heaven unpunished would not leave.
O false Lorenzo, are these thy flattering looks?
Is this the honor that thou didst my son?
And Balthazar, bane to thy soul and me,
Was this the ransom he reserved thee for?   60
Woe to the cause of these constrainèd wars,
Woe to thy baseness and captivity,
Woe to thy birth, thy body and thy soul,
Thy cursèd father, and thy conquered self!
And banned with bitter execrations be   65
The day and place where he did pity thee.
But wherefore waste I mine unfruitful words,
When naught but blood will satisfy my woes?
I will go plain me to my lord the king,
And cry aloud for justice through the court,   70
Wearing the flints with these my withered feet,
And either purchase justice by entreats,
Or tire them all with my revenging threats.
                                                    Exit.

[3.8]

Enter ISABELLA *and her Maid.*

ISABELLA
So that you say this herb will purge the eye,
And this the head?
Ah, but none of them will purge the heart;
No, there's no medicine left for my disease,
Nor any physic to recure the dead.   *She runs lunatic.*   5
Horatio! O where's Horatio?

59. **bane:** poison.
65. **banned:** cursed.
69. **plain me:** complain.
73. **tire:** plays on *tire* = "tear at the flesh" (a term from falcony, *OED* v^2 2).
5. **recure:** restore to health.

MAID
    Good Madam, affright not thus yourself
    With outrage for your son Horatio:
    He sleeps in quiet in the Elysian fields.
ISABELLA
    Why, did I not give you gowns and goodly things,   10
    Bought you a whistle and a whipstalk too,
    To be revengèd on their villainies?
MAID
    Madam, these humors do torment my soul.
ISABELLA
    My soul? poor soul thou talks of things
    Thou know'st not what—my soul hath silver wings   15
    That mounts me up unto the highest heavens.
    To heaven! ay, there sits my Horatio,
    Backed with a troop of fiery cherubins,
    Dancing about his newly healèd wounds,
    Singing sweet hymns and chanting heavenly notes,   20
    Rare harmony to greet his innocence
    That died—ay, died!—a mirror in our days.
    But say, where shall I find the men, the murderers,
    That slew Horatio? whither shall I run
    To find them out that murderèd my son?   25
                               Exeunt.

[3.9]

[Enter] BEL-IMPERIA *at a window.*
BEL-IMPERIA
    What means this outrage that is offered me?
    Why am I thus sequestered from the court?
    No notice? Shall I not know the cause
    Of this my secret and suspicious ills?
    Accursèd brother, unkind murderer,   5
    Why bends thou thus thy mind to martyr me?
    Hieronimo, why writ I of thy wrongs?
    Or why art thou so slack in thy revenge?
    Andrea, O Andrea, that thou sawest

---

8. **outrage:** mad or passionate behavior; violent outcry (*OED* n. 2a–b).
11. **whipstalk:** whipstock, the stock or staff to which a whiplash is attached.
13. **humors:** moods, displays of passion (*OED* n. 5).
21. **greet:** (1) honor; (2) bewail (*OED* v¹ 3d–e, v² 2).
22. **mirror:** model (of excellence, goodness).
3. **No notice:** kept ignorant.
5. **unkind:** unnatural.
6. **Why bends thou:** why do you devote.

Me for thy friend Horatio handled thus,   10
And him for me thus causeless murderèd.
Well, force perforce, I must constrain myself
To patience, and apply me to the time,
Till heaven, as I have hoped, shall set me free.
    Enter CHRISTOPHIL.

CHRISTOPHIL
Come, madam Bel-Imperia, this may not be!   15
                                      Exeunt.

[3.10]

    Enter LORENZO, BALTHAZAR, *and the Page.*
LORENZO
Boy, talk no further, thus far things go well:
Thou art assurèd that thou saw'st him dead?
PAGE
Or else, my lord, I live not.
LORENZO   That's enough.
As for his resolution in his end,
Leave that to him with whom he sojourns now.   5
Here, take my ring, and give it Christophil,
And bid him let my sister be enlarged,
And bring her hither straight.   *Exit Page.*
This that I did was for a policy
To smooth and keep the murder secret,   10
Which as a nine-days' wonder being o'erblown,
My gentle sister will I now enlarge.
BALTHAZAR
And time, Lorenzo; for my lord the duke,
You heard, enquired for her yester-night.
LORENZO
Why, and, my lord, I hope you heard me say   15
Sufficient reason why she kept away.
But that's all one, my lord: you love her?
BALTHAZAR   Ay.
LORENZO
Then in your love beware, deal cunningly,
Salve all suspicions, only soothe me up;

13. apply . . . time: behave as circumstances dictate.
4. his . . . end: the passing of final sentence upon him.
5. with . . . now: i.e., presumably the devil.
7. enlarged: set free.
13. time: in high time.
19. Salve: assuage. soothe me up: back me up.

And if she hap to stand on terms with us,   20
As for her sweetheart, and concealment so,
Jest with her gently: under feignèd jest
Are things concealed that else would breed unrest.
But here she comes.
      Enter BEL-IMPERIA.
           Now, sister—
BEL-IMPERIA   Sister? no—
Thou art no brother, but an enemy,   25
Else wouldst thou not have used thy sister so:
First, to affright me with thy weapons drawn,
And with extremes abuse my company;
And then to hurry me like whirlwind's rage,
Amidst a crew of thy confederates,   30
And clap me up where none might come at me,
Nor I at any to reveal my wrongs.
What madding fury did possess thy wits?
Or wherein is't that I offended thee?

LORENZO

Advise you better Bel-Imperia,   35
For I have done you no disparagement,
Unless, by more discretion than deserved,
I sought to save your honor and mine own.

BEL-IMPERIA

Mine honor! why, Lorenzo, wherein is't
That I neglect my reputation so   40
As you, or any, need to rescue it.

LORENZO

His highness and my father were resolved
To come confer with old Hieronimo
Concerning certain matters of estate
That by the Viceroy was determinèd.   45

BEL-IMPERIA

And wherein was mine honor touched in that?

BALTHAZAR

Have patience, Bel-Imperia, hear the rest.

LORENZO

Me next in sight as messenger they sent
To give him notice that they were so nigh;

---

20. **stand on terms:** argue about conditions, make difficulties.
28. **company:** companion (i.e., Horatio).
31. **clap me up:** arbitrarily imprison.
36. **disparagement:** dishonor, indignity.
40–41. **so As:** to the extent that.
44. **estate:** state.
48. **next in sight:** standing nearby.

Now when I came, consorted with the prince,   50
And unexpected, in an arbor there
Found Bel-Imperia with Horatio—

BEL-IMPERIA

How then?

LORENZO

Why then, remembering that old disgrace,
Which you for Don Andrea had endured,   55
And now were likely longer to sustain
By being found so meanly accompanied,
Thought rather—for I knew no readier mean—
To thrust Horatio forth my father's way.

BALTHAZAR

And carry you obscurely somewhere else,   60
Lest that his highness should have found you there.

BEL-IMPERIA

Even so, my lord, and you are witness
That this is true which he entreateth of.
You, gentle brother, forged this for my sake,
And you my lord, were made his instrument—   65
A work of worth, worthy the noting too!
But what's the cause that you concealed me since?

LORENZO

Your melancholy, sister, since the news
Of your first favorite Don Andrea's death,
My father's old wrath hath exasperate.   70

BALTHAZAR

And better was't for you, being in disgrace,
To absent yourself and give his fury place.

BEL-IMPERIA

But why had I no notice of his ire?

LORENZO

That were to add more fuel to your fire,
Who burned like Aetna for Andrea's loss.   75

BEL-IMPERIA

Hath not my father then enquired for me?

---

57. **meanly:** of low rank.
59. **forth:** out of.
63. **entreateth of:** treats of, explains.
64. **gentle:** well-born. **forged:** (1) fashioned; (2) fabricated.
66. **noting:** with the same play on *nothing* that Shakespeare exploits in *Much Ado about Nothing.*
70. **old wrath:** i.e., the anger Castile already felt because of the liaison with a man of lower rank. **exasperate:** aggravate, make more fierce.
72. **give . . . place:** allow his rage full scope (to exhaust itself).
75. **Aetna:** famously active volcano in Sicily.

LORENZO
    Sister he hath, and thus excused I thee.
       He whispereth in her ear.
    But, Bel-Imperia, see the gentle prince
    Look on thy love; behold young Balthazar,
    Whose passions by thy presence are increased,   80
    And in whose melancholy thou may'st see
    Thy hate, his love, thy flight, his following thee.
BEL-IMPERIA
    Brother you are become an orator—
    I know not I, by what experience—
    Too politic for me, past all compare,   85
    Since last I saw you; but content yourself,
    The prince is meditating higher things.
BALTHAZAR
    'Tis of thy beauty, then, that conquers kings;
    Of those thy tresses, Ariadne's twines,
    Wherewith my liberty thou hast surprised,   90
    Of that thine ivory front, my sorrow's map,
    Wherein I see no haven to rest my hope.
BEL-IMPERIA
    To love and fear, and both at once, my lord,
    In my conceit are things of more import
    Than women's wits are to be busied with.   95
BALTHAZAR
    'Tis I that love.
BEL-IMPERIA   Whom?
BALTHAZAR   Bel-Imperia.
BEL-IMPERIA
    But I that fear.
BALTHAZAR   Whom?
BEL-IMPERIA   Bel-Imperia.
LORENZO
    Fear your self?
BEL-IMPERIA   Ay, brother.
LORENZO   How?
BEL-IMPERIA   As those
    That what they love are loath and fear to lose.

---

81. **in . . . see:** whose melancholy is the result of.
89. **Ariadne's twines:** Presumably Kyd is confusing Ariadne, the Cretan princess whose
    thread enabled Theseus to escape the Minotaur's labyrinth, with Arachne, the weaver
    who was metamorphosed into a spider.
91. **front:** forehead.
94. **conceit:** opinion. **import:** importance, significance.

BALTHAZAR

Then, fair, let Balthazar your keeper be.   100

BEL-IMPERIA

No, Balthazar doth fear as well as we.

Et tremulo metui pavidum junxere timorem,

Et vanum stolidae proditionis opus.   *Exit.*

LORENZO

Nay, and you argue things so cunningly,

We'll go continue this discourse at court.   105

BALTHAZAR

Led by the lodestar of her heavenly looks,

Wends poor oppressèd Balthazar,

As o'er the mountains walks the wanderer,

Incertain to effect his pilgrimage.

Exeunt.

[3.11]

Enter two PORTINGALES, *and* HIERONIMO *meets them.*

1 PORTINGALE

By your leave, sir.

HIERONIMO

Addition 3

'Tis neither as you think, nor as you think,

Nor as you think—y'are wide all:

These slippers are not mine, they were my son Horatio's—

My son! and what's a son? A thing begot

Within a pair of minutes, thereabout,   [5]

A lump bred up in darkness, and doth serve

To ballast these light creatures we call women,

And at nine months' end creeps forth to light.

What is there yet in a son

To make a father dote, rave, or run mad?   [10]

Being born, it pouts, cries, and breeds teeth.

What is there yet in a son? He must be fed,

Be taught to go, and speak. Ay, or yet?

---

100. keeper (1) jailer; (2) one who keeps a mistress, lover.

102–03. *Et . . . opus:* They yoked tremulous dread to quaking dread, a futile act of stupid betrayal.

104. and: if.

106. lodestar: guiding star.

109. incertain to effect: unsure of achieving the goal of.

[2]. wide: wide of the mark.

[7]. light: frivolous; wanton (*OED* a[1] 14a–b).

Why might not a man love a calf as well?
Or melt in passion o'er a frisking kid   [15]
As for a son? Methinks a young bacon
Or fine little smooth horse-colt
Should move a man as much as doth a son;
For one of these in very little time
Will grow to some good use, whereas a son,   [20]
The more he grows in stature and in years,
The more unsquared, unbeveled he appears,
Reckons his parents among the rank of fools,
Strikes care upon their heads with his mad riots,
Makes them look old before they meet with age: [25]
This is a son:
And what a loss were this, considered truly?
Oh, but my Horatio
Grew out of reach of these insatiate humors:
He loved his loving parents,   [30]
He was my comfort, and his mother's joy,
The very arm that did hold up our house;
Our hopes were stored up in him;
None but a damned murderer could hate him.
He had not seen the back of nineteen year   [35]
When his strong arm unhorsed the proud Prince Balthazar,
That valiant, but ignoble Portingale
And his great mind, too full of honor,
Took him unto mercy.
Well, heaven is heaven still,   [40]
And there is Nemesis and Furies,
And things call'd whips,
And they sometimes do meet with murderers—
They do not always 'scape, that's some comfort.
Ay, ay, ay, and then time steals on,   [45]
And steals, and steals, till violence leaps forth
Like thunder wrappèd in a ball of fire,
And so doth bring confusion to them all.
Good leave have you: nay, I pray you go—
For I'll leave you; if you can leave me, so.

2 PORTINGALE
Pray you, which is the next way to my lord the duke's?

[16]. **young bacon:** piglet.
[22]. **unsquared, unbeveled:** rough, unfinished.
[38]. **great:** magnanimous (*OED* a 15). **too . . . honor:** too honorable for his own good.
[39]. **Took . . . mercy:** granted him mercy.
[41]. **Nemesis:** in Greek mythology, the spirit of retribution against those who display hubris (arrogant defiance of the gods). **Furies:** see note to 1.1.65.
[48]. **confusion:** destruction.
4. **next:** nearest.

HIERONIMO
  The next way from me.
1 PORTINGALE   To his house we mean.   5
HIERONIMO
  O, hard by, 'tis yon house that you see.
2 PORTINGALE
  You could not tell us if his son were there?
HIERONIMO
  Who, my lord Lorenzo ?
1 PORTINGALE   Ay, sir.
    He goeth in at one door and comes out at another.
HIERONIMO   O forbear,
  For other talk for us far fitter were.
  But if you be importunate to know,   10
  The way to him, and where to find him out,
  Then list to me, and I'll resolve your doubt.
  There is a path upon your left-hand side,
  That leadeth from a guilty conscience
  Unto a forest of distrust and fear—   15
  A darksome place and dangerous to pass:
  There shall you meet with melancholy thoughts,
  Whose baleful humors if you but uphold,
  It will conduct you to despair and death;
  Whose rocky cliffs, when you have once beheld,   20
  Within a hugy dale of lasting night
  That, kindled with the world's iniquities,
  Doth cast up filthy and detested fumes—
  Not far from thence, where murderers have built
  A habitation for their cursed souls,   25
  There in a brazen cauldron fixed by Jove
  In his fell wrath upon a sulfur flame,
  Yourselves shall find Lorenzo bathing him
  In boiling lead and blood of innocents.
1 PORTINGALE
  Ha, ha, ha!
HIERONIMO Ha, ha, ha!   30
  Why ha, ha, ha! Farewell good ha, ha, ha!   *Exit.*

---

5. **from**: in the opposite direction from.
8. **SD.** *He . . . another*: Usually taken to refer to the First Portuguese who exits in search of Lorenzo but immediately returns, not having found him. However it is at least equally possible that it is Hieronimo who leaves, the speed of his return indicating that his search is merely a mad charade.
12. **list**: listen.
18. **uphold**: persist in.
27. **fell**: cruel.

2 PORTINGALE
>Doubtless this man is passing lunatic,
>Or imperfection of his age doth make him dote.
>Come, let's away to seek my lord the duke.

Exeunt.

[3.12]

>*Enter* HIERONIMO *with a poniard in one hand, and
>a rope in the other.*

HIERONIMO
>Now sir, perhaps I come and see the king,
>The king sees me, and fain would hear my suit.
>Why, is not this a strange and seld-seen thing
>That standers-by with toys should strike me mute.
>Go to, I see their shifts, and say no more.   5
>Hieronimo, 'tis time for thee to trudge:
>Down by the dale that flows with purple gore
>Standeth a fiery tower, there sits a judge
>Upon a seat of steel and molten brass,
>And 'twixt his teeth he holds a fire-brand   10
>That leads unto the lake where hell doth stand.
>Away, Hieronimo, to him be gone:
>He'll do thee justice for Horatio's death.
>Turn down this path, thou shalt be with him straight,
>Or this, and then thou need'st not take thy breath.   15
>This way, or that way? Soft and fair, not so:
>For if I hang or kill myself, let's know
>Who will revenge Horatio's murder then?
>No, no! fie no! pardon me, I'll none of that.
>>*He flings away the dagger and halter.*
>This way I'll take, and this way comes the king,   20
>>*He takes them up again.*
>And here I'll have a fling at him—that's flat;

---

32. **passing:** extremely.
33. **imperfection . . . dote:** the frailty of old age makes him weak-minded.
3.12. SD. **poniard; rope:** Dagger and rope were stock properties signaling the impulse to suicide.
2. **fain would:** is eager to.
3. **seld:** seldom.
4. **toys:** see note to 3.2.[3].
5. **shifts:** subterfuges.
6. **trudge:** get moving.
7. **purple:** bloodred (*OED* a. 2d).
11. **lake:** the Acherusian lake (see note to 3.1.55).
14. **straight:** immediately.
14–15. **this . . . this:** i.e., choosing suicide by dagger or rope.
16. **Soft and fair:** hold on a moment.

And, Balthazar, I'll be with thee to bring,
And thee, Lorenzo! Here's the king; nay, stay!
And here, ay here, there goes the hare away.
     Enter KING, AMBASSADOR, CASTILE, *and* LORENZO.

KING
Now show, ambassador, what our viceroy saith: 25
Hath he received the articles we sent?

HIERONIMO
Justice, O justice to Hieronimo!

LORENZO
Back! see'st thou not the king is busy?

HIERONIMO
O, is he so?

KING
Who is he that interrupts our business?   30

HIERONIMO
Not I. [*Aside*] Hieronimo, beware! go by, go by.

AMBASSADOR
Renowned king, he hath received and read
Thy kingly proffers and thy promised league,
And, as a man extremely overjoyed
To hear his son so princely entertained,   35
Whose death he had so solemnly bewailed,
This for thy further satisfaction
And kingly love, he kindly lets thee know:
First, for the marriage of his princely son
With Bel-Imperia, thy beloved niece,   40
The news are more delightful to his soul
Then myrrh or incense to the offended heavens.
In person therefore will he come himself
To see the marriage rites solemnizèd,
And, in the presence of the court of Spain,   45
To knit a sure, inexplicable band
Of kingly love and everlasting league
Betwixt the crowns of Spain and Portingale.
There will he give his crown to Balthazar,
And make a queen of Bel-Imperia.   50

KING
Brother, how like you this our viceroy's love?

---

22. I'll . . . bring: I'll get even with you.
24. there . . . away: proverbial; Hieronimo fears he may lose his prey.
28. see'st: pronounced with two syllables.
31. go by: beware, don't get into trouble.
33. Thy: The Ambassador uses the singular form to emphasize the fact he speaks for the Portuguese ruler who is entitled to address the Spanish king as an equal. See also notes to. 1.4.2 and 2.4.18

CASTILE

No doubt, my lord, it is an argument
Of honorable care to keep his friend,
And wondrous zeal to Balthazar his son?
Nor am I least indebted to his grace,   55
That bends his liking to my daughter thus.

AMBASSADOR

Now last, dread lord, here hath his highness sent—
Although he send not that his son return—
His ransom due to Don Horatio.

HIERONIMO

Horatio! who calls Horatio?   60

KING

And well remembered—thank his majesty.
Here, see it given to Horatio.

HIERONIMO

Justice! O justice, justice, gentle king!

KING

Who is that? Hieronimo?

HIERONIMO

Justice, O justice! O my son, my son,   65
My son, whom naught can ransom or redeem!

LORENZO

Hieronimo, you are not well advised.

HIERONIMO

Away, Lorenzo, hinder me no more!
For thou hast made me bankrupt of my bliss.
Give me my son, you shall not ransom him.   70
Away! I'll rip the bowels of the earth,
     He diggeth with his dagger.
And ferry over to th'Elysian plains,
And bring my son to show his deadly wounds.
Stand from about me!
I'll make a pickaxe of my poniard,   75
And here surrender up my marshalship:
For I'll go marshal up the fiends in hell
To be avenged on you all for this.

KING

What means this outrage?
Will none of you restrain his fury?   80

---

52. **argument**: demonstration, proof.
56. **bends**: directs.
58. **that**: in order that.

HIERONIMO

    Nay soft and fair—you shall not need to strive:
    Needs must he go that the devils drive.   *Exit.*

KING

    What accident hath happed Hieronimo?
    I have not seen him to demean him so.

LORENZO

    My gracious lord, he is—with extreme pride   85
    Conceived of young Horatio his son,
    And, covetous of having to himself
    The ransom of the young Prince Balthazar—
    Distract and in a manner lunatic.

KING

    Believe me, nephew, we are sorry for't: 90
    This is the love that fathers bear their sons.
    But, gentle brother, go give to him this gold,
    The prince's ransom; let him have his due,
    For what he hath Horatio shall not want;
    Haply Hieronimo hath need thereof.   95

LORENZO

    But if he be thus helplessly distract,
    'Tis requisite his office be resigned,
    And given to one of more discretion.

KING

    We shall increase his melancholy so.
    'Tis best that we see further in it first;   100
    Till when, ourself will not exempt the place.
    And, brother, now bring in the ambassador
    That he may be a witness of the match
    'Twixt Balthazar and Bel-Imperia,
    And that we may prefix a certain time   105
    Wherein the marriage shall be solemnized,
    That we may have thy lord the viceroy here.

AMBASSADOR

    Therein your highness highly shall content
    His majesty, that longs to hear from hence.

KING

    On then, and hear you, lord ambassador.   110
                                  Exeunt.

---

100. **see . . . it:** investigate the matter further.
101. **exempt:** abolish (*OED* v.1). **place:** office, position.
102. **bring in:** introduce to the proceedings.
105. **prefix:** appoint.

Addition 4

[3.12A]

Enter JACQUES *and* PEDRO.

JACQUES   I wonder, Pedro, why our master thus
    At midnight sends us with our torches' light,
    When man and bird and beast are all at rest,
    Save those that watch for rape and bloody murder?

PEDRO
    O Jacques, know thou that our master's mind   [5]
    Is much distraught since his Horatio died,
    And, now his aged years should sleep in rest;
    His heart in quiet, like a desperate man,
    Grows lunatic and childish for his son;
    Sometimes, as he doth at his table sit,   [10]
    He speaks as if Horatio stood by him,
    Then, starting in a rage, falls on the earth,
    Cries out "Horatio! Where is my Horatio?"
    So that, with extreme grief and cutting sorrow,
    There is not left in him one inch of man. [15]
    See where he comes.

      Enter HIERONIMO.

HIERONIMO
    I pry through every crevice of each wall,
    Look on each tree, and search through every brake,
    Beat at the bushes, stamp our grandam earth,
    Dive in the water, and stare up to heaven,   [20]
    Yet cannot I behold my son Horatio.
    How now? who's there? spirits, spirits?

PEDRO
    We are your servants that attend you, sir.

HIERONIMO
    What make you with your torches in the dark?

PEDRO
    You bid us light them, and attend you here.   [25]

HIERONIMO
    No, no, you are deceived—not I, you are deceived!
    Was I so mad to bid you light your torches now?
    Light me your torches at the mid of noon,

---

[4]. **watch**: keep watch.
[18]. **brake**: thicket.
[24]. **what make you**: what are you doing

Whenas the sun god rides in all his glory:
Light me your torches then.
PEDRO   Then we burn daylight.   [30]
HIERONIMO
Let it be burned: night is a murderous slut,
That would not have her treasons to be seen,
And yonder pale faced Hecate there, the moon,
Doth give consent to that is done in darkness,
And all those stars that gaze upon her face   [35]
Are aglets on her sleeve, pins on her train;
And those that should be powerful and divine
Do sleep in darkness when they most should shine.

PEDRO
Provoke them not, fair sir, with tempting words:
The heavens are gracious, and your miseries   [40]
And sorrow makes you speak you know not what.

HIERONIMO
Villain, thou liest, and thou doest naught
But tell me I am mad. Thou liest, I am not mad:
I know thee to be Pedro, and he Jacques.
I'll prove it to thee—and were I mad, how could I?   [45]
Where was she that same night when my Horatio
Was murdered? She should have shone. Search thou the book:
Had the moon shone, in my boy's face there was a kind of grace,
That I know—nay, I do know, had the murderer seen him,
His weapon would have fallen and cut the earth,   [50]
Had he been framed of naught but blood and death.
Alack, when mischief doth it knows not what,
What shall we say to mischief?
          Enter ISABELLA.

ISABELLA
Dear Hieronimo, come in a-doors:
O, seek not means so to increase thy sorrow.   [55]

HIERONIMO
Indeed, Isabella, we do nothing here:
I do not cry—ask Pedro and ask Jacques—
Not I indeed, we are very merry, very merry.

---

[30]. **burn daylight:** Pedro plays on the literal sense of a familiar expression for wasting time.
[33]. **Hecate:** Greek goddess of magic, identified by Elizabethans with the moon and as
the patron of witchcraft.
[36]. **aglets:** metallic tags on the laces used to attach sleeves and other parts of a garment;
any metallic ornaments or spangles. **pins:** dress fastenings; spangles; metallic ornaments;
brooches.
[47]. **book:** almanac.
[52]. **mischief:** wickedness, evil.

ISABELLA
    How? Be merry here, be merry here:
    Is not this the place, and this the very tree,   [60]
    Where my Horatio died, where he was murdered?
HIERONIMO
    Was—do not say what: let her weep it out.
    This was the tree, I set it of a kernel,
    And when our hot Spain could not let it grow,
    But that the infant and the human sap   [65]
    Began to wither, duly twice a morning
    Would I be sprinkling it with fountain water;
    At last it grew, and grew, and bore and bore,
    Till at the length
    It grew a gallows, and did bear our son: [70]
    It bore thy fruit and mine—O wicked, wicked plant!
       One knocks within at the door.
    See who knocks there.
PEDRO   It is a painter, sir.
HIERONIMO
    Bid him come in, and paint some comfort,
    For surely there's none lives but painted comfort.
    Let him come in; one knows not what may chance.   [75]
    God's will, that I should set this tree!—but even so
    Masters ungrateful servants rear from naught,
    And then they hate them that did bring them up.
       Enter the Painter.
PAINTER
    God bless you, sir.
HIERONIMO   Wherefore? why, thou scornful villain,
    How, where, or by what means should I be blest?   [80]
ISABELLA
    What wouldst thou have, good fellow?
PAINTER   Justice, madam.
HIERONIMO
    O ambitious beggar, wouldst thou have that
    That lives not in the world?
    Why, all the undelvèd mines cannot buy
    An ounce of justice, 'tis a jewel so inestimable: [85]
    I tell thee,
    God hath engrossed all justice in his hands,
    And there is none, but what comes from him.

---

[60]. **this . . . tree:** The arbor in which Horatio was hanged seems to have remained on stage
   throughout the performance (see notes to 3.6.106 SD; 4.2.5 SD; 4.3 SD; 4.4.88 SD).
[74]. **painted:** i.e., illusory.

PAINTER
> O, then I see
> That God must right me for my murdered son.   [90]

HIERONIMO
> How, was thy son murdered?

PAINTER
> Ay, sir; no man did hold a son so dear.

HIERONIMO
> What, not as thine? that's a lie
> As massy as the earth: I had a son,
> Whose least unvalued hair did weigh   [95]
> A thousand of thy sons; and he was murdered.

PAINTER
> Alas, sir, I had no more but he.

HIERONIMO
> Nor I, nor I; but this same one of mine,
> Was worth a legion—but all is one.
> Pedro, Jacques, go in a-doors; Isabella go,   [100]
> And this good fellow here and I
> Will range this hideous orchard up and down,
> Like to two lions reavèd of their young.
> Go in a-doors, I say!
>> *Exeunt* [ISABELLA, PEDRO, JACQUES].
>> *The Painter and* HIERONIMO *sit down.*
> Come let's talk wisely now: was thy son murdered?   [105]

PAINTER   Ay, sir.

HIERONIMO   So was mine. How do'st take it: art thou not sometimes mad? Is there no tricks that comes before thine eyes?

PAINTER   O Lord, yes sir.

HIERONIMO   Art a painter? canst paint me a tear, or a wound,   [110]
a groan, or a sigh? canst paint me such a tree as this?

PAINTER   Sir, I am sure you have heard of my painting: my
name's Bazardo.

HIERONIMO   Bazardo! afore God, an excellent fellow! Look
you sir, do you see, I'd have you paint me in my gallery, in   [115]
your oil colors matted, and draw me five years younger
than I am—do ye see, sir, let five years go, let them go,
like the Marshal of Spain—my wife Isabella standing by

---

[94]. **massy:** weighty, huge.
[99]. **legion:** a vast multitude.
[103]. **reavèd:** bereaved.
[108]. **tricks:** illusions (*OED* n. 1c).
[110–51]. **Art . . . forth:** On the tradition of revenge paintings, see the Introduction (pp. xxix–xxxi).
[116]. **matted:** dull (*OED* v. 2).

me, with a speaking look to my son Horatio, which should
intend to this, or some such like purpose: "God bless thee, [120]
my sweet son," and my hand leaning upon his head thus,
sir. Do you see? May it be done?

PAINTER   Very well, sir.

HIERONIMO   Nay, I pray mark me, sir. Then sir, would I have
you paint me this tree, this very tree. Canst paint a doleful cry? [125]

PAINTER   Seemingly, sir.

HIERONIMO   Nay, it should cry: but all is one. Well sir, paint
me a youth, run through and through with villains' swords,
hanging upon this tree. Canst thou draw a murderer?   [130]

PAINTER   I'll warrant you, sir. I have the pattern of the most
notorious villains that ever lived in all Spain.

HIERONIMO   O, let them be worse, worse: stretch thine art,
and let their beards be of Judas his own color, and let their
eyebrows jutty over—in any case observe that. Then sir, [135]
some violent noise, bring me forth in my shirt, and my
gown under mine arm, with my torch in my hand, and my
sword reared up thus, and with these words: "What noise
is this? Who calls Hieronimo?" May it be done?

PAINTER   Yea, sir.   [140]

[HIERONIMO]   Well sir, then bring me forth, bring me
through alley and alley, still with a distracted countenance
going along, and let my hair heave up my night-cap. Let
the clouds scowl, make the moon dark, the stars extinct, the
winds blowing, the bells tolling, the owl shrieking, the [145]
toads croaking, the minutes jarring, and the clock striking
twelve. And then at last, sir, starting, behold a man hanging,
and tottering, and tottering—as you know the wind will
wave a man—and I with a trice to cut him down; and
looking upon him by the advantage of my torch, find it to be [150]
my son Horatio. There you may [paint] a passion, there you
may show a passion. Draw me like old Priam of Troy, crying
"The house is a-fire, the house is a-fire as the torch over my
head." Make me curse, make me rave, make me cry, make me
mad, make me well again; make me curse hell, invocate [155]
heaven, and in the end, leave me in a trance, and so forth.

[119]. speaking: eloquent, expressive.
[128]. all is one: no matter.
[134]. Judas . . . color: (supposedly) red.
[135]. jutty: jut, overhang.
[137–38]. torch . . . sword: see note to 2.5.1 SD. and the 1615 title-page woodcut (p. xxii).
[147]. starting: jumping with fright.
[148]. tottering; swinging from a gallows (OED v.1b).
[149]. wave: cause to sway, with a play on wave in the wind=be hanged (OED v. 1b,d).
  with a trice: in a trice.

PAINTER   And is this the end?

HIERONIMO   O no, there is no end: the end is death and
      madness. As I am never better than when I am mad, then
      methinks I am a brave fellow, then I do wonders; but reason   [160]
      abuseth me, and there's the torment, there's the hell. At the
      last, sir, bring me to one of the murderers: were he as strong
      as *Hector*, thus would I tear and drag him up and down.

> *He beats the* Painter *in, then comes out again with a book in his
> hand.*

[3.13]

Enter HIERONIMO *with a book in his hand.*

HIERONIMO

Vindicta mihi!

Ay, heaven will be revenged of every ill,   *Rom. 12*

Nor will they suffer murder unrepaid:

Then stay, Hieronimo, attend their will,

For mortal men may not appoint their time.   5

Per scelus semper tutum est sceleribus iter.

Strike, and strike home, where wrong is offered thee,

For evils unto ills conductors be,

And death's the worst of resolution;

For he that thinks with patience to contend   10

To quiet life, his life shall easily end.

Fata si miseros juvant, habes salutem:

Fata si vitam negant, habes sepulchrum.

If destiny thy miseries do ease,

Then hast thou health, and happy shalt thou be;   15

If destiny deny thee life, Hieronimo,

Yet shalt thou be assurèd of a tomb;

If neither, yet let this thy comfort be:

Heaven covereth him that hath no burial.

And to conclude, I will revenge his death.   20

[157–58]. **is this . . . no end:** Like Kent's "Is this the promised end" (*King Lear* 5.3.264), these lines play on the apocalyptic suggestions of *end*, while anticipating the recurrent reference to dramatic ending, mortal ends, and endless punishment in Kyd's closing scenes (4.4.151–52, 4.5.1–2,34,40,43,48).

[160]. **brave:** excellent, splendid.

1. **Vindicta mihi:** Because the subsequent Latin quotations in this speech are from the plays of Seneca, it seems likely (as Boas suggests) that Hieronimo is reading from *Octavia* (*Vindicta debetur mihi*, 849); however, as the next two lines suggest, the phrase immediately reminds him of Romans 12.19: "Venegeance is mine, I will repay."

4. **attend their will:** await the working out of what they have decreed.

6. **Per . . . iter:** The safe way to [the successful achievement of] a crime is always through [the perpetration of] other crimes (from Seneca, *Agamemnon* l.115).

9. **worst of resolution:** the worst thing that can result from resolved conduct.

12–13. **Fata . . . sepulchrum:** loosly translated in lines 14–17 from Seneca, *Troades* lines 511–12.

But how? not as the vulgar wits of men,
With open, but inevitable ills,
As by a secret, yet a certain mean,
Which under kindship will be cloakèd best.
Wise men will take their opportunity,   25
Closely and safely fitting things to time;
But in extremes advantage hath no time,
And therefore all times fit not for revenge.
Thus, therefore, will I rest me in unrest,
Dissembling quiet in unquietness,   30
Not seeming that I know their villainies,
That my simplicity may make them think,
That ignorantly I will let all slip—
For ignorance, I wot, and well they know,
Remedium malorum iners est.   35
Nor aught avails it me to menace them
Who, as a wintry storm upon a plain,
Will bear me down with their nobility.
No, no, Hieronimo, thou must enjoin
Thine eyes to observation, and thy tongue   40
To milder speeches than thy spirit affords,
Thy heart to patience, and thy hands to rest,
Thy cap to courtesy, and thy knee to bow,
Till to revenge thou know when, where, and how.
          A noise within.
How now, what noise? what coil is that you keep?   45
          Enter a Servant.

SERBERINE
Here are a sort of poor petitioners
That are importunate, and it shall please you, sir,
That you should plead their cases to the king.

HIERONIMO
That I should plead their several actions—

21. **vulgar:** ordinary, common.
22. **With . . . ills:** "by open violence and [its] inevitable ill consequences" (Bevington's note).
23. **mean:** means.
24. **kindship:** kindness.
26. **Closely:** covertly.
27. **advantage:** opportunity.
32. **simplicity:** (seeming) innocence, naïveté.
34. **wot:** know.
35. *Remedium . . . est:* is an ineffective remedy for evils (adapted from Seneca, *Oedipus* l. 515; "*Iners malorum remedium ignorantia est*").
38. **nobility:** aristocratic rank.
41. **affords:** yields, allows.
45. **what . . . keep?:** what are you making such a fuss about?
46. **sort:** group, crowd (*OED* n.² 17–18).
47. **and:** if.
49. **actions:** lawsuits.

Why let them enter, and let me see them.   50
   Enter three Citizens and [BAZULTO] *an Old Man.*

I CITIZEN

So, I tell you this: for learning and for law,
There's not any advocate in Spain,
That can prevail, or will take half the pain,
That he will in pursuit of equity.

HIERONIMO

Come near, you men that thus importune me.   55
[*Aside*] Now must I bear a face of gravity,
For thus I used, before my marshalship,
To plead in causes as corregidor.
—Come on, sirs, what's the matter?

2 CITIZEN   Sir, an action.

HIERONIMO

Of battery?

I CITIZEN   Mine of debt.

HIERONIMO   Give place.   60

2 CITIZEN

No sir, mine is an action of the case.

3 CITIZEN

Mine an *ejectione firmae* by a lease.

HIERONIMO

Content you, sirs—are you determined,
That I should plead your several actions?

I CITIZEN

Ay sir, and here's my declaration,   65

2 CITIZEN

And here is my band.

3 CITIZEN   And here is my lease.
    They give him papers.

HIERONIMO

But wherefore stands yon silly man so mute,
With mournful eyes and hands to heaven upreared?
Come hither, father, let me know thy cause.

---

58. corregidor: advocate (properly the principal magistrate in a Spanish town).
60. Give place get out of the way.
61. action . . . case: "An action not within the limited jurisdiction of the [Court of] Common Pleas [that] needed a special writ to cover it" (Edwards's note).
62. ejectione firmae: "a writ to eject a tenant . . . before the expiration of his lease" (Edwards's note). **by:** with respect to, as concerns (*OED* prep. 27).
66. band: bond. **SD. They . . . papers:** the formal submission of these documents, in addition to their literal significance, serves as a reminder of Hieronimo's authority under the King. Compare the similarly formal moment in which the General gives the King a "paper" setting out the terms of peace with the Portuguese (1.2.92 SD). See also line 3.13.123 SD.
67. silly: poor, helpless, simple.
69. cause: grounds of action; legal case.

BAZULTO

O worthy sir, my cause but slightly known   70
May move the hearts of warlike Myrmidons,
And melt the Corsic rocks with ruthful tears.

HIERONIMO

Say father, tell me what's thy suit?

BAZULTO

No sir, could my woes
Give way unto my most distressful words,   75
Then should I not in paper, as you see,
With ink bewray what blood began in me.

HIERONIMO

What's here? "The humble supplication
Of Don Bazulto for his murdered son."

BAZULTO

Ay sir.

HIERONIMO   No sir, it was my murdered son,   80
O my son, my son! O my son Horatio!
But mine, or thine, Bazulto be content.
Here, take my handkercher and wipe thine eyes,
Whiles wretched I in thy mishaps may see
The lively portrait of my dying self,   85
    He draweth out a bloody napkin.
O no, not this: Horatio this was thine,
And when I dyed it in thy dearest blood,
This was a token 'twixt thy soul and me
That of thy death revengèd I should be.
But here, [*Draws out more objects*]
            take this, and this—what my purse?—   90
Ay, this, and that, and all of them are thine,
For all as one are our extremities.

1 CITIZEN

Oh, see the kindness of Hieronimo!

2 CITIZEN

This gentleness shows him a gentleman.

HIERONIMO

See, see, O see thy shame, Hieronimo: 95
See here a loving father to his son;
Behold the sorrows and the sad laments
That he delivereth for his son's decease!

---

71. **Myrmidons:** Achilles's ferocious followers in the *Iliad*. see note to 1.1.48–49.
72. **Corsic rocks:** the craggy rocks of Corsica (mentioned in Seneca's *Octavia* line 682).
    ruthful: full of pity.
77. **blood:** (1) passion; (2) the blood of his murdered son.
85. **lively:** lifelike; living.

If love's effects so strives in lesser things,
If love enforce such moods in meaner wits,   100
If love express such power in poor estates—
Hieronimo, whenas a raging sea,
Tossed with the wind and tide, o'erturneth then
The upper billows, course of waves to keep,
Whilst lesser waters labor in the deep,   105
Then shamest thou not, Hieronimo, to neglect
The sweet revenge of thy Horatio?
Though on this earth justice will not be found,
I'll down to hell, and in this passion
Knock at the dismal gates of Pluto's court,   110
Getting by force, as once Alcides did,
A troop of Furies and tormenting hags
To torture Don Lorenzo and the rest.
Yet, lest the triple-headed porter should
Deny my passage to the slimy strand,   115
The Thracian poet thou shalt counterfeit:
Come on, old father, be my Orpheus,
And if thou canst no notes upon the harp,
Then sound the burden of thy sore heart's grief,
Till we do gain that Proserpine may grant—   120
Revenge on them that murderèd my son.
Then will I rend and tear them thus and thus,
Shivering their limbs in pieces with my teeth.
He tears their papers with his teeth.

100. **meaner wits:** people of lower rank and intelligence.
102–05: **Hieronimo . . . deep:** A difficult passage: Hieronimo appears to mean that he
ought to be like a raging sea whose waves, driven onward by the "wind and tide" (of
passion), would overwhelm the "upper billows" that previously disturbed its surface,
whereas he is simply like those lesser currents that toil away in the deep within the
ocean (of the self), with no visible result. For alternative readings, see Edwards and
Mulryne.
102. **whenas:** seeing that, inasmuch as.
108. **Though . . . found:** see note to 3.13.139.
111. **Alcides:** Hercules.
114. **triple-headed porter:** Cerberus, the monstrous three-headed dog who guarded the
underworld.
116. **Thracian poet:** i.e., Orpheus (line 117), whose music persuaded Persephone (Proserpine) to release his wife, Eurydice, from Hades.
119. **sound:** (1) sound out, sing; (2) probe, measure. **burden:** (1) musical refrain or chorus;
(2) weight (of sorrow).
123. **Shivering:** ripping into fragments. **limbs . . . teeth:** Perhaps recalling the fate of
Orpheus when he was torn apart by the Maenads. **SD.** *Tears their papers:* Presumably
Hieronimo is to rip the petitioners' documents with his teeth. In the context of his invocation of Orphic myth, Hieronimo's berserk gesture has a peculiarly expressive power,
representing his surrender to the chaotic impulses of revenge, for Orpheus was often
treated as a figure for the ordering power of language and his music analogized to the
social harmony effected by the law, whose instrument Hieronimo has hitherto pro-
fessed to be. Compare 3.13.172.

1 CITIZEN
  O sir, my declaration!

                                    Exit HIERONIMO *and they after.*
2 CITIZEN   Save my bond!
      Enter HIERONIMO.
  Save my bond!   125
3 CITIZEN
  Alas, my lease! it cost me ten pound,
  And you, my lord, have torn the same.
HIERONIMO
  That cannot be, I gave it never a wound;
  Show me one drop of blood fall from the same:
  How is it possible I should slay it then?   130
  Tush no! run after, catch me if you can.
                    Exeunt all but [BAZULTO] *the old man.*
          BAZULTO *remains till* HIERONIMO *enters again, who,*
            staring him in the face, speaks.
HIERONIMO
  And art thou come, Horatio, from the depth
  To ask for justice in this upper earth?
  To tell thy father thou art unrevenged,
  To wring more tears from Isabella's eyes,   135
  Whose lights are dimmed with over-long laments?
  Go back, my son, complain to Aeacus,
  For here's no justice; gentle boy be gone,
  For Justice is exilèd from the earth;
  Hieronimo will bear thee company.   140
  Thy mother cries on righteous Rhadamanth
  For just revenge against the murderers.
BAZULTO
  Alas, my lord, whence springs this troubled speech?
HIERONIMO
  But let me look on my Horatio:
  Sweet boy, how art thou changed in death's black shade? 145
  Had Proserpine no pity on thy youth
  But suffered thy fair crimson-colored spring
  With withered winter to be blasted thus?
  Horatio, thou art older than thy father:
  Ah, ruthless fate, that favor thus transforms!   150

---

137. **Aeacus:** see note to 1.1.33.
139. **Justice . . . earth:** A common motif of the time, especially in revenge drama, refer-
    ring to the myth of Astraea, goddess of justice, who, with onset of the bloody Iron Age,
    became the last of the immortals to leave the earth.
141. **Rhadamanth:** see note to 1.1.33.
148. **blasted:** blighted.
150. **favor:** appearance, looks.

BAZULTO

Ah, my good lord, I am not your young son.

HIERONIMO

What, not my son? thou then a Fury art,
Sent from the empty kingdom of black night
To summon me to make appearance
Before grim Minos and just Rhadamanth   155
To plague Hieronimo, that is remiss
And seeks not vengeance for Horatio's death.

BAZULTO

I am a grievèd man and not a ghost,
That came for justice for my murdered son.

HIERONIMO

Ay, now I know thee, now thou nam'st my son: 160
Thou art the lively image of my grief;
Within thy face my sorrows I may see:
Thy eyes are gummed with tears, thy cheeks are wan,
Thy forehead troubled, and thy mutt'ring lips
Murmur sad words abruptly broken off,   165
By force of windy sighs thy spirit breathes,
And all this sorrow riseth for thy son;
And selfsame sorrow feel I for my son.
Come in, old man, thou shalt to Isabel:
Lean on my arm, I thee, thou me shalt stay,   170
And thou, and I, and she will sing a song,
Three parts in one, but all of discords framed—
Talk not of cords, but let us now be gone,
For with a cord Horatio was slain.

Exeunt.

[3.14]

Enter KING OF SPAIN, *Duke of* CASTILE, VICEROY, *and*
LORENZO, BALTHAZAR, DON PEDRO, *and* BEL-IMPERIA.

KING

Go brother, 'tis the Duke of Castile's cause:
Salute the Viceroy in our name.

CASTILE   I go.

VICEROY

Go forth, Don Pedro, for thy nephew's sake,
And greet the Duke of Castile.

PEDRO   It shall be so.

155. Minos: see note to 1.1.33.
170. stay: support.
172. discords: see note to 3.13.123 SD.

KING

And now to meet these Portuguese—   5
For as we now are, so sometimes were these,
Kings and commanders of the western Indies.
Welcome, brave viceroy, to the court of Spain,
And welcome all his honorable train.
'Tis not unknown to us, for why you come,   10
Or have so kingly crossed the seas;
Sufficeth it in this we note the troth
And more than common love you lend to us.
So is it that mine honorable niece—
For it beseems us now that it be known—   15
Already is betrothed to Balthazar;
And by appointment and our condescent,
Tomorrow are they to be marrièd.
To this intent we entertain thyself,
Thy followers, their pleasure, and our peace.   20
Speak men of Portingale, shall it be so?
If ay, say so—if not, say flatly no.

VICEROY

Renowned king, I come not as thou think'st,
With doubtful followers, unresolvèd men,
But such as have upon thine articles   25
Confirmed thy motion and contented me.
Know sovereign, I come to solemnize
The marriage of thy beloved niece,
Fair Bel-Imperia, with my Balthazar—
With thee, my son, whom sith I live to see,   30
Here take my crown, I give it her and thee;
And let me live a solitary life
In ceaseless prayers,
To think how strangely heaven hath thee preserved.

KING

See brother, see, how nature strives in him!   35
Come, worthy viceroy, and accompany

---

7. western Indies: here probably referring to the Portuguese colony of Brazil.
11. crossed the seas: A geographical blunder on Kyd's part, unless he envisages the
Portuguese traveling via Cadiz to Seville (where the Spanish court was sometimes
located).
12. troth: fidelity.
17. condescent: consent.
20. their: i.e., the couple's.
26. motion: proposal.
30. sith: since.
34. strangely: miraculously.
35. nature . . . him: he's overcome with emotion.

Thy friend with thine extremities:
A place more private fits this princely mood.

VICEROY

Or here or where your highness thinks it good.

Exeunt all but CASTILE *and* LORENZO

CASTILE

Nay stay, Lorenzo, let me talk with you.   40
Seest thou this entertainment of these kings?

LORENZO

I do my lord, and joy to see the same.

CASTILE

And knowest thou why this meeting is?

LORENZO

For her, my lord, whom Balthazar doth love,
And to confirm their promised marriage.   45

CASTILE

She is thy sister?

LORENZO   Who? Bel-Imperia?
Ay, my gracious lord; and this is the day
That I have longed so happily to see.

CASTILE

Thou wouldst be loath that any fault of thine
Should intercept her in her happiness.   50

LORENZO

Heavens will not let Lorenzo err so much

CASTILE

Why then, Lorenzo, listen to my words:
It is suspected—and reported too—
That thou, Lorenzo, wrong'st Hieronimo,
And in his suits towards his majesty   55
Still keep'st him back, and seeks to cross his suit.

LORENZO

That I, my lord—?

CASTILE

I tell thee, son, myself have heard it said,
When to my sorrow I have been ashamed
To answer for thee, though thou art my son.   60
Lorenzo, know'st thou not the common love
And kindness that Hieronimo hath won
By his deserts within the court of Spain?

---

37. **extremities:** overwhelming emotions.
39. **Or:** either.
50. **intercept:** interrupt; hinder, frustrate.

Or seest thou not the king my brother's care
In his behalf, and to procure his health?   65
Lorenzo, shouldst thou thwart his passions,
And he exclaim against thee to the king,
What honor were't in this assembly,
Or what a scandal were't among the kings
To hear Hieronimo exclaim on thee?   70
Tell me—and look thou tell me truly too—
Whence grows the ground of this report in court?

LORENZO
My lord, it lies not in Lorenzo's power
To stop the vulgar, liberal of their tongues:
A small advantage makes a water-breach,   75
And no man lives that long contenteth all.

CASTILE
Myself have seen thee busy to keep back
Him and his supplications from the king.

LORENZO
Yourself, my lord, hath seen his passions
That ill beseemed the presence of a king;   80
And for I pitied him in his distress,
I held him thence with kind and courteous words,
As free from malice to Hieronimo
As to my soul, my lord.

CASTILE
Hieronimo, my son, mistakes thee then.   85

LORENZO
My gracious father, believe me so he doth.
But what's a silly man, distract in mind,
To think upon the murder of his son?
Alas, how easy is it for him to err!
But, for his satisfaction and the world's,   90
'Twere good, my lord, that Hieronimo and I
Were reconciled, if he misconster me.

CASTILE
Lorenzo, thou hast said: it shall be so.
Go one of you and call Hieronimo.
                    Enter BALTHAZAR *and* BEL-IMPERIA.

---

65. health: well-being, welfare (*OED* n. 5a).
70. exclaim on: loudly denounce (*OED* v. 2b).
74. vulgar: common people. liberal of: free with.
75. advantage: i.e., for the water—a leak.
80. presence of: place of formal attendance upon.
87. silly: pitiable, feeble, helpless (*OED* adj. 1–2).
92. misconster: misconstrue.

BALTHAZAR

Come, Bel-Imperia, Balthazar's content,   95
My sorrow's ease, and sovereign of my bliss:
Sith heaven hath ordained thee to be mine,
Disperse those clouds and melancholy looks,
And clear them up with those thy sun-bright eyes
Wherein my hope and heaven's fair beauty lies.   100

BEL-IMPERIA

My looks, my lord, are fitting for my love,
Which, new begun, can show no brighter yet.

BALTHAZAR

New kindled flames should burn as morning sun.

BEL-IMPERIA

But not too fast, lest heat and all be done.
I see my lord my father.

BALTHAZAR   Truce, my love,   105
I will go salute him.

CASTILE   Welcome, Balthazar,
Welcome, brave prince, the pledge of Castile's peace;
And welcome, Bel-Imperia—how now, girl?
Why com'st thou sadly to salute us thus?
Content thyself, for I am satisfied: 110
It is not now as when Andrea lived,
We have forgotten and forgiven that,
And thou art gracèd with a happier love.
But, Balthazar, here comes Hieronimo.
I'll have a word with him.

Enter HIERONIMO *and a Servant.*

HIERONIMO   And where's the Duke?   115

SERBERINE Yonder.

HIERONIMO   Even so:
[*Aside*] What new device have they devisèd, trow?
Pocas palabras, mild as the lamb,
Is't I will be revenged? No, I am not the man.

CASTILE

Welcome, Hieronimo.   120

LORENZO

Welcome, Hieronimo.

BALTHAZAR

Welcome, Hieronimo.

HIERONIMO

My lords, I thank you for Horatio.

---

117. **trow:** do you suppose.
118. *Pocas palabras*: few words (Spanish).

CASTILE
  Hieronimo, the reason that I sent
  To speak with you, is this.
HIERONIMO   What, so short?   125
  Then I'll be gone; I thank you for't.
CASTILE
  Nay stay, Hieronimo! Go call him, son.
LORENZO
  Hieronimo, my father craves a word with you.
HIERONIMO
  With me, sir? Why, my lord, I thought you had done.
LORENZO [*Aside*]
  No, would he had!
CASTILE   Hieronimo, I hear   130
  You find yourself aggrievèd at my son
  Because you have not access unto the king,
  And say 'tis he that intercepts your suits.
HIERONIMO
  Why, is not this a miserable thing, my lord?
CASTILE
  Hieronimo, I hope you have no cause,   135
  And would be loath that one of your deserts
  Should once have reason to suspect my son,
  Considering how I think of you myself.
HIERONIMO
  Your son Lorenzo? Whom, my noble lord—
  The hope of Spain, mine honorable friend?   140
  Grant me the combat of them, if they dare:
      Draws out his sword.
  I'll meet him face to face to tell me so.
  These be the scandalous reports of such
  As love not me, and hate my lord too much.
  Should I suspect Lorenzo would prevent   145
  Or cross my suit, that loved my son so well?
  My lord, I am ashamed it should be said.
LORENZO
  Hieronimo, I never gave you cause.
HIERONIMO
  My good lord, I know you did not.
CASTILE   There then pause;
  And for the satisfaction of the world,   150

---

125. **so short?**: (1) have you so little to say?; (2) are you so rude?
136. **one . . . deserts**: someone as deserving as you.
141. **combat of them**: right to challenge them to combat.
145. **prevent**: forestall.

Hieronimo, frequent my homely house,
The Duke of Castile, Cyprian's ancient seat;
And when thou wilt, use me, my son, and it.
But here before Prince Balthazar and me,
Embrace each other, and be perfect friends.   155

HIERONIMO

Ay marry, my lord, and shall.
"Friends," quoth he? See, I'll be friends with you all—
Specially with you my lovely lord.
For divers causes it is fit for us
That we be friends: the world is suspicious,   160
And men may think what we imagine not.

BALTHAZAR

Why this is friendly done, Hieronimo.

LORENZO

And thus I hope old grudges are forgot.

HIERONIMO

What else? it were a shame it should not be so.

CASTILE

Come on, Hieronimo, at my request,   165
Let us entreat your company today.

                              Exeunt [all but HIERONIMO].

HIERONIMO

Your lordship's to command—Pha! keep your way:
Chi mi fa più carreze che non suole,
Tradito mi ha, o tradir mi vuole.

                                                          Exit.

[3.15]

[*Chorus*]

ANDREA

Awake, Erichtho! Cerberus, awake!
Solicit Pluto, gentle Proserpine,

---

151. **homely:** (1) hospitable; (2) humble (*OED* adj. 3; 4).
168–69. ***Chi . . . vuole:*** someone who shows me more affection than usual has either betrayed me, or wishes to betray me (Italian).
1. **Awake:** the audience are probably expected to remember Psalms 121.3–4: "he wyll not sleepe that kepeth thee. Beholde, he that kepeth Israel: wyll neither slumber nor sleepe." See also Calvin's *A Commentarie . . . vpon the First Booke of Moses Called Genesis*, trans Thomas Tymme (1578), which explains how, in the case of Babel, God "shewed himself a revenger by little and little" thereby demonstrating that "he doth oftentimes so beare with the wicked, that as one a sleepe he doth not only suffer them to take many wicked thinges in hand: but also he maketh them rejoyce at the successe of their wicked enterprises, that at the last he may make their fal the greater" (sig. Qvi).
Erictho: a necromantic sorceress from Thessaly. First mentioned in Lucan's Pharsalia (VI, 507–830), she later appears in Dante's *Inferno* (IX, 23), where Virgil's shade tells how she compelled him to bring back a spirit from the lowest depths of hell.

To combat Acheron and Erebus
For ne'er by Styx and Phlegethon in hell . . .

* * * * * * * * * * * * * *

Nor ferried Charon to the fiery lakes   5
Such fearful sights as poor Andrea sees!
Revenge, awake!

REVENGE   Awake, for why?

ANDREA
Awake, Revenge! for thou art ill-advised
To sleep away what thou art warned to watch.

REVENGE
Content thy self, and do not trouble me.   10

ANDREA
Awake, Revenge! if love, as love hath had,
Have yet the power or prevalence in hell!
Hieronimo with Lorenzo is joined in league,
And intercepts our passage to revenge.
Awake, Revenge! or we are woe-begone.   15

REVENGE
Thus worldlings ground, what they have dreamed, upon.
Content thy self, Andrea: though I sleep,
Yet is my mood soliciting their souls.
Sufficeth thee that poor Hieronimo
Cannot forget his son Horatio.   20
Nor dies Revenge although he sleep awhile,
For in unquiet, quietness is feigned,
And slumb'ring is a common worldly wile,
Behold, Andrea, for an instance how
Revenge hath slept, and then imagine thou   25
What 'tis to be subject to destiny.
        Enter a Dumb Show.

ANDREA
Awake, Revenge! reveal this mystery.

REVENGE
The two first, the nuptial torches bore,

---

3. **Erebus:** primeval darkness, the child of Chaos, commonly used as a synonym for hell.
4. **Styx and Phlegethon:** rivers of hell, like Acheron (see notes to 1.1.19 and 3.1.55). Edwards suggests that sense can be restored to this corrupt passage by restoring a missing line, something like "Was I distressed with outrage sore as this."
5. **Charon:** see note to 1.1.20.
16. **worldlings . . . upon:** mortals base their beliefs on mere dreams or fancies.
18. **my mood:** i.e., vindictive rage. **soliciting:** disturbing; importuning (*OED* v.1; v. 2). **their souls:** i.e., the souls of those who have been wronged.
27. **reveal this mystery:** explain the secret meaning [of this performance]; see note to 1.1.90.
28. **nuptial torches:** symbols of erotic passion.

As brightly burning as the mid-day's sun;
But after them doth Hymen hie as fast,   30
Clothèd in sable and a saffron robe,
And blows them out, and quencheth them with blood,
As discontent that things continue so.

ANDREA
Sufficeth me thy meaning's understood,
And thanks to thee and those infernal powers   35
That will not tolerate a lover's woe.
Rest thee, for I will sit to see the rest.

REVENGE
Then argue not, for thou hast thy request.

Actus Quartus.

[4.1]

Enter BEL-IMPERIA *and* HIERONIMO.

BEL-IMPERIA
Is this the love thou bear'st Horatio?
Is this the kindness that thou counterfeits?
Are these the fruits of thine incessant tears?
Hieronimo, are these thy passions,
Thy protestations, and thy deep laments   5
That thou wert wont to weary men withal?
O unkind father, O deceitful world!
With what excuses canst thou show thyself,
With what. . . . .
From this dishonor and the hate of men,   10
Thus to neglect the loss and life of him
Whom both my letters and thine own belief
Assures thee to be causeless slaughtered!
Hieronimo, for shame, Hieronimo,
Be not a history to after times   15
Of such ingratitude unto thy son.

30–31. Hymen . . . robe: Hymen, the god of marriage, here wears the ominous black of mourning over his celebratory saffron robes.

38. The early texts agree in printing "*Exeunt*" after this line, but Andrea's "I will sit to see the rest" (line 37) makes it plain that he and Revenge must remain on stage, as they have throughout. Perhaps the stage direction was intended for the performers in the dumb show.

9. The 1592 edition makes no sense here: the compositor's eye evidently skipped to the following line whose last six words are anticipated here. Boas suggests that Kyd's original must have read something like "With what devices seek thyself to save."

Unhappy mothers of such children then—
But monstrous fathers, to forget so soon
The death of those whom they with care and cost
Have tendered so, thus careless should be lost.   20
Myself, a stranger in respect of thee,
So loved his life, as still I wish their deaths;
Nor shall his death be unrevenged by me,
Although I bear it out for fashion's sake:
For here I swear in sight of heaven and earth,   25
Shouldst thou neglect the love thou shouldst retain
And give it over and devise no more,
Myself should send their hateful souls to hell,
That wrought his downfall with extremest death.

HIERONIMO

But may it be that Bel-Imperia   30
Vows such revenge as she hath deigned to say?
Why then, I see that heaven applies our drift,
And all the saints do sit soliciting
For vengeance on those cursed murderers.
Madam, 'tis true, and now I find it so: 35
I found a letter, written in your name,
And in that letter, how Horatio died.
Pardon, O pardon, Bel-Imperia,
My fear and care in not believing it,
Nor think I thoughtless think upon a mean   40
To let his death be unrevenged at full;
And here I vow—so you but give consent,
And will conceal my resolution—
I will ere long determine of their deaths
That causeless thus have murderèd my son.   45

BEL-IMPERIA

Hieronimo, I will consent, conceal,
And aught that may effect for thine avail,
Join with thee to revenge Horatio's death.

17–20. **Unhappy . . . lost:** Unless the text is corrupted here, the confused syntax may be intended to represent Bel-Imperia's disordered state of mind.
20. **tendered:** tenderly cherished (*OED* tender v² 3).
21. **in . . . thee:** compared to you.
24. **bear it out:** put up with it. **fashion:** outward ceremony, mere form (*OED* n. 7).
27. **devise:** plot, scheme.
32. **applies our drift:** consents to, supports our plot (*OED* apply v. 19; *OED* drift n. 5); perhaps with a play on the nautical meaning of *steers our slow course* (*OED* apply v. 22; *OED* drift n. 2a).
39. **care:** caution (*OED* n¹ 3a).
40. **mean:** see note to 3.3.23.
44. **determine of:** come to a judicial decision on (*OED* v. 5).

HIERONIMO

On then; whatsoever I devise,
Let me entreat you grace my practices—   50
For why, the plot's already in mine head.
Here they are.

    Enter BALTHAZAR *and* LORENZO.

BALTHAZAR   How now, Hieronimo?
What, courting Bel-Imperia?

HIERONIMO   Ay, my lord,
Such courting as, I promise you,
She hath my heart, but you, my lord, have hers.   55

LORENZO

But now, Hieronimo, or never
We are to entreat your help.

HIERONIMO   My help?
Why, my good lords, assure yourselves of me,
For you have given me cause—
Ay, by my faith have you.

BALTHAZAR   It pleased you   60
At the entertainment of the ambassador,
To grace the King so much as with a show;
Now, were your study so well furnishèd
As, for the passing of the first night's sport,
To entertain my father with the like,   65
Or any such-like pleasing motion,
Assure yourself it would content them well.

HIERONIMO

 Is this all?

BALTHAZAR   Ay, this is all.

HIERONIMO

Why then I'll fit you, say no more.
When I was young, I gave my mind   70

---

49. On . . . devise. This line is one syllable short, which may indicate a significant pause
after "On then," but as Edwards notes, there is much irregular verse in this scene,
which is a likely sign of textual corruption.
50. grace my practices: favor my stratagems (*OED grace* v. 2; *practice* n. 6).
60. Ay . . . you: The heavy irony in this line, combined with the pause indicated by the
metrically incomplete line 59, suggests that it may be intended as an aside.
62. grace: give pleasure to (*OED* v. 6).
63. furnishèd: stocked.
66. motion: Usually a puppet show; perhaps as an alternative to the regular forms of
theatrical performance denoted by "show" (line 62) or perhaps (as most editors suggest)
meant to refer generally to any form of entertainment—though *OED* offers no examples
of such a usage.
69. I'll fit you: (1) I'll provide what you need; (2) I'll punish you as you deserve (from
Edwards).

And plied myself to fruitless poetry:
Which, though it profit the professor naught,
Yet is it passing pleasing to the world.

LORENZO

And how for that?

HIERONIMO   Marry, my good lord, thus—
And yet methinks you are too quick with us—   75
When in Toledo there I studièd,
It was my chance to write a tragedy—
See here, my lords—   *He shows them a book.*
Which long forgot, I found this other day.
Now, would your lordships favor me so much   80
As but to grace me with your acting it—
I mean each one of you to play a part—
Assure you it will prove most passing strange
And wondrous plausible to that assembly.

BALTHAZAR

What, would you have us play a tragedy?   85

HIERONIMO

Why, Nero thought it no disparagement,
And kings and emperors have ta'en delight
To make experience of their wits in plays?

LORENZO

Nay, be not angry, good Hieronimo,
The prince but asked a question.   90

BALTHAZAR

In faith, Hieronimo, and you be in earnest,
I'll make one.

LORENZO   And I another.

HIERONIMO

Now, my good lord, could you entreat
Your sister Bel-Imperia to make one?
For what's a play without a woman in it?   95

---

72. **professor:** exponent, practitioner.
75. **too quick:** "too pressing; perhaps with a pun on *quick* meaning alive" (Mulryne's note).
83. **strange:** wonderful, astonishing, unexpected (with an ironic double entendre).
84. **plausible:** deserving of applause; pleasing, agreeable (*OED* n. 1–2).
85. **us:** the next speech suggests that Balthazar uses a haughty royal plural here.
86–88. **Nero . . . plays:** The emperor Nero was known to have been a passionate amateur actor; Hieronimo may also have covertly in mind the occasional Roman practice of killing condemned criminals in the course of a theatrical performance.
86. **disparagement:** dishonor, loss of dignity.
91. **and:** if.
92. **make one:** be one (of the cast).
95. **For . . . it:** An ironic metatheatrical joke: in English theaters all women's parts were played by boys.

BEL-IMPERIA

   Little entreaty shall serve me, Hieronimo,

   For I must needs be employed in your play.

HIERONIMO

   Why, this is well; I tell you, lordings,

   It was determined to have been acted

   By gentlemen and scholars too,   100

   Such as could tell what to speak.

BALTHAZAR

   And now it shall be played by princes and courtiers

   Such as can tell how to speak

   If, as it is our country manner,

   You will but let us know the argument.   105

HIERONIMO

   That shall I roundly. The chronicles of Spain

   Record this written of a knight of Rhodes:

   He was betrothed and wedded at the length,

   To one Perseda an Italian dame,

   Whose beauty ravished all that her beheld,   110

   Especially the soul of Suleiman,

   Who at the marriage was the chiefest guest.

   By sundry means sought Suleiman to win

   Perseda's love, and could not gain the same.

   Then gan he break his passions to a friend,   115

   One of his pashas whom he held full dear.

   Her had this pasha long solicited,

   And saw she was not otherwise to be won

   But by her husband's death, this knight of Rhodes,

   Whom presently by treachery he slew.   120

   She, stirred with an exceeding hate therefore,

   As cause of this slew Suleiman,

   And, to escape the pasha's tyranny,

   Did stab herself—and this the tragedy.

LORENZO

   O excellent!

---

97. **employed**: stress on the first syllable.

99. **determined**: intended.

101–103. **what to speak . . . how to speak**: the distinction is a social one, between "gentlemen and scholars," educated men concerned with content, and denizens of the court, whose primary concern is with formal elegance.

105. **argument**: plot.

106. **roundly**: to the full; without circumlocution; promptly (*OED* adv. 2; 4; 7).

106–24. **The chronicles . . . tragedy**: Hieronimo's play offers a much condensed version of this story, which may already have formed the subject of the tragedy *Soliman and Perseda*, probably by Kyd himself (see pp. xiii, xxvi).

115. **break**: confess.

BEL-IMPERIA   But say, Hieronimo,   125
  What then became of him that was the pasha?
HIERONIMO
  Marry thus: moved with remorse of his misdeeds,
  Ran to a mountain top and hung himself.
BALTHAZAR
  But which of us is to perform that part?
HIERONIMO
  Oh, that will I, my lords, make no doubt of it: 130
  I'll play the murderer, I warrant you,
  For I already have conceited that.
BALTHAZAR
  And what shall I?
HIERONIMO
  Great Suleiman, the Turkish Emperor.
LORENZO
  And I?   135
HIERONIMO
  Erasto, the Knight of Rhodes,
BEL-IMPERIA
  And I?
HIERONIMO   Perseda, chaste and resolute.
  And here, my lords, are several abstracts drawn
  For each of you to note your parts,   140
  And act it as occasion's offered you.
  You must provide a Turkish cap,
  A black mustachio, and a fauchion.
      Gives a paper to BALTHAZAR.
  You with a cross, like to a Knight of Rhodes.
      Gives another to LORENZO.
  And, madam, you must attire yourself   145
      He giveth BEL-IMPERIA *another.*
  Like Phoebe, Flora, or the huntress—
  Which to your discretion shall seem best.
  And as for me, my lords, I'll look to one,

---

127. **Marry:** why, to be sure (exclamation).
132. **conceited:** formed a conception of.
136. **Erasto:** In keeping with the ironic symmetries of revenge, Lorenzo will be forced to play the part that corresponds to that of his own victim, Horatio.
139. **abstracts drawn:** presumably the individual "parts" extracted and transcribed from the playbook. In the Elizabethan theater each actor was given a "part"—a manuscript roll ("role") on which his lines, together with the necessary cues, were inscribed.
140. **note:** learn.
141. **occasion:** opportunity.
143. **fauchion:** a broad curved sword "after the Turkish fashion" (*OED* n.).
146. **huntress:** perhaps pronounced with three syllables (*hunteress*) to complete the meter.

And, with the ransom that the viceroy sent,
So furnish and perform this tragedy   150
As all the world shall say Hieronimo
Was liberal in gracing of it so.

BALTHAZAR
Hieronimo, methinks a comedy were better.

HIERONIMO
A comedy?
Fie! comedies are fit for common wits,   155
But to present a kingly troupe withal,
Give me a stately written tragedy.
Tragedia cothurnata, fitting kings,
Containing matter, and not common things.
My lords, all this must be performed   160
As fitting for the first night's reveling.
The Italian tragedians were so sharp of wit
That, in one hour's meditation,
They would perform anything in action.

LORENZO
And well it may, for I have seen the like   165
In Paris, 'mongst the French tragedians.

HIERONIMO
In Paris? Mass! and well remembered!
There's one thing more that rests for us to do.

BALTHAZAR
What's that, Hieronimo? Forget not anything.

HIERONIMO
Each one of us must act his part   170
In unknown languages,
That it may breed the more variety—
As you, my lord, in Latin, I in Greek,
You in Italian; and, for because I know

---

150. **furnish**: provide for; deck out.
152. **gracing of**: adorning.
155–59 **comedies . . . things**: The social distinction between the worlds of comedy and tragedy was a commonplace, deriving originally from Aristotle's *Poetics* but repeated in recent texts such as Sir Philip Sidney's *Apology for Poetry* (c. 1579).
158. *Tragedia* . . . **kings**: Tragedy was habitually represented—e.g, as on the title page of Ben Jonson's *Works* (1616)—as a crowned figure wearing the buskins (*cothurni*, or thick-soled boots) derived from the costume of classical tragedians.
159. **matter**: substantial content (*OED* n. 11b).
163. **in . . . meditation**: after an hour's preparation.
164. **action**: acting, performance.
167. **Mass**: i.e., by the mass (a relatively mild blasphemy).
170–71. **act . . . languages**: Although scholars are divided as to whether Kyd intended this instruction to be carried out in actual performance, the publisher's note to the reader at 4.4.10, combined with the recurrent Babel motif (see pp. xviii–xix, xxvi, xxxviii), make it almost certain that this was his intention.

That Bel-Imperia hath practisèd the French,   175
In courtly French shall all her phrases be.

BEL-IMPERIA
You mean to try my cunning, then, Hieronimo?

BALTHAZAR
But this will be a mere confusion,
And hardly shall we all be understood.

HIERONIMO
It must be so, for the conclusion   180
Shall prove the invention and all was good;
And I myself in an oration—
And with a strange and wondrous show besides,
That I will have there behind a curtain—
Assure yourself shall make the matter known;   185
And all shall be concluded in one scene,
For there's no pleasure ta'en in tediousness.

The end justifies the means

BALTHAZAR
How like you this?

LORENZO   Why thus my lord
We must resolve to soothe his humors up.

BALTHAZAR
On then, Hieronimo! Farewell till soon.   190

HIERONIMO
You'll ply this gear?

LORENZO   I warrant you.

Exeunt all but HIERONIMO.

HIERONIMO   Why so,
Now shall I see the fall of Babylon *Babel*
Wrought by the heavens in this confusion.

---

177. cunning: (1) learning; (2) skill in deceiving, craft (*OED* n.1; 5b).
178–79. But . . . understood: cf. God's words in Genesis 11.7 (Geneva version) "Come on,
let vs goe downe, and there confound their language, that euery one perceiue not anothers
speache." (*Marginal gloss:* "By this great plague of the confusion of tongues, appeareth
Gods horrible iudgement against mans pride and vaine glorie").
181. invention: (1) devising or treatment of a subject; (2) device, contrivance, scheme
(*OED* n. 3b; 6).
185. matter: see note to line 159, but playing on the sense "material cause" (*OED* n. 15);
i.e., the murdered boy of Horatio.
189. soothe . . . up: humor him.
191. ply this gear: carry out this business.
192. fall of Babylon: Of the versions of the Bible available to Kyd, the Geneva Bible uses
Babel for the city of Babylon as well as for the impious Tower that brought about the confusion of languages, as does the prefatory "*descripcyon and successe of the kynges of Iuda
and Ierusalem*" in the Great Bible. The Bishop's Bible identifies Babylon with Babel in a
marginal gloss on Psalms 137; hence the destruction of the Tower of Babel and of the city
of Babylon under Belshazzar (Balthazar) were readily identified as precise reiterations of
God's wrath against the wicked. Protestant propaganda identified papal Rome with Babylon, and Spain, with its self-proclaimed *reyes catolicos* (catholic monarchs), was regarded
by the English as the militant arm of the papacy. See the Introduction (p. xxvi) and S. F.
Johnson "*The Spanish Tragedy* or Babylon Revisited," in *Essays on Shakespeare and Eliza-*

And if the world like not this tragedy,
Hard is the hap of old Hieronimo.   195

Exit.

[4.2]

Enter ISABELLA *with a weapon.*

ISABELLA

Tell me no more, O monstrous homicides!
Since neither piety nor pity moves
The king to justice or compassion,
I will revenge myself upon this place,
Where thus they murdered my belovèd son.   5
   She cuts down the arbor.
Down with these branches and these loathsome boughs
Of this unfortunate and fatal pine;
Down with them, Isabella, rend them up,
And burn the roots from whence the rest is sprung:
I will not leave a root, a stalk, a tree,   10
A bough, a branch, a blossom, nor a leaf,
No, not an herb within this garden plot,
Accursed complot of my misery.
Fruitless for ever may this garden be,
Barren the earth, and blissless whosoever   15
Imagines not to keep it unmanured!
An eastern wind commixed with noisome airs
Shall blast the plants and the young saplings;
The earth with serpents shall be pesterèd,
And passengers for fear to be infect,   20
Shall stand aloof, and, looking at it, tell:
"There, murdered, died the son of Isabel."
Ay, here he died, and here I him embrace:
See where his ghost solicits with his wounds
Revenge on her that should revenge his death!   25
Hieronimo, make haste to see thy son,

---

bethan Drama. *In Honour of Hardin Craig*, ed. Richard Hosley (London, 1962), pp.
23–36. 1962. See also note to 4.2.5 SD.
195. hap: fortune.
5. SD. She . . . arbor: For Isabella's action as a symbolic destruction of Babylon (whose
Hanging Gardens were among the wonders of the ancient world) op. cit., see S. F. Johnson
(pp. 26–27). Her cutting down of the arbor probably involved little more than a token strip-
ping of its leaves and branches because the property appears to be required again in 4.4.
7. unfortunate: inauspicious, ill-omened.
13. complot: plot, conspiracy.
17–19. An eastern . . . pestered: see Jeremiah 51.37 (Bishops' Bible): "Babylon shall become
an heape of stones, a dwellyng place for dragons, a fearefulnesse and wonderyng, and no
man shall dwell there."
20. infect: infected.

For sorrow and despair hath cited me
To hear Horatio plead with Rhadamanth.
Make haste, Hieronimo, to hold excused
Thy negligence in pursuit of their deaths,   30
Whose hateful wrath bereaved him of his breath.
Ah nay, thou dost delay their deaths,
Forgives the murderers of thy noble son,
And none but I bestir me—to no end.
And, as I curse this tree from further fruit,   35
So shall my womb be cursèd for his sake,
And with this weapon will I wound the breast
        She stabs herself.
The hapless breast that gave Horatio suck.   [*Exit.*]

[4.3]

Enter HIERONIMO; *he knocks up the curtain.*
Enter the DUKE OF CASTILE.

CASTILE
How now, Hieronimo, where's your fellows,
That you take all this pain?
HIERONIMO
O sir, it is for the author's credit
To look that all things may go well.
But, good my lord, let me entreat your grace   5
To give the king the copy of the play:
This is the argument of what we show.
CASTILE
I will, Hieronimo.
HIERONIMO
One thing more, my good lord.
CASTILE
What's that?   10

27. cited: summoned.
28. Rhadamanth: see note to 1.1.33.
38. SD. [*Exit*]: Edwards notes that because the compositor had run short of space at the
    bottom of this page, a stage direction may have been dropped but that line 38 gives
    Isabella a line on which to stagger off the stage.
4.3. SD. *knocks . . . curtain*: Editors usually follow Edwards in suggesting that Hieron-
    imo hangs the curtain over one of the stage doors, or perhaps across the central "discov-
    ery space." However because the framework of the arbor presumably remains on stage
    after Isabella's attack and because Hieronimo's speech at 4.4.88–112 seems to require
    that he display Horatio's body precisely as he found it ("Where hanging on a tree I found
    my son, / Through-girt with wounds, and slaughtered *as you see*," 4.4.111–12; emphasis
    added), it seems more likely that he uses it to screen off the arbor. If the arbor were
    placed in front of one of the three openings, Horatio's corpse could then be readily
    inserted from behind.
6–7. copy . . . argument: It seems that the King is to be presented with a full text of the
    play, prefaced (as printed plays often were) with an "argument" or plot outline. In this
    case Kyd may have in mind the "allowed copy," the precious manuscript passed for per-

HIERONIMO   Let me entreat your grace
  That, when the train are past into the gallery,
  You would vouchsafe to throw me down the key.

CASTILE
  I will, Hieronimo.

Exit CASTILE.

HIERONIMO
  What are you ready, Balthazar?   15
  Bring a chair and a cushion for the king
      Enter BALTHAZAR *with a chair.*
  Well done, Balthazar; hang up the title:
  Our scene is Rhodes—what, is your beard on?

BALTHAZAR
  Half on, the other is in my hand.

HIERONIMO
  Dispatch for shame, are you so long?   20

Exit BALTHAZAR.

  Bethink thy self, Hieronimo:
  Recall thy wits, recompt thy former wrongs
  Thou hast received by murder of thy son,
  And lastly, not least, how Isabel—
  Once his mother and thy dearest wife—   25
  All woe-begone for him hath slain herself.
  Behoves thee then, Hieronimo, to be revenged:
  The plot is laid of dire revenge;
  On then, Hieronimo, pursue revenge,
  For nothing wants but acting of revenge.   30

Exit HIERONIMO.

[4.4]

Enter Spanish KING, VICEROY, *the* DUKE OF CASTILE, *and
their train.*

KING
  Now, Viceroy, shall we see "The Tragedy
  Of Suleiman the Turkish Emperor,"

formance by the Master of the Revels, which an acting company would put into the
hands of the their "book holder" (see 4.4.9–10).
12–13. That . . . key: Editors are divided about the staging here: most follow Edwards in
supposing that "gallery" refers to the "long gallery," or the hall of a great house, and that
"throw me down" means simply "throw to the ground for me"; but Gurr has pointed out
that the *frons scenae* of the Rose playhouse had three angles, offering the on-stage audience quite viable sight lines from above. For the importance of the key, see 4.4.156.
17. title: presumably the title board often hung above the stage in Elizabethan theaters to
identify the play; though Hieronimo's next line suggests that, in this case, Kyd may
intend a locality board identifying that "[the]scene is Rhodes."
18–19. beard . . . half on: A large flowing beard will have been one of the markers of
Suleiman's Turkish identity.
22. recompt: recall.

Performed of pleasure by your son the prince,
My nephew, Don Lorenzo, and my niece.

VICEROY

Who, Bel-Imperia?   5

KING

Ay, and Hieronimo, our marshal,
At whose request they deign to do't themselves:
These be our pastimes in the court of Spain.
Here brother, you shall be the bookkeeper.
This is the argument of that they show.   10
      He giveth him a book.

*Gentlemen, this play of Hieronimo in sundry languages was thought
good to be set down in English more largely, for the easier understanding to every public reader.*

      Enter BALTHAZAR [*as* SULEIMAN], BEL-IMPERIA [*as* PERSEDA],
      and HIERONIMO [*as the* PASHA].

BALTHAZAR.

Pasha, that Rhodes is ours, yield heavens the honor,
And holy Mahomet, our sacred prophet;
And be thou graced with every excellence
That Suleiman can give, or thou desire.
But thy desert in conquering Rhodes is less   15
Than in reserving this fair Christian nymph,
Perseda, blissful lamp of excellence,
Whose eyes compel, like powerful adamant,
The warlike heart of Suleiman to wait.

KING

See, Viceroy, that is Balthazar, your son,   20
That represents the emperor Suleiman:
How well he acts his amorous passion.

VICEROY

Ay, Bel-Imperia hath taught him that.

CASTILE.

That's because his mind runs all on Bel-Imperia

HIERONIMO

Whatever joy earth yields betide your majesty.   25

---

9. **bookkeeper:** the "book holder" responsible for looking after the company's stock of
      play manuscripts, who also served as a prompter (see note to 4.3.6–7).
10. **SD.** see note to 4.1.170–71.
18. **adamant:** magnetic lodestone.
19. **wait:** attend on, serve [her].
22. **passion:** passionate speech (*OED* n. 6d).

BALTHAZAR
Earth yields no joy without Perseda's love.

HIERONIMO
Let then Perseda on your grace attend.

BALTHAZAR
She shall not wait on me, but I on her:
Drawn by the influence of her lights, I yield.
But let my friend, the Rhodian knight, come forth,   30
Erasto, dearer than my life to me,
That he may see Perseda, my beloved.
> *Enter* LORENZO [*as* ERASTO].

KING
Here comes Lorenzo; look upon the plot,
And tell me, brother, what part plays he?

BEL-IMPERIA
Ah, my Erasto, welcome to Perseda.   35

LORENZO
Thrice happy is Erasto that thou livest:
Rhodes' loss is nothing to Erasto's joy;
Sith his Perseda lives, his life survives.

BALTHAZAR
Ah, Pasha, here is love between Erasto
And fair Perseda, sovereign of my soul.   40

HIERONIMO
Remove Erasto, mighty Suleiman,
And then Perseda will be quickly won.

BALTHAZAR
Erasto is my friend, and while he lives,
Perseda never will remove her love.

HIERONIMO
Let not Erasto live, to grieve great Suleiman.   45

BALTHAZAR
Dear is Erasto in our princely eye.

HIERONIMO
But if he be your rival, let him die.

BALTHAZAR
Why, let him die: so love commandeth me;
Yet grieve I that Erasto should so die.

HIERONIMO
Erasto, Suleiman saluteth thee,   50

---

29. influence: "supposed flowing or streaming from the stars or heavens of an ethereal fluid acting upon the character and destiny of men" (*OED* n. 2a). **lights:** eyes (conventionally compared to stars).

And lets thee wit by me his highness' will,
Which is, thou shouldst be thus employed.   *Stab him.*
BEL-IMPERIA   *Ay me,*
Erasto! See, Suleiman, Erasto's slain!
BALTHAZAR
Yet liveth Suleiman to comfort thee.
Fair queen of beauty, let not favor die,   55
But with a gracious eye behold his grief
That with Perseda's beauty is increased,
If by Persed his grief be not released.
BEL-IMPERIA
Tyrant, desist soliciting vain suits:
Relentless are mine ears to thy laments   60
As thy butcher is pitiless and base,
Which seized on my Erasto, harmless knight;
Yet by thy power thou thinkest to command,
And to thy power Perseda doth obey;
But were she able, thus she would revenge   65
Thy treacheries on thee, ignoble prince: *Stab him.*
And on herself she would be thus revenged.   *Stab herself.*
KING
Well said, old marshal, this was bravely done!
HIERONIMO
But Bel-Imperia plays Perseda well.
VICEROY
Were this in earnest Bel-Imperia,   70
You would be better to my son than so.
KING
But now what follows for Hieronimo?
HIERONIMO
Marry, this follows for Hieronimo:
Here break we off our sundry languages,
And thus conclude I in our vulgar tongue: 75
Haply you think—but bootless are your thoughts—
That this is fabulously counterfeit,
And that we do as all tragedians do:
To die today, for fashioning our scene—
The death of Ajax, or some Roman peer—   80
And, in a minute starting up again,

51. **wit:** know.
68. **Well said:** bravo!
75. **vulgar tongue:** vernacular language.
76. **Haply:** perhaps. **bootless:** unavailing.
77. **fabulously:** fictitiously.
79. **for . . . scene:** for the acting out of our play.

Revive to please tomorrow's audience.
No, princes, know I am Hieronimo,
The hopeless father of a hapless son,
Whose tongue is tuned to tell his latest tale,   85
Not to excuse gross errors in the play.
I see your looks urge instance of these words—
Behold the reason urging me to this: *Shows his dead son.*
See here my show, look on this spectacle:
Here lay my hope, and here my hope hath end;   90
Here lay my heart, and here my heart was slain;
Here lay my treasure, here my treasure lost;
Here lay my bliss, and here my bliss bereft;
But hope, heart, treasure, joy, and bliss
All fled, failed, died, yea all decayed with this.   95
From forth these wounds came breath that gave me life;
They murdered me that made these fatal marks.
The cause was love, whence grew this mortal hate,
The hate, Lorenzo and young Balthazar,
The love, my son to Bel-Imperia.   100
But night, the coverer of accursed crimes,
With pitchy silence hushed these traitors' harms,
And lent them leave—for they had sorted leisure—
To take advantage in my garden plot
Upon my son, my dear Horatio: 105
There merciless they butchered up my boy
In black, dark night to pale, dim, cruel death.
He shrieks, I heard—and yet methinks I hear—
His dismal outcry echo in the air.
With soonest speed I hasted to the noise,   110
Where hanging on a tree I found my son,
Through-girt with wounds, and slaughtered as you see.
And grieved I, think you, at this spectacle?
Speak Portuguese, whose loss resembles mine:
If thou canst weep upon thy Balthazar,   115

85. **latest:** last.
87. **urge instance:** demand proof.
88. **SD. Shows . . . son:** see note to, 4.3.SD.
103. **sorted:** sought out.
111. **hanging on a tree:** self-consciously echoes a standard figure for Christ's crucifixion.
112. **Through-girt:** struck through.
114. **Portuguese:** addressed to a prince by a mere court official the adjective is extremely insulting.
115. **thou:** see note to 3.7.42. Hieronimo insolently employs the second person form when addressing the Viceroy (lines 135, 159, 177) but continues to use the respectful plural for Castile (lines 117, 170) until his last defiant speeches when he uses "thou" even to the king (lines 182, 185, 187, 200).

'Tis like I wailed for my Horatio.
And you, my lord, whose reconcilèd son
Marched in a net, and thought himself unseen,
And rated me for brainsick lunacy
With "God amend that mad Hieronimo!"—   120
How can you brook our play's catastrophe?
And here behold this bloody handkerchief,
Which at Horatio's death I weeping dipped
Within the river of his bleeding wounds:
It as propitious, see I have reserved,   125
And never hath it left my bloody heart,
Soliciting remembrance of my vow
With these, O these accursed murderers—
Which now performed, my heart is satisfied.
And to this end the pasha I became,   130
That might revenge me on Lorenzo's life,
Who therefore was appointed to the part
And was to represent the knight of Rhodes
That I might kill him more conveniently.
So, Viceroy, was this Balthazar, thy Son,   135
That Suleiman which Bel-Imperia,
In person of Perseda, murderèd—
Solely appointed to that tragic part
That she might slay him that offended her.
Poor Bel-Imperia missed her part in this,   140
For though the story saith she should have died,
Yet I of kindness, and of care to her,
Did otherwise determine of her end;
But love of him whom they did hate too much
Did urge her resolution to be such.   145
And, princes, now behold Hieronimo,
Author and actor in this tragedy,
Bearing his latest fortune in his fist,
And will as resolute conclude his part
As any of the actors gone before.   150
And, gentles, thus I end my play—
Urge no more words, I have more to say.
          He runs to hang himself.

---

117. **reconcilèd son:** Probably refers both to Lorenzo's reconciliation with Horatio, after
   the dispute over Balthazar's capture and to his seeming reconciliation with Hieronimo
   in 3.14.
118. **Marched . . . net:** proverbial for "deceit"; see Tilley N130.
119. **rated:** chided.
148. **Bearing . . . fist:** i.e., the rope with which he attempts to hang himself at line
   152.

KING
O hearken, Viceroy! Hold, Hieronimo!
Brother, my nephew and thy son are slain.
VICEROY
We are betrayed! My Balthazar is slain!   155
Break ope the doors, run save Hieronimo!
[*They break in and hold* HIERONIMO]
Hieronimo, do but inform the King of these events,
Upon mine honor thou shalt have no harm.
HIERONIMO
Viceroy, I will not trust thee with my life,
Which I this day have offered to my son.   160
Accursèd wretch,
Why stayest thou him that was resolved to die?
KING
Speak, traitor! Damned, bloody murderer speak!
For now I have thee I will make thee speak:
Why hast thou done this undeserving deed?   165
VICEROY
Why hast thou murderèd my Balthazar?
CASTILE
Why hast thou butchered both my children thus?

Addition 5

HIERONIMO
But are you sure they are dead?
CASTILE   Ay, slave, too sure.
HIERONIMO
What and yours too?
VICEROY
Ay, all are dead, not one of them survive.
HIERONIMO
Nay, then I care not. Come, and we shall be friends:
Let us lay our heads together.   [5]
See, here's a goodly noose will hold them all.

153. **Hold:** stop.
156. **Break . . . doors:** Presumably locked with the key that Castile promised to "throw down" for Hieronimo (4.3.13–14).
161. **Accursèd wretch:** addressed to one of the guards holding him.
165. **undeserving:** undeserved (*OED* ppl. a. 3)
Addition 5: replaces lines 168–91 but incorporates, in transposed order, lines 168–75 and 176–77.

VICEROY

   O damnèd devil, how secure he is!

HIERONIMO

   Secure? why doest thou wonder at it.

   I tell thee, Viceroy, this day I have seen revenge,

   And in that sight am grown a prouder monarch   [10]

   Than ever sat under the crown of Spain.

   Had I as many lives as there be stars,

   As many heavens to go to as those lives,

   I'd give them all—ay, and my soul to boot—

   But I would see thee ride in this red pool.   [15]

CASTILE

   Speak, who were thy confederates in this?

VICEROY

   That was thy daughter, Bel-Imperia ,

   For by her hand my Balthazar was slain—

   I saw her stab him.

HIERONIMO   O good words!

   As dear to me was my Horatio   [20]

   As yours, or yours, or yours, my lord, to you.

   My guiltless son was by Lorenzo slain;

   And by Lorenzo and that Balthazar

   Am I at last revengèd thoroughly,

   Upon whose souls may heavens be yet revenged   [25]

   With greater far than these afflictions.

   Methinks since I grew inward with revenge,

   I cannot look with scorn enough on death.

KING

   What, dost thou mock us, slave? Bring tortures forth!

HIERONIMO

   Do, do, do! and meantime I'll torture you: [30]

   [To VICEROY] You had a son, as I take it, and your son

   Should ha' been married to [To CASTILE] your daughter—

      ha, was't not so?

   You had a son too, he was my liege's nephew;

   He was proud and politic: had he lived,

---

[7]. **secure:** overconfident (*OED* a.1). In the context of "damnèd devil," the meaning may be colored by the theological sense of "security"—the sinful conviction that one is predestined to salvation and therefore cannot be damned.

[8]. **doest:** The scansion seems to require the disyllabic pronunciation suggested by the original spelling, rather than the usual monosyllabic contraction, "dost."

[9–11]. **I . . . Spain:** Although he modulates the insulting tone of Hieronimo's final address to the King (see lines 182, 185, 187, 189), the reviser is at pains to spell out the way in which revenge constitutes a usurpation of royal authority.

[12–14]. **Had . . . boot:** Imitating *Dr Faustus*, A-text, 1.3.104–05: "Had I as many souls as there be stars, / I'd give them all for Mephastophilis."

[27]. **inward:** intimate.

He might ha' come to wear the crown of Spain—   [35]
I think 'twas so. 'Twas I that killèd him,
Look you, this same hand, 'twas it that stabbed
His heart—do you see this hand?—
For one Horatio, if you ever knew him: a youth,
One that they hanged up in his father's garden,   [40]
[*To* VICEROY] One that did force your valiant son to yield,
[*To* CASTILE] While your more valiant son did take him
    prisoner.

VICEROY

Be deaf my senses, I can hear no more!

KING

Fall heaven, and cover us with thy sad ruins!

CASTILE

Roll all the world within thy pitchy cloud!   [45]

HIERONIMO

Now do I applaud what I have acted.
    Nunc iners cadat manus!
Now to express the rupture of my part,
First take my tongue, and afterward my heart.
    He bites out his tongue.

HIERONIMO

O good words!
As dear to me was my Horatio
As yours, or yours, or yours, my lord, to you.   170
My guiltless son was by Lorenzo slain;
And by Lorenzo and that Balthazar
Am I at last revengèd thoroughly,
Upon whose souls may heavens be yet avenged
With greater far then these afflictions.   175

CASTILE

But who were thy confederates in this?

VICEROY

That was thy daughter Bel-Imperia,
For by her hand my Balthazar was slain
I saw her stab him.

KING   Why speak'st thou not?

HIERONIMO

What lesser liberty can kings afford   180

---

[47]. *Nunc . . . manus*: Now let my hand fall idle.
[48]. **express . . . part**: Given that Hieronimo has effectively supplied the King and Vice-
    roy with all the information they need, the author of this revision clearly felt the need to
    supply some explanation for the old man's berserk gesture and turned it into a bitter
    metatheatrical comment on the theatricality of his revenge.

Than harmless silence? Then afford it me:
Sufficeth I may not, nor I will not tell thee.

KING

Fetch forth the tortures.
Traitor as thou art, I'll make thee tell.

HIERONIMO

Indeed thou may'st torment me, as his wretched son   185
Hath done in murdering my Horatio.
But never shalt thou force me to reveal
The thing which I have vowed inviolate;
And therefore, in despite of all thy threats,
Pleased with their deaths, and eased with their revenge,   190
First take my tongue, and afterward my heart.
    [*He bites out his tongue.*]

KING

O monstrous resolution of a wretch!
See, Viceroy, he hath bitten forth his tongue
Rather than to reveal what we required.

CASTILE

Yet can he write.   195

KING

And if in this he satisfy us not,
We will devise th'extremest kind of death,
That ever was invented for a wretch.
    Then he makes signs for a knife to mend his pen.

CASTILE

Oh, he would have a knife to mend his pen.

VICEROY

Here, and advise thee that thou write the troth.   200
    [HIERONIMO] *with a knife stabs the* DUKE *and himself.*

KING

Look to my brother! Save Hieronimo!
What age hath ever heard such monstrous deeds?
My brother and the whole succeeding hope
That Spain expected after my decease!
Go bear his body hence, that we may mourn   205

---

182. **thee:** see note to line 11, (see also lines 185, 187, and 189).
188. **thing . . . inviolate:** In light of the fact that the epilogue speech at the end of Hieronimo's play effectively revealed his sole "confederate," it is difficult to imagine what his
mysterious secret may be. Hieronimo's gesture of biting out his tongue probably derives
from accounts of the death of the Stoic philosopher Zeno, who bit out his tongue rather
than expose the details of a conspiracy, but here, in the context of the play's references
to the "confusion of tongues" at Babel, it is probably best read (like his use of the pen-
knife as an instrument of suicide rather than writing) as a repudiation of language—
traditionally the instrument of rationality and social order that set human beings apart
from animals—and so as a symbolic expression of the chaotic destructiveness of revenge.

The loss of our beloved brother's death,
That he may be entombed, whate'er befall:
I am the next, the nearest, last of all.

VICEROY

And thou, Don Pedro, do the like for us:
Take up our hapless son, untimely slain;   210
Set me with him, and he with woeful me,
Upon the mainmast of a ship unmanned,
And let the wind and tide haul me along
To Scylla's barking and untamèd gulf,
Or to the loathsome pool of Acheron,   215
To weep my want for my sweet Balthazar:
Spain hath no refuge for a Portingale.

The trumpets sound a dead march, the KING *of Spain*
mourning after his brother's body, and the VICEROY
of Portingale bearing the body of his son.

[4.5]

[*Chorus*]

ANDREA

Ay, now my hopes have end in their effects,
When blood and sorrow finish my desires:
Horatio murdered in his father's bower,
Vild Serberine by Pedringano slain,
False Pedringano hanged by quaint device,   5
Fair Isabella by herself misdone,
Prince Balthazar by Bel-Imperia stabbed,
The Duke of Castile and his wicked son,
Both done to death by old Hieronimo,
My Bel-Imperia fallen as Dido fell,   10
And good Hieronimo slain by himself:
Ay, these were spectacles to please my soul.
Now will I beg at lovely Proserpine
That by the virtue of her princely doom,

---

214. **Scylla's . . . gulf:** Scylla and Charybdis were two mythical sea monsters (in fact a rock and a whirlpool) that devoured unwary sailors off the coast of Sicily. Scylla was reputed to bark, or to be surrounded by barking dogs.
215. **Acheron:** see note to. 1.1.19.
216. **want for:** loss of.
217. SD. *dead march:* funeral march.
4. **Vild:** vile (a term conveying social disdain as well as moral indignation).
5. **quaint:** cunning.
6. **misdone:** killed.
10. **Dido:** the legendary queen of Carthage (celebrated in Book 4 of Virgil's *Aeneid*), who kills herself after her desertion by Aeneas and to avoid marriage to another prince.
14. **doom:** judgment.

I may consort my friends in pleasing sort,   15
And on my foes work just and sharp revenge.
I'll lead my friend Horatio through those fields
Where never-dying wars are still inured;
I'll lead fair Isabella to that train,
Where pity weeps but never feeleth pain;   20
I'll lead my Bel-Imperia to those joys
That vestal virgins and fair queens possess;
I'll lead Hieronimo where Orpheus plays,
Adding sweet pleasure to eternal days—
But say, Revenge (for thou must help, or none),   25
Against the rest how shall my hate be shown?

REVENGE
This hand shall hale them down to deepest hell,
Where none but furies, bugs, and tortures dwell.

ANDREA
Then, sweet Revenge, do this at my request:
Let me be judge and doom them to unrest;   30
Let loose poor Tityus from the vulture's gripe,
And let Don Cyprian supply his room;
Place Don Lorenzo on Ixion's wheel,
And let the lovers' endless pains surcease—
Juno forgets old wrath and grants him ease;   35
Hang Balthazar about Chimera's neck,
And let him there bewail his bloody love,
Repining at our joys that are above;
Let Serberine go roll the fatal stone,
And take from Sisyphus his endless moan;   40
False Pedringano, for his treachery,
Let him be dragged through boiling Acheron,

---

15. **consort:** accompany.
18. **inured:** practiced (*OED* v. 3).
19. **train:** body of persons, company (*OED* n. 11).
22. **vestal virgins:** in ancient Rome the priestesses of Vesta, who took unbreakable vows of chastity.
23. **Orpheus:** see note to 3.13.116. The magical power of Orpheus's music was frequently cited in the Renaissance as a trope for the ordering capacity of human art.
31. **Tityus:** son of Gaia, the earth goddess, this giant was condemned to have his liver eternally devoured by vultures as a punishment for his attempted rape of Leto.
32. **And . . . room:** It is not clear why Castile, whose only offence has been to frown on his daughter's love for Andrea, should be singled out for so terrible a punishment; perhaps it is intended to exemplify the arbitrary and indiscriminate character of revenge.
33. **Ixion:** king of the Lapiths, who, for his attempt to seduce Juno, was bound for all eternity to a fiery wheel.
34. **surcease:** cease.
36. **Chimera:** Fire-breathing female monster from classical mythology.
40. **Sisyphus:** mythical Greek king punished for his sins by having to roll an enormous boulder up hill for eternity—only to see it repeatedly roll back down.

And there live dying still in endless flames,
Blaspheming gods and all their holy names.
REVENGE
   Then haste we down to meet thy friends and foes,   45
   To place thy friends in ease, the rest in woes.
   For here, though death hath end their misery,
   I'll there begin their endless tragedy.   *Exeunt.*

FINIS.

Collation

1.1.2 wanton] wonted *1615*
82 horn] *Hawkins*; Hor *1592*; Horror *1599*

1.2.53 rain] *Collier*; ran *1592*
56 *Arma sonant armis*] *1633*; *Anni sonant annis 1592*
83 waning] *1603*; wauing *1592*
100 SD] *Dodsley*; *after 99 1592*
101 the trumpet] *1615*; this trumpet *1592*
130–131 Two . . . them] *Manly*; duckets / . . . know / Our *1592*

1.3.9 SD] *1623*; *after 11 1592*
29 is] *Dodsley*; *not in 1592*

1.4.35 wielding] *Schick*; welding *1592*; wilding *1602*

2.1.27 beauty's] *1615*; beauteous *1592*
41 *qui*] *Collier*; *que 1592*
48 banishment] *Dodsley*; punishment *1592*
67 SD] *1602*; *not in 1592*
77 SD] *1602*; *not in 1592*

2.2.6 SD *above*] *Edwards*; *Balthazar* aboue *after 17 1592*
33 war] *Dodsley*; warring *1592*

2.3 SD Nobles *and* Attendants] &c *1592*
49 thought] *1615*; thoughts *1592*

2.4.35 wars] *Dodsley*; warre *1592*

2.5 SD *carrying . . . torch*] &c. *1592*
[13] he] *Edwards*; me *1602*; me he *1603*
[20–4]] *as prose 1602*
[30–31]] *one line 1602*
[36] pure] *1615*; poore *1602*
[37] Dear Hieronimo] *begins line 38 in 1602*
[44] O God!] *begins line 45 in 1602*
48 stayed] *1603*; stainde *1592*

3.1.4 heat] hate *1599*
30 SD Halberdiers] Halberts *1592*
58–61 Stay . . . entrance] *Schick*; *1592 lines* Stay . . . Maiestie, / Lay . . .
    Viluppo. / Embassadour . . . entrance
69 SD VICEROY] King *1592*
91 Wherein] *Hazlitt*; Or wherein *1592*
96 shameless] *Cairncross*; shamelesly *1592*

3.2.13 wakes] *Dodsley*; wake *1592*
15 Solicits] *Dodsley*; Solicite *1592*
23 See . . . may] *Manly*; *1592 lines* See . . . man / Some mean
23 SD] *1592 prints* Red incke *after line 25*
26 For] *1602*; *Bel.* For *1592*
32 What] *1602*; *Hiero* What *1592*
65–66 O . . . lordship] *om. 1602*

[5] it is] *Schick*; tis *1602*
[5–7]] *Manly*; *as prose 1602*

83 Saint Luigi's] S. Liugis *1592*
94 Che . . . Jerome] *Che le Ieron 1592*
94–98 Che. . . . lord] *this ed.*; *1592 lines* Che . . . Ieron. / My Lord./ Goe . . .
  forthwith, / Meet . . . Parke, / Behind . . . boy. / I . . . Lord
95 go to] *this ed.*, to *1592*
98 LORENZO] *1602*; *not in 1592*
109–10] *Hawkins*; *as one line 1592*
116 'tis] *1599*; its *1592*

3.4.18 SD] *1615*; *not in 1592.*
50–51 What . . . distress] *Manly*; What . . . vs? / He . . . distres *1592*
70–71] *Hazlitt*; *as one line 1592*
76 fee] *conj. Edwards*; see *1592*
82–83 E quel . . . basterà] *Hawkins, Schick*; Et quel que voglio Ii nessun le sa, /
  Intendo io quel me bassara *1592*

3.5 SD Page] *this ed.*; Boy *1592*

3.6.16 SD Page] *this ed.*; Boy *1592*
40] *1615 inserts* Enter Hangman *after this line.*
40–42 And . . . gear] *this ed.*; *1592 lines* Come . . . ready? / To . . . knave? /
  To . . . geere
43–47 O . . . flat] *as prose Schick*; *1592 lines* O . . . habit. / So . . . rope. / But
110 heavens] *1592*; heaven *1603*

3.7.15 empyreal] *Schick*; imperiall *1592*

3.10.24–25 But . . . Thou] *Manly*; But . . . comes. / Now Sister. / Sister . . .
  enemy *1592*
98–99 Fear . . . those] *Manly*; *one line 1592*
102 Et] *Hawkins*; Est *1592*

3.11.[26–30] This . . . parents *Boas*; *1602 lines* This . . . truly. / O . . . these /
  Insatiate . . . parents
[37]] *after line 39 1602*
[39–40] *one line 1602*
[39] unto] *Manly*; vs to *1602*
[45–47] Ay . . . fire] *Schick*; *1602 lines* I . . . steales, and steales / Till . . .
  thunder / Wrapt]

8–9] *Hazlitt*; *one line 1592*
30–31] *one line 1602*

3.12.46 inexplicable] *1594*; inexecrable *1592*; inextricable *Hawkins*
74–75] *one line 1592*
79–80] *one line 1592*
101 not exempt] *Edwards*; exempt *1592*; hold exempt *Hazlitt*; execute *Collier conj.*

3.12a.[22] spirits, spirits] sprits, sprits *1592*
[33] Hecate] *1623* (*Heccat*); Hee-cat *1602*
[36] aglets] agglots *1610*; aggots *1602*
[40–41] The . . . what] *Boas*; *1602 lines* The heauens . . . sorow / Makes
[46–47] Where . . . book] *1602 lines* Where . . . Murdered? / She
[48–49] *1602 lines* Had . . . know / Way
[61] died] *1603*; hied *1602*
[69–70] *Boas*; *one line 1602*
[72] knocks] *1603*; knocke *1602*
[76–77] God's . . . naught] *Boas*; *1602 lines* Gods . . . tree / But
[86–87] *Edwards*; *one line 1602*
[89–90] *Edwards*; *one line 1602*
[115] me in my] *Lamb*; me my *1602*
[149] wave] *1603*; weave *1602*
[151] [paint]] *this ed.*; *not in 1602*; show *Dodsley*

3.13.44 SD] *after 45 1592*
70, 74, 80 BAZULTO] *Senex 1592*
80–81 Ay . . . Horatio] *Manly*; *1592 lines* . . . oh my sonne. / My sonne
103 o'erturneth] *Hawkins*; ore turnest *1592*; ore-turned *1618*
123 SD He . . . teeth] *this ed.*; *Teare the Papers 1592*
143 BAZULTO] *Senex 1592*
150 fate] *Dodsley*; Father *1592*
151, 158 BAZULTO] *Ba. 1592*
160 my] *1592*; thy *1623*

3.14.1–2] *1610*; *as prose 1592*
1 tis] *1610*; it is *1592*
46–47 She . . . day] *Edwards*; *1592 lines* . . . Who . . . Lord, / And
102 no brighter] *1594*; brighter *1592*
105–07 I . . . peace] *Manly, Schick*; *1592 lines* Father / Truce . . . him. / Welcome . . . Prince, / The
114–17 But . . . trow] *this ed.*; *1592 lines* him. / And . . . Duke? / Yonder. / Euen . . . tro
128 LORENZO] *1602*; *not in 1592*
130–131] *as one line 1592*
144 love] *1610*; loues *1592*
149–50] *as one line 1592*
163 thus] *Dodsley*; that *1592*
168 Chi] *Manly, Schick*; *Mi. Chi. 1592*
168 *fa più carreze*] *Hawkins*; *fa? Pui Corezza 1592*
168 *suole*] *Hawkins*; *sule 1592*
169 *mi ha*] *Hawkins*; *viha 1592*
169 *o tradir mi*] *Hawkins*; *otrade 1592*
169 *vuole*] *Hawkins*; *vule 1592*

3.15 SD Chorus] *this ed.*; Enter *Ghoast* and *Reuenge 1592*
3 Acheron] *Hawkins*; *Achinon 1592*
3 Erebus] *Hawkins*; *Ericus 1592*
4 in hell] *Schick*; *ends line 3 in 1592*
9 To sleep] *1594*; Thsleep *1592*

4.1.9 With what . . .] With what dishonour and the hate of men, *1592*
52–61 Here . . . ambassador] *Schick*; *1592 lines* are, / How . . . *Bel-imperia.* / I my . . . promise you / She . . . hers. / But . . . your helpe. / My helpe . . . me. / For you . . . haue you. / It pleasde . . . Embassadour.
125–26 O excellent . . . pasha] *Boas*; *1592 lines* O excellent. / But . . . him / That . . . Bashaw?

136 Erasto] *this ed.;* Erastus *1592*
182–83] *1602; lines transposed in 1592*
189 We must resolve] *ends* line 188 *in 1592*
191–92 Why . . . Babylon] *as one line 1592*

4.4.52 Ay me] *begins line 53 1592*
58 Persed his] *this ed.;*Persedaes *1592; Perseda his Schick; Perseda Manly*
156 SD] *1602; not in 1592*
161 Accursed wretch] *Begins line 162 in 1592*

[9] revenge] *Dodsley;* reueng'd *1602*
[19] O good words] *begins line 20 in 1602*
[31], [32], [41], [42] SD] *this ed., not in 1592*
[39] a youth] *begins line 40 in 1602*
168 O good words] *Begins line 169 in 1602*
185 Indeed] *Begins line 185 in 1592*
191 SD] *from Addition 5, 1602; not in 1592*
200 SD] *this ed.;after line 201 1592*
201 KING] *Boas; before line 202 1592*
213 haul] *Edwards;* hall *1592;* hale *1594*
214 gulf] *1623;* greefe *1592*
217 SD VICEROY] *this ed.;* KING *1592*

4.5 SD Chorus] *this ed.; Enter* Ghoast *and* Reuenge *1592*
1, 29 ANDREA] *Ghoast 1592*

CONTEXTS

Sources and Biography

VIRGIL

[Aeneas in the Underworld][†]

On they went, hidden in solitary night, through gloom,
through Dis's empty halls, and insubstantial kingdom,
like a path through a wood, in the faint light
under a wavering moon, when Jupiter has buried the sky
in shadow, and black night has stolen the colour from things.
Right before the entrance, in the very jaws of Orcus,
Grief and vengeful Care have made their beds,
and pallid Sickness lives there, and sad Old Age,
and Fear, and persuasive Hunger, and vile Need,
forms terrible to look on, and Death and Pain:
then Death's brother Sleep, and Evil Pleasure of the mind,
and, on the threshold opposite, death-dealing War,
and the steel chambers of the Furies, and mad Discord,
her snaky hair entwined with blood-wet ribbons.
In the centre a vast shadowy elm spreads its aged trunks
and branches: the seat, they say, that false Dreams hold,
thronging, clinging beneath every leaf.
And many other monstrous shapes of varied creatures,
are stabled by the doors, Centaurs and bi-formed Scylla,
and hundred-armed Briareus, and the Lernean Hydra,
hissing fiercely, and the Chimaera armed with flame,
Gorgons, and Harpies, and the triple bodied shade, Geryon.
At this, trembling suddenly with terror, Aeneas grasped
his sword, and set the naked blade against their approach:
and, if his knowing companion had not warned him
that these were tenuous bodiless lives flitting about
with a hollow semblance of form, he would have rushed at them,

† From Virgil, *Aeneid* VI, lines 268–901, trans. A. S. Kline. © 2002. All rights reserved. Reprinted by permission of the translator. Andrea's account of his underworld journey is modeled on this famous Virgilian passage.

and hacked at the shadows uselessly with his sword.
From here there is a road that leads to the waters
of Tartarean Acheron. Here thick with mud a whirlpool seethes
in the vast depths, and spews all its sands into Cocytus.
A grim ferryman watches over the rivers and streams,
Charon, dreadful in his squalor, with a mass of unkempt
white hair straggling from his chin: flames glow in his eyes,
a dirty garment hangs, knotted from his shoulders.
He poles the boat and trims the sails himself,
and ferries the dead in his dark skiff,
old now, but a god's old age is fresh and green.
Here all the crowd streams, hurrying to the shores,
women and men, the lifeless bodies of noble heroes,
boys and unmarried girls, sons laid on the pyre
in front of their father's eyes: as many as the leaves that fall
in the woods at the first frost of autumn, as many as the birds
that flock to land from ocean deeps, when the cold of the year
drives them abroad and despatches them to sunnier countries.
They stood there, pleading to be first to make the crossing,
stretching out their hands in longing for the far shore.
But the dismal boatman accepts now these, now those,
but driving others away, keeps them far from the sand.
Then Aeneas, stirred and astonished at the tumult, said:
'O virgin, tell me, what does this crowding to the river mean?
What do the souls want? And by what criterion do these leave
the bank, and those sweep off with the oars on the leaden stream?
The ancient priestess spoke briefly to him, so:
'Son of Anchises, true child of the gods, you see
the deep pools of Cocytus, and the Marsh of Styx,
by whose name the gods fear to swear falsely.
All this crowd, you see, were destitute and unburied:
that ferryman is Charon: those the waves carry were buried:
he may not carry them from the fearful shore on the harsh waters
before their bones are at rest in the earth. They roam
for a hundred years and flit around these shores: only then
are they admitted, and revisit the pools they long for.'
The son of Anchises halted, and checked his footsteps,
thinking deeply, and pitying their sad fate in his heart. . . .
So they pursued their former journey, and drew near the river.
　　　　　　　　 * * * [Charon] turned the stern
of the dark skiff towards them and neared the bank.
Then he turned off the other souls who sat on the long benches,
cleared the gangways: and received mighty Aeneas
on board. The seamed skiff groaned with the weight
and let in quantities of marsh-water through the chinks.

At last, the river crossed, he landed the prophetess and the hero
safe, on the unstable mud, among the blue-grey sedge.
Huge Cerberus sets these regions echoing with his triple-throated
howling, crouching monstrously in a cave opposite.
Seeing the snakes rearing round his neck, the prophetess
threw him a pellet, a soporific of honey and drugged wheat.
Opening his three throats, in rabid hunger, he seized
what she threw and, flexing his massive spine, sank to earth
spreading his giant bulk over the whole cave-floor.
With the guard unconscious Aeneas won to the entrance,
and quickly escaped the bank of the river of no return.
Immediately a loud crying of voices was heard, the spirits
of weeping infants, whom a dark day stole at the first
threshold of this sweet life, those chosen to be torn
from the breast, and drowned in bitter death.
Nearby are those condemned to die on false charges.
Yet their place is not ordained without the allotted jury:
Minos, the judge, shakes the urn: he convenes the voiceless court,
and hears their lives and sins. Then the next place
is held by those gloomy spirits who, innocent of crime,
died by their own hand, and, hating the light, threw away
their lives. How willingly now they'd endure
poverty and harsh suffering, in the air above!
Divine Law prevents it, and the sad marsh and its hateful
waters binds them, and nine-fold Styx confines them.

* * *

the Sibyl,
his companion, warned him briefly saying:
'Night approaches, Aeneas: we waste the hours with weeping.
This is the place where the path splits itself in two:
there on the right is our road to Elysium, that runs beneath
the walls of mighty Dis: but the left works punishment
on the wicked, and sends them on to godless Tartarus.'
Deiophobus replied: 'Do not be angry, great priestess:
I will leave: I will make up the numbers, and return to the darkness.
Go now glory of our race: enjoy a better fate.'
So he spoke, and in speaking turned away.
Aeneas suddenly looked back, and, below the left hand cliff,
he saw wide battlements, surrounded by a triple wall,
and encircled by a swift river of red-hot flames,
the Tartarean Phlegethon, churning with echoing rocks.
A gate fronts it, vast, with pillars of solid steel,
that no human force, not the heavenly gods themselves,
can overturn by war: an iron tower rises into the air,
and seated before it, Tisiphone, clothed in a blood-wet dress,

keeps guard of the doorway, sleeplessly, night and day.
Groans came from there, and the cruel sound of the lash,
then the clank of iron, and dragging chains.
Aeneas halted, and stood rooted, terrified by the noise.
'What evil is practised here? O Virgin, tell me: by what torments
are they oppressed? Why are there such sounds in the air?'
Then the prophetess began to speak as follows: 'Famous leader
of the Trojans, it is forbidden for the pure to cross the evil threshold:
but when Hecate appointed me to the wood of Avernus,
she taught me the divine torments, and guided me through them all.
Cretan Rhadamanthus rules this harshest of kingdoms,
and hears their guilt, extracts confessions, and punishes
whoever has deferred atonement for their sins too long
till death, delighting in useless concealment, in the world above.
Tisiphone the avenger, armed with her whip, leaps on the guilty
       immediately,
lashes them, and threatening them with the fierce
snakes in her left hand, calls to her savage troop of sisters.
Then at last the accursed doors open, screeching on jarring hinges.
You comprehend what guardian sits at the door, what shape watches
the threshold? Well still fiercer is the monstrous Hydra inside,
with her fifty black gaping jaws. There Tartarus itself
falls sheer, and stretches down into the darkness:
twice as far as we gaze upwards to heavenly Olympus.
Here the Titanic race, the ancient sons of Earth,
hurled down by the lightning-bolt, writhe in the depths.
And here I saw the two sons of Aloeus, giant forms,
who tried to tear down the heavens with their hands,
and topple Jupiter from his high kingdom.
And I saw Salmoneus paying a savage penalty
for imitating Jove's lightning, and the Olympian thunder.
Brandishing a torch, and drawn by four horses
he rode in triumph among the Greeks, through Elis's city,
claiming the gods' honours as his own, a fool,
who mimicked the storm-clouds and the inimitable thunderbolt
with bronze cymbals and the sound of horses' hoof-beats.
But the all-powerful father hurled his lighting from dense cloud,
not for him fiery torches, or pine-branches' smoky light
and drove him headlong with the mighty whirlwind.
And Tityus was to be seen as well, the foster-child
of Earth, our universal mother, whose body stretches
over nine acres, and a great vulture with hooked beak
feeds on his indestructible liver, and his entrails ripe
for punishment, lodged deep inside the chest, groping
for his feast, no respite given to the ever-renewing tissue.

Shall I speak of the Lapiths, Ixion, Pirithous,
over whom hangs a dark crag that seems to slip and fall?
High couches for their feast gleam with golden frames,
and a banquet of royal luxury is spread before their eyes:
nearby the eldest Fury, crouching, prevents their fingers touching
the table: rising up, and brandishing her torch, with a voice of
    thunder.
Here are those who hated their brothers, in life,
or struck a parent, or contrived to defraud a client,
or who crouched alone over the riches they'd made,
without setting any aside for their kin (their crowd is largest),
those who were killed for adultery, or pursued civil war,
not fearing to break their pledges to their masters:
shut in they see their punishment. Don't ask to know
that punishment, or what kind of suffering drowns them.
Some roll huge stones, or hang spread-eagled
on wheel-spokes: wretched Theseus sits still, and will sit
for eternity: Phlegyas, the most unfortunate, warns them all
and bears witness in a loud voice among the shades:
"Learn justice: be warned, and don't despise the gods."
Here's one who sold his country for gold, and set up
a despotic lord: this one made law and remade it for a price:
he entered his daughter's bed and a forbidden marriage:
all of them dared monstrous sin, and did what they dared.
Not if I had a hundred tongues, a hundred mouths,
a voice of iron, could I tell all the forms of wickedness
or spell out the names of every torment.'
When she had spoken of this, the aged priestess of Apollo said:
'But come now, travel the road, and complete the task set for you:
let us hurry, I see the battlements that were forged
in the Cyclopean fires, and the gates in the arch opposite us
where we are told to set down the gifts as ordered.'
She spoke and keeping step they hastened along the dark path
crossing the space between and arriving near the doors.
Aeneas gained the entrance, sprinkled fresh water
over his body, and set up the branch on the threshold before him.
Having at last achieved this, the goddess's task fulfilled,
they came to the pleasant places, the delightful grassy turf
of the Fortunate Groves, and the homes of the blessed.
Here freer air and radiant light clothe the plain,
and these have their own sun, and their own stars.
Some exercise their bodies in a grassy gymnasium,
compete in sports and wrestle on the yellow sand:
others tread out the steps of a dance, and sing songs.
There Orpheus too, the long-robed priest of Thrace,

accompanies their voices with the seven-note scale,
playing now with fingers, now with the ivory quill.
Here are Teucer's ancient people, loveliest of children,
great-hearted heroes, born in happier years,
Ilus, Assaracus, and Dardanus founder of Troy.
Aeneas marvels from a distance at their idle chariots
and their weapons: their spears fixed in the ground,
and their horses scattered freely browsing over the plain:
the pleasure they took in chariots and armour while alive,
the care in tending shining horses, follows them below the earth.
Look, he sees others on the grass to right and left, feasting,
and singing a joyful paean in chorus, among the fragrant
groves of laurel, out of which the Eridanus's broad river
flows through the woodlands to the world above.
Here is the company of those who suffered wounds fighting
for their country: and those who were pure priests, while they
       lived,
and those who were faithful poets, singers worthy of Apollo,
and those who improved life, with discoveries in Art or Science,
and those who by merit caused others to remember them:
the brows of all these were bound with white headbands.
As they crowded round, the Sibyl addressed them,
Musaeus above all: since he holds the centre of the vast crowd,
all looking up to him, his tall shoulders towering above:
'Blessed spirits, and you, greatest of Poets,
say what region or place contains Anchises. We have
come here, crossing the great rivers of Erebus, for him.'
And the hero replied to her briefly in these words:
'None of us have a fixed abode: we live in the shadowy woods,
and make couches of river-banks, and inhabit fresh-water meadows.
But climb this ridge, if your hearts-wish so inclines,
and I will soon set you on an easy path.'
He spoke and went on before them, and showed them
the bright plains below: then they left the mountain heights. * * *
So they wander here and there through the whole region,
over the wide airy plain, and gaze at everything.
And when Anchises has led his son through each place,
and inflamed his spirit with love of the glory that is to come,
he tells him then of the wars he must soon fight,
and teaches him about the Laurentine peoples,
and the city of Latinus, and how to avoid or face each trial.
There are two gates of Sleep: one of which is said to be of horn,
through which an easy passage is given to true shades, the other
gleams with the whiteness of polished ivory, but through it
the Gods of the Dead send false dreams to the world above.

After his words, Anchises accompanies his son there, and,
frees him, together with the Sibyl, through the ivory gate.
Aeneas makes his way to the ships and rejoins his friends:
then coasts straight to Caieta's harbour along the shore.
The anchors are thrown from the prows: on the shore the sterns rest.

JACQUES YVER

[Soliman and Perseda]†

This damsel of whom my discourse shall determine was born in the
Isle of Rhodes, descended of the most honorable family in the
whole country, educated in all good nouriture,[1] as bountifully as
might possibly be desired; who, as soon as she grew to the knowledge of good and evil, fell in liking of the behaviour and courtesy of
a young stripling, born likewise in the same city, so accomplished
in all perfections of nature as, by due desert, he was fancied of this
beautiful minion,[2] and battered the first breath in her tender heart,
who with the only glances of her alluring eye, was able to mollify
the most savage and indurate fantasies bearing life. The damsel
* * * was named Perseda, and her young friend Erastus, unto whom
his father and mother newly deceased had left abundance of wealth,
and, by their last testament, bequeathed the governance and education of this orphan unto his uncle, who, by good adventure, was
neighbour unto the fair Perseda, whereby these younglings ordinary frequented company. * * * This couple, as they grew in age, so
increased their beauty and comeliness, like the rosebuds, which in
the heart of the spring sprout and spread abroad their beautiful
blossoms. And with their bodies likewise increased and augmented
their new conceived love. * * * Thus in their tender years the parents and friends on both parties conceived a secret hope, that destiny would confirm a match betwixt this likely couple. * * * And I
suppose if each man's opinion might have take[n] place, these two
creatures had been accounted the offspring of angels: but the heavens would not permit a paradise on earth.

* * *

[Before the lovers can be married, Erastus unluckily becomes involved
in a quarrel with a jealous rival, whom he kills in the ensuing duel.]

---

† From Jacques Yver, *A Courtly Controversy of Cupid's Cautels*, trans. Sir Henry Wotton,
  1578. Cautels: deceits, sleights, stratagems.
1. Upbringing.
2. Mistress.

This slain gentleman being of noble parentage, and greatly friended by reason of his good qualities, which entertained and acquainted him among the best, was much bewailed of many, and revenge of his death so earnestly pursued, as if Erastus (notwithstanding his favour and credit in Rhodes) had not by speedy escape saved himself, he had dangerously avoided the marks of too late repentance. Alas, behold the man in flight to shun the summons of death, banished his country and friends, deprived of all worldly pleasure and commodities, who even now possessed all joy, honor, and earthly felicity: Fortune hath full well sufficient occasion to content her unconstancy, having for her pleasure reduced this poor lover from the mount of mirth to the vale of misery. But this grievous disaster was nothing noisome to his stomach, in comparison of the absence of Perseda, whose remembrance and displeasure more pinched his heart, than the torments of a thousand deadly pangs. * * * In the meantime, only accompanied with his trusty servant Pistan, he journeyed towards Constantinople, where he was not so soon arrived as known of divers lords and knights, who being witness of his virtue and valor that day the jousts and tourneys were solemnized at Rhodes, entertained him according to his merits, making so great estimation of his prowess, as the published fame thereof sounded in the ears of Soliman, emperor of Turkey, unto whose magnificence Erastus was presented by the Coronel of his armies, with commendation to be the most valiant, hardy, and expert knight-at-arms living. Soliman entertained him, and employed his new soldier in petty exploits, which he executed with such effect as he gained greater estimation with the emperor by his acts, than reports ministered cause of liking. So that, as well for the assurance of his fidelity as for his sovereign valiantness already experimented, he constituted him Colonel of his Janissaries (which we call Captain of the Guard). * * *

[A]mong other secret affairs belonging to the commonwealth of the Empire, it was * * * determined * * * to invade and conquer the noble and puissant Isle of Rhodes, which was supposed to be the invincible key of Christendom. Hereupon the whole council resolved and concluded Erastus was supposed the meetest man among them to undertake the enterprise.; who, after due reverence unto the Emperor Soliman, humbly besought his highness that, although just occasion urged him to seek revenge against his ungrateful country, whereunto he lived in exile, nevertheless that it would please his majesty to pardon him, that he might not be assistant in any expedition so unlawful, not for any disobedience that remained in him—for he sought but occasion to testify and make apparent his faithful service—but because his duty rather consented to receive cruel death. Soliman advisedly considering his request, wonderfully commended his good nature. * * * Wherefore Soliman in person took his voyage with an huge army, conducting all his galleys, galliots and galliasses,[3] which were infinite, before Rhodes, where his presence took such effect as, executing divers secret practices, the island was rendered under his obeisance in the month of June, and in the year of our salvation, a thousand, five hundred, twenty and two, as far as I remember. And, although the inhabitants showed themselves very wilful, the victorious emperor notwithstanding—in favour of his gentle knight, of whom he was always mindful—used more benignity towards them, than the rigor of wars doth usually permit.

* * *

It was a custom among the Turks, at the taking of any town upon the enemy, to make choice of the most accomplished damsel in beauty and personage among all the captive virgins to present unto the principal captain, supposing they could not offer him a more honorable portion of the booty and pillage. This moved them to choose Perseda, whom they found in a religious monastery of close nuns, whether she was retired to demean[4] a solitary life, her delights being clearly abandoned through the disaster and exile of Erastus her dear friend. This nymph the Turkish troupe presented before the emperor Soliman, who presently frying in the flame of this celestial lamp, viewing the desolate damsel lapped[5] in lamentations, and almost drowned in the streams of despair, which distilled abundantly from her crystal eyes, immediately commanded she should be conveyed with great pomp toward Constantinople, showing in her presence, his gracious countenance and bountiful liberality unto all her kindred, how far off or near soever they were allied unto her, to the end he might thereby win her favor, and pacify her sorrows. Our captive departed from Rhodes and arrived at Constantinople, was lodged among young damsels, nourished, maintained, and taught by old cunning eunuchs to sing, dance, play on instruments, and to speak the Arabian tongue, committed to their charge, as a principal trreasure to delight the emperor. In this cage Soliman supposed his mournful turtle might prune at pleasure her feltered[6] plumage. At his return he went to visit his prisoner, beholding with great admiration the gifts wherewith Nature had rendered her view wonderful. And, although pensiveness had exceedingly blemished her beauty, decaying it as a sharp shower fadeth the garden flowers, yet felt he his fantasy inflamed with * * * love. * * * This amorous emperor, after many loving embracings and gorgeous gifts proffered unto our desolate Perseda * * * the damsel,

3. Small and large galleys.
4. Lead.
5. Wrapped.
6. Matted, tangled.

resolved rather to die chaste than live dishonoured, for answer of his demand, disbursed abundance of tears and sighs * * * which caused Soliman somewhat to temper his affections; who, leaving her in this ecstasy, departed her chamber, staying without the door, which was no sooner shut, but she opened her mouth, complete with sorrowful lamentations, and disgorging soaking sighs * * * sometime she bewailed her parents, then her country, now her friends and beloved companions—but all so pitifully as the emperor, who harkened attentively her whole discourse, in despite of nature was urged to compassion, which until then never harbored in his flinty Turkish breast, and constrained him to be partaker of her dolor. But above the rest, his heart was drowned in pity, whenas unfortunate Perseda, folding her languishing arms about the neck of her maid, Agatha, after the end of her former complaint, began thus to exclaim: 'Ah, my trusty friend, have I not in one moment exchanged all my delights forever, to lead a life overwhelmed with miseries? Yea, such a life as my envious fortune hath reserved for my last reward. But. alas, among so many evil haps as oppress me, there is not one to finish my irksome loathed life! Oh, how comfortable were the pinching pangs of death to my soul! Yea, how easily should my bones be lodged in my grave, if, before I resign my languishing ghost, my dimmed eyes might view mine Erastus, or my dulled senses once understand any inkling where or how he is bestowed. Ah, Erastus, Erastus, my dear friend Erastus, what mishap doth hinder us to live happily together amid our miseries! * * * The which I will testify with the price of my blood, the only worthy witness to ratify my constant amity to the end this voluntary sacrifice of my body may appease the malice of fortune, the sovereign goddess of worldlings, and exempt my virginity from the puissance of an emperor. * * *' Wherewithal a flood of tears troubled with a storm of sobbing sighs interrupted her speech, and with a mortal fury she drew a knife from under her gown, which she had provided for the purpose, fearing to be prevented, by the force whereof (like unto Lucretia) she resolved to finish her woeful life; and all dismayed, with a trembling hand, she set the point thereof upon her lily breast, a perfect fortress of chastity. When the King, marvellously amazed to view her furious enterprise, rushed open the door, and at one leap saved his cruel friend, crying: 'Ah, dear darling, wherefore wilt thou so unkindly harm the thing which deserveth so carefully to be preserved? * * *' The poor damsel like a thief taken with the fact, astonished, and much grieved to be found in this estate, but more discontented, having failed the execution of her attempt, letting the knife fall from her quivering fingers, fixed her eyes upon the earth, without the utterance of any speech. Then the King remembering how affectuously he heard her record the name of Erastus oftentimes in her lamentation, speedily dispatched a post with commandment from his majesty to repair to the court with all expedition. * * * Being arrived, he presently pressed to the emperor's presence, who, willing him to arise from the earth, led him to view the desolate beauty, from whom he had taken the knife, and committed under sure guard, because he perceived her ears stopped, and heart hardened against all persuasions of consolation. The emperor demanding if he knew the damsel, Erastus, astonished as one newly risen from sleep, knew not whether he waked or dreamed; nevertheless, to play true or false, running towards his recovered Perseda, [he] cast his displayed arms about her neck, locking mouth to mouth so close with the pleasant key of extreme joy, as thereby the souls of these two lovers were near unloosed from their bodies. * * *

Then Erastus, embracing the knees of the emperor Sultan, said: 'Sir, I most humbly beseech you, pardon your servant if, vanquished by too excessive love, he hath had no power to prefer the observation of his lord's commandment, before his impatient desires; for I confess, gracious prince, my duty deserved greater diligence in answering your demand. But I felt my fancies so enforced by the renewing of an ancient fire, kindled in me from my youth through the perfections of this damsel as, thereby forgetting myself, it is not strange if I have also forgotten my duty. Notwithstanding, sir, I suppose if your noble heart hath ever tasted, and experimented true love, mine offence shall find excuse before your majesty. The damsel, on the other side, having changed her face of funerals into a nuptial countenance, beholding the emperor with an eye wherein love, perfection, and reverence bathed their limbs, by little and little unbridling her tongue, briefly discovered unto him the whole estate of the love betwixt her and Erastus, the which they had never changed for all the divers injuries of envious fortune, but had reserved always entire and undefiled in the secret of their hearts, as the corn preserved in the earth from the cold of nipping frosts. Affirming, in fine, that she esteemed her disaster fortunate that, with the presence of her desired Erastus, have so well paid and rewarded her painful travails, as she should ever acknowledge herself very well contented and satisfied, and that his sight should serve instead of a favorable bark to harbor her in the last port of her miseries, rendering thanks unto the emperor for the benefit she then received of him, which was partly a recompense for the destruction of her country. Soliman, beholding the effect of this unseparable love, embraced the two lovers, marvellously astonished to understand so strange adventures. * * * Then, turning towards the princes which accompanied him, he said: 'By Mahound,[7] my lords, I have long mused by what means I might sufficiently recompense

7. Medieval term for Muhammad (imagined as an idol).

the services done to me, by this poor gentleman, considering the perilous travails he hath endured in mine affairs, never sparing to adventure his life in most manifest dangers. Wherein my mind is at this present much satisfied, sith[8] occasion is offered so aptly to acknowledge and reward the same, in making him possessor of my Christian prisoner.' Then, beholding Erastus, he said: 'Sir knight, sith your love is so sincere towards this damsel, as is apparent, I give her unto you as lover and lawful espouse; although I am enforced to confess that her beauty, wherein she surpasseth the most excellent of Asia, hath until this present had authority to command me. But in this behalf I will vanquish my proper affections to give you triumph over my victory: assuring you, that your advantage and commodity, hath more puissance[9] in me, than mine own.' Whereunto Erastus answered: 'My lord, I humbly thank the heavens, which have planted a heart so noble and virtuous in the breast of my sovereign King to have power to bridle his will, the which is unto you a trophy more glorious than if you had conquered the occident empire. * * *' Immediately the marriage was celebrated with great solemnity and magnificence, which the emperor honoured in person, with his whole court. But cursed be that honour whereby great dishonor ensueth, and horrible mischief is committed! Soliman gave great and rich gifts, and constituted our bridegroom lieutenant and governor of the isle of Rhodes, whither our fortunate lovers, within few days after the wedding was ended, parted with consent of the whole signory.[1] O what tongue can utter the joyful delights this couple received, enjoying at will that which they had so long desired. * * * [But] they alas lived not long in this amorous delight, so unconstant are the fruits of this world, wherein we search surety and stability; yet that which ought to be found strangest is, that the marriage day which seemed most fortunate was most unhappy, cloaking under a coloured sweetness the bitter poison which procured the piteous death of them both. * * * [T]he emperor Soliman, touched to the quick with the darts of her eyes (the languishing heads whereof were bathed in the sugared venom of her delicate devices) yielded his vanquished liberty to the mercy of this divine beauty; and love, whom he pretended to resist, planted his proud foot upon the prince's head so as—whether by the supposed favor he received at her hand, who sought that day to honor him with all her endeavour, which he construed to proceed of love (as lovers take everything for their advantage), or for that he stood too near this pleasant fire, he felt his heart so warmed, and his former intent so altered, as all his determination was wholly to please his pardoned captive, who, by a cruel revenge, now

8. Since.
9. Power.
1. Governing council.

imprisoned him so straightly as—although (reviving his ancient virtue) he was resolved to deliver her—yet with joined hands he was enforced to require grace. So as this grief by little and little grew so great, having taken root by his consent, as in a while neither continuance of time (which breedeth oblivion) nor the distance of his lover's abode, nor yet the remembrance of the services received of Erastus * * * could not dissuade him from bitter repentance of his too frank offer and unadvised liberality, by the which he departed from a jewel more precious and worthy of estimation unto him than the half of his empire. Thus finding no remedy in his natural constancy, lastly concluded to give the bridle unto his rebellious and untamed affections, esteeming nothing impossible for him to compass, hoping that Perseda, vanquished by his benefits, would render him in the end a gracious recompense. * * *

[I]gnorant whereupon to resolve, he purposed for his comfort to impart his grief unto his cousin Brusor, Beglerbeg of Serbia, who like the other Princes * * * envied Erastus extremely, because he had been more advanced by the emperor than their ambition could tolerate. Now after long deliberation and counsel in the matter, it was supposed between them a thing unpossible to allure the rebellious and obstinate Perseda, unless she were first deprived of Erastus, 'which,' quoth he, 'will be easily compassed, notwithstanding the love and favor he hath obtained among the garrisons * * * so that your majesty will send for him by your straight commandment, the which I am certain he will not disobey, but make his speedy repair with his whole family; and, being present, I will find occasion he shall be accused of revolt and rebellion; whereupon being committed to prison for the offence, judgement and execution of death may ensue.' The emperor, joyfully embracing this wicked councillor, commended exceedingly his invention, and dispatched him presently to practise the execution of his devilish device. * * * Brusor, under colour of secret and weighty affairs allured and led poor Erastus to Constantinople, where he was no sooner alighted from his horse but the marshal of the emperor's household attached and committed him close prisoner under sure guard. The king * * * resolved to strike while the iron was hot, with speed prosecuted the process against the poor gentleman; and, by false witnesses of purpose provided, Erastus was accused and convicted of treason and rebellion, for that he had consented (said they) to deliver the isle of Rhodes into the possession of the Christians; for which offence, judgement passed upon him, and by the emperor's commandment he was beheaded. Wherewith those whose minds had virtue in recommendation were so miscontented as they could not refrain to murmur and raise sedition. But Perseda, who could not long forbear the company of her young husband, shook off her sickness, purposing to meet him homeward. But, alas, her journey was soon stayed by a sudden report of the treason so lewdly conspired, and the lamentable death which ensued. * * * [B]ruising her white breast and tearing her yellow hair, she imagined what sudden death might dispatch her with least pain (sith in this life there was no hope of grace to be expected for her relief). When poor Pistan—her trusty servant, newly returned after the death of his good master—seeing he could neither comfort nor dissuade her from her pretended mischief, spake thus: 'Madam, sith you will persevere in rigour against your person, at least, I beseech you, defer the execution thereof until you have revenged the death of the best knight that ever bare lance, and testified what power his innocency hath possessed in you even after his death. Then will we depart and carry joyful tidings unto the paradise of blessed souls where my master attendeth our coming.' These words somewhat appeased her fury, whereby, taking a manly courage, she assembled succors, mustered soldiers, and made provision of necessary furniture to resist the power of barbarous Soliman, who made no long abode with great ordinance to approach and invade this invincible chastity, like as the roaring lion devoureth the fearful hind. But, contrary to his expectation, the castle was so well defended as he knew neither where he was nor what to do, now cursing his tyranny, then his licentious desires, the only occasion of so great mischiefs. Nevertheless, he determined to go through what so befell thereof, and to see the end whatsoever it cost him. Wherein he had been deceived if the woeful Perseda, consenting to live so long after the loss of her dear friend * * * had not aided him, lingering happily to testify unto the ashes of Erastus * * * how his death extinguished not their eternal love: whereby * * * after many lamentations, of force to move the dumb towers of the fortress to pity her distress, she mounted to the top of a vault, where, bending her watered eyes and woeful hart with joined hands unto the heavens, she prayed her Creator to receive her pure and clean soul betwixt his arms into the company of his soul. * * * Then casting her bedewed eyes towards the sea side, she perceived the Turks preparing their power to assault and enter the castle. Among whom espying and knowing Soliman, with a stern voice she exclaimed: 'Ah, mischievous barbarian, thou cruel and ungrateful wretch of mine Erastus' benefits, whose services thou hast so tyrannously recompensed, imbrue[2] thy bloody paws and glut thy greedy paunch with the blood of thy faithful servant, whom thou hast not wholly murdered: behold here his one half yet living. Finish, therefore, thy wicked brutish tyranny—at least if it have an end.' This said, she advanced her head and breast above the battlements of the wall, making semblance to discharge this canon shot against the Turks, who, taking her for some soldier, loosed a volley of shot, among the

2. Stain, defile.

which two bullets sent from a musket struck her through the stomach, wherewith the virtuous dame, feeling the approach of her death, sat down, crossing her arms and staying her head against a stone. * * *
The news of the lady's marvellous accident was not long concealed from them of the castle, who, astonished of so great constancy, mused not to complain such a loss; but, in playing double or quit, determined to imitate this notable virtue, lest they should seem in any respect inferior to women. Wherefore as well men as women armed them as joyfully as a bride putteth on her wedding apparel; and, orderly marching in fair ordinance under the conduct of good Pistan, issued out furiously, where, being weary of the great slaughter of their enemies, they skirmished so desperately as they yielded but only to death. * * * Thus the cruel tyrant took possession of the castle, whereinto entering fearfully, he found no creature but the pale body of courageous Perseda, resembling a rose which by age hath lost the red lively hue, looking so sweetly as a man would have said she slept, if her set eyes and loss of blood, streaming from her wounds, had not ministered manifest advertisement of certain death. Oh, who could express the sorrow of Soliman, seeing after so many travails, the beauty mortified for the which he lived? Alas, after he had a thousand times kissed her cold mouth, he drew his falchion, and, brandishing his * * * brand about him, he hurt and slew as many of his people as would abide, but speedily they fled his presence, and left him alone. At length, gathering his wits unto him, he devised by what means he might amend his fault, and accomplish some notable reparation unto the diseased souls of the two lovers, so cruelly offended. * * *
[The] monument is yet to be seen in Rhodes, within a chapel of black marble, in the top whereof the sorrowful Soliman (who, every day visiting his workmen, bathed the work with warm tears) commanded a pyramid of brass to be erected, in the height whereof he caused the traitor Brusor to be hanged, in guerdon of his wicked counsel. * * * When all things were accomplished to the emperor's contentation,[3] accompanied with all the princes, lords, and ladies of his court in mourning attire, he celebrated the obsequies and funeral pomps, casting flowers and perfumes, with so great lamentations as they seemed rather people judged to die and going to their graves than mourners lamenting the funerals of others. Behold how this poor barbarian, with a Persian sumptuousness and memorable honor of eternal fame, sought to repair his tyrannical cruelty committed, protesting to consume the remainder of his solitary life in sorrowful repentance, constituted from the funeral day for ever, a solemn feast to be solemnized, which to this day is nominated the

3. Satisfaction.

Feast of Lamentable Loves, and is yearly renewed in the pitiful
remembrance of the dead. In whose favor the emperor granted great
liberties, and gave general pardon unto the whole isle. But, in taking
breath, I had almost forgot how in this temple there was a broad
plate of fine gold of Ophir, wherein was written in azured letters the
whole history, with this Epitaph ensuing.

1

In passing by this place, my friend,
Disburse thy brinish tears,
Behold this peerless princely pile,
The which true record bears
How Soliman to work his will
Hath cut the fatal thread,
And made a woeful sacrifice
Of two that here lie dead.

2

Within this gorgeous stately tomb,
These creatures are enclosed,
On whom dame Nature in their life
Her golden gifts disposed:
In beauty, wit, and comely grace,
None living might compare
With these, whose love was linked in one,
Their virtues were so rare,

3

That heaven, with all the heavenly powers,
Grew jealous of these wights,[4]
And did suppose the earth too base
To yield them due delights:
They gave the world authority
These lovers to disdain,
That they amid their flowering youth
Might with the gods remain.

4

By Fortune, Envy, and by Death,
This couple caught their bane:
When hard mishap by princely power

---

4. Creatures.

Enforced a virgin's shame,
He, in redress of infamy,
This trophy did devise,
A memory perpetual
Where these two lovers lies.

5

O Soliman, thou Turkish prince,
Thy tyranny deplore:
Erastus with his Perseda
Doth joy for evermore,
Whose perfect love and amity,
True witness of thy blame,
Shall blazèd live eternally,
Triumphantly by fame.

By this piteous tragical history you may conjecture (gracious company) my saying to be true, that all lamentations, miscontentments, and misfortunes chancing in love proceed on the behalf of women, who harbor this mishap in them (yea, even the most perfect) of force to be always the original of some misfortune, although it be in their despite—as the example of our Perseda may verify, in whom it seemeth by the error of nature, a manly heart was lodged; for may any man find or desire a more firm and constant love than hers, which steadfastly endured until after death? And yet was her disaster so great, as twice she procured the ruin of her friend and herself.

ANONYMOUS

[The Earl of Leicester Betrays His Own Servant]†

* * * There was also, this last summer past, one Gates hanged at Tyburn,[1] among others, for robbing of carriers; which Gates had been lately clerk of my lord [Leicester]'s kitchen, and had laid out

---

† From Anonymous (perhaps Thomas Morgan and Robert Parsons), *The copie of a leter, vvryten by a Master of Arte of Cambrige, to his friend in London; concerning . . . some proceedings of the Erle of Leycester and his friendes in England* (1584). Published in the same year as Robert Parsons's savage *Leicester's Common-wealth*, this "letter" is one of a number of contemporary texts attacking the corrupt practices of Elizabeth's unpopular favorite, Robert Dudley, Earl of Leicester. The close parallel between Leicester's murderous deception of Gates and Lorenzo's tricking of Pedringano may mean that Kyd's audience was intended to recognize an echo of this contemporary scandal.
1. Gates's story is retold in a set of verses titled "Leicester's Ghost," attached to a later edition Robert Parsons's *Leicester's Common-wealth* (1641), which appears to make the connection between Leicester and Lorenzo explicit, when the earl is made to declare: "For his reprieval (like a crafty fox) / I sent no pardon, but an empty box" (B4v).

much money of his own (as he said) for my l[ord's] provision, being also otherwise in so great favor and grace with his l[ordship] as no man living was thought to be more privy of his secrets than this man, whereupon also it is thought that he presumed the rather to commit this robbery (for to such things doth my lord's good favor most extend); and, being apprehended and in danger for the same, he made his recourse to his honor for protection (as the fashion is) and that he might be borne out, as divers[2] of less merit had been by his lordship in more heinous causes before him.

The good earl answered his servant and dear privado[3] courteously, and assured him for his life, howsoever for outer show or compliment the form of law might pass against him. But Gates, seeing himself condemned, and nothing now between his head and the halter but the word of the magistrate—which might come in an instant when it would be too late to send to his lord—remembering also the final assurance of his said lord's word by his former dealings towards other men (whereof this man was too much privy), he thought good to solicit his case also by some other of his friends, though not so puissant as his l[ord] and master, who, dealing indeed both diligently and effectually in his affair, found the matter more difficult a great deal than either he or they had imagined, for that my lord of Leicester was not only not his favorer, but a great hastener of his death underhand, and that, with such care, diligence, vehemency, and irresistible means (having the law also on his side) that there was no hope at all of escaping: which thing when Gates heard of, he easily believed, for the experience he had of his master's good nature, and said that he always mistrusted the same, considering how much his lordship was in debt to him, and he made privy to his lordship['s] foul secrets—which secrets he would there presently have uttered in the face of all the world, but that he feared torments or speedy death, with some extraordinary cruelty, if he should have done; and therefore he disclosed the same only to a gentleman of worship, whom he trusted specially, whose name I may not utter for some causes. * * *

2. Various (people).
3. Favorite.

THOMAS NASHE

[Satiric Criticism of Kyd]†

It is a common practice nowadays, among a sort of shifting companions that run through every art and thrive by none, to leave the trade of noverint,[1] whereto they were born, and busy themselves with the endeavors of art, that could scarcely Latinize their neck verse if they should have need. Yet English Seneca read by candlelight yields many good sentences, as 'Blood is a beggar' and so forth; and, if you entreat him fair in a frosty morning, he will afford you whole Hamlets, I should say handfuls of tragical speeches. But, O grief! *Tempus edax rerum*[2]—what's that will last always? The sea exhaled by drops will in continuance be dry, and Seneca, let blood line by line and page by page, at length must needs die to our stage; which makes his famished followers to imitate the kid in Aesop, who, enamoured with the fox's new-fangles, forsook all hopes of life to leap into a new occupation; and these men, renouncing all possibilities of credit or estimation, to intermeddle with Italian translations—wherein how poorly have they plodded * * * let all indifferent gentlemen that have travelled in that tongue discern by their two-penny pamphlets. And no marvel though their home-born mediocrity be such in this matter; for what can be hoped of those that thrust Elysium into hell,[3] and have not learned, so long as they have lived in the spheres, the just measure of the horizon without an hexameter? Sufficeth them to botch up a blank verse with ifs and ands, and otherwhile for recreation after their candle-stuff, having starched their beards most curiously, to make peripatetical path into the inner parts of the city, and spend two or three hours in turning over French dowdy,[4] where they attract more infection in one minute, than they can do eloquence all days of their life by conversing with any authors of like argument.

† From Thomas Nashe, Preface to Robert Greene's *Menaphon*, Stationer's Register, August 23, 1589. From *Works*, ed. R. B. McKerrow, III:315–16. Nashe satirizes contemporary trends in tragic writing, mocking Kyd ('the kid in Aesop')—who may also have been the author of an early *Hamlet* tragedy—as a crude imitator of Seneca.
1. The making of writs.
2. Time the devourer of all things.
3. Perhaps a gibe at the geography of Andrea's underworld as well as an apparent echo of Marlowe's *Dr Faustus* (iii.58): "For he confounds hell in Elysium."
4. Shabbily dressed French women (prostitutes).

Revenge

From An Exhortation Concerning Good Order and Obedience to Rulers and Magistrates[†]

Almighty God hath created and appointed all things in heaven, earth, and waters, in a most excellent and perfect order. In heaven he hath appointed distinct and several orders and states of archangels and angels. In earth he hath assigned and appointed kings, princes, with other governors under them, in all good and necessary order. The water above is kept, and raineth down in due time and season. The sun, moon, stars, rainbow, thunder, lightning, clouds, and all birds of the air, do keep their order. The earth, trees, seeds, plants, herbs, corn, grass, and all manner of beasts, keep themselves in order: all the parts of the whole year, as winter, summer, months, nights, and days, continue in their order: all kinds of fishes in the sea, rivers, and waters, with all fountains, springs, yea, the seas themselves, keep their comely course and order; and man himself also hath all his parts both within and without, as soul, heart, mind, memory, understanding, reason, speech, with all and singular corporal members of his body, in a profitable, necessary, and pleasant order: every degree of people in their vocation, calling, and office, hath appointed to them their duty and order: some are in high degree, some in low, some kings and princes, some inferiors and subjects, priests and laymen, masters and servants, fathers and children, husbands and wives, rich and poor; and every one have need of other; so that in all things is to be lauded and praised the goodly order of God, without the which no house, no city, no commonwealth, can continue and endure, or last. For where there is no right order, there reigneth all abuse, carnal liberty, enormity, sin, and Babylonical confusion.

Take away kings, princes, rulers, magistrates, judges, and such estates of God's order, no man shall ride or go by the highway

---

[†] From the Anglican homily (1547). Published to be read from the pulpit, the Church of England's homilies were designed to limit the opportunities offered by individually composed sermons for the expression of heterodox opinion. The exhortation presents an orthodox opinion of the destructiveness of revenge, which threatens to subvert the divinely appointed order embodied in the state.

unrobbed, no man shall sleep in his own house or bed unkilled, no man shall keep his wife, children, and possessions in quietness, all things shall be common; and there must needs follow all mischief and utter destruction both of souls, bodies, goods, and commonwealths. But blessed be God that we in this realm of England feel not the horrible calamities, miseries, and wretchedness which all they undoubtedly feel and suffer, that lack this godly order: and praised be God that we know the great excellent benefit of God showed towards us in this behalf. God hath sent us his high gift, our most dear sovereign * * * with a godly, wise, and honourable council, with other superiors and inferiors, in a beautiful order, and godly.

Wherefore, let us subjects do our bounden duties, giving hearty thanks to God, and praying for the preservation of this godly order. Let us all obey, even from the bottom of our hearts, all their godly proceedings, laws, statutes, proclamations, and injunctions, with all other godly orders. Let us consider the Scriptures of the Holy Ghost, which persuade and command us all obediently to be subject, first and chiefly to the King's majesty, supreme governor over all, and the next to his honourable council, and to all other noblemen, magistrates, and officers, which by God's goodness be placed and ordered.

For Almighty God is the only author and provider for this forenamed state and order, as it is written of God in the Book of the Proverbs, 'Through me kings do reign, through me counsellors make just laws, through me do princes bear rule, and all judges of the earth execute judgment : I am loving to them that love me.' (Proverbs 8.15, 17).

Here let us mark well, and remember, that the high power and authority of kings, with their making of laws, judgments, and offices, are the ordinances, not of man, but of God; and therefore is this word (through me) so many times repeated. Here is also well to be considered and remembered, that this good order is appointed by God's wisdom, favour, and love, especially for them that love God; and therefore he saith, I love them that love me. Also in the Book of Wisdom we may evidently learn, that a king's power, authority, and strength is a great benefit of God, given of his great mercy, to the comfort of our great misery. For thus we read there spoken to kings. Hear, O ye kings, and understand: learn ye that be judges of the ends of the earth; give ear, ye that rule the multitudes, for the power is given you of the Lord, and the strength from the Highest (Wisdom 6.1–3). Let us learn also here, by the infallible and undeceivable word of God, that kings and other supreme and higher officers, are ordained of God, who is most Highest; and therefore they are here taught diligently to apply and give themselves to knowledge and wisdom, necessary for the ordering of

God's people to their governance committed, or whom to govern they are charged of God.

And they be here also taught by Almighty God, that they should acknowledge themselves to have all their power and strength, not from Rome, but immediately of God most Highest. We read in the Book of Deuteronomy, that all punishment pertaineth to God, by this sentence, 'Vengeance is mine, and I will reward' (Deuteronomy, 32.35). But this sentence we must understand to pertain also unto the magistrates which do exercise God's room in judgment, and punishing by good and godly laws here in earth. And the places of Scripture which seem to remove from among all Christian men judgment, punishment, or killing, ought to be understood, that no man (of his own private authority) may be judge over other, may punish, or may kill. But we must refer all judgment to God, to kings and rulers, and judges under them, which be God's officers to execute justice; and by plain words of Scripture have their authority and use of the sword granted from God; as we are taught by Saint Paul, that dear and chosen Apostle of our Savior Christ, whom we ought diligently to obey, even as we would obey our Savior Christ, if he were present.

Thus St. Paul writeth to the Romans: 'Let every soul submit himself unto the authority of the higher powers for there is no power but of God. The powers that be, be ordained of God. Whosoever therefore withstandeth the power, withstandeth the ordinance of God; but they that resist or are against it shall receive to themselves damnation. For rulers are not fearful to them that do good, but to them that do evil. Wilt thou be without fear of the power? Do well then, and so shall thou be praised of the same; for he is the minister of God for thy wealth. But, and if thou do that which is evil, then fear; for he beareth not the sword for naught, for he is the minister of God, to take vengeance on him that doth evil. Wherefore ye must needs obey, not only for fear of vengeance, but also because of conscience; and even for this cause pay ye tribute, for they are God's ministers, serving for the same purpose' (Romans, 13.1–6).

Here let us learn of St. Paul, the chosen vessel of God, that all persons having souls (he excepteth none, nor exempteth none, neither priest, apostle, nor prophet, saith St. Chrysostom,) do owe of bounden duty, and even in conscience, obedience, submission, and subjection to the high powers which be set in authority by God; forasmuch as they be God's lieutenants, God's presidents, God's officers, God's commissioners, God's judges, ordained of God himself, of whom only they have all their power, and all their authority. And the same St. Paul threateneth no less pain than everlasting damnation to all disobedient persons, to all resisters against this general and common authority, forasmuch as they resist not man but God; not man's device and invention, but God's wisdom, God's order, power, and authority.

*   *   *

But let us now hear St. Peter himself speak, for his words certify best our conscience: thus he uttereth them in his first epistle: 'Servants, obey your masters with fear, not only if they be good and gentle, but also if they be froward. For it is thankworthy, if a man for conscience toward God endureth grief, and suffereth wrong undeserved: for what praise is it when ye be beaten for your faults, if ye take it patiently? But when ye do well, if you then suffer wrong, and take it patiently, then is there cause to have thank of God: for hereunto verily were ye called; for so did Christ suffer for us: leaving us an example that we should follow his steps' (1 Peter, 2.18–21). All these be the very words of St. Peter.

Holy David also teacheth us a good lesson in this behalf, who was many times most cruelly and wrongfully persecuted of King Saul, and many times also put in jeopardy and danger of his life by King Saul and his people; yet he neither withstood, neither used any force or violence against King Saul, his mortal and deadly enemy: but did ever to his liege lord and master King Saul, most true, most diligent, and most faithful service (1 Samuel, 18.11, 14, 30; 19.10–11; 20.31; 24.2–7). Insomuch, that when the Lord God had given King Saul into David's hands in his own cave, he would not hurt him, when he might, without all bodily peril, easily have slain him; no, he would not suffer any of his servants once to lay their hand upon King Saul, but prayed to God in this wise: 'Lord, keep me from doing that thing unto my master the Lord's anointed: keep me that I lay not my hand upon him, seeing he is the anointed of the Lord: for as truly as the Lord liveth (except the Lord smite him, or except his day come, or that he go down to war, and perish in battle), the Lord be merciful unto me, that I lay not my hand upon the Lords anointed.'

*   *   *

Here is evidently proved, that we may not withstand, nor in any wise hurt an anointed king, which is God's lieutenant, vicegerent, and highest minister in that country where he is king.

An objection. But peradventure some here would say, that David in his own defence might have killed king Saul lawfully, and with a safe conscience.

An answer. But holy David did know that he might in no wise withstand, hurt, or kill his sovereign lord and king: he did know that he was but King Saul's subject, though he were in great favour with God, and his enemy King Saul out of God's favour. Therefore though he were never so much provoked, yet he refused utterly to hurt the Lord's anointed. He durst not, for offending God and his own conscience (although he had occasion and opportunity) once lay his hands upon God's high officer the king, whom he did know to be a person reserved and kept (for his office sake) only to God's punishment and judgment: therefore he prayeth so oft and so earnestly that he lay not his hands upon the Lord's anointed. And by these two examples, Saint David (being named in Scripture a man after God's own heart) giveth a general rule and lesson to all subjects in the world, not to withstand their liege lord and king; not to take a sword by their private authority against their king, God's anointed (1 Samuel, 26.11; Psalm 88), who only beareth the sword by God's authority, for the maintenance of the good, and for the punishment of the evil; who only by God's law hath the use of the sword at his command, and also hath all power, jurisdiction, regiment, correction, and punishment, as supreme governor of all his realms and dominions, and that even by the authority of God, and by God's ordinances.

*   *   *

Ye have heard before, in this sermon, of good order and obedience, manifestly proved both by the Scriptures and examples, that all subjects are bound to obey their magistrates, and for no cause to resist, or withstand, or rebel, or make any sedition against them, yea, although they be wicked men. And let no man think that he can escape unpunished that committeth treason, conspiracy, or rebellion against his sovereign lord the king, though he commit the same never so secretly, either in thought, word, or deed, never so privily, in his privy chamber by himself, or openly communicating and consulting with others. For treason will not be hid, treason will out at length: God will have that most detestable vice both opened and punished, for that it is so directly against his ordinance, and against his high principal judge and anointed in earth. The violence and injury that is committed against authority is committed against God, the commonweal, and the whole realm, which God will have known, and condignly or worthily punished one way or other; for it is notably written of the Wise Man in Scripture, in the Book called Ecclesiastes: 'Wish the king no evil in thy thought, nor speak no hurt of him in thy privy chamber: for the bird of the air shall betray thy voice, and with her feathers shall bewray thy words' (Ecclesiastes, 10.20). These lessons and examples are written for our learning: therefore let us all fear the most detestable vice of rebellion; ever knowing and remembering, that he that resisteth or withstandeth common authority, resisteth or withstandeth God and his ordinance, as it may be proved by many other places of holy Scripture.

MICHEL DE MONTAIGNE

From Of Cruelty[†]

I fancy virtue to be something else, and something more noble, than good nature, and the mere propension to goodness, that we are born into the world withal. Well-disposed and well-descended souls pursue, indeed, the same methods, and represent in their actions the same face that virtue itself does: but the word virtue imports, I know not what, more great and active than merely for a man to suffer himself, by a happy disposition, to be gently and quietly drawn to the rule of reason. He who, by a natural sweetness and facility, should despise injuries received, would doubtless do a very fine and laudable thing; but he who, provoked and nettled to the quick by an offence, should fortify himself with the arms of reason against the furious appetite of revenge, and after a great conflict, master his own passion, would certainly do a great deal more. The first would do well; the latter virtuously: one action might be called goodness, and the other virtue; for methinks, the very name of virtue presupposes difficulty and contention, and cannot be exercised without an opponent. It is for this reason, perhaps, that we call God good, mighty, liberal and just; but we do not call Him virtuous, being that all His operations are natural and without endeavour

* * *

The savages do not so much offend me, in roasting and eating the bodies of the dead, as they do who torment and persecute the living. Nay, I cannot look so much as upon the ordinary executions of justice, how reasonable soever, with a steady eye * * * even in justice itself, all that exceeds a simple death appears to me pure cruelty; especially in us who ought, having regard to their souls, to dismiss them in a good and calm condition; which cannot be, when we have agitated them by insufferable torments.

From Cowardice, the Mother of Cruelty[‡]

* * * What is it in these times of ours that makes our quarrels mortal; and that, whereas our fathers had some degrees of revenge, we now begin with the last in ours, and at the first meeting nothing is

---

† From *Essays* (1580), II.xi. The two excerpts printed here from Montaigne's *Essays*, written just a few years before Kyd's play, exemplify a contemporary humanist's attitude to revenge.
‡ From *Essays* (1580), II.xxvii.

to be said but 'kill'? What is this but cowardice? Everyone is sensible that there is more bravery and disdain in subduing an enemy, than in cutting his throat; and in making him yield, than in putting him to the sword: besides that the appetite of revenge is better satisfied and pleased because its only aim is to make itself felt: And this is the reason why we do not fall upon a beast or a stone when they hurt us, because they are not capable of being sensible of our revenge; and to kill a man is to save him from the injury and offence we intend him. * * * [S]o revenge is to be pitied, when the person on whom it is executed is deprived of means of suffering under it: for as the avenger will look on to enjoy the pleasure of his revenge, so the person on whom he takes revenge should be a spectator too, to be afflicted and to repent. "He will repent it," we say, and because we have given him a pistol-shot through the head, do we imagine he will repent? On the contrary, if we but observe, we shall find, that he makes mouths at us in falling, and is so far from penitency, that he does not so much as repine at us; and we do him the kindest office of life, which is to make him die insensibly, and soon; we are afterwards to hide ourselves, and to shift and fly from the officers of justice who pursue us whilst he is at rest. Killing is good to frustrate an offence to come, not to revenge one that is already past; and more an act of fear than of bravery; of precaution than of courage; of defence than of enterprise. It is manifest that by it we lose both the true end of revenge and the care of our reputation; we are afraid, if he lives he will do us another injury as great as the first; 'tis not out of animosity to him, but care of thyself, that thou gettest rid of him. * * * If we thought by virtue to be always masters of our enemies, and to triumph over them at pleasure, we should be sorry they should escape from us as they do, by dying: but we have a mind to conquer, more with safety than honour, and, in our quarrel, more pursue the end than the glory.

*   *   *

Our fathers contented themselves with revenging an insult with the lie, the lie with a box of the ear, and so forward; they were valiant enough not to fear their adversaries, living and provoked we tremble for fear so soon as we see them on foot. And that this is so, does not our noble practice of these days, equally to prosecute to death both him that has offended us and him we have offended, make it out? 'Tis also a kind of cowardice that has introduced the custom of having seconds, thirds, and fourths in our duels; they were formerly duels; they are now skirmishes, rencontres, and battles. * * * Third persons were formerly called in to prevent disorder and foul play only, and to be witness of the fortune of the combat; but now they have brought it to this pass that the witnesses themselves engage; whoever is invited cannot handsomely stand by as an idle spectator, for fear of being suspected either of want of affection or of courage.

*   *   *

What is it that makes tyrants so sanguinary? 'Tis only the solicitude for their own safety, and that their faint hearts can furnish them with no other means of securing themselves than in exterminating those who may hurt them. * * *

Tyrants, at once both to kill and to make their anger felt, have employed their capacity to invent the most lingering deaths. They will have their enemies despatched, but not so fast that they may not have leisure to taste their vengeance. And therein they are mightily perplexed; for if the torments they inflict are violent, they are short; if long, they are not then so painful as they desire; and thus plague themselves in choice of the greatest cruelty. Of this we have a thousand examples in antiquity, and I know not whether we, unawares, do not retain some traces of this barbarity.

FRANCIS BACON

Of Revenge[†]

Revenge is a kind of wild justice, which the more man's nature runs to, the more ought law to weed it out. For, as for the first wrong, it doth but offend the law; but the revenge of that wrong putteth the law out of office. Certainly in taking revenge a man is but even with his enemy; but in passing it over he is superior; for it is a prince's part to pardon. And Solomon, I am sure, saith it is the glory of a man, to pass by an offence. That which is past is gone and irrevocable; and wise men have enough to do with things present and to come; therefore they do but trifle with themselves that labor in past matters. There is no man doth a wrong for the wrong's sake, but thereby to purchase himself profit, or pleasure, or honor, or the like. Therefore why should I be angry with a man for loving himself better than me? And if any man should do wrong merely out of ill-nature—why, yet it is but like the thorn or briar, which prick and scratch because they can do no other. The most tolerable sort of revenge is for those wrongs which there is no law to remedy; but then let a man take heed the revenge be such as there is no law to

---

† From *Essaies*, Essay 4 (1625). Bacon's essay reflects his vocation as a lawyer and jurist: in contrast to the theologically based denunciations in the Anglican homilies, his hostility to the revenge ethic derives primarily from his conviction that it constitutes an implicit challenge to the rule of law.

punish—else a man's enemy is still beforehand, and it is two for one. Some, when they take revenge, are desirous the party should know whence it cometh. This is the more generous. For the delight seemeth to be not so much in doing the hurt as in making the party repent. But base and crafty cowards are like the arrow that flieth in the dark. Cosmus, duke of Florence, had a desperate saying against perfidious or neglecting friends, as if those wrongs were unpardonable: 'You shall read,' saith he, 'that we are commanded to forgive our enemies; but you never read that we are commanded to forgive our friends.' But yet the spirit of Job was in a better tune: 'Shall we,' saith he, 'take good at God's hands, and not be content to take evil also?' And so of friends in a proportion. This is certain, that a man that studieth revenge keeps his own wounds green, which otherwise would heal and do well. Public revenges are for the most part fortunate—as that for the death of Caesar, for the death of Pertinax, for the death of Henry the Third of France, and many more. But in private revenges it is not so. Nay rather, vindictive persons live the life of witches, who, as they are mischievous, so end they infortunate.

Contemporary Reception

ANONYMOUS

[The Ballad of *The Spanish Tragedy*]†

You that have lost your former joys,
And now in woe your lives do lead,
Feeding on nought but dire annoys,
Thinking your griefs all griefs exceed,
    Assure yourselves it is not so:
    Lo, here a sight of greater woe.

Hapless Hieronimo was my name
On whom fond Fortune smilèd long;
But now her flattering smiles I blame,
Her flattering smiles hath done me wrong.
    Would I had died in tender years,
    Then had not been this cause of tears.

I Marshal was in prime of years
And won great honour in the field,
Until that age with silvered hairs
My aged head hath overspread;
    Then left I war and stayed at home
    And gave my honour to my son.

Horatio, my sweet only child,
Pricked¹ forth by Fame's aspiring wings,
Did so behave him in the field

---

† From *The Spanish Tragedy Containing the Lamentable Murders of* Horatio *and* Bellim-
peria *With the pitifull Death of old* Hieronimo. *To the Tune of* Queene Dido (London,
1620). The author of this ballad—in which Hieronimo is made to recount his own
story, rather in the fashion of Andrea's ghost—clearly knew the play well because he
echoes its wording at several points. The ballad's existence is further testimony to the
extraordinary popularity of Kyd's tragedy until well into the seventeenth century.
1. Spurred.

That he Prince Baltazar captive brings,
   And with great honour did present
   Him to the King incontinent.[2]

The Duke of Castile's daughter then
Desired Horatio to relate
The death of her beloved friend,
Her love Andrea's woeful fate.
   But when she knew who had him slain,
   She vowed she would revenge the same.

Then more to vex Prince Baltazar,
Because he slew her chiefest friend,
She chose my son for her chief flower,
Thereby meaning to work revenge.
   But mark what then did straight befall
   To turn my sweet to bitter gall.

Lorenzo then to find the cause
Why that his sister was unkind,
At last he found within a pause
How he might sound her secret mind.
   Which for to bring well to effect
   To fetch her man he doth direct,

Who, being come into his sight,
He threat'neth for to rid his life,
Except straightways he should recite
His sister's love, the cause of strife.
   Compelled therefore to unfold his mind,
   Said, "With Horatio she's combined."

The villain then, for hope of gain,
Did straight convey him to the place
Where these two lovers did remain
Joying in sight of other's face;
   And to their faces they did impart
   The place where they should lay their heart.

Prince Baltazar with his compeers[3]
Enters my bower all in the night;

2. Immediately.
3. Associates.

And there my son slain they uprear
The more to work my greater spite.
  But as I lay and take repose:
  A voice I heard, whereat I rose;

And finding then his senseless form,
The murderers I sought to find;
But missing them I stood forlorn
As one amazèd in his mind,
  And rent and pulled my silvered hair,
  And cursed and banned each thing was there.

And that I would revenge the same,
I dipped a napkin in his blood,
Swearing to work their woeful bane
That so had spoiled my chiefest good;
  And that I would not it forget,
  I always at my heart it kept.

    The second part. To the same tune.

Then Isabella my dear wife,
Finding her son bereaved of breath,
And loving him dearer than life,
Her own hand straight doth work her death.
  And now their deaths both meet in one,
  My griefs are come, my joys are done.

Then franticly I ran about,
Filling the air with mournful groans
Because I had not yet found out
The murderers to ease my moans.
  I rent and tore each thing I got,
  And said and did I knew not what.

Thus as I passed the streets, hard by
The Duke of Castile's house, as then
A letter there I did espy
Which showed Horatio's woeful end,
  Which Bel-imperia forth had flung
  From prison where they kept her strong.

Then to the court forthwith I went
And of the King did justice crave;
But by Lorenzo's bad intent

I hindered was, which made me rave;
    Then vexèd more I stamped and frowned
    And with my poniard ripped the ground.

But false Lorenzo put me out,
And told the King then by and by
That franticly I ran about
And of my son did always cry,
    And said 'twere good I should resign
    My marshalship, which grieved my mind.

The Duke of Castile, hearing then
How I did grudge still at his son,
Did send for me to make us friends,
To stay[4] the rumour then begun;
    Whereto I straightway gave consent—
    Although in heart I never meant.

Sweet Bel-imperia comes to me,
Thinking my son I had forgot,
To see me with his foes agree—
The which I never meant, God wot.[5]
    But when we knew each other's mind,
    To work revenge a mean I find.

Then bloody Baltazar enters in,
Entreating me to show some sport
Unto his father and the King
That to his nuptial did resort;
    Which gladly I prepared to show
    Because I knew 'twould work their woe.

And from the chronicles of Spain
I did record Erastus' life,
And how the Turk had him so slain,
And straight revenge wrought by his wife.
    Then for to act this tragedy
    I gave their parts immediately.

Sweet Bel-imperia Baltazar kills
Because he slew her dearest friend,

4. Stop.
5. Knows.

And I Lorenzo's blood did spill,
And eke to hell his soul to hell did send.
    Then died my foes by dint of knife,
    But Bel-imperia ends her life.

Then, for to specify my wrongs,
With weeping eyes and mournful heart
I showed my son with bloody wounds,
And eke the murderers did impart.
    And said my son was as dear to me
    As thine, or thine, though kings you be.

But when they did behold this thing,
How I had slain their only sons,
The Duke, the Viceroy, and the King
Upon me all they straight did run.
    To torture me they do prepare,
    Unless I should it straight declare.

But that I would not tell it then
Even with my teeth I bit my tongue
And in despite did give it them
That me with torments sought to wrong.
    Thus, when in age I sought to rest,
    Nothing but sorrows me oppressed.

They, hearing well that I could write,
Unto my hand a pen did reach,
Meaning thereby I should recite
The author of this bloody fetch.[6]
    Then fainèd I my pen was naught,
    And by strange signs a knife I sought.

But when to me they gave the knife,
I killed the Duke then standing by,
And eke myself bereaved of life,
For I to see my son did hie.[7]
    The Kings that scorned my griefs before
    With nought can they their joys restore.

6. Device, trick.
7. Go.

Here have you heard my tragic tale
Which on Horatio's death depends,
Whose death I could anew bewail,
But that in it the murderers ends;
   For murder God will bring to light
   Though long it be hid from man's sight.

Printed at London for *H. Gosson*.

FINIS

CRITICISM

Stagecraft

MICHAEL HATTAWAY

From The Spanish Tragedy: Architectonic Design[†]

When he wrote *The Spanish Tragedy* Thomas Kyd not only found a theme that kindled the imagination of his audiences but devised a form that fully and spectacularly utilized the resources and conventions of the popular playhouses of the 1590s. Revenge is a perennial theme in popular literature: in Christian cultures it combines the lure of what is forbidden by religion and society with expectation, surprise, and the suspense of the hunt. It can, moreover, like Kyd's play, exploit the fascination with obsession, madness, and violence that for centuries filled ballads and chapbooks until they were replaced by popular newspapers and films. The play was also topical: like Shakespeare's Henry VI plays and Marlowe's *Edward II*, Kyd's work grew out of the strengthening Renaissance sense of national identity: it dramatized the state of a nation, in particular the way its destinies are shaped by politics, the specific personalities and actions of its rulers. (Lorenzo is the first 'Machiavellian' figure in English drama.) Spain was a Catholic country, England's arch-enemy, a country whose armada had attempted an invasion of England at about the time the play was probably written. Kyd created a sequence of dramatic images that displayed both the magnificence and the ephemerality of a secular and, to the Elizabethans, a totalitarian power, and was thus able to appeal to the chauvinism of native Protestants just as Shakespeare did in his dramatization of the defeat of the French in *1 Henry VI*. He mustered the support a mass audience will give to a heroic individual who sets himself against a network of contrivance and corruption—the number of references to the play or affectionately parodic quotations from it show that it occupied the collective consciousness of the Elizabethans in the way that the James Bond films did for a much later generation.

[†] From *"The Spanish Tragedy*: Architectonic Design" by Michael Hattaway as it appeared in *Elizabethan Popular Theatre* (London: Routledge, 1982), pp. 101–04, 106–11, 220. Reproduced by permission of Taylor & Francis Books UK. © 1982 Routledge & Kegan Paul.

161

Kyd along with Marlowe and the young Shakespeare had a sense of basic stagecraft that far exceeded that of their predecessors. Kyd's distinctive contribution was his sense of theatrical space. He used the two levels of the stage and gallery, the discovery space, and scenic properties, like the arbour in this play, in an economical and assured way, a way that enabled him not only to dramatize narrative but to create with visual devices as well as words the consciousness of his characters. He exploited the visual frames provided by elements of the tiring-house façade in a manner analogous to that of a film director today, bringing objects and dramatic tableaux into a field and focus shared by both character and spectator. He was able to give the plebeian members of the audience a sampling of the dramatic fare served up at Court—masques, dumb shows, and magniloquent declamations. He domesticated the learned and modernized the antique, even as he incorporated into the play the elements of street theatre and clownage of Pedringano's gallows scene. While attending scrupulously to the design of his plot, he built up archetypal images by using the conventions of dream, and worked towards subconscious layers of response by composing strong speech rhythms familiar in folk forms like ballads, using language as a kind of music, as well as by creating a strong visual pattern of repeated theatrical images.

Kyd was one of the first to learn how the physical arrangement of stage and tiring-house, the spatial relationship between players and spectators, made possible that combination of history and tragedy, the particular and the universal, that gives the popular drama of the Renaissance its distinctive resonances. Medieval drama was anachronistic and timeless: it made no attempt to emphasize the historical truth of its stories but concerned itself with morality and religious symbol. Its scenic devices and costumes were allegorical, its concerns were ethical, and players switched from dramatic dialogue to direct exhortatory address to the audience. Renaissance drama too used non-illusionistic properties and costumes, but the transition from *décor simultané*, playing spaces equipped with mansions that stood unmoved throughout the action (as in *The Castle of Perseverence*), to an empty space (on which similar devices if used might be displayed in sequence as the play unfolded) made possible the writing of plays concerned with time and change, with history. (Mansions could, as we have seen, be introduced into history—as with the tents on Bosworth Field at the end of *Richard III*—to universalize the predicament of the hero.) Although there was no physical division between audience and players in the popular playhouses, the elevation of the stage did create a special world, a world apart, and in this play Kyd seems not to have infringed its boundaries, his sense of the identity of 'Spain', by direct address to the audience. Moreover Kyd, like Marlowe and Shakespeare, found that the sheer size of the new permanent stages and the enlargement of the dramatic companies enabled him to dramatize the fates of nations rather than individuals, and the flexibility of theatrical conventions of time and space enabled him to realize particular moments in the kingdoms of men rather than the eternal presence of the kingdom of God. Particular moments of time and place could be fixed by indications in the dialogue, while the ethical status or freedom of the characters would be revealed by their position in relationship to the tiring-house façade. To put the matter in the crudest terms, personages with a propensity to evil might emerge from the cellarage, those that were not free to prosper, because of their evil actions or the superior power of contriving adversaries, stood beneath the gallery whence they might be regarded with compassion or contempt by classical deities or earthly potentates.

The achievement of *The Spanish Tragedy* was of course to be soon surpassed. It was quickly parodied by dramatists whose verse was more flexible and sophisticated and who could thereby create characters with a greater degree of individuality than any in Kyd's play, as well as scenes that opened on to wider areas of experience than that of the claustrophobic Iberian courts so obviously painted in primary moral colours. Yet that iconic, gestic style, the procession of 'painted tyrants' retained its hold on popular audiences and for some thirty years, from the time of its composition through the first decades of the seventeenth century, *The Spanish Tragedy* was one of the most successful plays of its age.

*   *   *

In this play scenes will repeat situations or gests, bringing the audience to the point where it would accept not only the validity of the player's art as a plausible form of experience but the reality of situations that are strange or improbable. Kyd's method of composition, then, is based on analogy, on the creation of *figurae*, and the architectonic arrangement of these gives the play its strong dramatic rhythm.[1]

Further evidence for this notion of scenic structure comes from entries in the *Stationers' Register* and the expanded titles (the forerunners of modern 'blurbs') on the titlepages of early editions, pages that were sometimes pasted up on posts about the city as advertisements. The entry of 6 October 1592 reads: 'A book which is called the Spanish Tragedy of Don Horatio and Bel-Imperia' and

---

1. See E. Auerbach, '*Figura*', in his *Themes from the Drama of European Literature*, New York, 1959, pp. 11–76.

the titlepage for the first six editions reads in part: 'The Spanish Tragedy, Containing the lamentable end of Don Horatio, and Bel-Imperia: with the pitiful death of old Hieronimo.' The 1615 edition adds the subtitle and the woodcut depicting one of the most memorable images of the play. Hieronimo bears his torch towards the arbour where the body of his son is hanging. Behind him is Bel-Imperia and behind her in a black mask is Lorenzo with drawn sword. What is notable about these descriptions is that they do not imply only a single hero but see the tragedy as that of a family or dynasty, and suggest that what would sell the play would be a reminder of those great *scenes* in the play that had caught the imagination of the audiences. Like audiences at operas now who anticipate with pleasure favourite arias or pieces of spectacle, the Elizabethans did not see the play only through the eyes of the hero or assume that it was shaped about his consciousness. Rather it was for them a sequence of performed actions. Indeed Kyd may be said to have gained his effect by adding theatrical action to the long declamatory sequences developed by the academic dramatists and English Senecans; to have, in effect, created the 'scene' as the elemental dramatic unit. Without *The Spanish Tragedy* for a model, Shakespeare would not have written a play like *Richard III* in which so many scenes are based around a simple bold incident—or gest—of the kind we have described.

* * *

Kyd was remembered by contemporaries not only for the high relief of his scenic construction but for his language. It is easily recognizable as rhetorical in that he often employs the boldest and simplest of the figures of sound: isocolon, or repetition of clauses of approximately the same length, parison, parallel placing of corresponding grammatical units of these clauses, and paramoion, similarity of sound in the parallel clauses. Kyd, who took these academic devices into the popular playhouses, sought from the declamation of his lines a musical and emotional effect. There is a sure sense of simple rhythms in Kyd, and his sound patterns, even if they tend towards the hypnotic, are a compelling part of his dramatic climaxes.[2]

It might be claimed that the rolling rhythms and surging movements of the speeches lead only to mannerism and monotony. Kyd himself gives a description of his manner when Hieronimo claims he wants

---

2. For a contrary view see S. W. Dawson, *Drama and the Dramatic*, London, 1970, pp. 22–3 and Jonas A. Barish, 'The Spanish Tragedy or The Pleasures and Perils, of Rhetoric', in J. R. Brown and Bernard Harris (eds), *Elizabethan Theatre*, London, 1966.

> stately-written tragedy,
> *Tragedia corthurnata*, fitting kings,
> Containing matter, and not common things. (IV.i.159–61)

*   *   *

Like that of all his contemporaries, Kyd's art is self-conscious in that it draws attention to its own method. In his conversation with Bazulto Hieronimo describes an extreme of passion that demands bravura playing:

> Thou art the lively image of my grief:
> Within thy face, my sorrows I may see.
> Thy eyes are gummed with tears, thy cheeks are wan,
> Thy forehead troubled, and thy mutt'ring lips
> Murmur sad words abruptly broken off,
> By force of windy sighs thy spirit breathes,
> And all this sorrow riseth for thy son:
> And selfsame sorrow feel I for my son.
> Come in old man, thou shalt to Isabel,
> Lean on my arm: I thee, thou me shalt stay . . .
>   (III.xiii.162–71)

We may deduce from the 'theatricality' of this that Kyd made no attempt to pretend that the action of the play was not taking place on the stage. 'Lively' means energetic, hard in outline. Moreover Kyd calls, as we shall see, for two players to act the part of spectators, looking down from above to the action on the stage below. For them the play is 'real' in that Andrea is satisfied by the acts of revenge that take place, but, paradoxically, it is also a dream. So we hear at the end of the Ghost's speech as he describes Proserpine:

> Forthwith, Revenge, she rounded thee in th'ear,
> And bade thee lead me through the gates of horn,
> Where dreams have passage in the silent night.
> No sooner had she spoke but we were here,
> I wot not how, in twinkling of an eye. (I.i.81–5)

There were two gates of sleep in the underworld: through those of ivory, false visions emerged, through those of horn, true visions. The figure recurs ironically when Hieronimo, after hearing the outcries at his son's murder, reasons: 'I did not slumber, therefore 'twas no dream' (II.v.5). The device is another way of creating the familiar Elizabethan conceit that what is strange may yet be true, inviting actors to play out the play's conventions with confidence.

A second device that sets the play firmly within the structure of theatrical art is apparent in the opening speeches. Following classical example, Kyd introduced narrative into his plays, and characters are thus called upon to act as prologue and choruses. Moreover these narratives do not simply use the third person but employ the device of *prosopopeia* or impersonation. As in some of Brecht's theatre, a player acting one character has to impersonate another. So Andrea, narrating his journey to the underworld, tells of his meeting with the infernal judges, Minos, Aeacus, and Rhadamanth:

> To whom no sooner gan I make approach,
> To crave a passport for my wand'ring ghost,
> But Minos, in graven leaves of lottery,
> Drew forth the manner of my life and death.
> 'This knight,' quoth he, 'both lived and died in love,
> And for his love tried fortune of the wars,
> And by war's fortune lost both love and life . . .' (I.i.34–40)

Beyond the symmetrical stylization of the verse we notice a deliberate use of archaic formulae ('quoth he') and, more interesting perhaps, self-dramatization as Andrea refers to himself as both 'I' and 'my . . . ghost'. As was characteristic of popular drama, the player remains distinct from the character he plays; he is therefore called upon to tell as well as to show, to indicate by physical gesture and inflexion of voice his and the author's attitude to the genre that is created and to the mode of theatrical illusion.

With regard to the literary dimension of the play, Kyd was bringing to a popular audiences elements of the highest and most aristocratic genres, the epic and the romance. Andrea has ventured in the footsteps of epic heroes through the underworld, Pedringano plays the servant go-between in the love affairs of Bel-Imperia. Kyd was making accessible to the people by his dramatization what had been available only to the most literate. The lines of Latin that stud the play would have been pleasingly familiar to the judicious, exotic fare for the general. They are also related to the conventions of Renaissance emblem books in which a Latin motto was illustrated by an engraving and amplified by verses in the vernacular. Again there is a similarity to Brecht's dramaturgy: the Latin tags or passages resemble the captions he put on stage to turn image to emblem.

Kyd even gave Hieronimo a fourteen-line Latin dirge to recite (II.v.) as he contemplates suicide after the death of his son. Perhaps these lines were there simply to please those with a taste for rhetorical declamation but they also point towards an interesting if not wholly successful experiment with dramatic language. In IV.i. Hieronimo promises the court that the play of Soliman and Perseda will be performed in sundry tongues:

> Each of us must act his part
> In unknown languages,

That it might breed the more variety.
And you, my lord, in Latin, I in Greek,
You in Italian, and for because I know
That Bel-Imperia hath practisèd the French,
In courtly French shall all her phrases be. (IV.i.172–8)

Although 'variety' was a quality to be striven after—according to
the rhetoricians (*OED*, 2c)—'that it may breed the more variety' is
a lame and queer explanation, especially as, according to custom, a
'book' of the play had to be handed to the King as the highest personage present that he at least might follow the action. When we
come to the text of the play within the play, however, we find the
following note appended:

> Gentlemen, this play of Hieronimo in sundry languages,
> was thought good to be set down in English more largely,
> for the easier understanding to every
> public reader. (IV.iv.10)

There are several possible explanations for this: (1) Kyd in fact
intended that the play be performed in English; (2) we can take the
note at its face value and conjecture that the publisher had the foreign tongues translated for his readers; or (3) that the English version represents a revision by Kyd after puzzlement in the playhouse,
or else intervention by another hand, perhaps the author of the
additions. After the play within the play, however, the text reads;

> Here break we off our sundry languages
> And thus conclude I in our vulgar tongue (IV.iv.74–5)

which makes the second conjecture at least plausible. Why, though,
should Kyd have essayed this strange device? Perhaps the play was in
several languages so that it would appear as though the performers
did not know exactly what was afoot, but in performance the device
might have a different effect. I have suggested that one of Kyd's great
fascinations was for memorable speech-rhythms and cadence and it
is possible that he was trying to see whether he could employ a theatre language that would, to the unlettered at least, communicate by
its mere sound. Anyone who has enjoyed a performance of a Greek
play without knowing the language knows, to his surprise perhaps,
how this can happen. The story of Soliman and Perseda is simple
enough, after all, to be communicated through mime. What an audience who did not understand the dialogue would experience would be
the ritual shape of this inset action and perhaps thereby the mythic
dimension of the whole play.[3] It is the culmination of a movement

---

3. See S. F. Johnson, 'The Spanish Tragedy, or Babylon Revisited', in R. Hosley (ed.),
Essays on Shakespeare and Elizabethan Drama, Columbia, Mo., 1962, pp. 23–36.

from the pronounced narrative elements of the opening of the play, through the manifest dramatic conflicts and on-stage violent action of the middle, towards a species of music that suggests that the action includes more than merely the characters, that it creates its own mythic order.

Before attending to the unfolding action of the play it is necessary to examine further one final component, Kyd's use of specific dramatic emblems or speaking pictures. These occur with a regular rhythm throughout the play. We see Balthazar marched captive between Lorenzo and Horatio, the Portuguese Viceroy leaving his throne and throwing himself to the ground in grief, the court at a banquet (cf. the banquet in Cambises, 965–1042) watching Hieronimo's masque of the English champions, Alexandro bound to the stake to be burnt, the hanging of Pedringano, Hieronimo with poniard and rope contemplating suicide, the mad scenes, and the great dumb show in which nuptial torches are dowsed in blood. They need little comment but should not be dismissed as mere pandering to a vulgar taste for inexplicable dumb show and noise. As we have seen, they can serve as structural devices:[4]

> The scenes may remind the audience of a cause and effect relationship: Hieronimo, cutting down the lifeless body of his son (II.v.), and Isabella, cutting down the arbour itself (IV.ii.). The scenes may be in ironic contrast: Hieronimo applauded as the master of the 'device', the show concerning past military exploits, by which the court is entertained in Act One, and Hieronimo applauded for the bloody show of 'Soliman and Perseda' in which Balthazar, Lorenzo, and Bel-Imperia meet death before the eyes of the uncomprehending court ('*King.* Well said, old Marshal, this was bravely done!' IV.iv.68.)

These relationships could have been made by quoting the blocking of the scenes in question. They have also a general effect, for these and many of the other scenes of the play are both artificial, and, for the Elizabethans, examples of the shows of their 'real' world. They have their origins in the pageantry of the court, the street dramas of executions, the illustrations to theological and moral tracts. They are images or icons that combine the everyday and the fictional, the real and the artificial, and which, by this combination, achieve their particular dramatic, eidetic effects. Only recently, through the work of Brecht and Artaud, have dramatic critics been able to react without condescension or embarrassment to the basic satisfaction this kind of popular show can provide. *The Spanish Tragedy* had a subtitle, 'Hieronimo's mad again'; later *Philaster* was

---

4. E. M. Tweedie, '"Action is Eloquence": The Staging of Thomas Kyd's *Spanish Tragedy*', S.E.L., XVI, 1976, pp. 223–39.

to be commonly known by its subtitle, 'Love lies a-bleeding', which was illustrated on its titlepage with a woodcut depicting the Country Gentleman looking proudly upon the wounded princess with Philaster disappearing through the woods. These 'naive' images are the stuff of popular drama.

*   *   *

The Language of the Play

JONAS A. BARISH

From *The Spanish Tragedy,* or The Pleasures and Perils of Rhetoric[†]

The Spanish Tragedy is, as has long been recognised, a repository of 'patterned' speech. What has perhaps been less well recognised is that this speech derives, for the most part, not so much from the dramatic as from the nondramatic verse of Kyd's predecessors and contemporaries among the poets. Specifically, it seems to represent Kyd's adaptation of the rhetoric of the 'middle style', the rhetoric of the schemes, tropes and figures, as enshrined in the poetical miscellanies of the later sixteenth century and codified in the manuals of style. The figures had as their purpose simply to please, 'to avoyd sacietie [sic], and cause delight: to refresh with pleasure, and quicken with grace the dulnesse of mans braine' (Wilson's *Art of Rhetoric*, p. 180), and thus to assist the poet in his aim of persuasion. Doubtless it was the acknowledged delightfulness of the figures that led Kyd to employ them so bountifully in *The Spanish Tragedy* that the play might almost have served, like Sidney's *Arcadia*, as a text on which to base a rhetorical lexicon, but it was wholly a consequence of his feeling for the connection between language and gesture that he was able to take devices that had often proved intractable in the hands of other playwrights, and turn them into vital constructive elements. Unlike his predecessors, Kyd used the figures of rhetoric not simply to decorate the action but to articulate it.

*　*　*

It was playwrights like Kyd who helped bring into being our present sense of the dramatic. What Kyd does is to make functional the schemes and tropes of the figured style. He pares away the fatty amplification that writers like Mundy did not even recognize as

[†] From *"The Spanish Tragedy,* or The Pleasures and Perils of Rhetoric" by Jonas A. Barish as it appeared in *Elizabethan Theatre* (London: Edward Arnold, 1966), pp. 59, 65–83. Reprinted by permission.

encumbering, and what remains he remanages so as to fit it for its new context. When he borrows directly, he improves. Lorenzo's notorious echoing of a sonnet by Thomas Watson represents, simply on the level of versification, a distinct advance:

> My lord, though Bel-imperia seem thus coy,
> Let reason hold you in your wonted joy:
> In time the savage bull sustains the yoke,
> In time all haggard hawks will stoop to lure,
> In time small wedges cleave the hardest oak,
> In time the flint is pierc'd with softest shower,
> And she in time will fall from her disdain,
> And rue the sufferance of your friendly pain.
> BALTHAZAR.   No, she is wilder, and more hard withal,
> Than beast, or bird, or tree, or stony wall.
>
> (II. i. 1)

Watson's version ran thus:

> In time the Bull is brought to weare the yoake;
> In time all haggred Haukes will stoope the Lures;
> In time small wedge will cleave the sturdiest Oake;
> In time the Marble weares with weakest shewres:
>   More fierce is my sweet *love*, more hard withall,
>   Then Beast, or Birde, then Tree, or Stony wall.[1]

'The oftener it is read of him that is no great clarke', declares Watson patronisingly in his headnote to the sonnet, 'the more pleasure he shall have in it', thus emphasising the auricular drubbing to which he will subject his vulgar readers. Kyd provides dramatic context for the lines, and uses them to score a dramatic point. The familiar conflict in the mind of the Petrarchan lover, between the spectacle of his mistress' cruelty and the hope that she may relent, turns into a lively interchange between the confident Lorenzo, unimpressed by the genuineness of his sister's indifference toward Balthazar, and the despairing Balthazar, already daunted by the conviction of his own worthlessness. Kyd resists the temptation to shovel a complete poem, with its own beginning, middle and end, into his play; where Munday, following Watson, would have spun twelve lines more of schematic parallels on the properties of bulls, hawks, oaks and flints, Kyd cuts short the amplification, makes the quatrain a vivid moment of persuasion in Lorenzo's speech and allots only the despondent rejoinder to Balthazar. In addition, he confers a new compactness and energy on the familiar images by curbing the stream of monosyllables, reducing the shower

---

1. *The Hekatompathia, or Passionate Century of Love* (1582), facs. ed. S. K. Heninger, Jr. (1964), p. 61.

of sibillants and practising other small but significant metrical improvements.

When, in short, we turn from the sporadic and halting attempts of earlier playwrights to *The Spanish Tragedy*, we find that the figures have ceased being mere aimless embroidery. They no longer represent self-indulgence on the playwright's part, nor do they suggest a flagging imagination. They now work actively to order the materials of the play. In addition to being 'auricular' and 'rhetorical', they have conceptual force. They help articulate the relationships among the characters; they aid the plot to incarnate itself as a physical event on a physical stage. At the same time, they gradually serve the playwright to turn a critical eye on language itself. Words come to oppose physical events as well as to buttress them, and in the tension between speech and act lies much of the tragic force of the plot.

The tendency for most of the schemes of antithesis, parallel, and balance to carve experience into dualities, triads, tetrads, and the like—in short, to impose a symmetrical patterning on phenomena—pervades the language of *The Spanish Tragedy* from the start, long before the figures, as figures, begin to press themselves on our notice. The solemn periphrasis with which the ghost of Don Andrea makes his entry lodges us at once in a realm of precise distinctions and complementary rejunctions:

> When this eternal substance of my *soul*
> Did live imprison'd in my wanton *flesh*,
> *Each* in their function *serving other's* need, . . .
> (I. i. 1, my italics)

Andrea elaborates the body-soul dualism in two successive lines, and then in a third reunites the separated halves into a mutually co-operative union. The use of the word 'flesh' rather than 'body', in contrast to 'soul', slightly mutes the rhetorical emphasis of the opposition, without affecting its conceptual import. Death is next viewed as a divisive power that cleaves in sunder not the body and soul, as we might expect, but the speaker and his mistress:

> But in the harvest of my summer joys
> Death's winter nipp'd the blossoms of my bliss,
> Forcing divorce betwixt my love and me.
> (I. i. 12)

Here a new series of antitheses—between summer and winter, harvest and frost, life and death—runs obliquely against the earlier opposition of flesh and soul and the splintered unity of the lovers arrived at in the final line. The mode of thinking is continuously antithetical and disjunctive, but the disjunctions at this moment remain slightly out of phase with one another, so that they do not crystallise into obvious patterns.

Andrea's description of his visit to the underworld, based on the voyage in Book VI of the *Aeneid*, condenses and abridges Virgil's account; it also regularises and patterns it. At the threshold of Hades, Aeneas meets only Minos among the infernal judges; Rhadamanth appears further on, in Tartarus; and Aeacus is not mentioned at all. Kyd makes Andrea's arrival in Hades the occasion of a ceremonious debate in which all three judges, sitting as a high tribunal, ponder the fate of their new charge. They comprise a perfect trinity of thesis, antithesis and synthesis. Aeacus recommends that Andrea, a lover, be sent to the fields of love; Rhadamanth proposes to send him, as a soldier, to dwell with martialists; Minos, finally, arbitrates the difference by referring the question to Pluto. The journey toward Pluto deals in a like manner with infernal geography; on the right, the path leading to the fields of lovers and warriors; on the left, the steep descent to hell; in between, the entrance to the Elysian fields, where Pluto holds court. The arrangement revises Virgil's plan of the region so as to satisfy Kyd's liking for symmetrical patterns and the reconciliation of opposites.

The epic narrative of the victory of Spain over Portugal is conducted along similar lines. When, in the account of the Spanish general, the opposing armies set forth, they confront each other in a six-fold sequence of identical gestures:

> Both furnish'd well, both full of hope and fear,
> Both menacing alike with daring shows,
> Both vaunting sundry colours of device, . . . [etc.]
> (I. ii. 25)

The battle itself proceeds like a tournament. Each aggressive move made by one side is countered by an equivalent defensive manœuvre from the other:

> I brought a squadron of our readiest shot
> From out our rearward to begin the fight:
> They brought another wing to encounter us.
> Meanwhile our ordnance play'd on either side,
> And captains strove to have their valours tried.
> (I. ii. 35)

First the assault from the rear of one army, then the riposte from the flank of the other. First the challenge and answer of the ordnance, then the striving of the anonymous captains. When the smoke clears enough to enable us to discern and identify individual combatants, the same arrangement prevails. First,

> Don Pedro, their chief horseman's colonel,
> Did with his comet bravely make attempt
> To break the order of our battle ranks.
> But Don Rogero, worthy man of war,
> March'd forth against him with our musketeers,
> And stopp'd the malice of his fell approach.
>
> (I. ii. 40)

So, Don Pedro with his cavalry must oppose Don Rogero with his musketry; the first launches an attack which is repulsed by the energy of the second. Kyd allots three lines to each opponent: the first gives the identity of the officer, the second indicates the nature of the troops in his command, the third specifies the purpose of his mission.

And so with the rest of the description; group is pitted against group in symmetrical antagonism. Kyd has done more than 'straighten out' Grimald's contorted lines in 'The Death of Zoroas' on which he may have based his narrative (H. Baker, p. 77); he has nearly reimagined the scene. Instead of an impenetrable confusion, he visualises a battle of nearly heraldic formality. Even the description of a field strewn with the dead acquires an ordered clarity:

> On every side drop captains to the ground,
> And soldiers, some ill-maim'd, some slain outright:
> Here falls a body scinder'd from his head,
> There legs and arms lie bleeding on the grass,
> Mingled with weapons and unbowell'd steeds,
> That scattering overspread the purple plain.
>
> (I. ii. 57)

There is no gainsaying the total effect of horror, but it is a controlled and lucid horror, achieved by the patient laying on of apposite details, like bricks, usually in pairs: first the captains, then the soldiers; first the maimed, then the slain; first the decapitated bodies, then the disembodied limbs; first the weapons, then the steeds. Turmoil and hubbub are rendered with a certain pictorial sharpness of outline by the antithetic rhetoric, as in a tapestry, while the free play of detail helps keep the symmetries unobtrusive.

After the battle the antitheses and oppositions surge more insistently into view, and begin to mesh more closely with the stage action. As the king finishes hearing the reports from the campaign, the victorious Spanish army crosses the stage, with Balthazar led between Lorenzo and Horatio. The two Spanish warriors, flanking their prisoner, provide a visual image of their rivalry for the honour of his capture. The king inquires into the circumstances of the capture:

> KING.   But tell me, for their holding makes me doubt,
>   To which of these twain art thou prisoner?
> LORENZO.   To me, my liege.
> HORATIO.   To me, my sovereign.
> LORENZO.   This hand first took his courser by the reins.
> HORATIO.   But first my hand did put him from his horse.
> LORENZO.   I seiz'd his weapon and enjoy'd it first.
> HORATIO.   But first I forc'd him lay his weapons down.
> KING.   Let go his arm, upon our privilege.
>
> (I. ii. 152)

The plot here involves a symmetrical antagonism, mimed simultaneously in the language and in the stage action. At the king's bidding, the Spanish knights release their captive, who now explains his position for himself:

> KING.   Say, worthy prince, to whether didst thou yield?
> BALTHAZAR.   To him in courtesy, to this perforce:
>   He spake me fair, this other gave me strokes:
>   He promis'd life, this other threaten'd death:
>   He wan my love, this other conquer'd me:
>   And truth to say I yield myself to both.
>
> (I. ii. 160)

Again the antitheses in the language are mirrored by the antithetic gestures with which Balthazar designates his captors, as he particularises by turns their treatment of him. His final line, surprisingly, collapses the vivid contrast back into a noncommittal unity. Here we meet one of the perils of rhetoric. It is true that Balthazar is merely answering the king's question, and that he has, in fact, surrendered to both Horatio and Lorenzo. It hardly follows, however, from the opposition between courteous and peremptory treatment elaborated in the first four lines, that he should end by casually abandoning the distinction. The sharply registered preference for the one who offered gentle usage cannot be so limply disowned without making retrospective nonsense of the rest of the speech. Kyd's penchant for the reconciliation of opposites seems to have led him to enfeeble the force of his own disjunction at a crucial moment. And this leads to the further suspicion that the odd ascription of harsh behaviour to Horatio and generous behaviour to Lorenzo springs itself from the passion for disjunctions.

The king next mediates the contention by awarding Balthazar's weapon and horse to Lorenzo, but his ransom to Horatio; the custody of him to Lorenzo, but his armour to Horatio. All claims are scrupulously adjudicated, both the rights and rewards arising from the combat itself, and the larger issues arising from the unequal social rank of the rivals. The latter, in fact, interfere with the for-

mer, and prevent true justice; the king awards the armour to Horatio as a compensation for depriving him of the prisoner himself.
The competing claims of the two knights, then, can be regulated
only in part, even by a king renowned for his equity. When conflicts
arise in a situation more resistant to justice, such as the rivalry
between Horatio and Balthazar for the favours of Bel-imperia, tragedy ensues, and justice flees to heaven.

For the moment, however, justice is done as it was in Hades:
competing extremes are moderated by compromise. The patterning
in the language, clearly, is more than a perfunctory verbal manœuvre;
it reflects the patterning in the plot, and helps to delineate it. In
the episodes leading up to the murder, the patterns become more
pronounced; Kyd uses them to reinforce the relationships on the
stage, to intensify the mood, and to underline the varying temper-
aments of the *dramatis personae*. When Bel-imperia finishes her
first frank avowal of love to Horatio in II. ii, our attention shifts to
Lorenzo and Balthazar, hidden, by pre-arrangement, above, to spy
on the lovers:

> BALTHAZAR.   O sleep mine eyes, see not my love profan'd,
>   Be deaf my ears, hear not my discontent,
>   Die heart, another joys what thou deserv'st.
> LORENZO.   Watch still mine eyes, to see this love disjoin'd,
>   Hear still mine ears, to hear them both lament,
>   Live heart, to joy at fond Horatio's fall.
>
> (II. ii. 18)

Balthazar's speech and Lorenzo's belong to the kind of 'conceited
verse' that Fraunce praised in Sidney, where the same grammatical
scheme recurs a number of times in sequence, with its key words—
subject, verb, object—shifted like interchangeable blocks. Each
speaker pursues a formula of systematic invocation, directing his
eyes, ears and heart in turn to react to love, to sorrow, and to joy.
But the two speeches are also antithetical, and Lorenzo's forms an
answer to Balthazar's. Balthazar invites his faculties to abandon
their function, to wrap him in insensibility and death. Lorenzo, following the same grammatical scheme, instructs *his* senses to redou-
ble their activity. The first speech expresses defeatism and passivity,
the second violence and aggression; so that while the symmetry
reflects the close partnership between the two eavesdroppers, the
antitheses reflect the contrast in their dispositions, the self-abandon
of the one and the vindictive energy of the other.

These speeches, perhaps, should be spoken like incantations.
During the speaking of them, there is nothing for Horatio and Bel-
imperia to do but remain silent and motionless below. When they
resume their interrupted duet, Kyd capitalises brilliantly on the

interval of enforced silence. Bel-imperia is still waiting for an answer to her declaration of love; Horatio is still lost in his own thoughts.

> BEL-IMPERIA.   Why stands Horatio speechless all this while?
> HORATIO.   The less I speak, the more I meditate.
> BEL-IMPERIA.   But whereon dost thou chiefly meditate?
> HORATIO.   On dangers past, and pleasures to ensue.
> BALTHAZAR.   On pleasures past, and dangers to ensue.
> BEL-IMPERIA.   What dangers and what pleasures dost thou
>   mean?
> HORATIO.   Dangers of war, and pleasures of our love.
> LORENZO.   Dangers of death, but pleasures none at all.
> BEL-IMPERIA.   Let dangers go, thy war shall be with me.
>   (II. ii. 24)

Even more strikingly than before, the patterned language here, with its intricacies of repetition and echo, translates itself into stage rhetoric. Balthazar and Lorenzo, unseen, unheard, give the reply to Horatio and Bel-imperia, grimly converting each cheerful presage into a menacing one. The repetitions bind the two levels of the stage together into a unity, and charge the love dialogue with heavy irony. Caught up as we are in the vigorous rhythm of the patterning, we scarcely notice such blemishes as the fatuousness of Bel-imperia's question, 'What dangers and what pleasures dost thou mean?'

In the wooing scene in the arbour, the intimate reciprocity between word and stage gesture becomes even closer:

> BEL-IMPERIA.   If I be Venus, thou must needs be Mars,
>   And where Mars reigneth there must needs be wars.
> HORATIO.   Then thus begin our wars: put forth thy hand,
>   That it may combat with my ruder hand.
> BEL-IMPERIA.   Set forth thy foot to try the push of mine.
> HORATIO.   But first my looks shall combat against thine.
> BEL-IMPERIA.   Then ward thyself, I dart this kiss at thee.
> HORATIO.   Thus I retort the dart thou threw'st at me.
> BEL-IMPERIA.   Nay then, to gain the glory of the field,
>   My twining arms shall yoke and make thee yield.
> HORATIO.   Nay then, my arms are large and strong withal:
>   Thus elms by vines are compass'd till they fall.
> BEL-IMPERIA.   O let me go, for in my troubled eyes
>   Now may'st thou read that life in passion dies.
> HORATIO.   O stay awhile and I will die with thee,
>   So shalt thou yield and yet have conquer'd me.
>   (II. iv. 34)

Here the language dictates physical gesture nearly line by line; the governing analogy between love and war completes itself in a series of bodily movements. The hand, the foot, the lips, the glance of each lover advance with ceremonious gravity, to be parried by their counterparts from the other, just as the sallies of the Portingale troops were repulsed by the counter-assaults of the Spaniards. As with infernal justice, as with the campaign between the neighbouring kingdoms, as with the dispute over the capture of Balthazar, initial oppositions are here more than ready to merge into a dialectal unity, when the killers rush in with drawn swords and rend the fabric of reconciliation for good. Open antagonisms can be mediated and compromised; stealth cannot. From this point on the dialectic retreats into the inner spirit of Hieronimo, as he wrestles to reconcile his impulse toward revenge with the sanctions against it.

In all these cases we find Kyd using imaginatively and incisively the same rhetorical materials used so inanely and ineffectively by Mundy and the author of *The Rare Triumphs*. Sometimes, however, the use of the figures involves Kyd in the sort of decorative writing in which the decorativeness obscures narrative clarity instead of sustaining it. Balthazar's celebrated Euphuistic lament in II. i, though it establishes him as a despairing Petrarchan wooer, does so at some strain to the known facts of the plot; most of its details have the air of having been improvised hastily, and none too accurately, for the occasion. A more damaging illogicality creeps into the symmetrical flourish at the end of the same scene, when Balthazar expresses his fury with Horatio:

> I think Horatio be my destin'd plague:
> First in his hand he brandished a sword,
> And with that sword he fiercely waged war,
> And in that war he gave me dangerous wounds,
> And by those wounds he forced me to yield,
> And by my yielding I became his slave.
> Now in his mouth he carries pleasing words,
> Which pleasing words do harbour sweet conceits,
> Which sweet conceits are lim'd with sly deceits,
> Which sly deceits smooth Bel-imperia's ears,
> And through her ears dive down into her heart,
> And in her heart set him where I should stand.
> Thus hath he ta'en my body by his force,
> And now by sleight would captivate my soul: . . .
>   (II. i. 118)

It is of at least passing interest to notice Kyd's especial fondness for this figure of climax, or 'Marching figure', as Puttenham terms it (p. 208). Its propulsive forward motion makes it in a sense intrinsically dramatic, lends it particular power to create sequences of cause and effect. Kyd ordinarily uses it as he does here, to forge a chain in which A brings about B brings about C, each effect becoming in turn a new cause. His partiality to the figure reflects the causality ingrained in his thinking, his penchant for intrigue and concern for motivation, and the densely sequential texture of his language in general.

A chain, however, is no stronger than its weakest link, and the present ladder contains a number of shaky rungs, offences against the facts of Kyd's own story. We know that Horatio gave no dangerous wounds to Balthazar. Had he done so, we should have heard about them earlier, and, strictly speaking, they would have made it impossible for Balthazar to appear before the king to explain the circumstances of his capture. If Horatio did not dangerously wound Balthazar, by the same token he did not, with those wounds, force Balthazar to yield. And least of all did he, by the alleged wounds, make Balthazar his 'slave'; he has not even acquired nominal custody, much less privilege of restraint over him.

Of the second half of the dyptych, lines 124–9 may be allowed as the resentful fantasies of an envious rival, though we may notice that they are founded on mere conjecture; Balthazar has no information about what prompted Bel-imperial to love Horatio. It is the concluding couplet, however, that effects a final divorce between sound and sense: 'Thus hath he ta'en my body by his force, / And now by sleight would captivate my soul'. Here the pressure of the antithetic patterning requires attributing 'sleight' to Horatio in his wooing, to match the 'force' of his soldiership, and it requires, even more bizarrely, charging him with the aim of enslaving Balthazar's 'soul', to correspond to his previous capture of his 'body'. At the moment of the ringing final rhyme on 'soul', the rhetorical pattern thus reaches its satisfying auricular conclusion, and the plain prose sense of the speech, as a reflection of the humble facts of the narrative, collapses into absurdity.

The failure here, if it is not to be ascribed to a deliberate attempt to show Balthazar as the victim of his own words, as I think it is not, illustrates the tendency of figural rhetoric to strew hidden reefs in the path of its own smooth sailing. The figures develop an impetus of their own, which can carry them athwart the dramatic current as well as along with it. The danger lies not, as an older school of critics might have said, in the fact that 'passion runs not after' exact schemes and tropical symmetries, but in the tendency of the schemes and symmetries to coerce thought. They bend somewhat reluctantly to quick shifts in feeling; they pursue a statelier, more galleon-like course; they tend to promote an effect of ritualized abstraction, so that it takes a sure hand to keep them obedient to all the particulars of a given dramatic context. Perhaps there is some justice in Moody Prior's charge that 'ostentatiously rhetorical art of any sort endows almost any sentiments with an academic, generalised quality' (p. 51).

Kyd is nevertheless often strikingly successful in projecting even extreme emotion within the bristling geometry of the figures. Hieronimo's much parodied outburst in III. ii brings to the stage, for a moment of clamorous passion, a scheme derived ultimately from Petrarch, which Sidney had already used, or would shortly use, in *Astrophil and Stella*:

> O teares, no teares, but raine from beautie's skies,
>   Making those Lillies and those Roses grow,
>   Which ay most faire, now more then most faire show,
> While gracefull pitty beauty beautifies.
> O honied sighs, which from that breast do rise,
>
>   O plaints conserv'd in such a sugred phraise,
>   That eloquence it selfe envies your praise,
> While sobd out words a perfect Musike give.
>   Such teares, sighs, plaints, no sorrow is, but joy:
>   Or if such heavenly signes must prove annoy,
> All mirth farewell, let me in sorrow live.
>   (*Poems*, ed. W. A. Ringler (1962), p. 231)

Sidney's use of the figure creates a sense of majestic calm. Each quatrain, through a spacious suspension, elaborates on one of the beloved's attributes of sorrow—her tears, her sighs, her plaints—and all three are made to converge at length under the sign of joy rather than sorrow. The theme of the poem is the transformation of apparent sorrow into pleasure through the beloved's beauty. Kyd, by packing the three successive apostrophes into three successive lines, and stressing the correspondences between them, achieves an effect of swollen passion breaking loose:

> O eyes, no eyes, but fountains fraught with tears;
> O life, no life, but lively form of death;
> O world, no world, but mass of public wrongs,
> Confus'd and fill'd with murder and misdeeds;
> O sacred heavens! If this unhallow'd deed . . .
>   (III. ii. 1)

In Sidney, the lady's manifestations of sorrow remain on the same level of importance and intensity; they do not evolve, except perhaps in the direction of increasing articulateness. Kyd proceeds climactically, through circles of widening significance: eyes, life, world, heavens—organ, organism, social milieu, cosmos. The theme is the progressive perversion of all order and health into disease and disorder through the murder of Horatio. Each of the first three members of the series represents a realm felt to be deranged by the murder. In the case of the final realm, the heavens, the question is left open—left, indeed, for the heavens themselves to answer.

Hieronimo's sense of cosmic dislocation leads him to a second series, in which he enumerates forces that spur him to revenge: the night, the ugly fiends, the cloudy day. Finally, in a recapitulation—what Puttenham would term a 'collection'—of the sort adopted by Sidney in line 12 of his sonnet, Hieronimo gathers together all the phenomena he has discoursed upon, and appeals to them for aid in the discovery of the identities of his son's killers:

> Eyes, life, world, heavens, hell, night, and day,
> See, search, shew, send, some man, some mean, that may—
> (III. ii. 22)

At which point, the stage direction informs us, 'A letter falleth.' Hieronimo's recapitulation thus serves a dramatic as well as a rhetorical purpose. It constitutes a plea for action, and it leads up to a significant bit of stage business, the dropping of Bel-imperia's letter with its disclosure about the murderers. What is remarkable is that Kyd has worked out the schematism of the speech with a high degree of precision—no rhetorical treatise of the day would have had to apologise for offering it in illustration of the figures it uses—yet with enough flexibility in detail, especially prosodic detail, to make it convincing as an expression of Hieronimo's grief. What Elizabethan audiences found exciting and memorable in the language of *The Spanish Tragedy* was precisely such moments of high artifice as these. The numerous parodies of Hieronimo's lament, and of Balthazar's complaints, testify to the auricular impact of Kyd's theatrical tropes—testify, that is, to the pleasures of rhetoric, as well as, by their scorn, to its perils.

One problem faced by the bereaved Hieronimo throughout is how to find adequate expression for his feelings. When we meet him first, after the battle in Act I, he only with difficulty refrains from pleading his son's cause against Lorenzo. He refrains not out of any mistrust of his own eloquence, but because the king's well-known wisdom makes eloquence unnecessary; the king can be counted on to decide justly. Despite its evident scrupulosity, however, the king's justice, bending as it does to the pressure of the world's prejudices, inspires little confidence. Hieronimo, along with the rest, accepts it without protest, but it is not long before he is plunged into a situation in which he can find neither justice nor relief for his anguished feelings. The latter, indeed, becomes as cardinal a necessity as the former, and a main spur to revenge; revenge alone can provide a satisfactory outlet for his grief and outrage. 'Where shall I run to breathe abroad my woes', he cries, entering distractedly shortly after the murder,

> My woes, whose weight hath wearied the earth?
> Or mine exclaims, that have surcharg'd the air
> With ceaseless plaints for my deceased son?
> (III. vii. 1)

The immensity of Hieronimo's desolation demands cosmic scope for its utterance. Even his adjutants, the compassionate winds, who have vexed nature in his behalf, have wrought too feebly, for 'still tormented is my tortur'd soul/With broken sighs and restless passions'. Words, even when they denote extremest woe, remain words. Even when reinforced by the eloquence of the blustering winds, verbal plaints remain insufficient to express the fullness of grief. Still less can they bring about justice or revenge. Words, indeed, as Hieronimo comes to feel, are 'unfruitful', and yet, they are all he has.

> But wherefore waste I mine unfruitful words,
> When naught but blood will satisfy my woes?
> I will go plain me to my lord the king,
> And cry aloud for justice through the court,
> Wearing the flints with these my wither'd feet,
> And either purchase justice by entreats
> Or tire them all with my revenging threats.
>
> (III. vii. 67)

If language cannot be made to relieve his feelings, or accomplish justice, at least it can be turned into a weapon of harassment, and used to disturb the peace of mind of his foes.

The fact that his cries go unheard—partly through his own imprudence, partly through Lorenzo's cunning—deepens Hieronimo's skepticism toward the efficacy of speech. The decision to revenge, which crystallises in the *Vindicta mihi* soliloquy (III. xiii. 1), carries with it the realisation that henceforth, in order to combat those who have violated the natural current between speech and feeling, he must tamper with it himself. Having been driven, by abnormal circumstances, to adopt a course of action abhorrent to him, he must embrace the unnatural methods that will enable him to accomplish his purpose. He must enjoin his eye to 'observation', and his tongue. 'To milder speeches than [his] spirit affords' (III. xiii. 40). From this moment on, he must turn language into something opaque and deceptive, instead of revelatory and transparent.

The apparition of Don Bazulto, the forlorn *senex* who stands mutely by at the sessions, proffering the humble supplication for his murdered son, acquaints Hieronimo with a kind of silent eloquence that he recognises as more potent than mere speech. Convinced of the futility of spoken words, Don Bazulto refuses to give voice to his distress. Instead, he presents the supplication. Ink must 'bewray', he explains, what blood began; passion must be reduced to formal writ, to documentary petition, to visible emblem. As the writ serves Bazulto, so the bloody napkin dipped in Horatio's wounds serves Hieronimo, as a mute testimony or dumb significant, helping to express the inexpressible. The old man himself, returning to the stage to confront

Hieronimo alone, suddenly becomes an image in a hallucination, the ghost of Horatio, until Hieronimo awakens to the realisation that he is staring at a simulacrum of himself. The scene bears fresh witness to Kyd's power to make figured rhetoric convey intensity of feeling:

> Ay, now I know thee, now thou nam'st thy son,
> Thou art the lively image of my grief:
> Within thy face, my sorrows I may see.
> Thy eyes are gumm'd with tears, thy cheeks are wan,
> Thy forehead troubl'd, and thy mutt'ring lips
> Murmur sad words abruptly broken off,
> By force of windy sighs thy spirit breathes,
> And all this sorrow riseth for thy son:
> And selfsame sorrow feel I for my son.
>
> (III. xiii. 161)

Gazing at the old man gradually becomes, for Hieronimo, a process of self-discovery, an act of mirror-gazing. As on previous occasions, the patterned rhetoric participates deeply in the configuration of action: the anaphora, the repetitions, the near-identity of the two last lines, all express the growing identity felt by Hieronimo between himself and Bazulto. Bazulto is his semblable, as the audience already knows. The patterning in the language allows Hieronimo to make the discovery himself, as the two bereft old fathers stare hopelessly into each other's faces.

By this time, words scarcely avail Hieronimo at all, either as vehicles of woe, or vessels of truth. Like Lorenzo, he will henceforth keep his own counsel: '*pocas palabras*, mild as the lamb' becomes the motto (III. xiv. 118); a distrust of all language replaces his former fluent security with it. When asked to contribute some 'pleasing motion' to entertain the visiting Portingales, he answers with a bit of autobiography:

> When I was young, I gave my mind
> And plied myself to fruitless poetry:
> Which though it profit the professor naught,
> Yet is it passing pleasing to the world.
>
> (IV. i. 71)

Hieronimo may arraign the fruitlessness of poetry out of bitter experience. His skill has in fact already diverted the court once before, in the show of knights and scutcheons in Act I, but it has not enabled him to give proper utterance to his grief, or to secure justice, earthly, celestial or infernal. The play commanded for the visiting monarch will allow him, at last, to validate his poetical talent by translating it into action—reprehensible action, to be sure, but action none the less. For once, fruitless poetry will bear fruit.

And it will do so in terms suitable both to the distracted poet and to the ceremonious audience. Suitable to the distracted poet in being an incomprehensible medley of tongues, expressive of the chaos in Hieronimo's spirit; suitable to the court in being '*tragedia cothur-nata*, fitting kings' (IV. i. 160)—appropriate in stateliness and style to the pompous occasion it is intended to honour.

In view of the sustained emphasis in *The Spanish Tragedy* on ver-bal artifice, it seems reasonable to think that the original audience did indeed hear the play within a play spoken 'in sundry languages'. An audience that had already listened to various miscellaneous scraps of Latin, Italian, and Spanish in the course of the afternoon, including Hieronimo's 14-line dirge recited over the bleeding body of Horatio, would not have been likely to balk at the brief polyglot interlude of *Soliman and Perseda*. Even if the original script, in its sundry languages, ran to the same length as its English translation, the plot had already been fully explained in advance; it would twice be interrupted for further explanation while in progress, would be interrupted a third time for a spectacular stabbing and was capable of being mimed vividly throughout so as to heighten and clarify its essential gestures.[2]

The effect, perhaps, would have been to suggest the extremes to which language can evolve, the lengths to which verbal ingenuity can be carried and how unintelligible words can become when they lose their moorings in the realities they are meant to express. The jabber-ing in four languages turns the whole phenomenon of speech under a strange phosphorescent glare, revealing it as a kind of disembodied incantation, a surrealistic dance of abstractions, divorced from roots in lived existence. Hieronimo's experience has involved a progressive alienation of language, a breakdown of the links between rhetoric

---

2. The presence of a puzzling note from the printer at IV. iv. 10, to the effect that the playlet would be '*set down in English . . . for the easier understanding to every, public reader*,' together with some other oddities of this scene, have led editors to suspect textual corruption in this portion of the play. Edwards (pp. xxxiii–xl) advances an inge-nious and intricate hypothesis concerning the copy in an attempt to account for the difficulties: (1) In order to shorten *The Spanish Tragedy* for performance, Kyd revised the original ending by striking out the English playlet and substituting a pantomime with a few snatches of gibberish ('*sundry languages*'). But the original ending had already been printed in the first edition of the play, now lost, (2) The printer of the extant 1592 edition, when setting up this part of the play, had recourse both to the earlier printed text and to Kyd's manuscript revision. Confused, he failed to see that he was dealing with alternate versions of the same scene, and so printed them as successive episodes, but did recognise the discrepancy between Hieronimo's promise of sundry languages and the actual English provided in the earlier text, and so inserted his note to explain the anomaly.

My own view, which concurs generally with that of S. F. Johnson, 'The Spanish Trag-edy, or Babylon Revisited', in *Essays on Shakespeare and Elizabethan Drama*, ed. R. Hos-ley (1963), is that the printer's note may he taken at face value, and that the finale of the play is essentially intelligible as it stands. Certain problems remain, chiefly the discrep-ancy between Hieronimo's speech of explanation to the court and his subsequent refusal to explain, coupled with references to a mysterious 'vow' he has made, but it is doubtful whether the problems require a hypothesis so drastic as that of Edwards.

and reality. To this alienation the playlet forms a fitting climax. It acts out the insubstantiality of words, sets them at loggerheads with motives and at cross-purposes with each other, shows them as the fantasms they threaten to become, and cancels them out, finally, by a stroke of the sword. The disclosure of Horatio's mutilated body provides a more devastating climax, a silent spectacle of woe for which words serve humbly as interpreters again:

> See here my show, look on this spectacle:
> Here lay my hope, and here my hope hath end:
> Here lay my heart, and here my heart was slain:
> Here lay my treasure, here my treasure lost:
> Here lay my bliss, and here my bliss bereft:
> But hope, heart, treasure, joy and bliss,
> All fled, fail'd, died, yea, all decay'd with this.
>   (IV. iv. 89)

The patterned litany, with its insistent anaphora on the adverb 'here', pins us relentlessly to this moment in time and this point in space. It enforces repeatedly on us the reality of the visible, palpable fact and so, momentarily, restores the wholeness of the fractured image.

Having thus published to the world what heretofore he confided only to the winds, the night, and the churlish heavens, Hieronimo ends with the declared determination to 'as resolute conclude his part / As any of the actors gone before'. When, at the king's command, the guards bar his flight, he concludes his long agony by biting out his tongue. The final lunatic gesture betrays the final despair at the uselessness of talk, the berserk resolve to have done with language forever. And not spoken language only—the knife he is given to mend his pen he plunges into his heart; the last instrument available to facilitate expression he uses savagely to annul all further possibility of expression.

The Spanish Tragedy, then, with its thickets of figural rhetoric, is also to some degree a critique of rhetoric, an assessment of the limits of impassioned speech. We might term it a theatrical digression on a familiar Senecan text: *Curae leves loquuntur; ingentes stupent.* Language, including the patterned language borrowed from the sonneteers, proves able to meet the expressive requirements of epic narration in Act I, and the portrayals of love and hate in Act II. With the murder of Horatio, the world's equilibrium is upset; justice goes awry, and language with it. An unnatural state of divorce sets in between thought and word, word and deed; speech deteriorates as an instrument of reality and an agent of truth. In the distracted climax, it horribly apes the confusions of the world, sending them back magnified and further deformed as from a distorting mirror. The Babel-Babylon playlet does not so much reflect the visible ceremony of the Spanish court as its inner ethical chaos.

Action, in nondramatic poetry, remains of necessity verbal action. The poet, rebuffed by his mistress or the world, withdraws, perhaps, into frustration, or comes to terms with his plight rhetorically—through argument or retort, through objurgation, defiance, or self-inflicted melancholy. In the drama, words must be affirmed or denied by other acts—coupled with blows, or mingled with kisses. Under normal conditions, words and acts complete and complement each other: a half-angry, half-submissive Balthazar displays both anger and submissiveness to his captors and his captor king, and yields himself to both; a proud Hieronimo beguiles the triumphant court with vignettes of an earlier epoch when England invaded the Iberian peninsula. When the healthy reciprocity between words and acts is fractured, they develop independent and dangerous lives of their own; instead of confirming and corroborating each other, they delude and destroy. When the divorce becomes chronic, it leads, ultimately, to the splintering, shattering finale of *The Spanish Tragedy*, in which all communication breaks down, the community collapses in horror, and the stage is left littered with silent corpses for whom there is nearly no-one alive to mourn.

*   *   *

BIBLIOGRAPHY

Moody E. Prior. *The Language of Tragedy.* New York: Columbia University Press, 1947.

George Puttenham. *The Arte of English Poesie*, London, 1589.

Thomas Watson. *Hekatompathia.* London, 1582.

Thomas Wilson. *The Art of Rhetoric.* Ed. G. H. Mair. Oxford: Clarendon Press, 1909.

Metadramatic Readings

DONNA B. HAMILTON

From *The Spanish Tragedy*: A Speaking Picture[†]

Work on *The Spanish Tragedy* has been primarily a process of learning from and then revising the conclusions which Fredson Bowers reached in *Elizabethan Revenge Tragedy*. Bowers' questioning of the relation of the Ghost-Revenge frame to the rest of the play, and his assertion that Hieronimo becomes an unsympathetic villain-revenger, remain the central issues with which subsequent interpretations grapple.[1] In those recent studies which have most successfully gone beyond Bowers' conclusions, the chief advance has come about largely as a result of an interest in the play's reiterative structure, an approach which permits us to adjust our focus away from revenge as the core of the plot and direct it to the theme of justice.[2] In pointing out how the actions within the play mirror each other ironically, structural studies have seized upon the devices of the Ghost-Revenge frame and the play-within-the-play as the central symbols through which the structure and subsequently the meaning are made clear. Two frequent assumptions of those who discuss these devices are: (1) that the play incorporates three audiences (we in the theater, Andrea and Revenge, and the court audience at Hieronimo's play) on various levels of awareness; and (2) that there are as many authors and plays as there are audiences, the authors being Kyd, Revenge,

† From "*The Spanish Tragedy*: A Speaking Picture" by Donna B. Hamilton as it appeared in *English Literary Renaissance* 4 (1974): 203–17. Reprinted by permission of John Wiley and Sons.
1. *Elizabethan Revenge Tragedy* (Princeton, 1940), pp. 68–71, 77–82.
2. See Philip Edwards, ed., *The Spanish Tragedy* (London, 1959), pp. l-lxi; S. F. Johnson, "*The Spanish Tragedy*, or Babylon Revisited," *Essays on Shakespeare and Elizabethan Drama in Honor of Hardin Craig*, ed. Richard Hosley (Columbia, Mo., 1962), pp. 23–36; G. K. Hunter, "Ironies of Justice in *The Spanish Tragedy*," *Renaissance Drama*, 8 (1965), 89–104; Ejner J. Jensen, "Kyd's *Spanish Tragedy*: The Play Explains Itself," *JEGP*, 64 (1965), 7–16; Arthur Freeman, *Thomas Kyd: Facts and Problems* (London, 1967), pp. 80–101; and Peter B. Murray, *Thomas Kyd* (New York, 1969), pp. 28–54.

and Hieronimo.[3] As a refinement of this approach, I suggest that there are only two authors, Kyd and Hieronimo, and that Revenge does not direct or control anything, but represents the element of disorder and destruction that operates in the affairs of mortal men. The following analysis proposes that grasping the differences between the role of Revenge and the role of Hieronimo not only offers another solution to the objections Bowers initially raised but, more importantly, helps us to concentrate on Kyd's perception of the function of the poet and the relationship of art to life.

In *The Spanish Tragedy*, Kyd provides England with her first major tragedy, as well as with one of the first defenses of the play as an art form. However, the play undertakes its defense more along distinctly Aristotelian than broadly Horatian lines, for in acknowledging the profit which man receives from art, its concern is more specifically with art as an experience which helps man come to terms with the conditions of his world than with art as an instrument for morality.[4] Rather than focusing on the teaching of what it is to be or not to be a good man in a flawed world, the play explores what kinds of responses can make it possible for man to endure the pain and suffering which such a world has in store. The focal point of this exploration is Hieronimo. Once he recognizes that gods and institutions do not exert an absolute control over man's destiny, his search for a meaningful response leads him to art, which, by mirroring his experiences, also helps him to learn their universal quality, a lesson which gives him some relief from his torment. Throughout Hieronimo's struggle to select the best form in which to cast his perceptions, Kyd seems to be using the Renaissance notion of poetry as a speaking picture for the touchstone against which to judge Hieronimo's success. As Hieronimo moves from the oratory of the soliloquies, to painting (in the Painter addition), to metaphor and song in the Bazulto scene, and finally to the playlet of the last scene, the conclusion inevitably emerges that drama is the form most capable of expressing the human experience because it is both *poesis* and *pictura*, and has, as well, real sound and action.[5]

3. Besides the essays listed in n. 2, see also the interesting analyses of Barry B. Adams, "The Audiences of *The Spanish Tragedy*," *JEGP*, 68 (1969), 221–36; Harriett Hawkins, "Fabulous Counterfeits: Dramatic Construction and Dramatic Perspectives in *The Spanish Tragedy, A Midsummer Night's Dream*, and *The Tempest*," *Shakespeare Studies*, 6 (1970), 51–65; and Scott McMillin, "The Figure of Silence in *The Spanish Tragedy*," *ELH*, 39 (1972), 27–48.
4. For a discussion of Renaissance attempts to deny Aristotle's distinctiveness and make him conform to the Horatian mainstream of literary criticism, see Marvin Herrick, *The Fusion of Horatian and Aristotelian Literary Criticism 1531–1555*, Illinois Studies in Language and Literature, 32 (1946), 39–47.
5. For the Renaissance paragone between *poesis* and *pictura* and some comments on the place of drama in this contest, see Jean Hagstrum, *The Sister Arts* (Chicago, 1958), pp. 57–92; D. J. Gordon, "Poet and Architect: The Intellectual Setting of the Quarrel Between Ben Jonson and Inigo Jones," *Journal of the Warburg and Courtauld Institutes*, 12 (1949), 152–78; William S. Heckscher, "Shakespeare in His Relationship to the

While Hieronimo's experiences will occupy most of this discussion, it is necessary to reconsider first the development of the frame, so that the dependency of these two parts can be clarified. For Kyd gives credibility to Hieronimo's judgment of his situation, and significance to his search for order and relief through artistic responses, by placing his story within the frame of Andrea and Revenge, where the audience can witness man-made chaos obtusely mistaken for divinely ordained events.

In the frame episode, Andrea, who, I suggest, will change during the course of the play, searches in a thoroughly casual and unworried manner for a resting place in the underworld. Because he has no opinion at this point about what his future either will be or should be, his narrative carries no indication that revenge might be in order. When the three judges of the dead are unable to agree on his resting place, Minos sends him to Pluto. With smiling ease and a playful spirit, Proserpine gains from Pluto the chance to name Andrea's future. Her decision to give him to Revenge is not prescriptive, but descriptive. She names what the future will be because she knows how men turn circumstances into chaos. We might compare the function of Kyd's frame to that of the gods that frame some Greek tragedies; in both cases the frames are universalizing agents which indicate that the main action of the play depicts general truths about man and life. In the words of H. D. F. Kitto, speaking of the gods in Sophocles' plays, they "typify what does happen rather than what 'ought' to happen" and therein suggest "the general balance of things."[6] Revenge is a name for those qualities in men which turn "their friendship into fell despite, / Their love to mortal hate, their day to night, / Their hope into despair, their peace to war, / Their joys to pain, their bliss to misery" (I.5.6–9).[7] In the course of the play hate, despair, war, pain, and misery do predominate over love, hope, peace, and bliss. The frame, then, universalizes this condition by the presence of Revenge, but it also presents in the figure of Andrea one who is as unaware as are his earthly counterparts that Revenge is not a law prescribed or insisted upon by the gods, but a pattern in life maintained by human error. Andrea's attitude in the frame typifies the habits of thought and behavior which lead characters in the main action to assume that the plans they make, the orders they give, and even the revenges they require are somehow predetermined and justified by forces beyond themselves.

Visual Arts: A Study in Paradox," *RORD*, 13–14 (1970–71), 5–71; John M. Steadman, "Iconography and Renaissance Drama: Ethical and Mythological Themes," *RORD*, 13–14 (1970–71), 73–122; and Renesselaer W. Lee, *Ut Pictura Poesis: The Humanistic Theory of Painting* (New York, 1967).
6. *Form and Meaning in Drama* (London, 1956), p. 74.
7. All quotations of *The Spanish Tragedy* are from Edwards' edition.

Casual at the outset, Andrea becomes increasingly involved emotionally as the action progresses and his hopes do not materialize. Instead of seeing justice work itself out through the destruction of Balthazar, he sees "league, and love, and banqueting" (1.5.4) among those he now regards as his enemies. Then he observes Horatio slain and with this atrocity the "abuse" of "fair Bel-imperia" (II.6.3–4). Revenge's reply to Andrea's distress, "Thou talk'st of harvest when the corn is green" (II.6.7), emphasizes that events come to their fruition according to nature, implying that in this life it is as natural for Horatio and Bel-imperia to be slain as it is for Balthazar. Again the issue is what is, not what ought to be.

That Andrea still does not understand and persists in his notion that Revenge is prescribing and controlling events becomes entirely clear in the fourth Chorus. Andrea, having just witnessed the reconciliation of Hieronimo and Lorenzo, fails to recognize that the reunion is merely a "device" to placate those suspicious that Lorenzo has wronged Hieronimo. Blaming the sleeping Revenge for this further travesty of justice, Andrea calls upon him to resume control:

> Hieronimo with Lorenzo is join'd in league
> And intercepts our passage to revenge:
> Awake, Revenge, or we are woe-begone! (III.15.15–17)

Revenge's reply, "Thus worldlings ground, what they have dream'd, upon," categorizes the insubstantiality of Andrea's interpretation both of Hieronimo and Lorenzo's reconciliation and of Revenge's relationship to events. When Revenge explains, "though I sleep, / Yet is my mood soliciting their souls," he is speaking again of himself as a quality in men, not himself as a creature in control of men. His final statement is the most clear and the most terrifying:

> Behold, Andrea, for an instance how
> Revenge hath slept, and then imagine thou
> What 'tis to be subject to destiny. (III.15.26–28)

To be subject to destiny, Revenge says, is merely to be at the mercy of whatever occurs. Destiny is what happens. The nuptial dumb show that enters simply states what the outcome will be, just as Proserpine did in the opening scene. Andrea, as uncomprehending as ever, assumes again that supernatural forces are in control and thanks Revenge and "those infernal powers / That will not tolerate a lover's woe." Andrea's assumption that an order is being imposed on events from without accounts for the pleasure he receives once the harvest has been reaped at the end of Act IV: "Ay, now my hopes have end in their effects, / When blood and sorrow finish my desires" (IV.5.1–2). The casualness of his first scene is a deliberate and shocking contrast to the bloodthirsty self-righteousness of his last scene. Misconstruing "what is" for "what ought to be" has led Andrea away from his initially relaxed acceptance of his death to a conviction that superhuman forces control men's fates, and finally to the claim that, once he knows the will of those powers, he has the right and power himself to execute their will and determine tragedies of others: "Then, Sweet Revenge, do this at my request, / Let me be judge, and doom them to unrest" (IV.5.29–30). The irony lies in the audience's awareness that the people in the central action have acted on their own initiative, prescribing dooms of others and thus predetermining their own, with the same confidence and self-righteousness which Andrea exhibits in the play's end. The degree to which he imitates their activities and grows to be identical to them, even when he is in a unique position to gain a superior perspective, spells man's doom, and names again revenge, misery, and pain as indeed man's "endless tragedy" (IV.5.48).

By juxtaposing what Revenge knows about life to what Andrea believes to be true, Kyd illustrates the ease with which man creates illusions that will give authority to his beliefs. In the main plot, the same point is made by allowing large patterns of error and duplicity to emerge alongside the characters' habitual proliferation of rituals and ceremonies. The Spanish General's praise of Heaven's justice as he narrates the battle, the Viceroy's lament for the dead Balthazar in which he blames "blind Fortune," the tribunal scene in which the King honors both Lorenzo and Horatio for bringing in Balthazar, the ongoing negotiations between the Spanish King and the Portuguese ambassador, the decision to achieve political unity by uniting Bel-imperia and Balthazar in marriage, Hieronimo's trial of Pedringano, Pedringano's scornful confidence that the box contains his pardon, even Horatio's explanation that Don Andrea fell because of the envy of "wrathful Nemesis," are all governed by the assumption that earthly events consistently reflect a preordained order. But the validity of this assumption in each instance is undercut as Kyd makes the audience aware of other dimensions of the truth. Only the audience knows that the various accounts of the battle conflict, that Balthazar is alive when Villuppo accuses Alexandro, that Lorenzo and Balthazar are conspiring against Horatio, that Lorenzo's order to Pedringano to kill Serberine will automatically lead to Pedringano's death too, and that Bel-imperia and Hieronimo have vowed to get revenge. The juxtaposition of ceremony and faith to conspiracy and error establishes an ironical structure through which the ceremonies are rendered ludicrous because they neither reflect reality nor have any power to produce a desirable situation. They merely film the ulcer that infects unseen. The central theme, that man creates his own chaos, with injustice as the result, is thus illustrated over and over, gathering its impact from the force of multiple repetitions of a single idea.[8] The numerous single incidents provide the audience with the information they need to grasp the general perception of human destiny which the play presents, and to discover that this view is identical to the one which is conveyed by the casual, knowing gods and the sleepy, patient Revenge.

That much in life is destructive or incomprehensible does not, however, alter man's compulsive search for order and meaning. Discerning a pattern, or even creating one by establishing a ceremony, simplifies, makes concrete, and provides direction for the variously complex and contradictory aspects of experience—and with this human impulse Kyd seems sympathetic. Alongside the ceremonies, strategies, and loyalties of family and state, Kyd places the artistic response as another variety of man's attempts to come to terms with experience through ritual and pattern. But he suggests that the artistic response can be superior to those other attempts by being honest and by admitting that man's grief is man-made while at the same time furnishing him with a means of making his own relief. Hieronimo is Kyd's vehicle for exploring the process and the validity of the artistic response. It is also through Hieronimo's involvement in art that we realize how very intimately the play is bound to Renaissance ideas of the means and purposes of art. As Hieronimo's distrust of authority grows, his inclination to impose his own order increases. In the act of imposing his own order, he is doing what the artist does; he is imitating nature. Just as a poem or a painting or a play gains in quality when it is informed with a profound truth, so too are Hieronimo's artistic experiences more valuable as he moves farther and farther away from the reiteration of his experiences and closer to an interpretation of those experiences, or, in other words, as he acts less like the historian and more like the poet. At his very best, in the concluding playlet, Hieronimo will come close indeed to fulfilling the Renaissance poetic ideal by creating, in Sidney's words, "a representing, counterfeiting, or figuring foorth: to speak metaphorically, a speaking picture."[9] Watching Hieronimo move toward that ideal, and then sadly fall short, is interesting and instructive.

By way of introducing the theme of art, Kyd implies all of these ideas in that scene in Act I where Hieronimo presents the masque that he has promised the King, "in honour of our guest, / To grace our banquet with some pompous jest" (1.4.136–37). That the

---

8. Hunter, p. 91, usefully compares the repetitive structure of Kyd's play to the "multiple unity" of the Tudor interlude, as discussed in David M. Bevington, *From* Mankind *to* Marlowe (Cambridge, Mass., 1962).

9. *Apologie for Poetrie, Elizabethan Critical Essays*, ed. G. Gregory Smith, I, (Oxford, 1904), 158. Gregory Smith, I, 386–87, n. 8, gives additional Renaissance references to the theme of poetry as a speaking picture. On imitation, see Madeleine Doran, *Endeavors of Art* (Madison, 1954). pp. 70–84, and Herrick, pp. 7–38.

sketches of various figures conquering Portugal and Spain are not historically accurate has frequently been noted. Arthur Freeman, responding to those who have disparaged Kyd for these "errors," suggests that Kyd is using here a tradition of popular history.[1] Surely Freeman is on the right track, and most likely Kyd intended that his audience recognize the choice of a popular account over a more objective chronicle history as a deliberate effort on Hieronimo's part to touch nature with art so that it would be more useful. Hieronimo is doing what Sidney says a poet must do and what a historian is incapable of doing:

> But if the question be for your owne use and learning, whether it be better to have it set downe as it should be, or as it was, then certainely is more doctrinable the fained *Cirus* in *Xenophon* then the true *Cyrus* in *Justine*, and the fayned *Aeneas* in *Virgil* then the right *Aeneas* in *Dares Phrigius*. As to a Lady that desired to fashion her countenance to the best grace, a Painter should more benefite her to portraite a most sweet face, wryting *Canidia* upon it, then to paynt *Canidia* as she was, who, *Horace* sweareth, was foule and ill favoured.
>
> If the Poet doe his part a-right, he will shew you in *Tantalus*, *Atreus*, and such like, nothing that is not to be shunned; in *Cyrus, Aeneas, Ulisses*, each thing to be followed; where the Historian, bound to tell things as things were, cannot be liberall (without hee will be poeticall) of a perfect patterne.[2]

By suggesting the possibilities that Portugal might be subject to a more formidable enemy than Spain and that Spain might also suffer a defeat, the masque places the immediate situation of Portuguese defeat and Spanish victory into a perspective which mitigates both the Portuguese shame and the smug Spanish confidence. The presentation of carefully shaped examples allows the more general, universal notion to emerge that Portugal and Spain are both vulnerable and can both benefit from unity. The aesthetic experience has clarified the real life situation, and the effect of the experience is a combination of comfort and pleasure. As the King puts it, "My lord of Portingale, by this you see / That which may comfort both your king and you, / And make your late discomfort seem the less" (I.4. 147–49), and he later adds, "Hieronimo, I drink to thee for this device, / Which hath pleas'd both the Ambassador and me" (I.4.173). The wedding plans which follow are an effort to profit from what has been learned. Although their effort fails because it is at the mercy of Bel-imperia's and Hieronimo's revenges, which are set in motion against it, yet the masque remains a significant introduction to the

1. Freeman, pp. 55–56.
2. *ECE*, I, 168.

way the play and Hieronimo conceive of art as Nature's mirror, not merely reflecting but also transmuting and organizing the image.

Hieronimo's masque has revealed his wisdom as a diplomat, but it will prove much more difficult for him to achieve a like perspective and a like comfort when he experiences a personal crisis. From the time he discovers Horatio dead until the end of the play, his needs are twofold, to punish the murderers and to find some means of relieving his unbearable grief:

> Here Isabella, help me to lament,
> For sighs are stopp'd, and all my tears are spent.
> . . . . . .
> To know the author were some ease of grief,
> For in revenge my heart would find relief. (ii.5.36–37; 40–41)

Although he has spent his time as chief judiciary providing order and justice for others, no person or power will provide the same service for him when he is in need. Consequently, his determination to get the justice of heaven or earth to avenge Horatio's murder is accompanied by an increasing sense that any salve to the wound he has suffered must come from himself. Much of the remaining action of the play involves his trial-and-error search for such comfort and relief.

In the next scene the elaborate form of the "O eyes, no eyes, but fountains fraught with tears" soliloquy conveys Hieronimo's effort to organize his emotions and to externalize his grief by verbalizing it. Clemen's important analysis of the first half of the soliloquy reveals its "mathematical exactness":

> It opens with three apostrophes, all three identical in syntax and structure and all three at once turned into negatives, the whole sequence broadening out from what is of close personal concern to the speaker ("eies," "life") to the more comprehensive conception of the "world"; thence the speech proceeds to a further apostrophe, "O sacred heauens", an invocation to the highest of all abstractions which is differentiated from the preceding apostrophes by the epithet ("sacred") appended to it. This leads up to three if-clauses, each one twice the length of the one before, and each in turn an amplification of the same idea, until at last we come to the predicate of this multiple conditional clause. This predicate, "pass", is given a special emphasis by the two corresponding participles, "vnreveald" and "vnrevenged." The whole sentence, gathering weight as it proceeds, is brought to an end with the great question concerning justice, which closes with yet another conditional clause introduced by "if"; and this—surely, like line 23, quite deliberately—is given a line which is extra long, linked with the preceding line both by the rhyme and by the two-fold repetition of words.

The second half of the speech has the same tripartite organization, and again there is a carefully controlled parallelism
in the syntactic structure of the sentences.[3]

The manner in which the soliloquy is slow to start yet "gathers weight
as it proceeds" portrays Hieronimo's hesitation and struggle, but at
the same time his increasing success, in achieving a more satisfactory verbal expression of his woe. Even though the relief such oratory
affords Hieronimo is relatively insignificant, Kyd's careful orchestra-
tion of this soliloquy and the one following ("Where shall I run to
breathe abroad my woes," III.7.1–18) prepares the audience for Hieronimo's pursuit of relief by way of other art forms.

When the soliloquy is interrupted by the mysterious appearance of
Bel-imperia's letter, Hieronimo's attention is again drawn to the specific task of achieving revenge. But his ability to pursue it is truncated
by the conviction that this task belongs to an authority beyond him
which should respond automatically. When no response is forthcoming, he resists the full impact of the truth by promising to provide justice to those who come under his official provenance: "And though
myself cannot receive the like, / Yet will I see that others have their
right" (III.6.37–38). For Hieronimo, the hanging of Pedringano is a
ritual which reassures him that justice is possible at least on an individual level. Yet the delivery of Pedringano's letter naming his cohorts
in crime reveals instead that Hieronimo's justice has been shortsighted
and incomplete, and as much of a jest as was Pedringano's belief that
he would be saved. Now the see-saw of Hieronimo's allegiances tips
again toward seeking the assistance of a higher authority:

> But wherefore waste I mine unfruitful words,
> When naught but blood will satisfy my woes?
> I will go plain me to my lord the king. (III.7.67–69)

It is the King's rejection (III.12) which sets Hieronimo permanently
onto the course he will pursue to the end of the play.

That Kyd saw this rejection as a crucial structural feature in the
drama is clear, first of all, from the strategic placing of the *Vindicta
mihi* soliloquy, in which Hieronimo shrugs off traditional beliefs
and takes up the revenge himself, immediately following the incident of the King's rejection. After this soliloquy comes the Bazulto
scene, which, because it is another opportunity for Hieronimo to
act as justicer, stands in contrast to the Pedringano scene. Having
failed in his initial assessment of Pedringano's situation and having
been rejected by the King, Hieronimo must now depend solely on
his own inner resources to calm his desperation. He makes no
effort to deal with Bazulto in the limited judicial terms. He even

---

3. Wolfgang Clemen, *English Tragedy Before Shakespeare* (London, 1961), pp. 271–72.

tears up the petitions. Left without religion, philosophy, or the example of historical event which can soothe his woe, Hieronimo instinctively turns to a subjective and figurative response—the poet's response. The bereaved Bazulto appears to Hieronimo as "The lively portrait of my dying self" (III.13.85). In seeing an analogy between his grief and Bazulto's, Hieronimo discerns a pattern which subsumes and clarifies his experience. Hieronimo does not ask Bazulto to tell about his own past; he does not ask for history. Rather, Hieronimo assigns actions to Bazulto which will portray the implications of Horatio's kind of death. The first section of Hieronimo's instructions to Bazulto, where he tells him to go to hell and request revenge, expresses the injustice which the events embody. The second section, where Hieronimo sees Bazulto as Horatio, emphasizes the fact of Horatio's being dead and the irrepressible and horrible image of the physical change which death brings to his boy:

> Sweet boy, how art thou chang'd in death's black shade!
> Had Proserpine no pity on thy youth?
> But suffer'd thy fair crimson-color'd spring
> With wither'd winter to be blasted thus?
> Horatio, thou art older than thy father:
> Ah ruthless fate, that favour thus transforms!
>   (III.13.146–51)

The third episode, where Hieronimo suggests that Bazulto may be a Fury come to call him to revenge, emphasizes Hieronimo's torturous sense of guilt for not having avenged his son's death. As the scene concludes, Hieronimo again recognizes Bazulto's separate identity as one whose son has been murdered and repeats the relationship he perceives between them: "Thou art the lively image of my grief" (III.13.162). That his effort to deal with his felt woe has become entirely personal, and no longer the search for a response from a public institution, is emphasized when Hieronimo invites Bazulto to come away from the public place, where the petitioners have sought his official service, and presumably into his private quarters. There, as Hieronimo explains to Bazulto, they will provide mutual support and comfort for each other through the unity of discordant song:

> Come in old man, thou shalt to Isabel,
> Lean on my arm: I thee, thou me shalt stay,
> And thou, and I, and she, will sing a song,
> Three parts in one, but all of discords framed.
>   (III.13.170–73)

In the sounds of dissonant chords, they hope to formalize their chaos and thereby control the impulse to madness that grows stronger as the realization of life's pain and injustice grows clearer.

When placed in this context, Kyd's allusion to Orpheus earlier in the scene can be seen to function on various levels. On the one hand, it simply embodies Hieronimo's plea that someone might sometime effect a just response from the gods:

> The Thracian poet thou shalt counterfeit:
> Come on, old father, be my Orpheus,
> And if thou canst no notes upon the harp,
> Then sound the burden of thy sore heart's grief,
> Till we do gain that Proserpine may grant
> Revenge on them that murdered my son. (III.13.116–21)

The allusion to Orpheus, the symbol of art, order, and reason, also emphasizes from the outset that Hieronimo is deliberately using Bazulto as a vehicle to order his experience. Hieronimo is drawing an analogy not only between himself and Bazulto, but also between himself and Orpheus, who regained Eurydice from the underworld, but only to lose her again, and who eventually suffered the cruel death of dismemberment at the hands of the Bacchides. But standing in juxtaposition to Orpheus' painful experiences is his capacity for charming the beasts through poetry and song. He exists as a symbol for the possibilities of reason and order in civilization as well as of man's capacity for spiritual renewal despite the constant threat of destruction by outside forces. He represents the ideal toward which Hieronimo and Kyd strive—an artistic response which will engulf the chaos and allow human endeavor to continue.

That Kyd's contemporaries understood the author's point is suggested by the addition of the Painter episode, which was inserted between the King's rejection and the *Vindicta mihi* soliloquy. The scene considers what possibility there may be for finding solace in an art form other than the poetry or music of the Bazulto scene. Hieronimo requests that the Painter "paint some comfort, / For surely there's none lives but painted comfort" (ll. 73–74). Aware that his unrelieved grief is affecting his sanity, he inquires how the Painter, whose son has also been murdered, deals with this kind of loss: "How dost take it? Art thou not sometimes mad? Is there no tricks that comes before thine eyes?" (ll. 109–11). The size of Hieronimo's distress finds expression in the large and detailed order which he gives to the Painter. He asks the Painter to paint emotions ("a groan, or a sigh" and "a speaking look"), sounds ("a doleful cry," "some violent noise"), and sequential actions, including the actual events before, during, and after Horatio's murder, as well as an imagined future when Hieronimo will kill the murderers. There is, however, something wrong with Hieronimo's request. He is asking not for interpretive painting, but history in painted form; he wants the painter to paint the events precisely as they happened, and consequently, the painting suggests little relief to him: "O no, there is no end: The end is death and madness" (l. 163). The point to be made here is that good painting, like good poetry, must capture the universal. And if history is going to be used at all, it must always be molded so that it can best portray the universal, as Hieronimo successfully did when he presented the masque for the King and the Portuguese early in the play.

But even when a painting accomplishes its task well, there is inherent in its nonverbal and silent form a limitation that does not, of course, go undetected in Renaissance literary criticism. Jonson, who may or may not have written the Painter episode, comments in *Timber* on this limitation of painting:

> *Poetry*, and *Picture*, are Arts of a like nature; and both are busie about imitation. It was excellently said of *Plutarch, Poetry* was a speaking Picture, and Picture a mute Poesie. For they both invent, faine, and devise many things, and accommodate all they invent to the use, and service of nature. Yet of the two, the Pen is more noble, then the Pencill. For that can speake to the Understanding; the other, but to the Sense.[4]

Conversely, even if poetry is more capable of speaking to the "Understanding," it lacks the visual effect which a painting can make. Poetry's picture remains a picture in the mind, not in the eye. When applied to drama, however, the "ut pictura poesis" idea is not a metaphoric description, as it is when applied to poetry, but rather a literal description. By having Hieronimo register his dissatisfaction with a mute production, the author of the Painter episode prepares us for the fact that Hieronimo's search for a more complete medium will end when he turns to drama. Hieronimo demands that the Painter "stretch thine art" in portraying the villain and asserts that the painted cry must not exist only "Seemingly," as the Painter tells him it will. "Nay, it should cry," Hieronimo insists. Hieronimo insists that the picture really speak, and only dramatic art can do that, as Thomas Heywood, in his discussion of the limitations of both painting and poetry, points out:

> A Description is only a shadow received by the eare but not perceived by the eye: so lively portrature is meerely a forme seene by the eye, but can neither shew action, passion, motion, or any other gesture, to moove the spirits of the beholder to admiration: but to see a souldier shap'd like a souldier, walke, speake, act like a souldier: to see a *Hector* all besmered in

4. *Ben Jonson* [Works], ed. C. H. Herford, Percy and Evelyn Simpson, VIII (Oxford, 1947), 609–10. For Jonson's opinion stated elsewhere that the effect of the word is superior to that of a visual spectacle, see "The Prologue For The Stage" in *The Staple of News* (VI, 28a), and the prefatory lines to *Hymenaei* (VII, 209).

blood, trampling upon the bulkes of Kinges. A *Troylus* return-
ing from the field in the fight of his father Priam. . . . To see as
I have seene, *Hercules* in his owne shape hunting the Boare . . .
Oh these were fights to make an Alexander.[5]

While it is often assumed that the Painter episode was intended
to replace the Bazulto scene, it remains possible that it was indeed
an addition, designed to contrast to and thereby emphasize what
Hieronimo is accomplishing in perceiving Bazulto as an "image."
The Bazulto scene, with its emphasis on metaphor, generalization,
interpretation, and comfort, is a decided advance over the literal-
ism Hieronimo asks for and the dissatisfaction he receives from the
Painter. In fact, if the Painter scene and the Bazulto scene are both
retained, they form a powerful trilogy with the concluding play
scene, the preparations for which begin at the start of Act iv. The
progression from painting to poetry and song and finally to drama
is a steady one. The literal and mute picture is exchanged for metaphor and sound, which in turn are replaced by a dramatized narrative, counterfeiting and interpreting Horatio's murder.

Hieronimo's playlet goes beyond his other attempts by being truly
a speaking picture, with visual, auditory, narrative, and figurative
effects combined to present his situation more completely than can
any other medium. Plot, properties, costume, and acting style all
concern him. All parts are devised to contribute to the whole, even
the seemingly foolish plan to have all the actors speaking in different
languages, "for the conclusion / Shall prove the invention."[6] Hieronimo's reluctance to turn his play over to "*princes* and *courtiers,* / Such
as can tell *how* to speak," when the work's quality more befits "*gentlemen* and *scholars* too, / Such as could tell *what* to speak" (my ital-
ics), indicates that his primary concern lies not with the manner, but
the meaning which the drama can carry. Hence he has chosen tragedy because its ability to convey "matter" is superior both to "fruitless
poetry: / Which . . . profit[s] the professor naught," and to comedy,
which contains "common things." To be absolutely sure that the play
is understood, he will himself "in an oration, / And with a strange
and wondrous show besides . . . make the matter known."

Upon the conclusion of the playlet, the King and Viceroy, still
unaware that real murders have occurred before their eyes, inanely
compliment the performance. Presenting the "matter," Hieronimo
sets out to make known how this art form relates to life. Having
given them an imitation, he presents an individual historical account

5. *An Apology for Actors* (London, 1612), sigs. b3v–[b4].
6. The confusion of tongues is a simple concern in Jonas Barish, "*The Spanish Tragedy*,
or The Pleasures and Perils of Rhetoric," *Elizabethan Theatre*, Stratford-Upon-Avon
Studies, 9 (London, 1966), pp. 59–85, and in S. F. Johnson (see n. 2).

of that horrid evening when he found Horatio dead, after which he explains the dire effect on himself: "But hope, heart, treasure, joy and bliss, / All fled, fail'd, died, yea, all decay'd with this" (IV.4.94–95). It is his way of telling them that his play has presented them with a lively image of his own grief, which in turn is a product of his acquaintance with a cruel universe. To this example of himself, he joins three more examples, the deaths of Lorenzo, Balthazar, and Bel-imperia. Thus, the situation is now reversed as Hieronimo's historical experience, and his play's imitation of it, suddenly become mirrors of the experiences of two more fathers, who for the first time must register the fact that Hieronimo's situation "resembles" theirs. Just as Hieronimo has lost his hope for earthly and heavenly justice, so too do Castile and the Viceroy now lose their hope that order might be achieved through a marriage ceremony. When Hieronimo asks, "How can you brook our play's catastrophe?" he is asking them to respond to the spectacle on two levels. Literally, he is asking how they can endure the fact of their children's deaths. Figuratively, he is asking how they can profit from the truths which the play has presented. They respond to the truth with questions which resist it, just as Hieronimo once stubbornly resisted the evidence that injustice is not a deviation from the norm. But the truth has been told and there is "no more to say." By killing Castile and himself, Hieronimo furnishes those who remain with two more examples on which to base a conclusion. Finally, the King and the Viceroy formulate what they have learned: hope is destroyed; only death and sorrow exist. Unfortunately, Hieronimo cannot endure his play's catastrophe because he has not allowed it merely to counterfeit life or to depict something that might be, but has made it life itself. Despite his attempt to transcend his experiences, he has become too much a part of the disorder to escape its worst implications. Hence Hieronimo dies, for though he finds a way to figure the complexity of his vision, he exchanges the release possible through art's presentation of universal truth for the desire of a particular event, the death of his son's murderers. In so doing, he sacrifices the balm of art to the singularity of history.

The ending scene of Andrea and Revenge reminds us that Hieronimo's play is contained within this frame and that the frame itself is part of an even larger construct. Andrea's inappropriate and unseeing response to the catastrophe of the play's end interrupts the audience's involvement with Hieronimo, and gives the audience an opportunity to gain a perspective on the impact of the work as a whole. Because *The Spanish Tragedy* contains both Andrea and Hieronimo, its matter stretches beyond what either one alone or both characters together can embody. What the play achieves can be brought into perspective by a backward glance at the scene where Isabella cuts down the arbor and kills herself. Her despair in perceiving how much life costs and how little it yields impels her to physical onslaught against Nature's casual and instinctive growth:

> Fruitless for ever may this garden be,
> Barren the earth, and blissless whosoever
> Imagines not to keep it unmanur'd! (IV.2.14–16)

The play suggests that it remains within the dramatist's power to act unlike Isabella, to cultivate rather than to destroy Nature, and therein become a maker who contributes something real to man's ability to endure and to profit from experience. In imitating Nature, Kyd has successfully given shape to what otherwise can appear random and imbecilic. Nature so adorned neither destroys others nor need be destroyed itself.

Justice and Revenge

G. K. HUNTER

From Ironies of Justice in *The Spanish Tragedy*[†]

The assumption that *The Spanish Tragedy* is usefully categorized as a "revenge play" and that this categorization gives us a means of differentiating what is essential in the text from what is peripheral—this has governed most that has been said about Kyd's play. And this is a pity, because the play when looked at in these terms shows up as rather a botched piece of work.

It is no doubt an inevitable part of the tendency of literary historians that they should look everywhere for indications of historical progress. Certainly this has caused them to search among the "amorphous" (i.e., nonmodern) dramatic forms of the Elizabethans for signs and portents of the coming of Scribe and the "well-made" play. The revenge motif, in particular, has been seen as important because (to quote Moody Prior) it

> had the advantage of imposing a fairly strict pattern on the play. It thus assisted in discouraging multiple narratives and irrelevant episodes, and, in general, acted as a check on the tendency toward diffuseness and digression which was a common defect of popular Elizabethan drama.[1]

Percy Simpson, in the same general terms, sees the revenge motif as imposing on Elizabethan dramaturgy the Aristotelian virtues of beginning, middle, and end: "The beginning is effectively supplied by the murder; the end should be effectively supplied by the vengeance. The problem for the working dramatist was skilfully to bridge the gap between the two."[2]

Unfortunately this pattern of progress shows the actual products it seeks to explain as rather unsatisfactory parts of the very progression

---

† From "Ironies of Justice in *The Spanish Tragedy*" by G. K. Hunter as it appeared in *Renaissance Drama* 8 (1965), pp. 89–104. Reprinted by permission.
1. Moody E. Prior, *The Language of Tragedy* (New York, 1947), p. 47.
2. Percy Simpson, "The Theme of Revenge in Elizabethan Tragedy," British Academy Shakespeare Lecture for 1935, p. 9.

which is adduced to explain them. Prior finds *The Spanish Tragedy* to be ensnared in the very "multiple narratives and irrelevant episodes" that the revenge motif was supposed to discourage. He speaks of "the disproportionate amount of preliminary preparation necessary before Hieronimo is introduced as the avenging agent,"[3] and also of "the introduction of the story of the treacherous noble in the Portuguese Court, which has no bearing on the main action."[4] Fredson Bowers tells us that "the ghost has no real concern with the play" and that "the fundamental motive for the tragic action . . . is not conceived until midway in the play."[5] Simpson has much the same attitude. After the passage quoted above, he goes on to apply it to Kyd:

> Now Kyd, who had a keen eye for dramatic situation and, in his happy moments, a powerful style, does at critical points fumble the action. His main theme, as the early title-page announces, is "the lamentable end of Don Horatio," avenged at the cost of his own life by his aged father Hieronimo. But the induction brings in the ghost of Horatio's friend, Don Andrea, and the personified figure of Revenge.[6]

Later Simpson speaks more unequivocally of

> the disconnectedness, the waste of opportunity, and the dramatic unevenness of much of the writing.[7]

This attitude toward the revenge play in general and *The Spanish Tragedy* in particular has persisted in criticism. Philip Edwards' recent and excellent edition of the play (1959) speaks of the "prolix early scenes" and tells us that "it is very hard to justify the sub-plot . . . the relevance of theme is very slight" (p. liii). But at the same time as these attitudes persist, their historical foundations are disappearing. The assumption that the Elizabethan play inherited from the Tudor interlude a diffuse form which reflects mere incompetence—this becomes increasingly difficult to sustain in the light of recent studies of the interlude by Craik,[8] Spivack,[9] Bevington,[1] and Habicht.[2] These, in their different ways, present the interlude as a serious form, in which flat characterization, repetitiveness, and dependence

3. Prior, pp. 46f.
4. *Ibid.*, p. 46.
5. F. T. Bowers, *Elizabethan Revenge Tragedy* (Princeton, 1940, 1959), p. 71.
6. Simpson, pp. 9ff.
7. *Ibid.*, p. 14.
8. T. W. Craik, *The Tudor Interlude* (Leicester, 1958).
9. Bernard Spivack, *Shakespeare and the Allegory of Evil* (New York, 1958).
1. D. M. Bevington, *From Mankind to Marlowe* (Cambridge, Mass., 1962).
2. Werner Habicht, "Sénèque et le théâtre pré-Shakespearien," in *Sénèque et le théâtre de la Renaissance*, ed. Jacquot (Paris, 1964) and *Studien zur Dramenform vor Shakespeare* (Winter Verlag, Heidelberg, 1968.)

on a multiplicity of short episodes are not defects, but rather means perfectly adapted to express that age's moral and religious (rather than psychological or social) view of human destiny. Persons are seen to be less important than theme; they exist to illustrate rather than represent; and narrative line gives way to the illustration of doctrine. * * *

If *The Spanish Tragedy* is seen not so much as the harbinger of *Hamlet* (not to mention Scribe), but more as the inheritor of a complex and rich tradition of moralizing dramaturgy, the actual structure of the play begins to make more sense, and the traditional strictures that Prior and Simpson re-echo lose much of their relevance. The text of the play does not appear to give its complete attention to the enactment of revenge. True. But this may be because the play is not centrally concerned with the enactment of revenge. Much more obsessive is the question of justice. Indeed we may hazard an initial statement that if revenge provides the plot line of the play (i.e., play structure as seen from Scribe's point of view), justice provides the thematic center of the play (i.e., play structure as seen from the point of view of the Tudor interlude).

The centrality of the concept of justice serves to explain much of the so-called "preliminary preparation" of the first two acts. The play opens with Don Andrea, who has been slain in the late war between Spain and Portugal. Don Andrea's journey after death is through an infernal landscape devoted to working out justice. He is set before Minos, Rhadamanthus, and Aeacus, the judges of the classical afterlife; they are unable to resolve his legal status and refer him to a higher authority—to the monarchs of the underworld, Pluto and Proserpine. On his way to their court he passes through the enactments of Hell's precisely organized justice—horribly poetic justice indeed:

> Where bloudie furies shakes their whips of steele,
> And poore *Ixion* turnes an endles wheele;
> Where vsurers are choakt with melting golde,
> And wantons are imbraste with ouglie Snakes,
> And murderers grone with neuer killing wounds,
> And periurde wightes scalded in boyling lead,
> And all foule sinnes with torments ouerwhelmd.
>
> (I.i.65–71)[3]

But Don Andrea is not allowed to complete his search for justice amid the palpable abstractions of Hell. What the higher court orders is that he should be sent back to earth to observe how the gods operate *there,* and for this purpose he is given Revenge as his companion and guide:

---

3. The text of quotations from *The Spanish Tragedy* is that of F. S. Boas (Oxford, 1901, 1955).

> Forthwith, *Revenge*, she rounded thee in th' care,
> And bad thee lead me through the gates of Horn,
> Where dreames haue passage in the silent night.
> No sooner had she spoke, but we were heere,
> I wot not how, in twinkling of an eye.
>   REVENGE
> Then know, *Andrea*, that thou art ariu'd
> Where thou shalt see the author of thy death,
>
> .   .   .   .
>
> Depriu'd of life by *Bel-imperia*.
>
> (I.i.81–87, 89)

Revenge here seems to bear the same relation to justice as Talus (in Book V of *The Faerie Queene*) does to Artegall—that is, he is the emotionless and terrifyingly nonhuman executive arm of the legality that is being demonstrated. But Revenge, unlike Talus, does not act in his own person; his presence guarantees that the human action will work out justly, but he is not seen to make it do so. The departure of Andrea and Revenge through the gates of horn, Virgil's *porta*—

> *Cornea, qua veris facilis datur exitus umbris*—

and their arrival at the Spanish court, can indeed be seen as dramatic equivalents to the introductory sequences of medieval dream allegory. The play may be viewed in this sense as what Andrea dreams, as an allegory of perfect justice: "The gods are indeed just; and now you shall see how their justice works out." We are promised a mathematical perfection of total recompense, where justice and revenge are identical. From this point of view the human beings who appear in Andrea's dream—the characters of the play, scheming, complaining, and hoping—are not to be taken by the audience as the independent and self-willed individuals they suppose themselves to be, but in fact only as the puppets of a predetermined and omnicompetent justice that they (the characters) cannot see and never really understand. But *we* (watching the whole stage) must never lose sight of this piece of knowledge.

The concern with justice in the opening scenes establishes an ironic set of responses for the audience and an ironic mode of construction for the play. The structure, indeed, may remind us of a Ptolemaic model of the universe, one level of awareness outside another level of awareness and, outside the whole, the unsleeping eye of God.

The disjunction between what the audience knows and what is known in the Spanish court is established straightaway when the "play proper" starts. The Spaniards congratulate themselves on the late victory and stress the unimportance of the losses:

> All wel, my soueraigne Liege, except some few
> That are deceast by fortune of the warre.
>
> (I.ii.2–3)

And again: "Victorie, my Liege, and that with little losse." *We*, seeing Andrea sitting on the stage, know that the "little losse" can be too easily discounted and that the "some few" may yet blemish the complacency of the court and the overconfident assumption that justice is already achieved:

> Then blest be heauen, and guider of the heauens,
> From whose faire influence such iustice flowes.
>
> (I.ii.10–11)

We now see assembled before us the characters who are to be involved in the final demonstration of justice, centrally Don Balthazar, who is to die (we have been told) by the hand of Bel-imperia. But what we see in the opening scenes is no movement that can be understood as leading toward the death of Balthazar. What happens involves Balthazar with a variety of different kinds of justice, but the play is obviously more interested in exploring thematic comprehensiveness than in moving toward any narrative consequence.

The problem of deciding justly between competing claims to truth, which has appeared already in the dispute between Aeacus and Rhadamanthus, recurs in the contest between Lorenzo and Horatio, who dispute which of them, in law, has Balthazar as prisoner; and the king shows a Solomon-like wisdom in making a just decision:

> Then by my iudgement thus your strife shall end:
> You both deserue, and both shall haue reward.
> Nephew, thou tookst his weapon and his horse:
> His weapons and his horse are thy reward.
> *Horatio,* thou didst force him first to yeeld:
> His ransome therefore is thy valours fee; [etc.].
>
> (I.ii.178–183)

Expectation is tuned into a competency of human justice that *we* know cannot finally be sustained against the meddling of divine justice in this human scene.

The next scene introduces the Portuguese episode so famous for its irrelevance to the main action. The first scene of the "play proper" showed the Spaniards rejoicing over their victory and absorbing Balthazar into their court life. What the second (Portuguese) scene does is to show us the other side of the coin—the Portingales bewailing their defeat. And actually the Portuguese scenes serve as a continuous counterpoint against the earlier stages of *The Spanish Tragedy*, not only setting Portuguese sorrow against the Spanish mirth of the first scene, but later inverting the counterpoint and setting the

viceroy's joy at his son's recovery against Hieronimo's cry of sorrow
and demand for vengeance. Moreover, the long aria of grief put into
the viceroy's mouth in I.iii gives the first statement of what is to
become the central theme of *The Spanish Tragedy*, certainly the central and most famous impulse in its rhetoric—that frantic poetry of
loss and sense of universal injustice which was to give Hieronimo
his fame. We can see that, in spatial terms, the viceroy prepares the
way for Hieronimo by living through the same class of experience—
the loss of a son. Hieronimo makes this point quite explicitly when
he says at the end of the play:

> Speake, Portaguise, whose losse resembles mine:
> If thou canst weepe vpon thy *Balthazar*,
> Tis like I wailde for my *Horatio*.
>
> (IV.iv.114–116)

The viceroy does not weep at this point, when Balthazar is really
dead, but the opening scenes and the speeches in which he bewails
his supposed death sustain our sense of what Hieronimo is referring to. Moreover, the connection between national sin and individual sorrow which seems to be implied in the main story of
Hieronimo and Horatio is quite explicit in the Portuguese episode:

> My late ambition hath distaind my faith;
> My breach of faith occasiond bloudic warres;
> Those bloudie warres haue spent my treasure;
> And with my treasure my peoples blood;
> And with their blood, my ioy and best beloued,
> My best beloued, my sweete and onely Sonne.
>
> (I.iii.33–38)

But this scene of sorrow does more than prepare for the second
and central lost son, Don Horatio; it establishes an ironic counter-
current inside the framework of the general information that has
been given us by Andrea and Revenge. Not only is it deeply ironic to
see the viceroy bewailing the death of a son, who is at that moment
involved in the murder of another son, Horatio, and the bereavement
of another father (and we should note that this second bereavement
is one which cannot, this time, be avoided as if by a miracle [see III.
xiv.34]). But more, the general framework of the play tells us that it is
ironic even when the viceroy changes from lamentation to rejoicing;
for *we* know that the relationship with Bel-imperia which looks so
auspicious from inside the play will be the actual cause of his death.

The short fable of human fallibility and divine concern which
supplies the narrative (as against the thematic) substance of the
Portuguese episode—this feeds into the main plot an expectation

that ". . . murder cannot be hid: / Time is the author both of truth and right, / And time will bring this trecherie to light" (II.v.58–60); it strengthens the expectation which Revenge and Andrea arouse by their very presence—that wrong must soon, and inevitably, be followed by retribution. It is no accident that places the second Portuguese scene (III.i)—which shows Alexandro rescued from death, as if by miracle, at the very last moment—immediately after the death of Horatio and the first sounds of Hieronimo's passion: "What out-cries pluck me from my naked bed, [etc.]" (II.v.i) The discovery of Horatio is the center of the main plot, being the reenactment in real life of the death which began the action of the play; for Don Horatio is, as it were, the living surrogate for the ghost Andrea. As he was friend and revenger to Andrea on the battlefield, so he has taken on the role of lover to Bel-imperia, and so too he falls victim to Balthazar (and his confederates). And this is the point in the play where the sense of just gods directing a revenge on Balthazar is at its lowest ebb. As Andrea understandably exclaims to Revenge:

> Broughtst thou me hether to encrease my paine?
> I lookt that *Balthazar* should haue beene slaine:
> But tis my freend *Horatio* that is slaine,
> And they abuse fair *Bel-imperia*,
> On whom I doted more then all the world,
> Because she lou'd me more then all the world.
>
> (II.vi.1–6)

The reinforcement of the justice theme at this point is, therefore, particularly useful. Even if the Portuguese episode had no other function, this one would seem to justify it.

Andrea was returned to earth by the just gods, to witness a parable of perfect recompense, a parable which would reenact the story of his life, but cleared of the ambiguities and uncertainties that had surrounded him. The death of Horatio re-presents the death of Andrea, but presents it as a definite crime (as the death of Andrea was not) and makes Balthazar into a definite criminal (as in the battle he was not). More important, the death of Horatio raises up an agent of recompense who has the best claim to justification in his action—the father of the victim and a man renowned for state service, the chief judicial functionary of the court. Kyd goes out of his way to show Hieronimo in this function and to make the first citizen tell us that

> . . . for learning and for law,
> There is not any Aduocate in Spaine
> That can preuaile, or will take halfe the paine
> That he will in pursuit of equitie.
>
> (III.xiii.51–54)

Hieronimo is justly at the center of *The Spanish Tragedy* because he is constructed to embody perfectly the central question about justice that the play poses: the question, "How can a human being pursue the path of justice?" Hieronimo is constructed to suggest both complete justification of motive (his outraged fatherhood) and the strongest advantages in social position. And as such he is groomed to be the perfect victim of a justice machine that uses up and destroys even this paragon. Herein lies the truly cathartic quality of *The Spanish Tragedy*: If this man, Kyd seems to be saying, fails to find any secure way of justice on earth, how will it fare with you and me? For Hieronimo, for all his devotion to the cause of justice, is as much a puppet of the play's divine system of recompense as are the other characters in the action. He is stuck on the ironic pin of his ignorance; we watch his struggles to keep the action at a legal and human level with involvement, with sympathy, but with assurance of their predestinate failure:

> Thus must we toyle in other mens extreames,
> That know not how to remedie our owne;
> And doe them iustice, when uniustly we,
> For all our wrongs, can compasse no redresse.
> But shall I neuer liue to see the day,
> That I may come (by iustice of the heauens)
> To know the cause that may my cares allay?
> This toyles my body, this consumeth age,
> That onely I to all men iust must be,
> And neither Gods nor men be iust to me.
> DEPUTY
> Worthy *Hieronimo*, your office askes
> A care to punish such as doe transgresse.
> HIERONIMO
> So ist my duety to regarde his death,
> Who, when he liued, deserued my dearest blood.
>   (III.vi.1–14)

He calls on heavenly justice; what he cannot know is that his agony and frustration are part of the process of heavenly justice. As his madness takes him nearer and nearer the nightmare world of Revenge and Andrea, this mode of irony is reinforced. Hieronimo tells us:

> Though on this earth iustice will not be found,
> He downe to hell, and in this passion
> Knock at the dismall gates of *Plutos* Court,
> . . . .
> Till we do gaine that *Proserpine* may grant
> Reuenge on them that murd<e>red my Sonne.
>   (III.xiii.108–110, 120–121)

What he cannot know is that this is precisely what Don Andrea has already done—indeed the explanation of the whole action of the play up to this point. Again and again he calls on the justices of Hell:

> Goe backe, my sonne, complaine to *Eacus*,
> For heeres no iustice; gentle boy, be gone,
> For iustice is exiled from the earth:
> *Hieronimo* will beare thee company.
> Thy mother cries on righteous *Radamant*
> For iust reuenge against the murderers.
>   (III.xiii.137–142)

> . . . thou then a furie art,
> Sent from the emptie Kingdome of blacke night,
> To sommon me to make appearance
> Before grim *Mynos* and iust *Radamant*,
> To plague *Hieronimo* that is remisse,
> And seekes not vengeance for *Horatioes* death.
>   (III.xiii.152–157)

But these infernal judges have already acted. All that Hieronimo can see is that he, the justice, the magistrate, the proponent of civil order, is living in a world where justice is impossible, where

> . . . neither pietie nor pittie mooues
> The King to iustice or compasion,
>   (IV.ii.2–3)

and where heavenly justice does not seem to be filling in the lacuna left by the failure of civil justice:

> O sacred heauens, if this vnhallowed deed,
> If this inhumane and barberous attempt,
> If this incomparable murder thus
> Of mine, but now no more my sonne,
> Shall vnreueald and vnreuenged passe,
> How should we tearme your dealings to be iust,
> If you vniustly deale with those, that in your iustice trust?
>   (III.ii.5–11)

The heavens are not asleep, in fact, but their wakefulness has a different aspect from that which mortals expect. Hieronimo knows the orthodox Christian doctrine of Romans XII.19, which tells us ("Vindicta mihi, ego retribuam, dicit Dominus") to leave revenge to God:

> *Vindicta mihi.*
> I, heauen will be reuenged of euery ill;
> Nor will they suffer murder vnrepaide.

> Then stay, *Hieronimo*, attend their will:
> For mortall men may not appoint their time.
> (III.xiii.1–5)

But no more than Andrea can he apply this knowledge or relate it to what is happening to himself and to those around him. Andrea feels that everything is going the wrong way:

> I lookt that *Balthazar* should haue beene slaine:
> But tis my freend *Horatio* that is slaine.
> (II.vi.2 ff.)

And when (in the next act) he finds that Revenge has actually been sleeping while the wicked continued their triumph, Heaven's conspiracy with injustice seems to be complete. But Revenge is coldly contemptuous of these passionate human outcries:

> Thus worldlings ground, what they haue dreamd, vpon.
> Content thy selfe, *Andrea*; though I sleepe,
> Yet is my mood soliciting their soules.
>
> . . . .
>
> Nor dies *Reuenge*, although he sleepe awhile;
> For in vnquiet quietnes is faind,
> And slumbring is a common worldly wile.
> Beholde, *Andrea*, for an instance, how
> *Reuenge* hath slept, and then imagine thou
> What tis to be subiect to destinie.
>   [*Enter a dumme shew.*]
> (III.xv.17–19,22–27)

The menace and even horror of Revenge's outlook, for those who are "subject to destiny," needs to be stressed. The presence of a justice machine in this play is no more cozily reassuring than in Kafka's *Strafkolonie*. For the irony of its operation works against Andrea and Hieronimo no less than against Lorenzo and Balthazar.

All in *The Spanish Tragedy* are caught in the toils of their ignorance and incomprehension, each with his own sense of knowledge and power preserved intact, and blindly confident of his own (baseless) understanding, even down to the level of the boy with the box (III.v). This episode—the only clearly comic piece of business in *The Spanish Tragedy*—catches the basic irony of the play in its simplest form. The boy's preliminary explanation of the trap set up, and his key sentence, "Ist not a scuruie iest that a man should iest himselfe to death?" establishes the usual Kydian disjunction in the levels of comprehension. Throughout the following trial scene (III. vi) the boy stands pointing to the empty box, like a cynical emblem of man's hope for justice; and yet the irony has also (as is usual in the play) further levels of complexity. For Lorenzo, the organizer of the ironic show which seals Pedringano's lips even while it betrays his body to the hangman, is himself a victim, not only in the larger irony of Revenge's scrutiny but also in the minor irony that it is his very cleverness that betrays him: It is Pedringano's letter that confirms Hieronimo's knowledge of the murderers of Horatio. Lorenzo, indeed, as Hieronimo remarks, "marcht in a net and thought himselfe unseen" even at the time he was entrapping others.

Hieronimo prides himself on his devotion to justice and his thoroughness as a judge, but he serves divine justice by ceasing to be just at all in any human sense. The feeling of incomprehension, of not knowing where he is, in terms of the standards by which he has ordered his life—this drives him mad; but even here he reinforces the play's constant concern with justice by his mad fantasies of journeys into the hellish landscape of infernal justice.

> *Hieronimo,* tis time for thee to trudge:
> Downe by the dale that flowes with purple gore,
> Standeth a firie Tower; there sits a iudge
> Vpon a seat of steele and molten brasse, [etc.]
> (III.xii.6–9)

His incomprehension is inescapable because it is a function of his humanity. His madness is a direct result of the collision of his human sense of justice with the quite different processes of divine justice; for it is a fearful thing to fall into the hands of a just God. The absorption of the human into the divine justice machine is the destruction of the human, and Hieronimo becomes the instrument of Revenge by becoming inhuman. He becomes part of the hellish landscape of his imagination. In the play of Soliman and Perseda that he organizes we have yet another reenactment of the situation that began with Don Andrea. Bel-imperia (certainly resolute even if not certainly chaste) plays the part of "Perseda chaste and resolute." Balthazar, the princely lover who hoped to win Bel-imperia from her common lovers (Andrea, Horatio), plays the Emperor Soliman, who hopes to win Perseda from her common love. The crimes and killings in the play are organized by the Bashaw or Pasha, and this is the part to be played by Hieronimo himself. When asked, "But which of us is to performe that parte?" he replies:

> O, that will I, my Lords, make no doubt of it:
> Ile play the murderer, I warrant you,
> For I already haue conceited that.
> (IV.i.130–133)

The Spanish Tragedy as a whole has continuously set the marionette-like action of the man whose destiny is predetermined against the sense of choice or willpower in the passionate and self-confident individual. Continuously we have had actors watching actors but being watched themselves by still other actors (watched by the audience). We watch Revenge and Andrea watching Lorenzo watching Horatio and Bel-imperia; we watch Revenge and Andrea watching Hieronimo watching Pedringano watching the boy with the box; and at each point in this chain what seems free will to the individual seems only a predetermined *act* to the onlookers.

In the play within the play, in Hieronimo's playlet of Soliman and Perseda, this interest reaches its climax. The illusion of free will is suspended. The four central characters are absorbed into an action which acts out their just relationships *for them*. The net has closed, character has become role, speech has changed to ritual; the end is now totally predetermined. The play itself is a flat puppet-like action with a total absence of personal involvement; but as the characters intone their flat, liturgical responses to one another there is an enormous *frisson* of irony or disparity between what they say and what *we* know to be meant.

Hieronimo himself has become *instrument* rather than agent. *He* knows that his life has been absorbed into the ritual and that he cannot escape back into humanity, and he accepts this Hegelian kind of freedom (freedom as the knowledge of necessity) with a resolution at once noble and inhuman. At the end of his play he comes forward to speak his own epilogue:

> Heere breake we off our sundrie languages,
> . . . .
> And, Princes, now beholde *Hieronimo*,
> Author and actor in this Tragedie,
> Bearing his latest fortune in his fist;
> And will as resolute conclude his parte
> As any of the Actors gone before.
> And, Gentles, thus I end my play.
>   (IV.iv.74,146–151)

Commentators on the denouement of *The Spanish Tragedy* usually concentrate on the human *mess* which follows Hieronimo's failure to complete his life in ritual, noticing the break in the pattern rather than the pattern itself. But I think that the nature of the final actions is only kept in focus if we see them as measuring the gap between the dream of justice and the haphazard and inefficient human actions that so often must embody it. This is a recurrent interest of a writer like Seneca. When he describes the suicide of Cato Uticensis, his greatest hero, he is not content to relate his fortitude in doing the deed; he stresses the horror of Cato's failure to finish himself off in one clean blow. What he is concerned to show is the persistence of Cato's will to die, in spite of his own inefficiency. And I think a similar concern to contrast the will to martyrdom with the *mess* of actual martyrdom can be seen at the end of *The Spanish Tragedy*.

A martyr is rather exceptional if his suffering is not prolonged and humanly degrading; a martyr whose soul had been antiseptically abstracted from his body would be rather unlike those whose histories thronged the Elizabethan imagination, whether from *The Golden Legend* or from its local equivalent, Foxe's *Acts and Monuments*. We should remember that it was not simply Zeno who anticipated Hieronimo by biting out his own tongue, but St. Christina as well. Much ink has been spilled in sympathy for Castile, who is struck down at the end of the play, simply because he stands too close to the protagonist. But Castile is, of course, identified with the tormenters who seek to interrupt the ritual and prevent it from completing itself. It is Castile who suggests that torture is still of use, to compel Hieronimo to *write* the names of his confederates. And the death of Castile confers another dramatic advantage: It transfers mourning to the highest personage on the stage. The king of Spain has hitherto been concerned with the miseries of existence only at second hand. Now, at the end of the play, he himself becomes a principal mourner, as is indicated well enough in the final stage direction:

> The Trumpets sound a dead march, the King of Spaine mourning after his brothers body, and the King of Portingale bearing the body of his sonne.

In the final episode we return to the justice of Hell, where the characters of the play now supply the classical examples of sin and wickedness with which the play began ("Place *Don Lorenzo* on *Ixions* Wheele," [IV.v.33]). A last judgment places everyone where he morally belongs (as in the *Last Judgment* play at the end of the mystery cycles), but we would do less than justice to the complexity of this play if we did not notice that humanity has been sacrificed so that justice can be fulfilled. Revenge has been completed; we have seen what Fulke Greville describes as the mode of modern tragedy: "God's revenging aspect upon every particular sin to the despair and confusion of mortality."

218

LORNA HUTSON

From Hieronimo, Justice and Dramatist[†]

. . . [I]t was in Latin dramatic writing, not in vernacular legal practice, that there could be a developing awareness of the tragic, as
well as comic, uses of false inference, the 'supposes' and 'surmises'
that are mimetically and emotionally effective in theatre and fiction. *The Spanish Tragedy* was probably written and first performed
between 1585 and 1590. By 1585 its author, Thomas Kyd, was writing for the Queen's Men, the most privileged and successful of the
theatre companies at that time.[1] The favoured genre of the Queen's
Men's pre-eminent writer, Robert Wilson, was, as McMillin and
Maclean explain, the 'medley', which featured a predominantly
visual style of performance, expounding action by means of costumes, shields, tableaux, and eloquent gestures. 'The unmistakeable
sign', write McMillin and Maclean, 'is crucial to this system—the
gesture no eye can misread, the accent no ear can misunderstand.'[2]
Kyd learned how to use this kind of theatre well: in the second
scene of *The Spanish Tragedy*, the Spanish army has to '*enter and
pass by*' as a visual demonstration of having returned victorious and
undiminished by battle with the Portuguese (1.2.110). But Kyd was
also ambitious to do something new: he married the visual, emblematic theatre of the Queen's Men with a newly intricate dramaturgy
of suspicion and probable conjecture, a dramaturgy of the *mistak-
able* rather than unmistakable sign. This innovation of Kyd's was
long ago identified by Alfred Harbage as the adaptation to tragic
situations of the plot techniques of Roman intrigue comedy, and
Lukas Erne has more recently claimed Kyd as the first dramatist to
represent human causality skilfully on-stage.[3]

There is, nevertheless, a strange laboriousness in Kyd's concern
to demonstrate causality in the movement of action from Hieroni-

† From "Hieronimo, Justice and Dramatist" by Lorna Hutson as it appeared in *The
Invention of Suspicion* (Oxford: Oxford UP, 2007), pp. 277–87. Reprinted by permission of Oxford University Press.
1. See Thomas Kyd, *The Spanish Tragedy*, ed. J. R. Mulryne (London: A & C Black, 1989),
pp. xi, xiii–xiv. References to act, scene, and line of this edition are henceforth given in
the text.
2. Scott McMillin and Sally-Beth Maclean, *The Queen's Men and their Plays* (Cambridge:
Cambridge University Press, 1998), 127.
3. Alfred Harbage, 'Intrigue in Elizabethan Tragedy', in *Essays On Shakespeare and Elizabethan Drama in Honour of Hardin Craig*, ed. Richard Hosley (London: Routledge &
Kegan Paul Ltd., 1963), 37–44; Lukas Erne, *Beyond the Spanish Tragedy* (Manchester:
Manchester University Press, 2001), 4. Erne omits any consideration of Gascoigne and
Whetstone, understandably in view of the fact that *Supposes* is a translation, and *The
Glasse of Government* and *Promos and Cassandra* are unlikely to have been staged,
though Gascoigne's grasp of dramatic causality is superior to Kyd's.

mo's first discovery of the murder of his son, through his slow cor-
roboration of evidence as to who were the killers, to his final,
meticulous enactment of revenge as the following of a scripted plot.
As T. S. Eliot noted, Kyd's interest in plot does not come from Seneca: '"Plot" in the sense in which we find plot in the *Spanish Tragedy* does not exist for Seneca at all . . . *The Spanish Tragedy*, like
the series of Hamlet plays, including Shakespeare's, has an affinity
to our detective drama.'[4] What seems particularly intriguing,
though, is the strangely obtrusive way in which a topography of
justice—a vision of the other world as a series of emblematically
distinct torments, each fitting a particular crime—is slowly, as the
play goes on, transposed into the concept of a movement across this
worldly space—a 'journey' or 'middle way', involving a series of
crossroads—which becomes, in turn, a metaphor for the weighing
of alternatives, for reasoning probably, for decision making, and for
plotting a course of action. This last concept materializes, of course,
in the book of Hieronimo's play, which he distributes 'in several
abstracts drawn' (4.1.141), determining the parts—and several
dooms—allotted to Horatio's murderers, brilliantly insisting as he
does so that the King, as bewildered spectator, should make an
effort to follow it: 'Here comes Lorenzo; look upon the plot, | And
tell me, brother, what part plays he?' (4.4.33–4).

The problem with an interpretation of the play that focuses exclu-
sively on the simultaneously inciting and retarding effects of remembrance of the dead is that it smoothes over the weirdness of Kyd's
insistent metaphorical transposition of a hellish topography of justly
distributed torments into the almost ploddingly slow process of judicial decision making on the basis of probable conjecture. This aspect
of the play, though less immediately appealing than its representation of Hieronimo's passionate moments of remembrance, is nevertheless crucial, for it is the public-spirited care that Hieronimo takes
in his role as an investigator of the 'causes' of others that likewise
distinguishes his deliberations at the crossroads of decision making
about how best to pursue justice for his beloved son, and these
moments, in turn, powerfully enlist our sympathy for him, and ensure
a kind of satisfaction in the appalling end.

Kerrigan observes that when Hieronimo first apprehends the sick-
ening horror of the sight in his arbour where his son hangs lifeless,
he takes from his son's body a memento, and makes a vow: 'See'st
thou this handkercher besmeared with blood? | It shall not from me
till I take revenge' (2.5.51–2). While his wife speaks the rhetoric of
providential disclosure: 'The heavens are just, murder cannot be

4. T. S. Eliot, 'Introduction', in *Seneca His Tenne Tragedies translated into English* [1581]
   ed. Thomas Newton (London: Constable and Co. Ltd., 1927), p. xxiii.

hid', Hieronimo himself implicitly assumes that heavenly agency (2.5.57). Two short scenes later, however, he is completely at a standstill, the murder remains 'unrevealed' by the sacred heavens, and fiends that should be tormenting the murderers are inhabiting not hell, but Hieronimo's night thoughts, 'sally[ing] forth' and framing his 'steps to unfrequented paths', driving him on 'to seek the murderer' (3.2.5–21). He has, though, no idea where to begin when, providentially or diabolically, 'A letter falleth', addressed to him. Kerrigan notes the visual resemblance of this letter, written in blood ('red ink'), to the 'bloody handkercher', and concludes that it is 'another memento, inciting revenge'.[5]

Such a reading of the bloody letter, however, produces the play's action as repetitive series rather than causal sequence. The letter is not a memento at all, but evidence—though highly suspect evidence, at first—of the identity of Horatio's killers. Hieronimo keeps it not to remind him of his son, and to stir thoughts of vengeance, but in order that he might continue to 'try' or test its assertions by corroborating what it says with other forms of evidence. From the moment he reads it, he subjects its contents to sceptical scrutiny: 'My son slain by Lorenzo and the prince! | What cause had they Horatio to malign?' (3.2.33–4). Equally, though, he wonders what motive Bel-imperia could have for accusing her own brother: 'Or what might move thee, Bel-imperia, | To accuse thy brother, had he been the mean?' (3.2.35–6). It is all too fishy: just as Hieronimo's first thought on encountering a body in his arbour was to suspect a plan 'to lay the guilt on me' (2.5.11), so, now, he suspects that he is betrayed, 'And to entrap thy life this train is laid' (3.2.38).

The letter fulfils Hieronimo's wish for 'some mean' to turn nightmare into direction—the word, as Kerrigan excellently glosses it, offers the sense of 'both "opportunity" and "middle course"', thus recalling 'the path along which Minos sent Andrea to Revenge'.[6] Andrea's path lay between a field on the right, where lay lovers and martialists, and a steep descent on the left, which

> Was ready downfall to the deepest hell,
> Where bloody Furies shake their whips of steel,
> And poor Ixion turns an endless wheel;
> Where usurers are choked with melting gold,
> And wantons are embraced with ugly snakes,
> And murderers groan with never-killing wounds,
> And perjured wights scalded in boiling lead,
> And all foul sins with torments overwhelmed.
>
> (1.1.64–71)

---

5. John Kerrigan, *Revenge Tragedy* (Oxford: Clarendon Press, 1996), 176.
6. Kerrigan, *Revenge Tragedy*, 176.

"Twixt these two ways', says Andrea, 'I trod the middle path' (1.1.72). This third *way*—Kyd's invention, for in book 6 of the *Aeneid* there are only two ways, the right to Elysium, the left to Tartarus—corresponds to the notion of Purgatory as a third *place*, the locus of torment not as damnation but as trial and purification. It is suggestive, then, that Kyd should transpose this idea of a 'middle way' back, via Andrea's watching of the play, into the probable 'means' or opportunities by which the action progresses, as Hieronimo proceeds to try 'by circumstances' the testimony of the letter (3.2.47). It is indeed as if Kyd, like Thomas Cooper, has metamorphosed the purifying idea of a Purgatorial 'satisfaction' for sin after death into the probative idea of God's working through the people and the officers of justice to discover evidence 'for our satisfaction', ensuring that we do not 'pervert Iustice, and condemn the innocent'.[7]

It is important, then, to realize, that the scene intervening between Hieronimo's discovery of his son's body and the opportune falling of the letter in his path is not so much indicative of time passing as admonitory of the consequences of failure to examine evidence. Act 3, Scene 1, brings the ambassador from Spain to Portugal, to inform the Viceroy of his son's welfare in Spain, and to begin negotiations for an alliance between Spain and Portugal by marrying the Viceroy's son to Castille's daughter. The Viceroy, of course, had, at the ambassador's entrance, just been giving one of his nobles, Alexandro, his passport to the 'lake' of hell, as a 'homicide', for killing his son. The audience is fully aware of how the Viceroy got his evidence for conviction: in Act 1, Scene 3, he lay prostrate with fears for his son's fate in the wars against Spain. Alexandro intervened with a reasoned likelihood: 'No doubt, my liege, but still the prince survives' (1.3.43). This nobleman developed the probability of his comforting supposition in successive stichomythic responses to the Viceroy's conviction of the contrary:

> VICEROY Survives! ay where?
> ALEXANDRO In Spain, a prisoner of mischance of war.
> VICEROY Then have they slain him for his father's fault.
> ALEXANDRO That were a breach of common law of arms.
> VICEROY They reck no laws that meditate revenge.
> ALEXANDRO His ransom's worth will stay from foul revenge.
> VICEROY No, if he lived the news would soon be here.
> ALEXANDRO Nay, evil news fly faster still than good.
> (1.3.43–50)

7. Thomas Cooper, *The Cry and Revenge of Blood* (London, 1620), sig. F3ᵛ.

Alexandro's conjectures are supported not by what he purports to have seen or heard, but their probability is inherent as they develop arguments from law (the death of Balthazar would be a breach of the law of arms), from commonplaces (bad news travels quickly), and from political experience (why kill a prince, whose ransom will be valuable?) to build up a convincing case. His enemy, Viluppo, by contrast, pours into his sovereign's ear a forged tale, backed by repeated assertions of personal witness: 'Then hear the truth which these mine eyes have seen', he begins, and proceeds to describe how Alexandro apparently discharged a pistol in the Prince's back. The Viceroy asks what became of his son's corpse? 'I saw them', Viluppo embellishes confidently, 'drag it to the Spanish tents' (1.3.59–75).

What Hieronimo decides to do, then, with the 'mean' or way afforded by the fallen letter is crucially, if somewhat laboriously, defined against the Viceroy's precipitate condemnation of Alexandro on the strength of Viluppo's evidence. At the end of his invention of arguments of suspicion concerning the letter, Hieronimo decides on a course of action: to 'Close, if I can with Bel-imperia | To listen more, but nothing to bewray' (3.2.51–2). In case Bel-imperia is part of the trap, he plans to reveal nothing of what he knows, and to gather what he can from her demeanour. With the almost over-neat irony characteristic of Kyd, however, Hieronimo's very caution provokes suspicion on the part of Lorenzo, and precipitates a false inference: Lorenzo, hearing from Pedringano, Bel-imperia's man, that Hieronimo has enquired of the whereabouts of his mistress, falsely supposes that Serberine, Balthazar's servant, has betrayed them. Even though Pedringano points out the unlikelihood of this, Lorenzo proposes to have Pedringano murder Serberine, for 'This sly enquiry of Hieronimo | For Bel-imperia breeds suspicion | And this suspicion bodes a further ill' (3.2.108–10). To Balthazar he seems about to reveal the whole plot, 'For I suspect', he begins, 'and the presumption's great, | That by those base confederates in our fault, | . . . We are betrayed' (3.4.9–11). Interrupted by the news of Pedringano's slaughter of Serberine, Lorenzo knows that everything now rests on the former being condemned to death, and silenced forever: 'now or never ends Lorenzo's doubts', he says, as he departs to arrange things with Pedringano's executioner (3.5.79).

The ironies, however, compound, as Hieronimo is appointed judge in Pedringano's case. Of course this puts Hieronimo in remembrance: 'This makes me to remember thee, my son', he says, as Pedringano mounts the scaffold (3.6.98). But the emotional effects of remembering cannot be separated from the ironies of discovery, as Hieronimo, though lamenting that he must 'toil in other men's extremes' without providing for his own 'redress' (4.6.1–4), nevertheless finds himself in receipt of more corroborating

evidence as a result of his judicial efforts. Pedringano's letter to
Lorenzo, brought to Hieronimo by a terrified hangman, dispels all
his doubts as to the veracity of Bel-imperia's letter:

> Now see I what I durst not then suspect,
> That Bel-imperia's letter was not feigned . . .
> Now may I make compare, twixt hers and this,
> Of every accident; I ne'er could find
> Till now, and now I feelingly perceive,
> They did what heaven unpunished would not leave.
>
> (3.7.49–56)

Though Hieronimo's journey to revenge may be punctuated by painful remembrance, its sequence and progress are determined by this
cautious investigatory process and the retaliation it duly provokes.
Once he has corroborated Bel-imperia's letter, he has his evidence,
but the problem has now become how he is to turn this private
knowledge into public accusation. 'I will', he proclaims, in words
remembered and imitated by Shakespeare in *Titus Andronicus*, 'go
plain me to my lord the king | And cry aloud for justice in the court,
| Wearing the flints with these my withered feet' (3.7.69–71).

Once again, sequence is rendered into space, and investigation or
deliberation into a choice of paths to worlds other than this, or to
the traversing of a place where judgment is enacted as pain and torment. So in Act 3, Scene 11, when Hieronimo meets two 'Portingales', who are asking for directions to Lorenzo's house, he tells
them 'List to me, and I'll resolve your doubt'.

> There is a path upon your left-hand side,
> That leadeth from a guilty conscience
> Unto a forest of distrust and fear,
> A darksome place, and dangerous to pass:
> There shall you meet with melancholy thoughts,
> Whose baleful humours if you but uphold,
> It will conduct you to despair and death;
> Whose rocky cliffs when you have once beheld
> Within a hugy dale of lasting night,
> That, kindled with the world's iniquities,
> Doth cast up filthy and detested fumes,
> Not far from thence, where murderers have built
> A habitation for their cursed souls,
> There, in a brazen cauldron, fixed by Jove
> In his fell wrath upon a sulphur flame,
> Yourselves shall find Lorenzo bathing him
> In boiling lead and blood of innocents.
>
> (3.11.12–29)

In one way, of course, we understand that Hieronimo is here trying
to convey to these Portuguese strangers that he knows that the
Duke of Castille's son—soon to be their prince's brother-in-law—is
guilty of murder. The knowledge means nothing to them, of course;
'Doubtless this man is passing lunatic', says one (3.11.32). In
another way, however, this lurid topography of guilt, pain, and punishment is Hieronimo's imaginative projection of the hopes he has
of bringing Lorenzo to justice. By this time, however, it is the very
invocation of these landscapes of everlasting torment itself that is
beginning to cancel out the feeling, in the play, that reliance on
divine justice might be an option. In the next scene, indeed, Hieronimo comes on with props that emblematically signify his need to
decide between two 'paths' to justice. One, which involves suicide, is
figured as 'trudging' to appeal to the judge of the underworld. The
other involves appealing to the King of Spain, who is about to pass
over the stage. He speaks hypothetically of pursuing this second
route: 'perhaps I come to see the king, | The king sees me and fain
would hear my suit' (3.12.1–2). But then he anticipates being struck
'mute' by standers by, and opts for the alternative: not justice at the
King's hands, but suicide, to stand before the Eternal Judge. 'Away,
Hieronimo, to him be gone: | He'll do thee justice for Horatio's death.
| Turn down this path' (3.12.12–14). Yet post-mortem justice seems a
contradiction. It is not that Hieronimo dreads everlasting punishment
for suicide, but that he cannot imagine justice without his collabora-
tion, justice as taking place after death: 'For if I hang or kill myself,
let's know | Who will revenge Horatio's murder then?' (3.12.17–18).
So, flinging away the instruments of suicide, 'This way I'll take', he
says. The 'way' is not a wild or violent one; it is the path of judicial
due process: Hieronimo, a judge and plaintiff with a good deal of
evidence for his case, pleads for justice with his King.

Once again, with heavy but powerful irony, one 'mean' or opportunity works against another, and Hieronimo's maddened attempt
to reveal his evidence by digging in the earth to 'bring my son and
show his deadly wounds' only confirms the King's suspicions of his
madness, which Lorenzo is very happy to corroborate (3.12.73). Kyd
skilfully and plausibly hints that political considerations—the
impending alliance of Spain and Portugal planned in the marriage
of Balthazar to Bel-imperia—render Hieronimo inaudible at court,
and prevent awareness of anything so inconvenient as an arraign-
ment of the Prince of Portugal for murder, now that a peace treaty
has been signed.

Hieronimo has evidence and the ear of the King, but cannot get
justice. At the next deliberative crossroads, the famous 'Vindicta
mihi' speech, he pits God's injunction to patience in Romans 12:19
against Seneca's advice that the criminal's only guarantee of safety

is through further crimes, and decides on a stance of patience, a clandestine alertness to opportunities for revenge. Citizens come to him seeking justice—he is renowned for his 'pursuit of equity', which was a term coming to be used quite generally for the circumstantial consideration of evidence at common law: Thomas Cooper praises 'the Equity and solemnity of that honourable trial' at which those who murdered the Leesons were found guilty by the jury.[8] Hieronimo's conscientiousness as a public servant, however, does him no good. The devastatingly heedless destruction of good local governance by global political ambition is painfully and effectively expressed in Kyd's skilful juxtaposition of Hieronimo's wild destruction of his plaintiffs' evidences with the smug unawareness of a court rapt in the thought of the imperial consequences of diplomatic triumph: an imminent alliance between Spain and Portugal via the marriage of Castille's princess, Bel-imperia, and the concealed murderer, Prince Balthazar. How perfect, then, that Hieronimo's skill as a dramatic writer of intrigue should enable him to seize this new 'mean' or opportunity that his forensic skill as a reader of evidence was forced to miss. Hieronimo's earlier work as a dramatist at the Spanish court demonstrated his skill in the representational strategies of the 'medley', when he entertained the Portuguese ambassador with a playlet featuring three knights with scutcheons capturing three kings with crowns. His dramatic *pièce de résistance*, however, is an intricately plotted intrigue, already extant as a text in a book, which both requires audience attention to cause and effect and confounds that attention by being performed in sundry languages. And where the medley style was perfected by improvisation, Hieronimo's carefully scripted intrigue dictates a causally plotted course of action which his actors—the murderous noblemen—are *bound to follow, even to their deaths*. This fantasy of classical dramatic plotting as retribution for class injustice is brilliantly conceived, as Hieronimo turns aside Prince Balthazar's repeated expressions of nervous hesitation by appealing to the snob value of tragedy. 'What, would you have us play a tragedy?', exclaims Balthazar, and Hieronimo ripostes with the example of Nero, and 'kings and emperors' delighting in plays (4.1.86–8). Having related the argument and cast the play, Hieronimo replies again to Balthazar's reservations, 'Hieronimo, methinks a comedy were better.' 'Fie', says Hieronimo, with delicious irony, 'Comedies are fit for common wits: | But to present a kingly troop withal, | Give me a stately-written tragedy, | *Tragedia cothurnata*, fitting kings, | Containing matter, and not common things' (4.1.155–61). The Kings, princes, and aristocrats that were so unaware, or so wilfully despising of such 'common things'

8. See Cooper, *Cry and Revenge of Blood*, sig. G4[r].

as Horatio's death, Hieronimo's cause, or the love of Bel-imperia for a commoner like Andrea, are so beguiled by their faith in tragedy's aristocratic credentials that they enact upon one another the just punishment for murder that it was once Hieronimo's task, as Spain's Knight Marshall, to dispense as part of every citizen's legal right. How fitting, indeed: it is little wonder that, as Ben Jonson tells us, there were some who would still 'swear, *Jeronimo*, or *Andronicus* are the best plays' as many as thirty years later.

Violence and Death

MOLLY SMITH

From The Theater and the Scaffold: Death as Spectacle in *The Spanish Tragedy*[†]

I

Traditional criticism regards Kyd's *Spanish Tragedy* as important primarily for its historical position at the head of the revenge tradition. Its violence has frequently been attributed to Senecan models, and its dramatic deaths, including the spectacular *coup de theatre* in the closing scene, analyzed primarily for their influence on Shakespeare's dramaturgy. And yet, though the Senecan influence has been well documented, critics have paid little attention to contemporary cultural practices such as public executions and hangings at Tyburn to explain the play's particular fascination with the hanged man and the mutilated and dismembered corpse. No other play of the Renaissance stage dwells on the spectacle of hanging as Kyd's does, and the Senecan influence will not in itself account for the spectacular on-stage hangings and near-hangings in the play.[1]

During Elizabeth's reign, 6160 victims were hanged at Tyburn, and though this represents a somewhat smaller figure than those hanged during Henry VIII's reign, Elizabethans were certainly quite familiar with the spectacle of the hanged body and the disemboweled and quartered corpse. In Kyd's treatment of the body as spectacle, we witness most vividly the earliest coalescence of the theatrical and punitive modes in Elizabethan England. Kyd also heightens the ambivalence inherent in the public hanging as spectacle

---

[†] From "The Theater and the Scaffold: Death as Spectacle in *The Spanish Tragedy*" by Molly Easo Smith as it appeared in *SEL Studies in English Literature 1500–1700* 32.2 (Spring 1992): 217–31. Reprinted by permission.

1. Frank Adolino has recently argued for a more specific connection between the play's depictions of death and the St. Bartholomew's Day Massacre in Paris in 1572; see "'In Paris? Mass, and Well Remembered!': Kyd's *The Spanish Tragedy* and the English Reaction to the St. Bartholomew's Day Massacre," *The Sixteenth Century Journal* 21, 3 (Fall 1990): 401–409. For a discussion of relationships between public executions and Marlowe's dramaturgy, see Karen Cunningham, "Renaissance Execution and Marlovian Elocution: The Drama of Death," *PMLA* 105, 2 (March 1990): 209–222.

and deliberately weakens the frames that separated spectators from
the spectacle.

Kyd's merger of the spectacles of punishment and enacted tragedy was perhaps inevitable in light of the remarkable similarities in
the format and ends of these popular events in early modern England.
Indeed, the stage and the scaffold seem to have been closely related
historically.[2] The famous Triple Tree, the first permanent structure
for hangings in London, was erected at Tyburn in 1571, during the
same decade which saw the construction of the first public theater.[3] At Tyburn, seats were available for those who could pay, and
rooms could be hired in houses overlooking the scene; the majority
of spectators, however, stood in a semi-circle around the event,
while hawkers sold fruits and pies, and ballads and pamphlets
detailing the various crimes committed by the man being hanged.
Other kinds of peripheral entertainment also occurred simultaneously. In short, hangings functioned as spectacles not unlike tragedies staged in the public theaters.[4] The organization of spectators
around hangings and executions and in the theaters, and the simultaneous localization of these entertainments through the construction
of permanent structures, suggest the close alliance between these
communal worlds in early modern England. Evidence also suggests that theater and public punishment provided entertainment
to upper and lower classes and that both events were generally well
attended. Contemporary letters abound in accounts of executions
and hangings, details of which are interspersed among court gossip
and descriptions of Parliament sessions. In a letter to Dudley Carleton, for example, John Chamberlain describes the hanging of four
priests on Whitsun eve in 1612, noting with mild surprise the large
number of people, among them "divers ladies and gentlemen," who

2. I include both executions and hangings under the term scaffold, but the distinction
   between these two forms of punishment is important. Executions were reserved for the
   upper classes and important criminals, while criminals of the lower classes were
   hanged. When William Laud appealed his death sentence, for example, the only con-
   cession made was to revise the sentence from hanging to execution in recognition of
   the prisoner's social stature.
3. Whether James Burbage's Theatre in Shoreditch was the first public playhouse is a
   matter of some dispute. See for example, Herbert Berry's "The First Public Playhouses,
   especially the Red Lion," SQ 40, 2 (Summer 1989): 133–148, where he argues that the
   Red Lion (which critics such as Chambers have regarded as an inn) was an earlier playhouse deliberately ignored by Cuthbert Burbage because of a falling out between his
   father, James Burbage, and Brayne, the owner of the Red Lion. But as Berry himself
   acknowledges, the Red Lion "must have been a very pale shadow of the Theatre. . . . So
   far as one can see, it had no walls or roofs, and the turret was to rest on the plates on
   the ground rather than on secure footings, along with, one might guess, the stage and
   galleries" (p. 145). The "secure footing" at least was provided only with the erection of
   the Theatre in 1576.
4. For descriptions of public executions and hangings in early modern England, especially at Tyburn, see Alfred Marks, Tyburn Tree (London: Brown, n.d.), and John Lau-
   rence, A History of Capital Punishment (Port Washington: Kennikat, 1932). See also
   Albion's Fatal Tree, ed. Douglas Hay, Peter Linebaugh, et al. (New York: Random
   House, 1967), though it deals primarily with the eighteenth century.

had gathered to witness the event which took place early in the morning between six and seven.[5]

*   *   *

Presumably, the relationship between theater and the scaffold worked both ways: if dramatic deaths could suggest public maimings and executions, the latter could as easily and as vividly evoke its theatrical counterparts.

Indeed, contemporary narratives about public hangings and executions frequently insist on the theatrical analogy. Carleton, for example, in a letter to Chamberlain, details in vividly theatrical terms the trial and executions of several conspirators, including two priests, implicated in the plot to harm King James I shortly after his ascension to the throne in 1603. The letter moves from a casual narrative to a concentrated exposition of the drama as it unfolded. Carleton begins his account with the hangings of two papist priests: "The two priests that led the way to the execution were very bloodily handled; for they were cut down alive; and Clark to whom more favour was intended, had the worse luck; for he both strove to help himself, and spake after he was cut down. . . . Their quarters were set on Winchester gates, and their heads on the first tower of the castle." This was followed by the execution of George Brooke, whose death, Carleton notes wryly, was "witnessed by no greater an assembly than at ordinary executions," the only men of quality present being the Lord of Arundel and Lord Somerset.[6] Three others, Markham, Grey, and Cobham, were scheduled to be executed on Friday; Carleton narrates the sequence of events as it occurred, retaining information about their narrow escape from the gallows until the very end:

> A fouler day could hardly have been picked out, or fitter for such a tragedy. Markham being brought to the scaffold, was much dismayed, and complained much of his hard hap, to be deluded with hopes, and brought to that place unprepared. . . . The sheriff in the mean time was secretly withdrawn by one John Gill, Scotch groom of the bedchamber. . . . The sheriff, at his return, told him [Markham] that since he was so ill prepared, he should have two hours respite, so led him from the scaffold, without giving him any more comfort.[7]

Lord Grey's turn followed, and he spent considerable time repenting for his crimes and praying to be forgiven, all of which, Carleton points out, "held us in the rain more than half an hour." As in the

5. Thomas Birch, *The Court and Times of James the First*, ed. R.F. Williams, 2 vols. (London: Henry Colburn, 1849), 1:173.
6. Ibid., 1:27.
7. Ibid., 1:29.

case of Markham, however, the execution was halted, the prisoner being told only that the sequence of executions had been altered by express orders from the King, and that Cobham would die before him. Grey was also led to Prince Arthur's Hall and asked to await his turn with Markham. Lord Cobham then arrived on the scaffold, but unlike the other two, came "with good assurance and contempt of death." The sheriff halted this execution as well, telling Cobham only that he had to first face a few other prisoners. Carleton then describes the arrival of Grey and Markham on the scaffold, and the bewildered looks on the three prisoners who "nothing acquainted with what had passed, no more than the lookers on with what should follow looked strange one upon another, like men beheaded, and met again in the other world." "Now," Carleton continues, "all the actors being together on the stage, as use is at the end of the play," the sheriff announced that the King had pardoned all three. Carleton concludes his account by noting that this happy play had very nearly been marred "for John Gill could not go so near the scaffold that he could speak to the sherrif, . . . but was fain to call out to Sir James Hayes, or else Markham might have lost his neck."[8]

The metaphoric alliance between theater and public punishment, which permeates Carleton's narrative, might be regarded as fundamental in Renaissance England. The theater and the scaffold provided occasions for communal festivities whose format and ends emerge as remarkably similar; early plays such as Kyd's *Spanish Tragedy* register the close alliance between these popular activities especially vividly. But the influence of the scaffold may also account for a general dramatic fascination with the spectacle of death evident throughout the late sixteenth and early seventeenth centuries. In fact, the close alliance between theater and public punishment frames the great age of drama in England; after all, the period culminates with the greatest theatrical spectacle of all, the public execution of King Charles I.

Despite my collapse of the theatrical and punitive modes, however, an important distinction needs to be made between the festivity of theater and the spectacle of the scaffold. Theater establishes distance between spectacle and spectators, and festivity implicitly or explicitly invokes the frame to separate itself from everyday living. Indeed, distance in the theater and framing in festivity perform similar functions. However, the authenticity in the enactment of public punishment makes its distance considerably more nebulous. In fact, participants in public executions and hangings remained acutely aware of their profound relevance both to the authorities who orchestrated the performance and to the spectators

8. Ibid., 1:31–32.

who viewed it. Such awareness frequently resulted in conscious attempts by victims to manipulate and modify the distance that separated criminals from onlookers. In such circumstances, the formal efficacy of the execution diminished considerably and events could easily transform into celebration of the condemned victim's role as a defier of repressive authority.[9] * * * Executions where the margins remained tenuous and where festivity merged so fully with the enactment of terror may be especially important to an understanding of the drama of death on the Renaissance stage. In early plays such as Kyd's, in the concluding representation of theater within theater, for example, we witness a conscious manipulation of distance and framing, dramatic exposition of the precarious nature of public spectacle itself as an illustration of royal and state power. The inner play's exposition of the shallowness of state authority gains added potency from the composition of its audience, the royal houses of Spain and Portugal. Hieronimo, the author of the inner play, even taunts his audience's reliance on the framed nature of theatrical tragedy:

> Haply, you think, but bootless are your thoughts,
> That this is fabulously counterfeit,
> And that we do as all tragedians do:
> To die today, for fashioning our scene,
> The death of Ajax or some Roman peer
> And in a minute, starting up again,
> Revive to please tommorow's audience.
>
> (IV.iv.76–82)[1]

At this, its most clearly self-reflexive moment, Kyd's tragedy simultaneously indulges and exposes its reliance on the drama of terror, and, through the mixed reactions of its stage audience who at first applaud the tragedy for its realistic enactment and then condemn it for its gory authenticity, invites a reevaluation of the spectacle of terror itself.[2]

9. Michel Foucault, *Discipline and Punish: The Birth of the Prison*, trans. Alan Sheridan (New York: Vintage Books, 1977), p. 61.
1. Thomas Kyd, *The Spanish Tragedy*, ed. Philip Edwards (Cambridge, MA: Harvard Univ. Press, 1959). All further citations from the play are taken from this edition.
2. Recent Renaissance criticism has shown particular interest in the self-reflexive and subversive aspects of drama in the sixteenth and seventeenth centuries and established the fragility of distance between spectacle and spectator especially in Shakespeare's plays. Greenblatt, for example, redefines this sense of distance in the dramaturgy of successful playwrights such as Marlowe and Shakespeare as the creation of anxiety. Anxiety in the theater also accompanies the evocation of delight: "the whole point of anxiety in the theater is to make it give such delight that the audience will pay for it again and again. And this delight seems bound up with the marking out of theatrical anxiety as represented anxiety—not wholly real, either in the characters onstage or in the audience" (*Shakespearean Negotiations*, p. 135). In characteristic privileging of the Shakespearean text, he goes on to describe "a kind of perfection" in the manipulation of anxiety, "a startling increase in the level of represented and

II

The Spanish Tragedy was staged within a decade after the construction of both the Triple Tree and the Theatre, and this perhaps
accounts for the hangings, murders, and near deaths which abound
in the play.[3] Lorenzo and Balthazar hang Horatio in the arbor in a
spectacularly gruesome scene, Pedringano's death by hanging
occurs on stage, Alexandro narrowly escapes being burnt at the
stake, Villuppo exits the play presumably to be tortured and hanged,
and Hieronimo tries unsuccessfully to hang himself in the last
scene, though he duplicates the effects of a hanging by biting his
tongue out. Of all these, however, Horatio's gruesome murder in
the arbor remains the centerpiece; we come back to it again and
again through Hieronimo's recounting of it, and as if to reiterate its
centrality, the playwright exploits the value of the mutilated body
as spectacle by holding Horatio's body up to view either literally or
metaphorically several times in the course of the play.

Kyd thus exploits thoroughly the audience's voyeuristic interest
in the hanged and mutilated corpse, but he prepares us for his centerpiece, Horatio's murder in the arbor, even from the opening
scene through promises of torture, mutilation, and death. Repeated
promises of more blood and gore, in fact, distinguish Kyd's version
of the revenge play from Shakespeare's later rendering in *Hamlet*.
While in the later play, Hamlet Senior insists that the torments of
the netherworld are too horrible to be recounted (he is also forbidden to reveal its secrets), in the opening scene of Kyd's tragedy, Don
Andrea's ghost provides with relish a vivid and detailed account of
his sojourn through the underworld:

> Through dreadful shades of ever glooming night,
> I saw more sights than a thousand tongues can tell,
> Or pens can write, or mortal hearts can think.

---

aroused anxiety" in Shakespeare (*Shakespearean Negotiations*, p. 133). I would like to
suggest that despite the heightening of what he terms as "delight" in the best plays of
Shakespeare, the manipulation of anxiety in Shakespeare's works moves entirely in
one direction, that is, to reiterate and rearticulate the distance between theater and
spectator. Indeed, I will suggest that despite the sometimes fragile nature of this distance, Shakespeare's plays reveal an ultimately conservative tendency towards the
demarcation rather than destruction of clear boundaries. In the work of other dramatists such as Kyd and Marlowe, and later, Shirley and Ford, however, one encounters
the highly problematic staging of such anxiety and delight that Greenblatt celebrates
in Shakespeare. Mary Beth Rose seems to be making a similar point when she argues
that "given the variety of conceptual options in Jacobean culture, he [Shakespeare]
often chooses the conservative ones, a pattern that becomes obvious when we view
him not on his own, but in relation to his fellow playwrights" (*The Expense of Spirit:
Love and Sexuality in English Renaissance Drama* [Ithaca: Cornell Univ. Press, 1988],
p. 173).

3. The earliest and latest possible dates for the play are 1582 and 1592, respectively. I have
gone by the generally accepted date of 1586–87. For a discussion of the problems in dating
the play accurately, see Philip Edwards's introduction to his edition, pp. xxi–xxvii.

Three ways there were: . . .
. . . .
The left-hand path, declining fearfully,
Was ready downfall to the deepest hell,
Where bloody Furies shake their whips of steel,
And poor Ixion turns an endless wheel;
Where usurers are choked with melting gold,
And wantons are embraced with ugly snakes,
And murderers groan with never killing wounds,
And perjured wights scalded in boiling lead,
And all foul sins with torments overwhelmed.
                                                    (I.i.56–70)

The underworld, not constrained by economic considerations, retains ancient methods of public deaths such as boiling and drowning, punishments long abandoned in England as too costly and troublesome; indeed, at the end of the play, Don Andrea's ghost envisions similar elaborate deaths for his murdered enemies in the afterworld. The opening and concluding accounts of the underworld which frame the play emphasize the tragedy's links with the spectacle of public punishment, the primary purpose of which was to replicate torments awaiting the victim after death. The opening scene even concludes with Revenge promising us better entertainment than that detailed by Don Andrea, more blood and gore through the murder of the princely Balthazar by Don Andrea's "sweet" Bel-imperia.

Indeed, the very next scene provides more elaborate fare; the king's request for a "brief discourse" concerning the battle between Spain and Portugal elicits from his general a detailed description complete with similes and accounts of mutilated and dismembered bodies;

On every side drop captains to the ground,
And soldiers, some ill maimed, some slain outright:
Here falls a body sundered from his head,
There legs and arms lie bleeding on the grass,
Mingled with weapons and unbowelled steeds,
That scattering overspread the purple plain.
                                                    (I.ii.57–62)

The king's satisfied response to this narrative, which ultimately details Spain's success in battle, captures the value of death as entertainment, an idea emphasized throughout the play in a variety of ways.

The audience hears four different versions of the battle in succession in these opening scenes—by Don Andrea, the Spanish general, Horatio, and Villuppo in the Portuguese court—and each account either elicits pleasure from the listener as in the scene just described or reveals the delight and ingenuity of the speaker.[4] The latter seems true of Villuppo's account of Balthazar's death to the viceroy in the scene which follows. Jealous of Alexandro's success at court, Villuppo fabricates a tale about Balthazar's treacherous betrayal by Alexandro in the midst of battle. The temperamental and fickle viceroy responds to the tale of his son's death with "Ay, ay, my nightly dreams have told me this" (I.iii.76) and immediately has Alexandro imprisoned. Villuppo closes this scene with an aside in which he revels in the ingenuity of his "forged tale." However, Villuppo's fantastic narrative must remind the audience of the uncanny way in which art mirrors life, for we have already been promised Balthazar's death by Revenge; when his murder occurs later in the play, its sequence mimics Villuppo's account, for the unsuspecting Balthazar is killed by his supposed wife-to-be, Bel-imperia, at what appears to be the height of his success. Even the viceroy's claim about his prophetic dreams gains ironic accuracy as the scene provides a narrative account of events yet to occur.

We arrive thus, via numerous accounts of death and mutilation, to the scene in the arbor where Bel-imperia and Horatio meet. Already aware of Pedringano's betrayal, however, the audience would view the images of war and love in the opening section of this scene as ominous. Interestingly, Pedringano, like the hangman who sometimes remained masked and hooded, conducts the ceremony of the hanging in disguise with the aid of his assistant Serebrine, while Lorenzo gives orders and joins in the stabbing after Horatio has been hanged. Though stage directions remain unclear, we can assume that Baltha-zar and Bel-imperia witness the stabbing, for Bel-imperia responds immediately to the horrible crime. Their function as spectators parallels our own and underscores Kyd's exploitation of the event as public spectacle. Foucault's argument that in early modern Europe, "in the ceremonies of the public execution, the main character was the people, whose real presence was required for the performance" proves especially appropriate to this hanging performed on a raised stage for an audience whose arrangement in "the pit" and the balconies above recalls the scaffold, and which certainly indulges the spectators' voyeuristic interest in death as spectacle.[5] The double framing of this event—the audience as spectators watching an already framed event—also anticipates the play within the play in

4. The exception to this might be Horatio's account of Don Andrea's death to Bel-imperia, though it also raises questions of authenticity by modifying two earlier accounts we have heard, the first by Don Andrea's ghost and the other by the Spanish general. Discrepancies among the earlier narratives should caution us, however, that the scene provides yet another tale glossed by the teller to satisfy Bel-imperia, a listener with different allegiances from the king and viceroy.
5. Foucault, p. 57.

Act IV which more explicitly raises questions about the value of death as entertainment.

A few scenes later, we are treated to a review of this event and later to another hanging (Pedringano's), whose format, however, remains remarkably different from the one we have just witnessed. Before turning to the later hanging, I would like to consider briefly the play's uncanny reliance hereafter on the spectacle of Horatio's mutilated body.

We are never allowed to forget this spectacle, and characters keep reminding us of this event in various ways. In fact, after the staging of this gory death, the earlier revenge plot associated with Don Andrea is all but forgotten; Horatio's murder and the collusive revenge orchestrated by Bel-imperia and Hieronimo on his behalf take center stage. Horatio's body, hanged and mutilated before a full house, thus takes precedence over Don Andrea, whose death has been narrated rather than witnessed. Interestingly, Don Andrea's funeral rites were conducted by Horatio in a private ceremony, and all that remains of him is a bloody scarf; it might even be argued that the complete obliteration of Don Andrea's corpse and the repeated emphasis on Horatio's symbolically reiterates the precedence of the second revenge plot over the first. Even Don Andrea's bloody scarf is duplicated through the rest of the play by Horatio's handkerchief which Hieronimo dips in his son's blood and presents on stage several times as a reminder of his unavenged death. This token of death also recalls a conventional practice at hangings and executions; onlookers frequently dipped their handkerchiefs in the blood of the victim which was believed to carry curative and divine powers.[6]

Unlike in *Hamlet* where murdered corpses remain hidden behind curtains or stuffed under the stairwell, Kyd's play thus presents death in vivid detail and follows this up with an elaborate scene of discovery in which both Hieronimo and Isabella identify Horatio's corpse. The ghost, perhaps echoing the audience's reaction to these events, expresses dismay at witnessing Horatio's murder rather than Balthazar's as promised, but Revenge, relishing the bloody detour, insists on the relevance of these events as preambles to more cunning deaths yet to occur: "The end is crown of every work well done; / The sickle comes not till the corn be ripe" (II.v.8–9).

After this murder, the focus of the play shifts to the psychological dilemma faced by Hieronimo as he plans revenge. The most interesting aspect of his character hereafter becomes his mental absorption with duplicating his son's murder. At first, he tries to duplicate bodies by reenacting the event with himself as victim; in a vividly

---

6. Peter Linebaugh, "The Tyburn Riot Against the Surgeons," *Albion's Fatal Tree*, pp. 65–118, 109–110.

dramatic scene which takes place at court, he enters with a poniard in one hand and a rope in the other and debates his route to death:

> Turn down this path—thou shalt be with him [Horatio]
>   straight—
> Or this, and then thou need'st not take thy breath.
> This way or that way?
>
> (III.xii.14–16)

Tormented by his inability to accomplish revenge, he spends most of his time wandering in the arbor looking for his son; here, near the very tree on which Horatio was hanged, the painter Bazulto, seeking justice for his own son's murder, visits him. In a psychologically revealing moment explored in one of the "additions," Hieronimo requests Bazulto to paint the scene of Horatio's murder, complete with the victim's doleful cry and his own emotional frenzy at discovering his son's body. In language, Hieronimo re-creates the event for us yet again: "Well sir, paint me a youth run through and through with villains' swords hanging upon this tree"; and later, describing his discovery of the body, he wishes to "behold a man hanging: and tottering and tottering, as you know the wind will weave a man" (Addition, III.xiii. 131–32, 151–53). His desire to re-create events through painting at first and later through the drama at court contrasts sharply with Isabella's desire a few scenes later to destroy the arbor and the tree on which her son was murdered. Both scenes, however, serve to keep the gruesome murder firmly in our minds.

The play even provides a semi-comic version of this murder in another hanging a few scenes later. Pedringano's hanging also takes place on stage and provides a semi-comic and officially authorized spectacle, a direct contrast to Horatio's base and treacherous murder committed in secret and under cover of night. Through the attitudes of Pedringano who reaches his death with a merry jest, and the clown who cannot resist the event despite his sympathy for the deluded victim, the scene simultaneously exploits and satirizes the value of the public hanging as a reiteration of justice.

* * * As I suggested earlier, the public execution's social relevance depended so fully on its proper enactment through the collusion of all participants, including the hangman as an instrument of the law, the criminal as a defier of divine and sovereign authority, and spectators as witnesses to the efficacy of royal power and justice, and the slightest deviation could lead to redefinitions and reinterpretations of power relations between subjects and the sovereign. Indeed, this happened frequently enough to cause some concern to the authorities.[7]

---

7. In the eighteenth century, official concern about the efficacy of public executions and hangings in reinforcing royal and social authority became especially acute as these

The speech delivered on the scaffold by the victim provided an especially suitable opportunity for such manipulation; intended to reinforce the power of justice, it frequently questioned rather than emphasized legal efficacy. Chamberlain, for example, bemoans the custom of allowing the condemned to address the audience and cautions about the inherent danger of this practice; describing the bravely rendered speech by a priest who was hanged at Tyburn, he notes that "the matter is not well handled in mine opinion, to suffer them [condemned prisoners] to brave and talk so liberally at their execution."[8]

Pedringano's defiant attitude when faced with death reiterates the carnivalesque possibilities of the public execution. Duped by Lorenzo into thinking that he will be pardoned, Pedringano insists on mocking the authorities who sentence him. Even the hangman expresses shock at his callous indifference to death: "Well, thou art even the merriest piece of man's flesh that e'er groaned at my office door" (III.vi.81–82). Indeed, it might even be argued that despite his role as victim, Pedringano has the final say on this travesty of justice, for he exposes Lorenzo's crimes in a letter, and thus forces Hieronimo to confront the inadequacy of the judicial system. In his mockery from beyond the grave, Pedringano becomes a version of the grinning skeleton in the *danse macabre* as he exposes the futility of human endeavor. The clown's attitude also reiterates the inherent irony of this grotesque enactment of state justice. Having opened the empty box which supposedly contains a pardon sent by Lorenzo, the clown reacts to the trick with infinite glee; his reaction parodies similar responses towards death voiced throughout the play by many characters, among them Balthazar, Lorenzo, Villuppo, and Pedringano himself:

> I cannot choose but smile to think how the villain will flout the gallows, scorn the audience, and descant on the hangman, and all presuming of his pardon from hence. Will't not be an odd jest for me to stand and grace every jest he makes, pointing my finger at this box, as who would say, "Mock on; here's thy warrant." Is't not a scurvy jest that a man should jest himself to death?
>
> (III.v. 10–18)

Indeed, he expedites Pedringano's death by playing his part to perfection.

In effect, the clown's attitude in this scene parallels the court's applause for the "Tragedy of Soliman and Perseda" staged as part of Bel-imperia's nuptial ceremony. After the tragedy, Hieronimo holds up his son's body to the bewildered court as justification for the

---

occasions increasingly provided excuses for rioting and general merrymaking (Foucault, p. 68).

8. Birch, 1:215.

multiple deaths that have occurred: "See here my show; look on this spectacle" (IV.iv.89). The court's reaction as the truth unfolds changes from applause to anger and condemnation. Implicitly, Kyd invites the audience to reevaluate its response to the tragedy of evil so cunningly staged, for Hieronimo's theatrical production necessarily draws attention to the nebulous nature of the boundary that separates spectators from the spectacle.

*   *   *

Kyd's tragedy, in fact, closes by reminding us of yet another frame, that provided by Don Andrea and the ghost who have witnessed events with the theatrical audience, and whose pleased reactions underscore the value of death as entertainment. The ghost, in fact, catalogues the list of deaths with obvious relish:

> Aye, now my hopes have end in their effects,
> When blood and sorrow finish my desires:
> Horatio murdered in his father's bower,
> Vild Serebrine by Pedringano slain,
> False Pedringano hanged by quaint device,
> Fair Isabella by herself misdone,
> Prince Balthazar by Bel-imperia stabbed,
> The Duke of Castille and his wicked son
> Both done to death by old Hieronimo,
> My Bel-imperia fall'n as Dido fell,
> And good Hieronimo slain by himself.
> Ay, these were spectacles to please my soul.
>   (IV.v.1–12)

His response reminds us of several such reactions to death in the course of the play: the court witnessing the "Tragedy of Soliman and Perseda" had commended the actors; Villuppo had reveled in anticipation as he plotted the death of Alexandro; the clown had marveled at the plot to send Pedringano to his "merry" death. Revenge even concludes the play with promises of further torments for the villains in the underworld. Thus, the play blatantly presents its multiple deaths as dramatic entertainment, but through Hieronimo's taunting condemnation of his audience's expectations, it also raises questions about theater's very status as a framed spectacle and about the value of death as public entertainment.

*   *   *

Politics and Subversion

J. R. MULRYNE

From Nationality and Language in Thomas Kyd's *The Spanish Tragedy*[†]

Thomas Kyd's remarkable play *The Spanish Tragedy* acknowledges in its title a national identity other than its author's. Notoriously, its denouement presents a babel of languages—Latin, Greek, Italian, French—likely to have been unfamiliar, at least in colloquial form, to the great majority of its earliest audiences. Yet the play's critical record shows that with few exceptions modern interpreters have paid scant attention to the national politics of *The Spanish Tragedy*, or to the association of these politics with questions of linguistic difference. I want in this essay to sketch in the framework of political (and religious) associations that would attach to Spain and Spaniards in English minds of the 1580s, or a prominent faction among them at least, and to identify so far as I can how such associations might properly influence our understanding of the play. Much has been written about the play's immensely fertile treatment of revenge; about its wonderfully adroit structure of ironies; about its preoccupation with personal and social justice; about its melodramatic excitements and its hero's eloquent introspection (taken up and sophisticated in Shakespeare's *Hamlet*). I wish to take nothing away from any of these interpretations; I have indeed tried elsewhere to contribute to them.[1] I wish only to ask whether we can bring the play even more sharply into focus, and put ourselves more fully in touch with its original structure of feeling, if we attend to questions of nationality and language.

* * *

† From "Nationality and Language in Thomas Kyd's *The Spanish Tragedy*" by J. R. Mulryne as it appeared in *Travel and Drama in Shakespeare's Time*, ed. Jean-Pierre Maquerlot and Michele Willems (Cambridge: Cambridge UP, 1996), pp. 87–105. Copyright © 1996 Cambridge University Press. Reprinted with the permission of Cambridge University Press.
1. See the introduction to my edition of *The Spanish Tragedy* in the New Mermaids series, revised edition (London, 1989).

We do not know when *The Spanish Tragedy* was written and first performed.* * * Yet for present purposes this scarcely matters, for Hispanophobia was a strand in the English consciousness in the 1570s, and one that broadened and intensified as the 1580s led towards the Armada of 1588.[2] In the immediately following years, enmity between the nations increased rather than slackened. The sorry tale of the mythologizing of such prejudice, fuelled by accounts, true and fancied, of Spanish conspiracies against Elizabeth herself, has been eloquently told in William S. Maltby's *The Black Legend in England*.[3] Protestant opinion came to think of Spain and the Spanish not just in belligerent but apocalyptic terms; as Garrett Mattingly has it, to Englishmen in 1588 'the clash of the English and Spanish fleets in the Channel was the beginning of Armageddon, of a final struggle to the death between the forces of light and the forces of darkness'.[4] It is hard to think that Kyd's audience in the 1580s, at the Rose or elsewhere, was unaffected by such widely disseminated attitudes when attending a play set in the Iberian peninsula and called *The Spanish Tragedy*.

Two critics who have read *The Spanish Tragedy* in relation to current nationalistic views are Ronald Broude and Eugene Hill.[5] Broude argues that Kyd's play may be seen to turn on the fulcrum of Isabella's line (II.v.58):

> Time is the author both of truth and right.

He tells us:

> Time as the revealer of truth and bringer of justice was a topos well known in Humanist circles . . . It was particularly prominent in English Protestant thought . . . During the ominous 1580's and 90's . . . the *topos* enjoyed special currency and seemed to promise not only that England would come through individual trials but that Divine Providence would guide English Protestantism through all its perils to ultimate victory.

The narrative of *The Spanish Tragedy*, Broude says, functions to reveal this humanist (but here sectarian) *topos* in action. Four narrative threads bind the play together in a series of revelations. Innocence is vindicated, calumny is unmasked, secret murder is revealed and

---

2. For a carefully documented account of Anglo-Hispanic relations in the period see R. B. Wernham, *Before the Armada: the Growth of English Foreign Policy 1485–1588* (London, 1966).

3. (Durham, NC 1971), *passim*.

4. *The Defeat of the Spanish Armada* (Harmondsworth, 1988), pp. 10–11.

5. Ronald Broude, 'Time, Truth and Right in *The Spanish Tragedy*', *Studies in Philology* 68 (1971), 130–45; Eugene Hill, 'Senecan and Virgilian Perspectives in *The Spanish Tragedy*', *English Literary Renaissance* 15 (1985); 143–65.

avenged, and the wickedness of the Spanish royal house is brought to light. The play's ultimate catastrophe shows Time as not merely serial but providential. Broude takes this to mean that *The Spanish Tragedy* must have jingoistic appeal for its English audience:

> While the Spain of Kyd's play cannot be taken literally as the historical Spain, it may certainly be understood as symbolic of a nation in which wickedness and depravity reign . . . The disaster which befalls Kyd's Spain is thus representative of the doom awaiting all nations in which the laws of God are ignored . . . Viewed in this way, *The Spanish Tragedy* must have offered welcome comfort to the English of the '80's.[6]

Eugene Hill's splendid essay 'Senecan and Virgilian Perspectives in *The Spanish Tragedy*' seeks to place Broude's insights (which he largely endorses) within a cultural nexus which takes in, as Broude does not, the framing action of Andrea and Revenge. For Hill, *The Spanish Tragedy* evokes, foregrounds and enacts 'a *translatio studii*, an historical rearticulation of privileged cultural models', these models being the creative insights associated with Virgil (in the framing action largely) and with Seneca. Recent studies, Hill argues, have recovered something of the Elizabethan Seneca as a writer who 'has no peer among classical poets in conveying the texture of evil in a hopelessly corrupt polity'. Virgil, by contrast, evokes in the *Aeneid* the burying of a regretted past, and the foundation of an enduring kingdom. 'In Seneca,' Hill writes, 'we observe with horror a hell-bent royal house, foundering in corruption. In Virgil we participate with wonderment in a rite of passage which inaugurates a new era of history.' The Senecan emphasis of *The Spanish Tragedy* is plain enough; the Virgilian perhaps needs some clarification. The Senecan prologue of the play, Hill explains, has been rewritten as an inversion of Aeneid VI:

> in place of *pius* Aeneas . . . Kyd gives us proud Andrea . . . Aeneas is led into the underworld by the ever-vigilant Sybil . . . Andrea is taken from the underworld by Revenge, who falls asleep. Aeneas learns the glorious destiny of his Trojan line and sees the future Emperor of Rome; Andrea watches the downfall of the Spanish royal house . . .

Hill shows how such sentiments would chime with popular myth-making among the Elizabethans. Spain came to be regarded as a kingdom 'too arrogant to note that it is ripe for downfall', while England began to cherish imperialist visions of London as the new

---

6. Quotations from Broude *ibid.*, 131–2, 144–5.

Troy (following Rome) and Englishmen as the new Romans. Thus anti-Spanish propaganda achieves in Kyd's play a culturally secure expression, making the energies of Senecan theatre expressively present for the Elizabethan popular stage.[7]

It is pertinent to ask what difference such interpretations make to our reading and performing of *The Spanish Tragedy*. Certainly, the horrors of act IV take on for informed readers and audiences a different kind of seriousness. The sense of absurdity with which it is tempting to greet Hieronimo's murderous play transforms itself to horror, or chauvinistic delight, as one realizes that what is at stake is the destruction of a kingdom and the collapse of its systems of government. The outcome may be read as minatory (England may go the same path if she neglects justice and privileges birth); but it must surely be understood in good part as a confirmation of the weakness at the heart of a hated if envied and (superficially) rich and powerful enemy. In Kyd's play, the King of Spain himself makes evident the historical parallel, and prompts the audience to indulge their fantasies at Spain's expense:

> What age hath ever heard such monstrous deeds?
> My brother and the whole succeeding hope
> That Spain expected after my decease! . . .
> I am the next, the nearest, last of all.
>
> (IV.iv.202–8)

The dead march that ends the tragedy pays tribute to those killed in Hieronimo's playlet. But its rituals incorporate specifically the grief of the Spanish king and his Viceroy in Portugal, together with the political collapse of their kingdoms:

> *The trumpets sound a dead march*, the KING of SPAIN *mourning after his brother's body, and the* VICEROY OF PORTINGALE *bearing the body of his son.*
>
> (IV.iv.217 s.d.)

The balance of emotions here is quite difficult to gauge. Conventionally, the grief that focuses on the death of the hero is mitigated by a sense of order restored, and the dawn of a new day. Here, we grieve for Hieronimo, and take pleasure in the sweeping-away of malice and corruption. We welcome too the avenging of Horatio. But the unease (familiar in the writing of critic after critic) with which the exacting of vengeance is greeted can only be allayed by taking the wider, the *historical* view, and subsuming unease within the gratified contemplation of a corrupt polity burning itself out. Hieronimo is displaced

---

7. Quotations from Hill, 'Senecan and Virgilian Perspectives', pp. 144, 146, 147, 150, 156.

from the closing moments of the play—not only through death but through a diversion of attention—because, however heroic and sympathetic, his meanings are engulfed in a more comprehensive tragedy than his own; or perhaps in a greater comedy, for as Hill remarks 'a *Spanish* tragedy implies an *English* comedy'.[8]

There are further aspects of a historical reading of the play which are worth bringing to notice. Even those scholars who have touched on the matter have not sufficiently emphasized that the concluding masque is one given in honour of a dynastic marriage. Dynastic marriage was a prime instrument of political policy in the sixteenth century, and one not unknown to the Tudors. Entertainments to celebrate significant marriages were prominent public occasions. Kyd's play is emphatic about the importance of the intended marriage of Balthazar to Bel-imperia (whose very name must have been interpreted as allegory by some at least among the audience). Even with the restless presence of Hieronimo to interrupt him, the Portuguese ambassador manages to convey the high and solemn significance of the intended betrothal:

> Renowned king, he hath received and read
> Thy kingly proffers, and thy promised league, . . .
> First, for the marriage of his princely son
> With Bel-imperia, thy beloved niece
> The news are more delightful to his soul,
> Than myrrh or incense to the offended heavens.
> In person, therefore, will he come himself,
> To see the marriage rites solemnised;
> And, in the presence of the court of Spain,
> To knit a sure, inexplicable band
> Of kingly love, and everlasting league,
> Betwixt the crowns of Spain and Portingale.
> There will he give his crown to Balthazar,
> And make a queen of Bel-imperia.
>
> (III.xii.32–50)

This set-piece diplomacy represents quite patently a bid for stability and political strength in an alliance between the states of Spain and Portugal. In the 1580s such an alliance would have particular meanings for an Elizabethan audience, a point to which I shall return. For the moment, it is enough to stress the dramatic irony of these high hopes: the 'kingly love, and everlasting league' which the alliance promises issues instead in a funeral procession mourning the collapse of both kingdoms' succession. Before that, Kyd takes

---

8. *Ibid.*, p. 151.

the opportunity, on the Viceroy's arrival in Spain, to underline the weighty personal and political implications of the event:

KING

> And now to meet these Portuguese,
> For as we now are, so sometimes were these,
> Kings and commanders of the western Indies.
> Welcome, brave Viceroy, to the court of Spain,
> And welcome all his honourable train.
> 'Tis not unknown to us, for why you come,
> Or have so kingly crossed the seas:
> Sufficeth it, in this we note the troth
> And more than common love you lend to us.
> So is it that mine honourable niece,
> (For it beseems us now that it be known)
> Already is betrothed to Balthazar,
> And by appointment and our condescent
> To-morrow are they to be married . . .

VICEROY

> Renowned king, I come not as thou think'st,
> With doubtful followers, unresolved men,
> But such as have upon thine articles
> Confirmed thy motion and contented me.
> Know sovereign, I come to solemnise
> The marriage of thy beloved niece,
> Fair Bel-imperia, with my Balthazar—
> With thee, my son; whom sith I live to see,
> Here take my crown, I give it her and thee;
> And let me live a solitary life,
> In ceaseless prayers,
> To think how strangely heaven hath thee preserved.

(III.xiv.5–34)

This self-divesting together with the investiture of his son, followed by withdrawal into religion, should be the prelude to political order and religious peace. Of course, it is not.

I do not think criticism has sufficiently underlined how intense the ironic contradictions of dynastic anticipation and actual event really are. In Hieronimo's playlet the nominal bride, Bel-imperia, stabs to death, rather than embraces, the groom-to-be Balthazar. If this were not in itself sufficient to turn masque to anarchy, the improbable topic addressed by the marriage masque offers no less a mockery of conventional celebration. For *Soliman and Perseda*, Hieronimo's play, evokes the ancient conflict of Christian with Turk, but in a fashion scarcely appropriate, at least superficially, to the marriage alliance between Christian princes. Erasto, the Christian knight of Rhodes, becomes the victim of the Turkish emperor,

Soliman, by the hand of his bashaw. Kyd makes Hieronimo explicit about the costume design for both actors: Erasto must wear 'a cross like to a knight of Rhodes' (iv.i.146); Soliman is arrayed in 'a Turkish cap' and 'a black mustachio' and carries the Turkish symbol of a 'fauchion' (a curved sword) (lines 144–5). Such patent emblems must stand out even more vividly in a kind of dumb show if the play was indeed performed in 'sundry languages', and was therefore incomprehensible to many of its audience. Simon Shepherd has noticed how a brief fashion for plays on Turks developed in the 1580s and 1590s, and furthermore how Protestant propaganda was inclined to 'describe the alleged cruelty of Catholics in general and Spaniards in particular as Turkish', a point Richard Bauckham amplifies by quoting Protestant apologists to the effect that 'the turke and antichrist differ not but as the devil differeth from hel'.[9] Shepherd offers an interesting discussion of *The Battle of Alcazar, Selimus* and *Tamburlaine*, but not *The Spanish Tragedy* (though he immediately turns to Kyd's play to discuss the topic of 'Fathers'). Yet the relevance of anti-Turkish prejudice to *The Spanish Tragedy*, and of the association of Turkish anti-Christianity with the perceived anti-Christianity of Spain, is I believe real—at least as a prevailing habit-of-mind within which Kyd's audience might interpret the *Soliman and Perseda* playlet.

As is well known, Kyd wrote a full-length play entitled *Soliman and Perseda* (or rather, a significant number of scholars regard him as the author). Whether this play precedes or follows *The Spanish Tragedy* is not certain—most commentators have thought it comes later—but it can arguably provide a near-contemporary frame within which the playlet may be understood. The printed play's title is given as *Soliman and Perseda, Wherein is laide open Loves constancy, Fortunes inconstancy, and Deaths Triumphs*, and indeed a heavy emphasis is given to death's eventual triumph through the framing action shared by Death, Fortune and Love. The play concludes with an *ubi sunt* spoken by Death:[1]

> Where is *Erastus* now, but in my triumph?
> Where are the murtherers, but in my triumph?
> Where Iudge and witnesses, but in my triumph?
> Wheres falce *Lucina*, but in my triumph?
> Wheres faire *Perseda*, but in my triumph?
> Wheres *Basilisco*, but in my triumph?
> Wheres faithfull *Piston*, but in my triumph?

9. Simon Shepherd, *Marlowe and the Politics of Elizabethan Theatre* (London, 1986), p. 144. The quotation is from E. Sandys, *Sermons* (London, 1585), p. 346. See Richard Bauckham, *Tudor Apocalypse* (Appleford, 1978) p. 97.
1. The quotations from *Soliman and Perseda* are taken from Frederick S. Boas ed., *The Works of Thomas Kyd* (Oxford, 1901).

Wheres valiant *Brusor*, but in my triumph?
And wheres great *Soliman*, but in my triumph?
Their loues and fortunes ended with their liues,
And they must wait vpon the Carre of Death.
Packe, *Loue* and *Fortune*, play in Commedies;
For powerful *Death* best fitteth Tragedies.
(v.v.17–29)

Amusingly, and significantly, the one excluded victim is 'Cynthias friend', Queen Elizabeth herself, for

Death shall die, if he attempt her end,
Whose life is heauens delight, and *Cynthias* friend.

The play is not doctrinally extreme, for Soliman is allowed to be both honourable (in ceding Perseda to Erasto in acknowledgement of their love) and capable of remorse (after he has Erasto strangled on a false charge of treason). But the religious and political significance of his conquest of Rhodes *is* brought out quite emphatically:

For by the holy Alcaron I sweare
Ile call my Souldiers home from *Persia*,
And let the Sophie breath, and from the Russian broiles
Call home my hardie, dauntlesse Ianisaries,
And from the other skirts of Christendome
Call home my Bassowes and my men of war,
And so beleager *Rhodes* by sea and land.
That Key will serue to open all the gates
Through which our passage cannot finde a stop
Till it haue prickt the hart of Christendome,
Which now that paltrie Iland keeps from scath.
(I.v.7–17)

Soliman and Perseda would mean for Kyd's first audience, if we can take some guidance from the full-length play, not only a death-laden disaster, but a religious débâcle that struck at the very heart of Christendom—neither, on a superficial understanding, at all appropriate for a marriage alliance between two of the great Christian powers, Spain and Portugal.

I can best bring out—or perhaps exaggerate—the climate of association of the Turkish conquest of Rhodes (with Erasto standing for Rhodes) by referring to the most influential, without doubt, of all the Protestant polemicists, the martyrologist John Foxe. Foxe's *Acts and Monuments* inserts a lengthy digression into his Protestant martyrology, under the title 'The History of the Turks'. This is devoted to highlighting the Turks' 'cruel tyranny and bloody victories, the ruin and subversion of so many Christian Churches, with the horrible

murders and captivity of infinite Christians'.[2] The most prominent
of all the Turkish tyrants is Soliman, 'The Twelfth Emperor of the
Turks'. Soliman's great deeds have been made possible by neglect of
duty and doctrinal folly on the part of the Christian Church. In particular, the fault must be laid at the door of the Papacy:

> the public church, standing in such danger as it then did, by
> the invasion of the Turk, reason would, nature led, religion
> taught, time required, that a good prelate, forgetting lighter
> matters, should rather have laid his shoulder to the excluding
> of so great a danger, as then was imminent both to himself,
> and the universal church of Christ. But now, his quarrel being
> unjust, and the cause of Luther being most just and godly,
> what is to be said or thought of such a prelate, who, forbearing
> the Turk, whom in a time so dangerous he ought chiefly to
> have resisted, persecuted the truth which he should specially
> have maintained? (p. 52)

The major outcome of such heinous neglect and wrong-headedness
has been the conquest of the Isle of Rhodes:

> This Rhodes was a mighty and strong island, within the Med-
> iterranean sea; the inhabitants whereof, at the first, did man-
> fully resist the Turk, sparing no labour, nor pains for the
> defence of themselves and all Christendom. But afterwards,
> being brought to extremity, and pinched with penury, seeing
> also no aid to come from the Christians, they somewhat began
> to languish in themselves . . . Thus Solyman, with his great
> glory, and utter shame to all christian princes, and also ruin of
> all Christendom, got the noble isle of Rhodes, (p. 53)

Foxe goes on to explore the manifest (to him) cause of such Christian reversals. He finds himself drawn to a discussion of the iniquities of Rome, and a comparison of Rome with Babylon:

> The causes why we have so to judge, be divers: first, that the see
> of Rome hath been defended hitherto and maintained, with
> much blood; and therefore it may seem not incredible, but that it
> will not long continue, but be lost with blood again . . . Another
> cause is, the fulfiling of Apocalypse xviii., where it is written,
> 'That great Babylon shall fall, and be made an habitation of
> devils, and a den of unclean spirits, and a cage of filthy and
> unclean birds:' . . . What city this is, called Great Babylon,
> which, like a mill-stone, shall fall and burn, and be made a habi-
> tation of unclean spirits and beasts, let the reader construe. This
> is certain and plain, by these her kings and merchants standing

---

2. The Revd. S. R. Cattley, ed., *The Acts and Monuments of John Foxe: a New and Complete Edition*, 8 vols., (London, 1841), IV, p. 18.

afar off for fear, and beholding her burning, that the destruction of this city (what city soever it be) shall be seen here on
earth before the coming of the Lord's judgment . . . by which
merchants and kings of the earth, peradventure, may be signi-
fied the pope, the rich cardinals, the great prelates, and the fat
doctors, and other obedientiaries of the Romish see . . . And
when they shall see with their eyes, and hear with their ears,
the city of Rome to be set on fire and consumed by the cruel
Turks, the sight thereof shall seem to them piteous and lamentable, to behold the great and fair city of Rome . . . so to burn
before their eyes, and to come to such utter desolation, which
shall never be re-edified again, but shall be made a habitation
of devils and unclean spirits; that is, of Turks and heathen sul-
tans, and barbarous Saracens, &c. (p. 77)

The only conclusion Foxe can reach is that we must think of Rome
as we think of the Turks. His wonderfully prejudiced account
culminates in a historian's pretended detachment that can only
lead ultimately to a bracketing of Turk and Pope as figures for
Antichrist:

Now, in comparing the Turk with the pope, if a question be
asked, whether of them is the truer or greater Antichrist, it
were easy to see and judge, that the Turk is the more open and
manifest enemy against Christ and his church. But, if it be
asked whether of them two had been the more bloody and per-
nicious adversary to Christ and his members; or whether of
them hath consumed and spilt more christian blood, he with
sword, or this with fire and sword together, neither is it a light
matter to discern, neither is it my part here to discuss, who do
only write the history and the acts of them both. (p. 122)

If we accept the Hispanophobic prejudice drawn out by Broude and
Hill as pertinent to the play as a whole, then the relevance of the
Turkish tragedy of Soliman and Perseda to the play's portrayal of
the fall of the papist realm of Spain becomes obvious. The ironies
of the play's structure extend to the choice of a marriage masque
entirely appropriate to the dynastic ambitions of this corrupt papis-
tical state. The masque, in other words, when aptly read *confirms*
the betrayal of Christianity, Protestant-style, for which the play's
Spain stands.

Several further specific ironies can readily be elicited from this
adroitly-conceived anti-masque of Soliman and Perseda,[3] but the
most inclusive irony lies in Hieronimo's own anticipation of his
polyglot playlet's effect:

---

3. For an exposition of several of these ironies see Sacvan Bercovitch, 'Love and Strife in
   Kyd's *Spanish Tragedy*', SEL 9 (1969), 215–29.

Now shall I see the fall of Babylon
Wrought by the heavens in this confusion.
(IV.i.195–6).

—the confusion, that is, of the linguistically disordered playlet. S. F. Johnson has pointed out that in the Geneva Bible (a translation much favoured in Protestant circles in the 1580s) Babylon and Babel are represented by the same word, used interchangeably.[4] Bound with a 1586 edition of the Geneva Bible in the library of the Shakespeare Birthplace Trust is a copy of *Two right profitable and fruitfull Concordances, or large and ample Tables Alphabeticall* 'collected' by R. F. H. The book is itself undated, but the preface is signed '1578'. Under the concordance entry for Babylon, one finds what amounts to a short essay on the significance (and the conflation) of Babel and Babylon in the compiler's mind:

> Babel, and Babylon . . . so named of the confusion of tongues.
> Gene. II.4, 9 . . . All nacio[n]s have drunken of the wine of the
> wrath of the fornications of Babylon. Reuel. 18.3. It is become
> the habitation of deuils, and the holde of all foule spirits.
> Reuel. 18.2. Her merchants were the great men of the earth,
> and all nations were deceiued with her inchantments. Reuel.
> 18.23. Utter destruction is prophecied against her, and her
> favourers [*many* references] . . . The Prophets and Apostles
> rejoyce at her destructio[n]. Reue. 18.20.

The proud and prosperous city whose 'inchantments' deceived the world, and whose lewdness led to a downfall greeted with joyful satisfaction by Prophets and Apostles, makes its appearance, as the compiler notes, throughout the Bible. But the principal appearances are in Isaiah (centred on chapter 13) Jeremiah (especially chapter 51) and Revelations (chapters 17 and 18). The Geneva Bible guided its readers' reading (like a modernist narrator) by marginal glosses. Taken together, text and gloss form a powerful interpretive alliance. I can quote isolated instances only, though the significant effect is cumulative. Take Isaiah 13, where the page heading (either side of the running title) is 'A thanksgiuing Against Babylon'. The first ten verses are occupied with prophecy, showing how 'the day of the Lorde cometh, cruel, with wrath and fierce anger to lay the land waste' (verse 9). Verses 11, 16 and 18–20 run as follows:

> 11 And I will visite the wickednesse vpon the world, and their
> iniquitie vpon the wicked, and I will cause the arrogancie
> of the provde to cease, and will cast down the pride of
> tyrants . . .

4. '*The Spanish Tragedy* or Babylon Revisited' in *Essays on Shakespeare and Elizabethan Drama in Honor of Hardin Craig*, ed. Richard Hoseley (London, 1963), pp. 23–36.

16 Their children also shalbe broken in pieces before their eyes:
their houses shalbe spoyled, and their wiues rauished . . .
18 With bowes also shall they destroye the children, and shall
haue no compassion vpon the fruit of the wombe, and their
eyes shall not spare the children.
19 And Babel the glorie of kingdomes, the beautie & pride of
the Chaldeans, shall be as the destruction of God in Sodom
and Gomorah.
20 It shall not be inhabited for euer, neither shall it be dwelled
in from generation to generation . . .

There are two marginal glosses to verse 11. The first (at 'the world')
notes 'He compareth Babylon to the whole world, because they so
esteemed themselves, by reason of their great empire.' It is easy to
see how such a self-image could readily be associated with Spain
and Portugal, who notoriously thought to part the whole world
between them. The second gloss explains the word 'proude': 'He
noteth the principall vice, whereunto they were most giuen, as are
all y^t abound in wealth.' The association of pride, wealth and Spain
was habitual. When the verses of the text go on to emphasize, as
part of the desolation of Babylon, the loss of children and the coming emptiness of the city, it is difficult (with our present preoccupa-
tions) not to think of the ending of *The Spanish Tragedy*, and the
King's lament for 'My brother, and the whole succeeding hope /
That Spain expected after my decease!' One might expect a 1580s
audience to recognize a suggestive analogy. The Geneva Bible and
its commentators were content with no more than general applica-
tion, when glossing the Prophets. Sectarian commentary is reserved
for the marginal annotation of Revelations, and here combative
candour is unrestrained. Verse 19 of Revelations chapter 16 runs:

> And the great citie was deuided into three partes, and the
> cities of the nations fell: and great Babylon came in remem-
> brance before God, to give unto her the cup of the wine of the
> fierceness of his wrath.

The first gloss (explaining 'the great citie') runs:

> Meaning the whole of them that shall call themselues Chris-
> tians, whereof some are so in deede, some are papists, and
> vnder pretence of Christ, serve Antichrist, and some are New-
> ters, which are neither of the one side nor of the other.

The second gloss (attached to 'the cities of the nations') spells matters out equally plainly:

> Signifying al strange religions, as of the Iewes, Turks and
> others, which then shall fall with that great whore of Rome,
> and be tormented in eternall paines.

Perhaps this is altogether enough; but the commentator reserves his plainest prejudice for the appearance of the whore of Babylon herself. Commenting on chapter 17 verses 5, 6 ('I saw a woman drunken with the blood of Saints, and with the blood of the Martyrs of Jesus') he lets any remaining mask of modesty fall right away:

> The beast signifieth the ancient Rome: the woman that sitteth thereon the new Rome which is the Papistrie . . .

and of the woman herself:

> This woman is the Antichrist, that is, the Pope with the whole body of his filthie creatures, as is expounded, vers. 18. whose beautie only standeth in outward pompe and impudencie, and craft like a strumpet.

Such a creative misreading must be one of the plainest instances on record of subjectivity in textual analysis. But it *was*, patently, a shared subjectivity, dispersed among a sectarian (and political) faction, at the least, in Elizabeth's court. For the reader, and the audience, of *The Spanish Tragedy*, we might expect Babylon and Babel to be braced together inseparably, with the polyglot confusion of Hieronimo's play signifying the downfall of the whore of Babylon, the papist church itself and its most prominent contemporary representative, the nation of Spain. Thus the Soliman and Perseda playlet, Babel and Babylon at once, serves as appropriately expressive dramatic inset for the play's account of a Spanish tragedy.

It has not been argued, I think, that the downfall of Spain amid Babylonian linguistic confusion is even more firmly tied to Protestant doctrine of the late sixteenth century. Yet, just as the Virgilian anti-type brings out for Hill the Senecan horrors of Spain's collapse, so the biblical anti-type for Babylon (or Babel) is itself a pertinent implicit contrast for an alert Elizabethan audience. Again, it is one that expresses itself in terms of diversity of languages. The biblical anti-type to Babylonian confusion for an Elizabethan churchman is the wonderful clarification of languages that came with Pentecost. The Epistle for Whitsunday (or Pentecost) as required by the Book of Common Prayer (Acts chapter 2 verses 1–12) tells how cloven tongues of fire sat on each of the Apostles, who 'began to speake with other tongues, as the Spirit gave them utterance'. Miraculously, among the multinational community of Jerusalem 'euery man hearde them speake his owne language':

> 11 . . . we heard them speake in our owne tongues the wonderfull workes of God.
> 12 They were all then amased . . .

The confusion of Babylon is healed. The Gospel for Whitsunday (John chapter 14 verses 15–end) promises 'another Comforter . . . Euen yᵉ Spirit of trueth';[5] the Proper Preface at the Eucharist makes a connection with preaching the truth to all nations:[6]

> Through Jesus Christ our Lord, according to whose most true promise the holy Ghost came downe this day from heauen, with a sudden great sounde, as it had bene a mighty winde, in the likenes of fiery tongues, lighting upon the Apostles, to teach them, & to leade them to all truth, giuinge them both the gift of divers laguages, & also boldnes with feruent zeale, co[n]stantly to preach the Gospel unto all nations, whereby we are brought out of darkenesse & errour, into the cleare light, & true knowledge of thee, of thy sonne Jesus Christ.

Such a missionary achievement as this might well be ringing in the minds of a Protestant audience as the fitting English comedy to complement implicitly the conclusion of *The Spanish Tragedy*.

There remains one further aspect of the play that invites comment here. Our discussion has so far assumed that *The Spanish Tragedy* is situated in a single court, the court of Spain. In fact, the Iberian history of the play is divided between the court of Spain and the court of Portugal (even the list of dramatis personae makes the division plain). The play begins from a battle between Spain and Portugal and it culminates in a disastrous marriage-masque intended to celebrate the final alliance between the two countries. Ambassadors from Portugal visit the Spanish court. The Spanish Viceroy in Portugal and his entourage make their way to Spain to grace the wedding ceremonies between the heir of Portugal and the niece of the Spanish King. Several major scenes are set in Portugal. Yet critics have been reluctant to consider whether Hispano-Portuguese relations of the 1580s may have influenced an audience's response to the tragedy. Some have wished the division of the courts suppressed partially or altogether: 'The Portuguese court,' writes Philip Edwards 'could have been introduced more economically and the relevance of theme is very slight.'[7] Patterns of irony have been identified to account for Kyd's inclusion of a second court; and a clear case can be made. But it is appropriate to ask whether a more contemporary and political relevance may have been apparent to a first audience, and one that will have intensi-

5. Quotations are from the Geneva Bible (?1586).
6. From *The Booke of Common Prayer, with the Psalter or Psalms of David*, n.d. (signed in ink 1586, but perhaps 1578).
7. Philip Edwards, ed., *The Spanish Tragedy*, The Revels Plays (London, 1959) p. liii. Professor Edwards' more recent paper, 'Thrusting Elysium into Hell: the Originality of *The Spanish Tragedy*' (*The Elizabethan Theatre* 11 (1990), 117–32) takes a different view. The essay is a major contribution to the interpretation of Kyd's play.

fied an Englishman's satisfaction at the destruction of the enemy Spain.

For those aware of the news from Europe (and, in a climate of gathering neurosis about Spain, almost everyone must have been) Portugal in the 1580s was perceived as at once Spain's enemy and Spain's possession. In 1580, Philip II annexed Portugal for Spain. He had some defensible title to the Portuguese crown, after the childless death of his nephew Sebastian I in the battle of Alcazarquivir (4 August 1578), and the brief reign of the aged Cardinal Henry (died 31 January 1580). Philip's hopes of constitutional succession were dashed by the Cardinal's inconveniently early demise, and he was forced to take Portugal with some brutality in the battle of Alcantara in August 1580. The union of Spain and Portugal that resulted was a matter, as J. H. Elliott puts it, of 'acute international concern',[8] and for English foreign policy a major source of anxiety, providing Spain, as it did, with maritime power of intimidating scope.[9]

A principal focus of opposition to Philip was Don Antonio, bastard son of the Duke of Braganza. Antonio had himself proclaimed King by a section of the ruling Cortes; first Santarem and then Setubal and Lisbon declared for him. After the crushing military victories of Philip he escaped to France and then the Azores. For the next ten or twelve years, he was a persistent irritant on the European scene, seeking alliances and financial support from France, England and elsewhere. In a climate of considerable political instability, he was far from entirely unsuccessful in such overtures. In 1582–3 the Dutch–French–English alliance provided him with ships and munitions for his assaults on the Azores; eleven of the ships were English. Antonio was a personable as well as plausible figure, a scion, if an illegitimate one, of the Portuguese royal family, fluent in several languages.[1] *The Calendar of State Papers, Domestic Series* of the 1580s bear testimony to the interest he stirred in England: there are numerous references from 1581 on, especially among communications to and from Walsingham—ever alert to potential conspiracies. On frequent occasions he is named as not merely pretender but *King* of Portugal, and generally taken seriously—though always with a sense that he was, after all, a dispossessed mendicant. Elizabeth certainly took him seriously, at least in terms of his potential as a pawn in the anti-Spanish cause. He was not only received at court (though the wary Elizabeth was

8. J. H. Elliott, *Europe Divided, 1559–1598* (London, 1968), p. 278.
9. See, for example, J. H. Elliott, *Imperial Spain, 1469–1716* (Harmondsworth, 1970), p. 276, and R. B. Wernham, *Before the Armada*, especially pp. 356–7.
1. For relevant details of Spanish and Portuguese history in these years see Geoffrey Parker, *Philip II: a Biography* (London 1978), especially pp. 142–6; and H. V. Livermore, *Portugal: a Short History* (Edinburgh, 1973), especially ch. 4.

inclined to play down the significance of this) but given financial backing—for example, an account of extraordinary payments from the Exchequer between Lady Day and Michaelmas 1587 records 'To King Antonio towards payment of his debts £1,000'.[2] His most prominent activities were those associated with the long-anticipated assault on Lisbon in May and June 1589, carried out by Drake and Norris; here the *State Papers Venetian* give especially eloquent testimony to the threat posed to Spain by Antonio, with the Venetian Ambassador sending up to three dispatches a day to the Consiglio di Dieci and the Doge.[3] There seemed a real possibility that the people of Portugal (if not the nobles) would rise and proclaim Antonio King; in the event they failed to do so, to Spanish relief and English disgust.

As Elliott remarks, wherever Don Antonio went 'he denounced the King of Spain and his wickedness, and managed to enlist widespread sympathy for his claims to the throne'.[4] It is scarcely conceivable that a play dealing so tendentiously as (we have argued) *The Spanish Tragedy* does with the matter of Spain and Portugal in the 1580s can have been unaffected by the stir he caused. There is one possible hint in the text that Antonio was not entirely absent from Kyd's mind. In the Portuguese court in 1. iii, the Spanish Viceroy accuses the (honourable) figure of Alexandro:

> Was't Spanish gold that bleared so thine eyes . . .
> Perchance because thou art Terceira's lord,
> Thou hadst some hope to wear the diadem.
>
> (1.iii.76–8)

In the play, Alexandro is vindicated; Antonio had indeed some hope to wear the diadem; he was *not* Terceira's lord but in the *Calendar of State Papers, Foreign Series* there are numerous references that associate him with the island. For example, a letter from Cobham to Walsingham of 11 November 1581:

> I am advertised as follows of the affairs of Portugal: that the Isles of Terceiras show themselves so affectioned towards Don Antonio that they have executed the King of Spain and the Duke of Alva by 'picture' after condemning them by their 'order of process' for tyrants.[5]

Terceira proved a power-base for Antonio. Plainly, Antonio is *not* the play's Alexandro, though in the manner of Elizabethan plays a

---

2. *Calendar of State Papers, Domestic Series, 1581–1590* (London, 1865), p. 427.
3. Horatio F. Brown, ed., *Calendar of State Papers and Manuscripts, Existing in the Archives and Collections of Venice 1581–1591* (London, 1894).
4. Elliott, *Europe Divided*, p. 281.
5. A. J. Butler, ed., *Calendar of State Papers, Foreign Series, January 1581–April 1582* (London, 1907), p. 361.

passing compliment may have been intended. Nor is the history of the play the Hispano-Portuguese history of the 1580s. The play's initial battle is not Alcantara, and there was no dynastic marriage contemplated to correspond to the Bel-imperia/Balthazar marriage of *The Spanish Tragedy*. But the Portugal and Spain of the play perhaps bear a certain resemblance to the prejudiced English image of the international diplomacy of the decade—the Portuguese court, so fully compliant with the wishes of Spain, and under a Spanish Viceroy, may be thought to represent what Englishmen feared if, as the King of Spain in our play wishes it, 'Spain is Portugal, / And Portugal is Spain' (i.iv.132–3). The political prejudices of an Elizabethan audience (which of course included religious prejudices) may well have led to an understanding of *The Spanish Tragedy* as offering a commentary on the historical circumstances in which Englishmen found themselves in the 1580s and early 1590s.

The Play of Opposites

T. McALINDON

From Thomas Kyd: *The Spanish Tragedy*†

* * *

Although the characters of the play are excellently differentiated,
radical contradiction is something they all have in common. The
nature of this dualism is reflected in a proliferation of certain cog-
nate antithetical terms which never occur in conjunction but lead a
deceptively separate existence: 'gentle' and 'wild', 'ruthful' and 'ruthless', 'patience' and 'fury'. Its most sinister manifestation occurs in
the character of Lorenzo, the man of very gentle birth whose smooth
courtliness and jovial affability obscure the fact that he can be compared to a 'savage monster, not of human kind' (ii.v.19). Although
untroubled by any inner conflict between the contrary tendencies
in his nature (his reason and will are wholly at the service of his
desires), he can be acted as a credible and well-rounded character.
Aristocratic pride is what unkennels his barbarity. Resentful in the
first place at his displacement in the roll of military honour by a mere
gentleman such as Horatio, he is quietly outraged by the discovery
that this same upstart ('What, Don Horatio, our Knight Marshal's
son?'—ii.i.79) is secretly undoing a prospective marriage between
his sister and the Portuguese heir-apparent:[1]

Lorenzo's abrupt shifts of style from the ornate and the oblique
to the plain and the blunt, manifesting a sudden impatience with
the 'gentle' manner he is obliged to practise and go along with, contribute much to his credibility and liveliness as a stage character.
But his impatience also relates him to an antithesis fundamental to
the play's conceptual pattern: that which poises impulsive private
action against respect for time, custom, and law. The antithesis is
superbly dramatised in ii.i, a scene which Lorenzo controls from
start to finish and which, in its structure, rhythm, and sense, mirrors

---

† From "Thomas Kyd: *The Spanish Tragedy*" by T. McAlindon as it appeared in *English Renaissance Tragedy* (London: Macmillan, 1986), pp. 59–72, 74–77, 248–50. Reprinted by permission of Palgrave Macmillan.
1. Cf. Philip Edwards (ed.) *The Spanish Tragedy* (London: Methuen, 1959), pp. liv–lv.

the larger tragedy. It opens with Lorenzo talking in his most languid and courtly style, urging his love-lorn friend to listen to reason and accept that 'in time' (the phrase is given fivefold iteration) the lady will relent and 'rue the sufferance of your friendly pain' (ll. 1–8). The scene reaches its climax with Lorenzo's successful attempt, partly brutal ('What, villain, ifs and ands?'—l. 77) and partly suave, to extract from Pedringano the name of his sister's secret lover. And it ends with his business-like injunction to the verbose and plaintive Balthazar, 'Let's go my lord, your staying stays revenge' (l. 133). Lorenzo's relationship here with the manifestly impatient Balthazar ('For love resisted grows impatient'–l. 117) is identical to that between Revenge and Andrea, shown in the preceding choric scene: 'Be still, Andrea, ere we go from hence, I'll turn their . . . joys to pain, their bliss to misery' (I.v.5–9). Like Revenge's, Lorenzo's air of quiet patience is that of a man who always has his hand on the detonator that will remove all obstacles from his path. He is fundamentally opposed to time and ripeness. This is finely suggested by the circumstances of Horatio's murder, hanged from a tree in his father's arbour and finished off in a stabbing orgy that mocks coition: 'Ay, thus and thus, these are the fruits of love' (II.iv.55).

Although it makes him an embryonic Iago (and Balthazar another Roderigo), Lorenzo's demonic parody of patience or 'stillness' is a less important element in his characterisation than are his perverted gestures to the qualities proper to the just lord and master. In his first dealings with Pedringano, he asks for fearless telling of the truth in response to 'just demand', threatens punishment if the servant is 'perjur'd and unjust' in his replies, and promises liberal reward, social advancement, and friendship to boot if he meets with 'duteous service' (II.i.43–103): the foolish Pedringano might almost confuse him with his uncle the King, whose conduct has shown strict fidelity to the principles specified in this behavioural outline. However, the service required from Pedringano entails betraying the trust of Bel-imperia and then acting as spy against her; it is secured by a combination of blackmail, bribery, and murderous threats; and it is underwritten with an oath of secrecy to which the servant is forced to subscribe. Although he has no present political role, the prospective heir to the Spanish throne is a prototypal Jacobean tyrant in every respect: that is, he violently undoes the bonds of friendship and true love, turns service into a condition of bondage, generates in society a netherworld of dark secrets, and—as we shall presently observe—either frustrates the due process of legal justice or uses it to dispose of unwanted servants. His relationship with his sister, with the socially inferior but intrinsically nobler Horatio, and with the corrupted servant Pedringano anticipates the more fully developed relationship between Ferdinand, the Duchess, Antonio, and Bosola in *The Duchess of Malfi*.

It is one of the more satisfying ironies of the play that Lorenzo, who thinks he knows everyone's 'mind' and 'humour' (III.iii.76; iv.57), is finally undone because he seriously misreads his own sister. The doubleness of Bel-imperia's name is no accident. She is beautiful and intelligent, but she is also endowed with an imperious will and with passions she is not in the habit of restraining for long. Modern attitudes to sexual morality should not blind us to the fact that her introduction to us as 'a worthy dame' possessed 'in secret' is a laconic paradox (I.i.10). Those closest to her are almost comically unaware of her unofficial self, complacently ascribing to her only those attributes conventionally associated with feminine beauty. According to brother, father, and uncle, she is 'gentle' and 'will stoop . . . In time' (III.x.12; II.i.4–5); not 'froward' but 'coy . . . as becomes her kind' (II.iii.3–5); one of the 'young virgins' (l. 43). There are layers of dramatic irony in her reassuring words to Horatio concerning her servant Pedringano: 'he is as trusty as my second self' (II.iv.9).

Not that inconstancy in love can be ascribed to her. She does indeed seem to transfer her affections from the dead Andrea to Horatio with remarkable speed; but this is because Kyd manages the development in an awkwardly condensed manner, and not because it is meant to appear unworthy. And Kyd does enough to suggest that it is perfectly credible. It seems natural that a woman grieving for the death of a lover, and alienated from her family because of their hostility to him when alive, should be strongly attracted to the sensitive hero who shares her love for the dead man. But the situation is more complex than that. For Kyd, the really important psychological fact about Bel-imperia's relationship with Horatio, and about her subsequent behaviour, is that both are propelled by a churning tide of contrary emotions. Loving grief converts to fury and hatred, these quicken new love, and new love sustains old hatred: 'Yes, second love shall further my revenge. / I'll love Horatio, my Andrea's friend, / The more to spite the prince that wrought his end' (I.iv.66–8).[2] To express the matter in humoral and elemental terms (as does Kyd: see III.x. 68–75), melancholy can flow to choler, the tears of pity and love can become the fires of rage and destruction. This psychological syndrome affects Hieronimo, Isabella, and Balthazar, and so is central to the play (it is prominent in many later tragedies). It means, of course, that the impulse to revenge is conceived as a dire confusion of emotional and moral opposites.

2. See Peter J. Murray, *Thomas Kyd* (New York: Twayne: 1969), pp. 34–5.

Bel-imperia's outraged love gives her a key role in the unfolding tragedy. Indeed, it makes her very like a euhemerized version of one of those classical, female divinities who habitually whip men out of their restrained and pacifist ways down the paths of violence and madness, a 'wrathful Nemesis' (I.iv.16) or 'madding Fury' (III.x.33). Although Horatio was 'incens'd with just remorse' at the treacherous killing of his friend, his reaction was not extreme: he 'set forth against the prince. / And brought him prisoner from his halberdiers' (I.iv.28–9). But for Bel-imperia this subordination of personal feeling to a chivalrous ethic is the one blot on Horatio's heroic record: like Lady Macbeth, she would have her man do more than becomes a man—'Would thou hadst slain him that so slew my love' (l. 30). It is she too who takes the initiative in the love affair; and, although this is dictated by his social inferiority, it is also indicative of her masterful nature and her intent to commit him to a course where passionate love and passionate hate are one. Thus, when he is killed as a result of his entanglement with her, his father becomes the object of those fiery persuasions he himself was due to receive:

> Is this the love thou bear'st Horatio?
> Is this the kindness that thou counterfeits?
> Are these the fruits of thine incessant tears?
> Hieronimo, are these thy passions,
> Thy protestations and thy deep laments,
> That thou wert wont to weary men withal?
> O unkind father, O deceitful world!
>
> (IV.i.1–8)

I am not suggesting, however, that Horatio and Hieronimo are essentially victims of this passionate young woman. Hieronimo is delighted here to discover that she is so thoroughly commited to revenge: 'Why then, I see that heaven applies our drift, / And all the saints do sit soliciting' (ll. 32–3). Since Hieronimo used to think it was the 'ugly fiends' of Hell would 'solicit' him to take revenge (III.ii.15–16), it follows that his confusion of mind and heart is just as severe as hers. As for Horatio, once he has been given the come-hither by Bel-imperia, he needs no further encouragement: it is he who lightly remarks that looks and words are very pleasant 'where more cannot be had' (II.ii.4), thus initiating the erotic dialogue which leds directly to his death in the garden. Moreover, there are suggestions that in neglecting Balthazar and pursuing Bel-imperia he is betraying the trust of the King and Castile (see I.ii.98–100; iv.55–7, 174 s.d.). At any rate, a courtier in his position would know that having an affair with the Infanta is courting disaster for oneself and one's family: Lorenzo's bitter remarks about his ambition would not have sounded wholly inept to an Elizabethan audience. It is apparent that in this tragedy, as in *The White Devil*, everyone is in some degree his own and the next person's provocative demon.

Because of the baseness of both her brother and her royal suitor, Bel-imperia never forfeits our sympathy and admiration. The attitude, too, of her father and the King towards her love life contributes substantially to these positive feelings. It has to be emphasised that in virtually every respect these two brothers are models of justice and kindly concern: each seeks at crucial moments to resolve differences, make enemies friends, and acknowledge true merit. Their one fault lies in their unthinking assumption that Bel-imperia has no rights whatever in the choice or rejection of a suitor. Any opposition to their will in this matter threatens to crack the mould of their patient urbanity and humane justice. The King believes that young ladies 'must be rul'd by their friends' in matrimonial matters and urges Castile to 'win fair Bel-imperia from her will' (II.iii.42–3). He does not advise his brother how this should be done, but we can guess at Castile's preferred method. It would be a combination of emotional blackmail ('love him or forgo my love'—l. 8) and blind fury (that 'old wrath' which blighted the Andrea affair—III.x.70, 72)— like father, like daughter. In the playlet used by Hieronimo and herself to wreak vengeance on Balthazar and Lorenzo, Bel-imperia plays a 'fair Christian nymph' (IV.iv.16), and in a sense 'miss'd her part in this' (l. 140). But, given the way in which male authority disposes of Bel-imperia's natural rights as a woman, it is very apt that the Christian nymph should be driven to violence by a ruler whose name is that of a legendary, barbarous tyrant, Soliman (Suleiman) the Turk. Like *Othello*, *The Spanish Tragedy* presents a contrarious world where Christian gentlemen can quickly 'turn Turk' (*Othello*, II.iii.162) in their dealings with the women they love (as with each other).

Of course, it is only in the character of Hieronimo that sudden and extreme change is exposed as a tragic fact, both pitiable and terrible. Hieronimo does not become a prominent figure until the end of Act II and so cannot be deemed a tragic protagonist in the conventional sense. Rather he is the most important individual in a tragedy which focuses on the way in which the failings of many characters interact to produce collective disaster, and where society is as much the victim of the individual as the individual is of society: a tragic model of which much will be made in the seventeenth century.[3] Nevertheless, the tragic intensity of *The Spanish Tragedy* derives

---

3. It is often said that seventeenth-century tragedy differs from Elizabethan tragedy in that it is concerned more with the fate of society than with that of the individual. Failure to qualify this distinction by reference to *The Spanish Tragedy* may owe something to the fact that critics of Kyd's play have regularly ignored the significance of its title (though for a notable exception to the rule, see Murray, *Thomas Kyd*, pp. 64–5). A comparable Elizabethan play is *Julius Caesar*, which might more appropriately have

almost entirely from Hieronimo's agonised responses to the horrors
of a violently changing world—

> O world, no world, but mass of public wrongs,
> Confus'd and fill'd with murder and misdeeds
> (iii.ii.3–4)

—and from his consequent protest and disintegration.

Before he is transformed by his son's murder, Hieronimo is the
embodiment of all that is best in his own society. He is a father and
husband of loving heart, a man of law noted for his energetic yet
'gentle' pursuit of equity (iii.xiii.51–4, 93–4), and a courtly poet and
entertainer who uses his art for socially binding purposes. Because
of his obvious 'deserts', he has won not only royal favour but also 'the
common love / And kindness' of the court and the people (iii.xiv.61–2).
He is thus a figure of unity in whom the twin themes of love and
justice converge: very aptly, Kyd associates him with Orpheus.

*   *   *

Pointed repeatedly by means of appropriate imagery and allusion,
the broad analogy between Hieronimo and Orpheus stands out
clearly in Kyd's play and greatly expands the imaginative effect of
its themes. Hieronimo too is grief-stricken by the loss of a loved one
snatched from him in a most untimely death. He journeys repeatedly in his imagination to the Underworld, finds that the harmonious arts are of no avail, despairs of divine justice and benevolence,
and finally is destroyed in a holocaust of violence to which he has
been urged by a woman as deaf to Orphic harmonies as any Maenad
('Relentless are mine ears to thy laments'—iv.iv.60). On the other
hand, Orpheus dies in a vain attempt to overcome discord with concord; unlike Hieronimo, he is true to himself to the end. In fact Kyd
uses the myth ironically and contrariously as well as analogically
and panegyrically. Hieronimo is an Orpheus who falls: the spirit of
strife invades his soul, and he even perverts the Orphic ideal, confusing discord with harmony. This conception of his tragedy (and it
is the tragedy of the society which he represents) is richly complicated by means of the Renaissance idea of Orpheus as the father of
eloquence and so of civilisation itself. Orpheus, son of Apollo, was
held to be the first orator. He was the type of those who once used
their persuasive powers to induce men to abandon their 'wyld, stowre,
hard' ways in the wilderness and to live together 'in good order . . .
Like neybours in a common weale by iustyce vnder law', and who

---

been called *The Roman Tragedy*—'O, what a fall was there, my countrymen! / Then I,
and you, and all of us fell down' (iii.ii.190–1).

function at all times, by virtue of their 'honest eloquence', as 'props to uphold a state, and the onely keyes to bring in tune a discordant Commonwealth'.[4] Thus in the Renaissance not only poet and musician, but also lawyer, politician and courtier—self-conscious masters in the arts of language and 'civil conversation'—would all look to Orpheus as their patron and model.[5]

Kyd's appeal to the Orphic paradigm in its full significance is unmistakable. Hieronimo's first two speeches mark him out with almost programmatic emphasis as a man of loving heart who pleads effectively for justice by skilfully controlling and expressing his feelings (I.ii.116–20, 166–72). His last sentence and his last actions in the play define, in organic and sensationally emblematic terms, the self-destruction of an Orphic hero: 'First take my tongue', he exclaims to his bewildered audience, 'and afterwards my heart' (IV.iv.191); and he then bites out his tongue and plunges a knife in his breast. His tragedy is that of a man whose heart is poisoned by an event whose full horror he finds unendurable and inexpressible; the discovery of his son's bloody corpse hanging from a tree in the family arbour undoes the unity of his being and results in a malfunctioning and perversion of his noblest gifts.[6] Kyd's concentration on this process of degenerative change is so thorough that it is difficult to see how he could have wished us to endorse Hieronimo's revenge, since it is precisely the pursuit of a secret and violent form of retribution that constitutes the loss of Hieronimo's Orphic self. This is not to say that we are expected to sit in judgement on Hieronimo, or even that Kyd is interested in the moral problem of private revenge. His primary concern (in relation to this character) is to convince us of the terrible fact that the 'heart' of a loving, rational man can become 'envenom'd with such extreme hate' (III.i.15–16) that he will revel in violence. Kyd's imaginative energies are devoted not to the exploration of a moral problem but to a psychic upheaval in which the protagonist oscillates between the poles of his being until his darkest instincts take complete control, silencing his noble self or using it as their instrument. That some audiences and readers will always suppose we are to approve of what Hieronimo does in his distress is a measure of Kyd's success in communicating the intensity of his

---

4. *The XV Bookes of P. Ouidius Naso, entytuled Metamorphoses*, trs. Arthur Golding (London, 1567) Epistle, ll. 521–6; Peacham, *The Complete Gentleman*, p. 8.
5. See Kirsty Cochrane, 'Orpheus Applied: Some Instances of his Importance in the Humanist View of Language', *RES*, XIX (1968) 1–13.
6. Although the Orphic analogy has not been noticed, the significance of language in the tragedy has come in for a good deal of discussion. See, for example, Barish, in *Elizabethan Theatre*, SUAS IX, pp. 78–81; Scott McMillin, 'The Figure of Silence in *The Spanish Tragedy*', *ELH*, XXXIX (1972) 27–48; Carol McGinnis Kay, 'Deception through Words: A Reading of *The Spanish Tragedy*', *SP*, LXXIV (1977) 20–38.

hero's sufferings and, in particular, the condition of psychic—i.e. emotional, intellectual, and moral—confusion which makes him think his actions right and 'fit'.[7]

From the moment he discovers his son's corpse in II.iv until the end of the third act, when he has become calmly and totally committed to revenge, Hieronimo is an image of contrariety, uncertainty, and confusion. The fourth and last act is splendidly theatrical and richly symbolical, but the essence of the tragic drama lies in the tense psychomachia of the third act, where the characteristic qualities and values of Orphic man are assailed by their opposites and either overcome or seduced. Reason, communication, patience, hope, and respect for time give way to fury, silence, secrecy, dissembling, despair, and a wild desire to accelerate the moment of justice and death.

The conflict is not logically progressive; rather, it is a pattern which repeats itself over and over with mounting intensity until madness—or a kind of mad rationality—prevails. The essential features of the pattern are evident in Hieronimo's behaviour after the discovery of the body. It is Isabella and not he who says,

> The heavens are just, murder cannot be hid,
> Time is the author both of truth and right,
> And time will bring this treachery to light.
>
> (II.v.57–9)

Such thoughts have been banished from his consciousness for the time being. He thinks not of impersonal justice but of an act of retaliation which would bring 'relief' and 'joy' to his 'throbbing heart' (ll. 2, 40–1, 51–5). His advice is that they should cease or at least dissemble their grieving, and accordingly he determines that the body will not be buried until he has fulfilled his vow of revenge. Our commitment to Hieronimo as a serious and convincing dramatic character is severely strained here; but the flawed relationship between action and character does at least show Kyd's concentration on theme. We are to reflect at this point on the damage that will inevitably be done to the bereaved heart by the renunciation of communal mourning; on the function of funeral as the primary token of love and respect for the dead (see I.i.20–6; iv.34–41); and on the significance of ceremony as the antithesis of secrecy and a prerequisite for the well-being of individual and community. Hieronimo's refusal to bury his son fits oddly with his claim that the heavens

---

7. According to John D. Ratcliff, 'Hieronimo Explains Himself', *SP*, *liv* (1957) 118, Kyd 'looked upon Hieronimo as an honorable, justified revenger'. Ronald Broude maintains that the marriage slaughter is justified because Hieronimo is acting 'both as magistrate (he is still Knight Marshall of Spain) and as revenger of blood' or kin—'Time, Truth, and Right in *The Spanish Tragedy*', *SP*, LXVIII (1971) 141.

will be shown unjust if the murder 'Shall unreveal'd and unreveng'd pass' (III.ii.9). In fact it is a major reason for the King's failure to listen to him when he eventually decides to get justice within the law—the King does not even know that Horatio is dead. Far from helping him, Hieronimo's rejection of ritual and espousal of secrecy plays into the hands of Lorenzo, who has no doubts that secrecy is his best friend.

Hieronimo's sombre, Latin dirge does, however, bring the scene to a ceremonial conclusion. But it recalls the black incantations of witchcraft and confirms the ominous character of his reactions so far. For the first of many times, Hieronimo glances in two directions: towards (in Edwards's translation) 'the fair realms of light' where the sun-bred herbs provide medicine for pain, and towards the dark realm where sorceresses contrive poison and weave their spells by 'secret power' (II.v.67–73). Instinctively but solemnly he commits himself to the dark world and its heartless extremes: 'All things I shall attempt, even death, until all feeling is extinct in my dead heart' (ll. 74–5). This clearly anticipates the end of the tragedy, but so too does his belief that the solitary, unsung ritual is appropriate ('singing fits not this case'): it is his profoundly confused sense of what is fitting ('Why then I'll fit you'—IV.i.70) that accounts for his execution of the death sentence at the height of a marriage celebration.

In his next appearance, Hieronimo speaks the long, two-part soliloquy beginning 'O eyes, no eyes, but fountains fraught with tears' (III.ii.1) and broken with the discovery of Bel-imperia's letter. The elaborately patterned style of the first half indicates a reassertion of his Orphic self; it reflects a controlled endeavour to express great anguish and a corresponding effort to establish the possibility of true justice in a world that seems 'confus'd and fill'd with murder and misdeeds'. The plain, deliberative style of the second part is appropriate, too, for here Hieronimo is considering the possibility that the letter (naming the murderers) might be a trap, and reasoning towards the conclusion that it must be confirmed by circumstantial evidence before acted upon. But there are signs too that the controlled, judicious self is on the wane and that Hieronimo—to take up the metaphoric cue given in the first line—is a man whose vision of reality is being impaired by grief. The unmasking and punishment of Viluppo in the previous scene, and the King's unhesitant efforts to do justice to his soldiers and two of their quarrelling leaders, do not support his despairing conviction that the world is a chaos of 'public wrongs'. There is question-begging too in the argument that the letter must be authenticated before it is acted upon; it is, after all, a 'bloody writ' (l. 26) from an incarnate Fury, saying nothing about justice and law and calling only for revenge. Moreover the grieving part of the soliloquy culminates in a prayer for supernatural aid

which makes no distinction between 'heavens, hell, night, and day'
(l. 22). Hieronimo is ready for help from any quarter when it arrives—
'What means this unexpected miracle?' (l. 32)—from Bel-imperia.
One thinks of Hamlet goading himself to action with the thought that
he has been 'prompted to . . . revenge by heaven and hell' (ii.ii.580).

We find Hieronimo in his next appearance correcting public
wrongs in an exemplary fashion: rebuking his prisoner for contempt
of court, discharging the law 'for satisfaction of the world', and des-
patching the accused to execution because 'the fault's approv'd and
confess'd, / And by our law he is condemn'd to die' (*Spanish Tragedy*,
iii.iv.25, 34–41). Simultaneously, however, he is consumed with impatience for redress of his own secret grievance and with the belief
that 'neither gods nor men' are just to him (l. 10). His horror at the
misplaced jocularity of the condemned Pedringano provokes some
reflections which seem doubly apt. Precisely when it should be 'shrin'd
in heaven', Pedringano's soul (remarks Hieronimo) is 'still wand'ring
in the thorny passages / That intercepts itself of happiness' (ll. 91–4).
Pedringano, it should be recalled, 'went the wrong way' (iii.vii.22)
in the end because he was obedient to Lorenzo's injunction to 'be
merry still, but secret' (iii.iv.64). Judge and criminal are less distinct
here than would at first appear; and, as we shall see, time will blur
the distinction a little more.

Hieronimo's next appearance suggests a considerable lapse of time
in which 'restless passions' (iii.vii.11) have accomplished much. At any
rate, we have the clearest indication so far of a disfigured Orpheus.
Hieronimo imagines that his plaintive words 'have mov'd the leave-
less trees', but also that they have transformed the order of nature
into a temporal and spatial chaos: 'Disrob'd the meadows of their
flower'd green, / Made mountains marsh with spring-tides of my
tears' (ll. 6–8). The discovery of Pedringano's letter incriminating
Lorenzo and Balthazar—and rendering Bel-imperia's unnecessary—
prompts him at first to acknowledge that 'they did what heaven
unpunished would not leave' (l. 56). But then the mere thought of the
two murderers leads immediately to a bitter curse on the day when
Horatio pitied Balthazar, and so to the declaration that 'unfruitful
words' must be abandoned when 'naught but blood will satisfy my
woes' (ll. 65–8). The 'either . . . Or' decision which brings the scene
to an end ('justice by entreats' or 'revenging threats') seems, therefore,
an unreal commitment to alternatives. Hieronimo no longer wants
or believes in Orphic justice and is heading for 'unfrequented paths'
(iii.ii.17). Lorenzo will find it all too easy to frustrate his half-hearted
and inopportune efforts to get the King's ear.

The first onset of his madness coincides with a literal use of the
symbolism of uncertain travel and contrary directions: the action
emblematises his whirling confusion of mind. Asked by the Portu-

guese, 'which is the next way to my lord the duke's?', Hieronimo answers ambiguously. But when mention is made of Lorenzo, '*He goeth in at one door and comes out at another*' (s.d.), purporting now to 'resolve' the travellers' 'doubt' by directing them to 'the path upon your left-hand side' that leads 'Unto a forest of distrust and fear', and ultimately to 'despair and death' (III.xi.1–19). In Balthazar's phrase, he is guiding them by 'sorrow's map' (III.x.91).

This leads naturally to the next scene, where the problem of direction is once more Hieronimo's: 'This way, or that way? (III.xii.16): violence or law? His attempt to follow the right path and get the King's ear (as he passes in state with the Portuguese ambassador) is abandoned as abruptly as it is decided upon. Suddenly, Hieronimo gives way to an outburst of passionate frustration in which he publicly renounces his Orphic self:

> Stand from about me!
> I'll make a pickaxe of my poniard
> And here surrender up my marshalship:
> For I'll go marshal up the fiends in hell
> To be avenged on you all for this.
>
> (ll. 74–8)

Here is no poet with enchanting song, no orator with civil and persuasive words: Hieronimo is devil-driving and devil-driven, unintelligible to the King to whom he pleads for justice: 'What means this outrage? / Will none of you restrain his fury' (ll. 79–80).

But the climax of Hieronimo's 'incertain . . . pilgrimage' (III.x.109) takes place in the following scene, with its 'Vindicta mihi' soliloquy and its monologues prompted by the petitioners (who ask him to plead their cases with the King). Like III.xii, it begins with a quiet, deliberative speech, a kind of fragile rationality, and then moves into speech and gestures that enact a total metamorphosis of Orphic man. In the soliloquy, Hieronimo confronts for the first time the ethical implications of revenge, but passes immediately through absolute confusion of mind in the direction of the left-hand path. Citing in stark juxtaposition the Christian teaching on revenge ('Heaven will be reveng'd of every ill . . . attend their will') and the morality of a Senecan villainess ('Strike, and strike home, where wrong is offer'd thee'), he proceeds by a sad parody of rational argument to choose the latter: 'and to conclude, I will revenge his death' (III.xiii.1–20).[8] His confusion in the soliloquy as a whole is evinced

---

8. Fredson Bowers, in *Elizabethan Revenge Tragedy, 1587–1642* (Princeton, NJ: Princeton University Press, 1940) p. 77, and Eleanor Prosser, in *Hamlet and Revenge*, p. 50, have found transparent sophistry and logical contradiction in the '*Vindicta mihi*' soliloquy. John Ratcliffe (see p. 264n7) considers its reasoning perfectly coherent and acceptable. So too do Ernst Chickera in 'Divine Justice and Private Revenge in *The Spanish Tragedy*',

mainly by his reflections on time and patience. 'Mortal men may not appoint their time' (l. 4), yet 'wise men will take their opportunity, / Closely and safely fitting things to time' (ll. 25–6). He will 'enjoin' his 'heart to patience', but only in order that he may the better exact 'revenge' (ll. 42, 44).[9]

Hieronimo's confusion is externalised in the appropriate form of mistaken identity when the petitioners arrive. He takes the Old Man with the piteous eyes to be his son: 'Sweet boy, how art thou chang'd in death's black shade! . . . Ah ruthless fate, that favour thus transforms! (iii.xiii.146, 151). But he sees in him too 'the lively portrait of my dying self' (1.85), and so construes him as an inverted Orpheus, an agent of bestial and demonic fury committed to destroy the bonds of law:

> I'll down to hell, and in this passion
> Knock at the dismal gates of Pluto's court,
> Getting by force, as once Alcides did,
> A troop of Furies and tormenting hags
> To torture Don Lorenzo and the rest . . .
> The Thracian poet thou shalt counterfeit:
> Come on, old father, be my Orpheus,
> And if thou canst no notes upon the harp,
> Then sound the burden of thy sore heart's grief,
> Till we do gain that Proserpine may grant
> Revenge on them that murdered my son:
> Then will I rent and tear them thus and thus,
> Shivering their limbs in pieces with my teeth.
> (*Tear the papers.*)
>
>   (ll. 109–23)

Hieronimo's imaginary plot to make Orpheus an instrument of revenge anticipates the use to which he will put 'fruitless poetry' (iv.i.72) (cf. 'my unfruitful words') in the final scene. But it relates also to his decision in the present scene to apply his 'tongue to / Milder speeches' than his spirit affords (iii.xiii.40–1). From now on he will show himself an expert in the use of verbal art for the purposes of misleading and concealing. His elaborate reconciliation with Lorenzo–'honey'd speech' to appease Cerberus (l. 114; i.i.30)— deludes not only Castile and his son but even Bel-imperia, Isabella, and the Ghost. But Hieronimo's dedication to false words results naturally and disastrously in his failure to recognise true ones: Castile's kindly sentences are taken by him as sure indications of intended

---

MLR, lvii (1962) 231–2; David Laird, in 'Hieronimo's Dilemma', SP, lxii (1965) 137–46; and Ronald Broude, in SP, lxviii 137–8.

9. Cf. iii.ix.6–14, where Bel-imperia sees herself as a 'martyr' who must practise 'patience, and apply me to the time'–until she can accelerate the execution of 'revenge'!

treachery. Thus 'misconstered' (III.xiv.92) by the secretive judge, the innocent Duke will die with his guilty son.

Like Titus Andronicus, Brutus, and Othello, Hieronimo follows a dark path which entails a violation of all that is best in him. Like them, too, he is pitiably and terribly confused. And, although his noble image is not clearly restored at the end, we are kept conscious of it throughout. The 'monstrous resolution' (IV.iv.193) with which he carries through his plan for revenge and suicide is a pathological distortion of that constancy which he always showed in the pursuit of equity (III.xiii.53–4). Above all, his venomous hatred for Lorenzo and Balthazar, and consequent devotion to 'sweet revenge' (l. 107; IV.v.29), are inseparable from his undying devotion to 'Horatio, my sweet boy' (II.v.33): 'The cause was love, whence grew this mortal hate' (IV.iv.98).[1] Even in his moment of triumphant butchery, he is a haunting image of blasted love: 'He shrieks, I heard, and yet methinks I hear, / His dismal outcry in the air' (ll. 108–109).

* * *

Kyd (like Marlowe in *Tamburlaine the Great*) implicates in his tragedy the well-known interpretation of the union of Mars and Venus, and the birth therefrom of the goddess Harmonia, as an allegory of nature's fruitful and concordant discord. It is in [Act II, scene iv] that the extreme relevance of the myth to the action as a whole is brought into sharp focus; in fact the lovers' rendezvous is turned into a duet of Mars and Venus and made the imaginative centre of the play as well as the basis for its major peripeteia. Perfectly placed towards the end of Act II (in a four-act play), it has been well prepared for and is handled in a manner designed to maximise its effectiveness as a symbol of unity (albeit a unity flawed from within as well as threatened from without). The lovers meet here to consummate a 'vow'd . . . mutual amity' (II.ii.43) whose true beginning is on the battlefield, where Horatio was 'Friendship and hardy valour, join'd in one'. They have chosen time and place to fit their conception of the encounter as a moment of rare harmony, meeting in the bower when Venus begins to rise (II.ii.45) and the nightingale to 'frame sweet music' (II.iv.28–33). Casting themselves as Mars and Venus, they act out, in their formal conjunction of hands, feet, arms, and lips, and in their playful conceits, a lingering metamorphosis of martial confrontation into the kind of amorous strife that 'breaks no bond of peace'—'a warring peace or peaceful war' (II.ii.33, 38). For the climax of this manifest dramatisation of *discordia concors*, Kyd finds a singularly appropriate verbal medium, and proceeds to use the climax as the springboard for a reversal which is devastatingly

---

1. Cf. Murray, *Thomas Kyd*, pp. 33–4.

effective both as symbol and as theatre. Twenty-four lines of dialogue combining stychomythia (contrariety) and rhyme (concord),
and culminating in 'O stay a while and I will die with thee, / So shalt
thou yield and yet have conquer'd me', come to an abrupt end with
the intervention of the murderers and the curt injunction of Lorenzo:
'My lord, away with her, take her aside' (ii.iv.24–51).

The next device is the dumb show in which the Hymeneal torches
are suddenly drenched with blood. An obvious prefiguration of the
final device, it is symbolic not only of violent contrariety but also
of incomprehension and non-communication. The show has been
presented by Revenge in order to clarify the significance of the
developing acting for the baffled Andrea; but Andrea understands
the explanatory dumb show no better than he has understood the
spoken show, and not until Revenge awakes to 'reveal this mystery'
does he rest contented—'Sufficeth me, thy meaning's understood'
(iii.xv.29, 36). This echoes the moment when Hieronimo revealed
the mystery of his show to the King. And it echoes too the way in
which Lorenzo terminated the duet of Mars and Venus.

*   *   *

That the proud bond-breakers should both die in Babylonical confusion with one of them playing the part of a lover pleading 'vain
suits' to the 'Relentless . . . ears' of a mistress who kills him in earnest, is poetic justice indeed (iv.iv.59–60). But once more it seems that
Hieronimo has become identifiable with what he opposes. Despite
his 'oration' to the bewildered and horrified audience, and his wondrous strange show (Horatio's corpse) he fails to 'make the matter
known' fully. Having revealed that Lorenzo and Balthazar were
killed in earnest in the play for their murder of Horatio, he contemptuously denies that he was mad and then bites out his tongue leaving the King with no explanation as to why he, of all people, should
have sought justice in so barbarous a fashion. Thus the King's
'Speak . . . speak . . . I will make thee speak. . . . Why speak'st thou
not' echo his own desperate appeals in the silent garden-plot for an
explanation of mystery (ll. 163–4, 179, 104). Orpheus has helped to
reduce life almost to the condition of an inexplicable dumb show.

The symbolic complexity of the final device is greatly enhanced
by its association with decorum, the doctrine which demanded harmonious relationships and respect for differences in both life and
literature (dramatic and non-dramatic). References to decorum (grace,
fitness, pleasingness) occur throughout the play with almost ritual
regularity, their combined effect being to strengthen the play–life
analogy. However, the most overt and extended reference to propri-
ety occurs in Hieronimo's discussion with his fellow actors of the
forthcoming wedding-play. Balthazar remarks that a comedy would

be more appropriate to the occasion than a tragedy, but Hieronimo appeals beyond the circumstance of time to that of persons to justify the fitness of his choice (comedy for common wits, tragedy for royalty). His argument is secretly ironic (these people will get just what suits them), but it is also openly bantering; and the banter is typical of the jesting enthusiasm with which he conducts his tragic plot and handles his intended victims. This jesting spirit is yet another symptom of Hieronimo's self-loss. We are to remember the courtier whose 'pompous jest' (i.e. 'stately show') (I.iv.137) was perfectly attuned to persons and time, and above all the grave judge who was horrified by the way in which Pedringano, gulled by Lorenzo's 'quaint device' and 'jest' (IV.v.5; III.v.13–17), clowned his way into the hangman's noose: 'I have not seen a wretch so impudent! / O monstrous times, where murder's set so light' (III.vi.89–90). Whereas in his perverted sense of fitness Hieronimo is akin to Seneca's Atreus (a revenger obsessed with the decorum of his barbarous ritual),[2] in his lethal jocularity he becomes almost indistinguishable from Lorenzo, the hated enemy who played at murder and murdered play.

* * *

2. See *Seneca his Tenne Tragedies*, 179–80: 'Kept is in all the order due, least such a mischiefe gret / Should not be order'd well. . . . He is himself the priest. . . . No rites were left of sacrifice undone . . . , such a cruelty / It him delights to order well.' After Kyd, the planning and execution of murderous acts is frequently attended by a tragically confused or viciously perverse sense of ritual decorum: see, for example, *Titus Andronicus, Julius Caesar, Othello, Catiline, The Revenger's Tragedy, The White Devil, Women Beware Women.*

Iconography

ANDREW SOFER

From Absorbing Interests: Kyd's Bloody Handkerchief as Palimpsest[†]

* * *

See here my show; look on this spectacle!
—Hieronimo in *The Spanish Tragedy*

By comparison to its more famous cousin in *Othello*, the bloody handkerchief in *The Spanish Tragedy* has received very little critical attention, especially considering its originality. Perhaps the first bloody napkin on the commercial Elizabethan stage, the handkerchief occupies both parts of Kyd's story. When the two parts were performed in repertory, presumably the same property appeared in both plays.[1] In *The First Part of Hieronimo*, the handkerchief appears as the "scarf" which passes from Bel-imperia to Andrea to Horatio, and in *The Spanish Tragedy*, the scarf, now referred to as a "bloody napkin," passes from Bel-imperia to Horatio to Hieronimo. By turns failed love-charm, martial memento, and bloody revenge token, the property continually acquires new connotations for the spectator as it passes from hand to hand in performance. This cumulative absorption of meaning is augmented by moments at which the handkerchief metonymically invokes its medieval predecessors: the Corpus

---

† From "Absorbing Interests: Kyd's Bloody Handkerchief as Palimpsest" by Andrew Sofer as it appeared in *Comparative Drama* 34 (2000), pp. 139–48, 151–53. Reprinted by permission of the editors of *Comparative Drama*.

1. Philip Henslowe, *Henslowe's Diary* ed. R. A. Foakes (New York: Cambridge University Press, 2002) indicates that a performance of *The Spanish Tragedy* was immediately or very closely preceded by a performance of "spanes comodye donne oracoe" on five occasions in 1592 (March 13, 14, 30, 31; April 10, 14, 22, 24; May 21, 22). See Andrew S. Cairncross, Introduction, [*The Spanish Comedy*, or] *The First Part of Hieronimo* and *The Spanish Tragedy* [or *Hieronimo is Mad Again*] (Lincoln: University of Nebraska Press, 1967), xiv–xv. I accept Cairncross' contention, xix, that "*I Hieronimo is* a memorial version [of] a longer good text by Kyd, *The Spanish Comedy*, which preceded *The Spanish Tragedy* and combined with it to form a two-part play." All citations to Kyd's Spanish plays are to Cairncross' edition and are cited by scene (or act) and line parenthetically in my text.

Christi Veronica cloth, the liturgical *sudarium*, and the Host itself. To understand how Kyd uses the handkerchief as a mobile "object lesson" intended to reshape the spectator's emotional response to a disturbingly familiar prop, we must trace the handkerchief's movement both in concrete stage space and through processual stage time.

Kyd's handkerchief first appears in *The First Part of Hieronimo* (c. 1582–92) as a scarf, which Bel-imperia gives to her beloved Don Andrea just before he joins battle with Portugal over its neglected tribute to Spain.[2] As she ties the scarf around his arm, Bel-imperia's stately couplets establish the silken scarf as a courtly love token and at the same time endow the favor with apotropaic powers:

> Lend me thy loving and thy warlike arm,
> On which I knit this soft and silken charm
> Tied with an amorous knot: oh, may it prove
> Enchanted armor being charmed by love;
> That when it mounts up to thy warlike crest,
> It may put by the sword, and so be blest. (9.15–20)

Ironically, Bel-imperia's "enchanted" talisman fails in its mission. Although the Portuguese are defeated in battle, Andrea himself is slain, and his final words are a confident statement of immortality that can also be interpreted as an ironic comment on the charm's failed magic: "I keep her favor longer than my breath" (11.111). Andrea's pun foreshadows the literal and figural transferral of Bel-imperia's "favor" to his friend, Horatio.

Each time the property changes hands, its meaning for the spectator shifts. When Horatio discovers Andrea's body on the battlefield, he ties the now-bloody scarf about his own arm:

> This scarf I'll wear in memory of our souls,
> And of our mutual loves; here, here, I'll wind it,
> And full as often as I think on thee,
> I'll kiss this little ensign, this soft banner,
> Smear'd with foes' blood, all for the master's honor.
> (11.164–68)

Horatio unwittingly appropriates Bel-imperia's pledge of love as a memento of male comradeship, and his erotic affection for "this soft

---

2. I accept J. R. Mulryne's tentative identification of Bel-imperia's "scarf" with Horatio's bloody napkin in Thomas Kyd, *The Spanish Tragedy*, ed. J. R. Mulryne (New York: Hill & Wang, 1970), 24. Mulryne glosses Hieronimo's word "handkercher" as "handkerchief, small scarf."

banner" revises its formerly heterosexual valence.[3] (Interestingly, Horatio refuses to acknowledge that the scarf may contain Andrea's blood.) With the scarf attached to his own arm, Horatio visually becomes Andrea's surrogate in the eyes of the audience. Presumably he wears the token in the play's final scene when he is embraced by Andrea's ghost at the latter's funeral procession.

The two exchanges in *1 Hieronimo* establish the scarf as an ambiguous prop whose meaning shifts according to the needs of the scene. In the first exchange, the unspotted scarf is an enchanted love token; in the second, the bloodied scarf is a homoerotic (or at least homosocial) memento. For the spectator the second meaning does not erase the first; rather, the repeated action of tying the scarf increases the property's dramatic interest. Further, the scarf perversely ironizes the meanings ascribed to it by the characters. Instead of "[e]nchanted armor," it becomes a bloody token of ignoble slaughter (Andrea is outnumbered and overrun). The scarf ominously absorbs blood *instead of* magic, and the repeated stage business of tying the scarf suggests that a similar fate awaits Horatio.

Thus far, it would appear that the handkerchief is being stripped of its prior thaumaturgic powers and hence (in Diehl's terms) demystified. Certainly, the contract of enchantment proposed by Bel-imperia's spell is strikingly negated by Andrea's death. Instead of the eternal contract of grace offered to the community of the faithful by such cloths as Veronica's napkin, we find ourselves caught up in a narrative contract whose outcome is uncertain. The result is both pleasurable dramatic irony (we know more than the characters about the fatal piece of cloth) and eager anticipation (we remain unsure how *this* napkin's story will end).

In *The Spanish Tragedy* the bloody sign on Horatio's arm serves as a constant visual reminder of Andrea, whose vengeful ghost (together with Revenge) acts as chorus throughout.[4] The play repeats *1 Hieronimo's* courtly love exchange but with a significant difference: the prop is now stained with blood. Horatio explains to the bereaved Bel-imperia how Andrea's scarf came into his possession: "This scarf I pluck'd from off his lifeless arm, / And wear it in remembrance of my

3. In *The Spanish Tragedy*, Horatio will describe the comrades' friendship in terms that suggest an Achilles-Patroclus relationship:

> I took him up and wound him in my arms,
> And welding him unto my private tent,
> There laid him down and dew'd him with my tears,
> And sighed and sorrowed as became a friend. (1.4.34–37).

4. Since the handkerchief and Andrea himself are both present on stage for much of the time, Andrea's blood and body are weirdly bifurcated yet simultaneously staged. Compare the play's final, uneasy double focus on Horatio's hanging corpse and the bloody handkerchief in his father's hand.

friend" (1.4.42–43).[5] As if aware of the erotic implications behind
Horatio's action, Bel-imperia denies the possibility that Andrea would
have given up the love token voluntarily:

> I know the scarf, would he had kept it still!
> For had he lived, he would have kept it still,
> And worn it for his Bel-imperia's sake;
> For'twas my favor at his last depart. (1.4.44–47)

Bel-imperia then reappropriates the scarf as hers to give, offering
the scarf a second time:

> But now wear thou it both for him and me,
> For after him thou hast deserved it best. (1.4.48–49)

Despite her awkward disclaimer ("wear thou it both for him and
me"), Bel-imperia elides the scarf's function as martial memento by
inserting Horatio into the position of recipient formerly occupied
by Andrea. Indeed, Bel-imperia has fallen recklessly in love with
Horatio.

The staging of this scene, which closely parallels the exchange
between Bel-imperia and Andrea in the earlier play, is ambiguous.
Does Horatio merely point to the scarf on his arm, or does he try to
hand it back to Bel-imperia, only to have her insist that he keep it?
In either case, the token now becomes an unintentional emblem of
Bel-imperia's faithlessness to Andrea. The contrast between the
scarf's spotlessness in 1 Hieronimo and its soiled appearance in The
Spanish Tragedy may carry sexual connotations.[6] Andrea's ghost
confirms that his relationship with Bel-imperia was sexual ("In secret
I possess'd a worthy dame," [1.1.10]), thereby ironizing the King's
later reference to "Young virgins" (2.3.43) and Horatio's comparison
of Bel-imperia to the unfaithful goddess Venus (2.4.33). In this scene,
the bloodied, recycled scarf suggests that Bel-imperia herself is
second-hand goods.

Yet the bloody token symbolizes not only furtive sexuality but
impending disaster. During his tryst with Bel-imperia, Horatio is
strung up in his father Hieronimo's arbor and stabbed by the jealous
Balthazar, Bel-imperia's brother Lorenzo, and two confederates.

---

5. Horatio's explanation to Bel-imperia has the added explicatory function of filling in
   those spectators at The Spanish Tragedy who may be unfamiliar with 1 Hieronimo. The
   scene thus implies two different yet simultaneous narrative contracts: one for those
   who know that the scarf was given to Andrea by Bel-imperia, and one for those (like
   Horatio himself) who do not. Presumably the pleasure of being "in the know" may have
   stimulated repeat attendance at the play.
6. Compare the sleeve offered by Troilus to Cressida and later given by Cressida to Diomedes in Shakespeare's Troilus and Cressida. (Although Troilus determines to bloody
   the favor worn in Diomedes' helmet, as with so much else in the play this threat is never
   realized.) The soiled handkerchief as an emblem of sexual consummation runs from
   The Spanish Tragedy through Othello all the way to August Strindberg's Miss Julie (1888).

The scene is iconic in at least two ways. The lovers' bower of bliss becomes a gibbet: J. L. Styan notes that "the rope and the knife used in that order [provide] a version of common hanging and drawing that anyone who paid a gruesome visit to Tyburn would recognize for its popular theatrical value."[7] Moreover, to a contemporary audience the hanging and stabbing of Horatio by four men, on an arbor-property designed to resemble a tree, may well have suggested the Crucifixion on the "tree" dramatized by the Corpus Christi Passion Plays. Thus in the York Crucifixion play, Christ is stretched with ropes to fit the incorrectly bored holes and crucified by four soldiers "symmetrically arranged at the four points of the Cross"; later, in the York play of Christ's Death and Burial, *The blind Longeus goes to Jesus and pierces his side with the spear, and suddenly gains his sight.*[8] But whereas Christ's blood in the Corpus Christi play is both curative and salvific—the Centurion who witnesses the miracle instantly converts—Horatio's slaughter is merely a bloodbath. "These are the fruits of love," quips Lorenzo as the four confederates stab Horatio again and again while the horrified Bel-imperia, like the spectators, is forced to look on (2.4.55). In the starkest terms possible, the spectacle of stage blood is revised from a vehicle of spiritual renewal (modeled by the Centurion's reaction) to a vehicle of theatrical voyeurism (modeled by Bel-imperia's reaction).

As we have seen, the Corpus Christi "sudarye" in which Christ's body is wrapped becomes ocular proof of the Resurrection when it is discovered in the tomb. *The Spanish Tragedy* provides a parallel discovery scene when Hieronimo and his wife Isabella discover the "murd'rous spectacle" of their son's corpse hanging in the arbor (2.5.9). After cutting down his son's body and weeping over it, Hieronimo seizes on the object still attached to Horatio's lifeless arm:

> See'st thou this handkercher besmeared with blood?
> It shall not from me till I take revenge. (2.5.51–52)

It is just possible that Hieronimo refers not to Bel-imperia's scarf but to some new property. Nevertheless, the description of the "handkercher" matches the silken scarf "Smeard with foes' blood" in *1 Hieronimo* (11. 168), and it seems unlikely that a dramatist as savvy as Kyd would ignore the opportunity to ring the changes on a property already so resonant for the audience and visibly there for the

---

7. J. L. Styan, *The English Stage* (Cambridge: Cambridge University Press, 1975), 113–15. Styan adds: "The property 'arbour' was probably an arch of lattice (decorated with leaves and looking a bit like the 'tree' referred to later in the play), sturdy yet portable for convenient hangings; it possibly did double duty when Pedringano was hanged in 3.6. Such a prop is sketched on the title-page of the edition of 1615, where Hieronimo from his bed finds Horatio hanging, while Bel-imperia is pulled away by Lorenzo in a mask," 115.
8. "Christ's Death and Burial (York)," in *Medieval Drama*, ed. David Bevington (Boston: Houghton Mifflin, 1975), 572; 589.

taking. All Hieronimo must do is untie the freshly bloodied scarf from his son's arm, just as Horatio untied it from Andrea's in *1 Hieronimo*—yet another opportunity for ironic visual parallelism. Once again, the love-charm presages doom for the character who picks it up.

If the Corpus Christi cloth suggests the "felt absence" of Christ's body in the tomb, Kyd's handkerchief is now literally imbued with the substance of Hieronimo's dead son:

> Seest thou this handkercher besmeard with blood?
> It shall not from me till I take revenge.
> Seest thou those wounds that yet are bleeding fresh?
> I'll not entomb them till I have reveng'd.
> Then will I joy amidst my discontent;
> Till then my sorrow never shall be spent. (2.5.51–56)

Here the scene hinges on yet another visual allusion. As at a public execution, the actor playing Hieronimo dips the handkerchief in Horatio's wounds as he intones these lines, while Hieronimo's reference to the handkerchief together with a *refusal* to entomb his son's body suggests a new twist to the ancient cloth. On the one hand, Hieronimo's virtual canonization of his son invites us to see Horatio as a Christ-figure: Hieronimo describes the "harmless blood" dishonored within "this sacred bower" (2.3.29–27), and in the first addition of 1602 Hieronimo calls Horatio "pure and spotless" (2.5.[80]). On the other hand, we witness the Knight Marshal of Spain preparing to embark on a very un-Christian vendetta against those whom God should punish. Kyd deliberately invokes the *sudarium* motif in order to subvert it; instead of a sacred relic promising divine salvation, in Horatio's hands the prop becomes a bloodthirsty revenge token that gives an unholy charge to the revenger's intent.[9]

Once Hieronimo dips the handkerchief in his son's blood and conceals it on his person in 2.5, the handkerchief makes no explicit appearance until 3.13. Pressed into hearing petitioners' suits, including that of an old man whose son has been murdered. Hieronimo identifies with the senex Bazulto and sees in the latter's grief a mirror for magistrates:

> Oh my son, my son, O my son Horatio!
> But mine, or thine, Bazulto, be content.
> Here, take my handkercher and wipe thine eyes,
> Whiles wretched I in thy mishaps may see

9. On the complex Elizabethan attitude toward the code of blood-revenge, as against the Christian injunction against vengeance ("Vengeance is mine, saith the Lord"), see Fredson Thayer Bowers, *Elizabethan Revenge Tragedy 1587–1642* (1940; reprint, Gloucester, MA: Peter Smith, 1959), 1–40.

The lively portrait of my dying self.
>   *He draweth out a bloody napkin.*
Oh no, not this; Horatio, this was thine;
And when I dy'd it in thy dearest blood,
This was a token 'twixt thy soul and me
That of thy death revenged I should be. (3.13.81–89)

Hieronimo seems surprised to discover the handkerchief in his own hand and takes the bloody token as a reproach: "See, see, oh see thy shame, Hieronimo!/ See here a loving father to his son!" (3.13.95–96). The handkerchief reminds the audience, as well as Hieronimo, that the motor of the play is Hieronimo's thirst for vengeance; it is as if Hieronimo has forgotten the contract symbolized by the cloth. We cannot tell if the forgotten token is revitalized by Hieronimo's passion or vice versa.

In this scene, the handkerchief triggers a reversion from the Christian frame of the play thus far to the pagan cosmology of the play's Induction. Hieronimo envisages himself "[K]nock[ing] at the dismal gates of Pluto's court" to enlist Proserpine in his revenge cause (3.13.110), a cause Andrea's ghost has already informed us she supports (1.1.78 ff.). Hieronimo betrays his role as impersonal arbiter of justice and hallucinates that Bazulto is Horatio returned from the underworld. He descends into an animal fury and tears the petitioners' bonds with his teeth, seeming almost disappointed when they refuse to bleed. As a hinge between Christian and pagan frames of reference, Hieronimo's napkin anticipates Desdemona's exotic handkerchief in *Othello*, which introduces an eerie pagan coloring into the familiar Christian landscapes of that play.

Neither the magical totem conjured by Bel-imperia nor the ocular proof of divine grace embodied by the sudarium, Kyd's handkerchief thus far is a failed love-charm and a stalled revenge token. But it is in the bloody finale to *The Spanish Tragedy* that Kyd's subversion of medieval tradition becomes most truly apparent. Hieronimo's masque of *Soliman and Perseda* ends with a deliberate parody of the traditional climax of the Mass: the Elevation of the Host. Having staged a murderous entertainment for the Kings of Spain and Portugal which dispatches their heirs, Hieronimo unveils "a strange and wondrous show besides" (4.1.181). Drawing a stage curtain, Hieronimo reveals Horatio's corpse hanging once again from the arbor-property: "See here my show; look on this spectacle!" (4.4.89).[1] Hieronimo's

---

1. The arbor-property may double as a gallows to hang Pedringano in 3.6, cementing its association with death. It appears yet again as the "bower" in Hieronimo's garden in 4.2, when Isabella strips its branches and leaves before she stabs herself; it is then moved into place behind the curtain Hieronimo knocks up at the top of the next scene, ready for the discovery of Horatio's body at 4.4.88 where the stage direction reads, "*Shows his dead son.*"

"show" is a theatrical coup that forces his shocked audience to recognize that the murders in the masque of *Solimon and Perseda* were in earnest.

Turning his son's corpse into an explicitly theatrical emblem, Hieronimo enacts a bloody parody of the Corpus Christi Passion Play. Before his captive audience, he demonstrates how "hanging on a tree I found my son,/ Through-girt with wounds, and slaughter'd as you see" (4.4.111–12). Not content with displaying the body of the "Son," Hieronimo also elevates his blood. Brandishing the bloody handkerchief, Hieronimo travesties the ritual gesture of visual display common to the Mass and the religious drama of the *sudarium:*

> And here behold this bloody handkercher,
> Which at Horatio's death I weeping dipp'd
> Within the river of his bleeding wounds:
> It, as propitious, see, I have reserved,
> And never hath it left my bloody heart,
> Soliciting remembrance of my vow
> With these, oh, these accursed murderers!
> Which now perform'd, my heart is satisfied. (4.4.122–29)

In Hieronimo's grasp the property becomes a fetish: the meaning of Horatio's corpse is reduced to and in some way *replaced by* a bloody piece of cloth. If Hieronimo's onstage audience watched the masque from the gallery situated above the doors in the tiring house wall (as Martin White suggests), Hieronimo must elevate the napkin toward the gallery with his back to the playhouse audience—just like a Catholic priest officiating at Mass.[2]

Through Hieronimo, Kyd transfers our attention from the body itself to the absorbing property in the actor's hand. Hieronimo thus arrogates to the theater the priest's power to orchestrate a spectacle in which the body is conjured by a metonymic object. In a theatrical sleight-of-hand, the prop replaces the corpse as our locus of visual and dramatic interest. Kyd implies that the power of the theater is the power of surrogation: the ability to spin out a potentially infinite chain of metonymic displacements that echo each other (Hieronimo's/ Horatio's/Andrea's/Bel-imperia's handkerchief, Veronica cloth, *sudarium*, *linteum*, Host, Christ).[3] In the case of the handkerchief, the connecting thread is blood.

---

2. Martin White, *Renaissance Drama in Action: An Introduction to Aspects of Theatre Practice and Performance* (London: Routledge, 1998), 120.
3. In my thinking about surrogation, I am especially indebted to Joseph Roach, *Cities of the Dead: Circum-Atlantic Performance* (New York: Columbia University Press, 1996). Roach's notion of the *effigy*, an object (or actor) that "fills by means of surrogation a vacancy created by the absence of an original" and "hold[s] open a place in memory into which many different people may step according to circumstances and occasions," applies beautifully to the bloody handkerchief, 36.

Hieronimo's sacrilegious perversion of the Mass no doubt played into Kyd's spectators' fear and loathing of Catholic Spain. Like Vindice's use of Gloriana's skull in *The Revenger's Tragedy*, Hieronimo's appropriation of his son's corpse as a theatrical device is shocking, even repulsive.[4] Kyd's transgressive emblem betokens neither salvation nor resurrection. Instead, the "buried" *sudarium* and Host of the liturgical ceremony are transmuted into a bloody prop and a rotting corpse, whose embarrassing material residue evokes what Stephen Greenblatt has called *"the problem of the leftover*, that is, the status of the material remainder"* of bread and wine once the formula for consecration has been uttered.[5]

Huston Diehl also detects eucharistic satire in *The Spanish Tragedy* but locates it in the masque. For an Elizabethan audience, she argues, *Soliman and Perseda* would have been an object lesson on the theatrical meretriciousness of Catholic ritual: "By mystifying and privileging spectacle, literalizing mimetic action, and displaying 'real' bodies and blood, the play-within-the-play manifests the very qualities of the Roman Mass that the Calvinist reformers condemn when they complain that 'of the sacrament' the papists 'make an idol; of commemoration make adoration; instead of receiving, make a deceiving; in place of showing forth Christ's death, make new oblations of his death' (Foxe 5:303)."[6] Yet aside from the fact that Hieronimo's deployment of his "props" provides a more blatant parody of Catholic ritual than his murderous playlet, Diehl's belief that the masque models "true" Protestant seeing by dramatizing its opposite underestimates the shocking immediacy of Kyd's bloody spectacle. The spectator is far more likely to be swept up in the deadly action of the masque than to be busy deconstructing its theatricality. Moreover, instead of confronting the artificialty of the masque, through dramatic irony the offstage audience is made aware that the stage action is *real*. Lorenzo, Balthazar and the rest are murdered, even as the courtly audience applauds the actors' masterly execution. Whereas Diehl claims that *Soliman and Perseda* mimics the very qualities of the Mass condemned by the reformers, it actually reverses them. For the reformers, the Mass passes off the sign (Host) as the thing

---

4. There is even a touch of Tourneuresque black humor: the fact that Hieronimo has "reserved" the "propitious" handkerchief recalls the liturgical practice of "reserving" the consecrated Host for Easter communion.
5. Stephen Greenblatt, "Remnants of the sacred in Early Modern England," in *Subject and Object in Renaissance Culture*, ed. Margreta de Grazia, Maureen Quilligan, and Peter Stallybrass, Cambridge Studies in Renaissance Literature and Culture Ser. (Cambridge: Cambridge University Press, 1996), 337–45.
6. Huston Diehl, "Observing the Lord's Supper and the Lord Chamberlain's Men: The Visual Rhetoric of Ritual and Play in Early Modern England," *Renaissance Drama* n.s. 22 (1991): 162. Diehl quotes from *The Acts and Monuments of John Foxe*, ed. Stephen Reed Cattley (London: 1837–41).

itself (the Body of Christ), whereas Hieronimo disguises the thing itself (murder) as a sign (masque).

One likely index of Kyd's intended effect on the spectator is the reaction of Andrea's ghost. Rather than being purged by this tragedy of blood, he becomes addicted to its sensationalism. "Ay, these were spectacles to please my soul," Andrea comments, after summarizing each murder with relish (4.5.12). Like any other spectator, the ghost has become swept up in the action; indeed, Andrea has discovered a taste for blood and forgotten that all he desired at first was revenge against Balthazar alone (just as the spectator may have forgotten this original impulse for revenge). Reveling in the deaths of the good as well as the bad, Andrea appoints himself judge of the underworld and sadistically rehearses the various tortures drawn from pagan mythology that lie in store for Lorenzo, Balthazar, and the rest. No Christian redemption awaits these fallen creatures, only the "endless tragedy" promised by Revenge in the play's last line (4.5.48). Andrea's response to tragedy is not catharsis, but a thirst for more bloodshed. Kyd sardonically anticipates the reaction of his own spectators, who (judging by the genre's ensuing popularity) left *The Spanish Tragedy* with an unrestrained appetite for revenge tragedy.[7]

The Spanish Tragedy's handkerchief is no demystified idol, but a fetish endowed by Hieronimo with new and appalling life. Despite the inroads against idolatry made by Protestant reformers, Kyd's handkerchief—stripped of its prior thaumaturgic power, perhaps, but magic *in a new way*—celebrates the enduring capacity of theatrical objects to seduce audiences through an apparently limitless series of metonymic substitutions. Kyd exploits a received visual language (the Elevation of the Host, the ocular proof of the *sudarium*) for his own sensational ends. The old symbols are stripped of their former theological efficacy, but—much like a painted-over rood screen—the old Catholic imagery bleeds through. For Kyd, it was necessary to travesty sacred objects in order to reclaim them for his sensational theater. Through the figure of Hieronimo, Kyd thrusts his bloody "spectacle" in the face of those Puritans who would condemn theater as a temple of idolatry.

Of course, we will never know exactly how Elizabethan spectators reacted to Kyd's tragedy. A given playwright can only propose a particular theatrical contract—in this case, what I have called a contract of sensation, as opposed to the contracts of revelation and transformation proposed by the sight of sacred cloth on the medieval stage—and it is for the individual spectator to accept or reject that

---

7. In direct contrast, Diehl, "Observing the Lord's Supper," 164, argues that "Kyd's audiences have learned to distrust spectacles of blood."

contract. What we do know is that *The Spanish Tragedy* and its successors (including *Hamlet*) were immensely popular, suggesting that Andrea's addictive response proved contagious. While it is possible that some of *The Spanish Tragedy's* spectators left the playhouse with their suspicion of "Papist" idolatry confirmed, it is far more likely that Kyd's theatrically absorbing handkerchief thrilled its audience and left it thirsting for fresh blood.

Such a hypothesis seems confirmed by the slew of bloody handkerchiefs on the Elizabethan and Jacobean stage that followed in Kyd's wake.[8] Indeed, the holy figure embedded in the cloth still occasionally rises to the surface, and as ocular proof I close with an image from our own day. In John Pielmeier's *Agnes of God* (1982), a commercially successful attempt to revive the medieval genre of the saint's play, the pregnant nun Agnes "*presents a hand wrapped in a bloody handkerchief*" as evidence of her stigmata.[9] One last time, rising like a phoenix, the bloody piece of linen is displayed to an astonished audience as a spectacular sign of the phantom beneath the cloth.

8. Bloody handkerchiefs subsequently appear in John Lyly's *The Woman in the Moon* (1594–97), the anonymous *A Warning for Fair Women* (1596–1600), Shakespeare's *3 Henry VI* (1590–91), *As You Like It* (1599–1600), *Othello* (c. 1603), and *Cymbeline* (1609–10), Francis Beaumont and John Fletcher's *Cupid's Revenge* (1608), John Webster's *The Duchess of Malfi* (1612), and Sir John Denham's *The Sophy* (1641). On the Restoration stage, the bloody handkerchief featured in three gory tragedies, Nathaniel Lee's *Caesar Borgia* (1679), John Banks' *Vertue Betray'd* (1682), and Colley Cibber's *Xerxes* (1699), before being mocked as a stage cliché in Sir John Vanbrugh's *The Mistake* (1705). In the Georgian era, the handkerchief's contract of sensation was eclipsed by a contract of sentiment: Georgian audiences evidently preferred their "tragedy handkerchiefs" drowned in tears rather than in blood.

9. John Pielmeier, *Agnes of God* (Garden City, New York: Nelson Doubleday, 1982), cited by Gatton, "'There must be Blood,'" 89. I am grateful to Gatton's article for bringing the play to my attention.

Selected Bibliography

• Indicates works included or excerpted in this Norton Critical Edition

Editions

Boas, F. S., ed. *The Works of Thomas Kyd*. Oxford, 1901.
Cairncross, Andrew S. *The First Part of Hieronimo and The Spanish Tragedy*. London: Edward Arnold, 1967.
Calvo, Clara, and Jesus Tronchi, eds. *The Spanish Tragedy*. Arden Early Modern Drama. London: Bloomsbury, 2013.
Collier J. P. *Dodsley's Old Plays*. London, 1825. Vol. III.
Dodsley, Robert. *Select Collection of Old Plays*. London, 1744. Vol. II.
Edwards, Philip. *The Spanish Tragedy*. London: Methuen, 1969.
Edwards, P., ed. *The Spanish Tragedy*. The Revels Plays. Manchester: Manchester University Press, 1959.
Hawkins, Thomas. *Origins of the English Drama*. London, 1773. Vol. II.
Hazlitt, W. C. *Dodsley's Old Plays*. London, 1874. Vol. V.
Lamb, Charles. *Specimens of English Dramatic Writers*. 1808.
Manly, J. M. *Specimens of the Pre-Shakespearean Drama*. Boston, 1897. Vol. II.
Mulryne, J. R., ed. *The Spanish Tragedy*. London: A. & C. Black, 1989.
Mulryne, J. R., ed., rev. Gurr, A. J. *The Spanish Tragedy*. London: Methuen, 2009.
Schick, J. *The Spanish Tragedy*. London, 1898.

General Studies of Kyd

Barber, C. L. *Creating Elizabethan Tragedy: The Theater of Marlowe and Kyd*. Chicago: University of Chicago Press, 1988.
Edwards, P. *Thomas Kyd and Early Elizabethan Tragedy*. London: Longmans, Green, 1966.
Erne, L. *Beyond* The Spanish Tragedy: *A Study of the Works of Thomas Kyd*. Manchester: Manchester University Press, 2001.
Freeman, A. *Thomas Kyd: Facts and Problems*. Oxford: Clarendon Press, 1967.

Studies of The Spanish Tragedy

Adams, Barry B. "The Audience of *The Spanish Tragedy*." *Journal of English and Germanic Philology* 68 (1969): 221–36.
Aggeler, G. "The Eschatological Crux in *The Spanish Tragedy*." *Journal of English and German Philology* 86 (1987): 319–31.
Altman, Joel. *The Tudor Play of Mind: Rhetorical Inquiry and the Development of Elizabethan Drama*. Berkeley: University of California Press, 1978.
Ardolino, F. *Apocalypse and Armada in Kyd's Spanish Tragedy*. Kirksville: Sixteenth Century Journal Publishers, Northeast Missouri State University, 1995.

285

————. "Corrida of Blood in *The Spanish Tragedy.*" *Medieval and Renaissance Drama in English* 1 (1984): 37–49.

————. "'The Hangman's Noose and the Empty Box': Kyd's Use of Dramatic and Mythological Sources in *The Spanish Tragedy.*" *Renaissance Quarterly* 30 (1977): 339.

————. "The Influence of Spenser's *Faerie Queene* on Kyd's *Spanish Tragedy.*" *Early Modern Literary Studies* 7 (2002).

————. "'In Paris? Mass, and Well Remembered!': Kyd's *The Spanish Tragedy* and the English Reaction to the St Bartholomew's Day Massacre." *SCJ* 21 (1990): 401–19.

————. *Thomas Kyd's Mystery Play: Myth and Ritual in "The Spanish Tragedy."* New York: Peter Lang, 1985.

Baines, B. J. "Kyd's Silenus Box and the Limits of Perception." *Journal of Medieval and Renaissance Studies* 10 (1980): 41–51.

• Barish, Jonas A. "*The Spanish Tragedy,* or the Pleasures and Perils of Rhetoric." In *Elizabethan Theatre.* Ed. John Russell Brown (58–85). London: Edward Arnold, 1967.

Bate, Jonathan. "The Performance of Revenge: *Titus Andronicus* and *The Spanish Tragedy.*" In *The Show Within.* Ed. Francois Laroque (267–83). Montpellier: 1990).

Belsey, C. *The Subject of Tragedy: Identity and Difference in Renaissance Drama.* London: Methuen, 1985, pp. 75–79.

Bercovitch, S. "Love and Strife in Kyd's *Spanish Tragedy.*" *Studies in English Literature* 9 (1969): 226.

Bevington, D., ed. *The Spanish Tragedy.* Manchester: Manchester University Press, 1996.

Braden, Gordon. *Renaissance Tragedy and the Senecan Tradition: Anger's Privilege.* New Haven, Conn.: Yale University Press, 1985.

Broude, R. "Time, Truth, and Right in *The Spanish Tragedy.*" *Studies in Philology* 68 (1971): 130–45.

Chickera, E. D. "Divine Justice and Private Revenge in *The Spanish Tragedy.*" *Modern Language Review* 57 (1962): 228–32.

Clemen, W. *English Tragedy before Shakespeare: The Development of Dramatic Speech.* Trans T. S. Dorsch. London: Methuen, 1961.

Coursen, H. R. "The Unity of *The Spanish Tragedy.*" *Studies in Philology* 65 (1963: 768–82.

Craig, D. H. "Authorial Styles and the Frequencies of Very Common Words: Johnson, Shakespeare and the Additions to *The Spanish Tragedy.*" *Style* 26 (1992): 165–98.

Daalder, J. "The Role of 'Senex' in Kyd's *The Spanish Tragedy.*" *Comparative Drama* 20 (fall 1986): 247–60.

Dillon, J. "*The Spanish Tragedy* and Staging Languages in Renaissance Drama." *Research Opportunities in Renaissance Drama* 34 (1995): 15–40.

Dunn, K. "'Action, Passion, Motion': The Gestural Politics of Counsel in *The Spanish Tragedy.*" *Renaissance Drama* 31 (2002): 27–60.

Edwards, P. "The Theme and Structure of *The Spanish Tragedy.*" In *Shakespeare's Contemporaries.* Ed. N. Rabkin and M. Bluestone. Englewood Cliffs, N.J.: Prentice-Hall, 1961.

————. "'Thrusting Elysium into Hell': The Originality of *The Spanish Tragedy.*" In *The Elizabethan Theatre XI.* Ed. A. L. Magnusson and C. E. McGee (117–32). Port Credit, Ont.: P. D. Meany, 1985.

Empson, W. *Essays on Renaissance Literature.* Vol. 2. Ed. J. Haffenden. New York: Cambridge University Press, 1994.

Erne, L. "'Enter the Ghost of Andrea': Recovering Thomas Kyd's Two-Part Play." *English Literary Renaissance* 30 (2000): 339–72.

Feerick, J. "Groveling with Earth in Kyd and Shakespeare's Historical Tragedies." In *The Indistinct Human in Renaissance Literature.* Ed. Jean Feerick and Vin Nardizzi (231–52). New York: Palgrave Macmillan, 2012.

Garrido, C. Z. "Rhetoric and Truth in *The Spanish Tragedy.*" *The Sederi Yearbook* 12 (2001): 341–48.

Griffin, E. "Ethos, Empire, and the Valiant Acts of Thomas Kyd's Tragedy of 'the Spains'" *English Literary Renaissance* 31 (2001): 192–229.

Hadfield, A. "A Handkerchief Dipped in Blood in *The Spanish Tragedy*: An Anti-Catholic Reference?" *Notes and Queries* 46 (1999): 197–98.

———. "*The Spanish Tragedy*, the Alencon Marriage Plans, and John Stubbs's *Discoverie of a Gaping Gulf.*" *Notes and Queries* 245 (2000): 42–43.

———. "The Ur-Hamlet and the Fable of the Kid." *Notes and Queries* 53 (2006): 46–47.

Hallett, C. A., and E. S. Hallett. *The Revenger's Madness: A Study of Revenge Tragedy Motifs.* Lincoln: University of Nebraska Press, 1980.

• Hamilton, D. B. "*The Spanish Tragedy*: A Speaking Picture." *English Literary History* 4 (1974): 203–17.

Hammersmith, J. P. "The Death of Castile in *The Spanish Tragedy.*" *Renaissance Drama* 16 (1985): 1–16.

Happé, Peter. *English Drama before Shakespeare.* London: Longman, 1999.

Hartley, A. J. "Social Consciousness: Spaces for Characters in *The Spanish Tragedy.*" *CahiersE* 58 (2000): 1–14.

• Hattaway, Michael. *Elizabethan Popular Tragedy: Plays in Performance.* London: Routledge, 1982.

Hill, E. D. "Senecan and Vergilian Perspectives in *The Spanish Tragedy.*" *English Literary Renaissance* 15 (1985): 143–65.

Hillman, Richard. "Botching the Soliloquies in *The Spanish Tragedy.*" *Elizabethan Theatre* 15 (2002): 111–29.

Hopkins, L. "What's Hercules to Hamlet? The Emblematic Garden in *The Spanish Tragedy* and *Hamlet.*" *Hamlot Studies* 22 (1999): 114–43.

Horwich, R. "The Settings of *The Spanish Tragedy*'" *CEA Citic* 49. 2–4 (1987): 33–36.

• Hunter, G. K. "Ironies of Justice in *The Spanish Tragedy*'" *Renaissance Drama* 8 (1965): 89–104.

———. "Tacitus and Kyd's *The Spanish Tragedy.*" *Notes and Queries* 245 (2000): 424–25.

• Hutson, L. *The Invention of Suspicion: Law and Mimesis in Shakespeare and Renaissance Drama.* Oxford: Oxford University Press, 2007.

Jensen, E. J. "Kyd's *Spanish Tragedy*: The Play Explains Itself." *Journal of English and Germanic Philology* 64 (1965): 7–16.

Johnson, S. F. "*The Spanish Tragedy* or Babylon Revisited." In *Essays on Shakespeare and Elizabethan Drama. In Honour of Hardin Craig.* Ed. Richard Hosley (23–36). London: Routledge, 1962.

Joseph, B. L. "*The Spanish Tragedy* and *Hamlet*: Two Exercises in English Seneca." In *Classical Drama and Its Influence: Essays Presented to H. D. F. Kitto.* Ed. M. J. Anderson (121–34). London: Methuen, 1965.

Justice, S. "Spain, Tragedy, and *The Spanish Tragedy.*" *Studies in English Literature* 25 (1985): 271–88.

Kay, C. M. "Deception through Words: A Reading of *The Spanish Tragedy.*" *Studies in Philology* 74 (1977): 20–38.

Kerrigan, J. "Hieronimo, Hamlet and Remembrance." *Essays In Criticism* 31.2 (1981): 105–26.

———. *Revenge Tragedy: Aeschylus to Armageddon.* Oxford: Clarendon Press, 1996.

Kiefer, F. "Creating a Christian Revenger: *The Spanish Tragedy* and Its Progeny vs. *Hamlet.*" *Shakespeare Yearbook* 13 (2002): 159–80.

Kistner, A. L., and M. M. Kistner. "The Senecan Background of Despair in *The Spanish Tragedy* and *Titus Andronicus.*" *Shakespeare Studies* 7 (1974): 1–9.

Kline, Daniel. "The Circulation of the Letter in *The Spanish Tragedy.*" In *Tudor Drama before Shakespeare, 1485–1590.* Ed. Frank Kermode et al. 2004. New York: Palgrave.

Knutson, R. L. "Influence of the Repertory System on the Revival and Revision of *The Spanish Tragedy* and *Doctor Faustus*." *English Literary Renaissance* 18 (1988): 257–74.

Kohler, R. C. "Kyd's Ordered Spectacle." *Medieval and Renaissance Drama in English* 3 (1987): 27–49.

Laird, D. "Hieronimo's Dilemma." *Studies in Philology* 62 (1965): 137–46.

Maus, K. E. "*The Spanish Tragedy*, or, The Machiavel's Revenge." In *Revenge Tragedy: Contemporary Critical Essays*. Ed./S. Simkin (88–106). Basingstoke: Palgrave, 2001.

Mazzio, C. "Staging the Vernacular: Language and Nation in Thomas Kyd's *The Spanish Tragedy*." *Studies in English Literature* 38 (1993): 207–32.

• McAlindon, T. "*The Spanish Tragedy*" in *English Renaissance Tragedy*. Basingstoke: Macmillan, 1986.

McMillin, S. "The Book of Seneca in *The Spanish Tragedy*." *Studies in English Literature* 14.2: (1974): 201–08.

———. "The Figure of Silence in *The Spanish Tragedy*." *English Literary History* 39 (1972): 27–48.

Merriam, T. "Possible Light on a Kyd Canon." *Notes and Queries* 42 (1995): 340–41.

Muller, W. G. "Dissimulation as a Theme and Rhetorical Device in Kyd's *Spanish Tragedy*." *Arbeiten aus Anglistik und Amerikanistik* 10 (1985): 21–41.

• Mulryne, J. R. "Nationality and Language in Thomas Kyd's *The Spanish Tragedy*." In *Travel and Drama in Shakespeare's Time*. Ed. J.-P. Maquerlot and M. Williams (87–105). Cambridge: Cambridge University Press, 1996.

Murray, P. B. *Thomas Kyd*. New York: Twayne, 1969.

Neill, M. "English Revenge Tragedy." In *A Companion to Tragedy*. Ed. Rebecca Bushnell (328–50). London: Blackwell, 2005.

———. *Issues of Death: Mortality and Identity in English Renaissance Tragedy*. Oxford: Clarendon Press, 1997.

Owens, R. "Parody and *The Spanish Tragedy*." *Cahiers Elisabéthains* 71 (2007): 27–36.

Rist, T. "Memorial Revenge and the Reformation(s): Kyd's *The Spanish Tragedy*." *Cahiers Elisabéthains* 71 (2007): 15–25.

Sacks, P. "Where Words Prevail Not: Grief, Revenge, and Language in Kyd and Shakespeare." *English Literary History* 49 (1982): 576–601

Salkeld, D. "Kyd's Absalon." *Notes and Queries* 40 (1993): 177.

———. "Kyd and the Courtesan." *Notes and Queries* 245 (2000): 43–47.

Semenza, G. M. C. "*The Spanish Tragedy* and Metatheatre." In *English Renaissance Tragedy*. Ed. Emma Smith and Garrett Sullivan (153–59). Cambridge: Cambridge University Press, 2010.

———. "*The Spanish Tragedy* and Revenge." In *Early Modern English Drama: A Critical Companion*. Ed. G. A. Sullivan, P. Cheney, and A. Hadfield (50–60). New York: Oxford University Press, 2006.

Shapiro, J. "'Tragedies Naturally Performed': Kyd's Representation of Violence, *The Spanish Tragedy* (c.1587)." In *Staging the Renaissance: Reinterpretations of Elizabethan and Jacobean Drama*. Ed. D. Kastan and P. Stallybrass (99–113). New York: Routledge, 1991.

Siemon, J. R. "Sporting Kyd." *English Literary Renaissance* 24 (1994): 553–83.

Smith, E. "Author Versus Character in Early Modern Dramatic Authorship: The Example of Thomas Kyd and *The Spanish Tragedy*." *Medieval and Renaissance Drama in English* 11 (1999): 129–42.

Smith, E., ed. *The Spanish Tragedie*. London: Penguin, 1998.

• Smith, M. "The Theater and the Scaffold: Death as Spectacle in *The Spanish Tragedy*.'" *Studies in English Literature* 32 (1992): 217–32.

• Sofer, A. "Absorbing Interests: Kyd's Bloody Handkerchief as Political Palimpsest." *Comparative Drama* 34 (2000): 127–54.

Stevenson, W. *Shakespeare's Additions to Thomas Kyd's The Spanish Tragedy: A Fresh Look at the Evidence Regarding the 1602 Additions.* New York: Edwin Mellen Press, 2008.

Stockholder, K. "'Yet Can He Write': Reading the Silences in *The Spanish Tragedy.*" *American-Imago* 47 (1990): 93–124.

Watson, R. N. *The Rest Is Silence: Death as Annihilation in the English Renaissance.* (55–73). Berkeley: University of California Press, 1994.

Whigham, F. *Seizures of the Will in Early Modern English Drama.* (22–63). Cambridge: Cambridge University Press, 1996.

Wineke, D. "Hieronimo's Garden and 'the Fall of Babylon': Culture and Anarchy in *The Spanish Tragedy.*" In *Aeolian Harps: Essays in Literature in Honor of Maurice Browning Cramer.* Ed. D. G. Fricke and D. C. Fricke (65–79). Bowling Green, Ohio: Bowling Green University Press, 1976.

Woodbridge, Linda. *English Revenge Drama.* Cambridge: Cambridge University Press, 2010.

Zitner, P. "*The Spanish Tragedy* and the Language of Performance." In *The Elizabethan Theatre XI.* Ed. A. L. Magnusson and C. E. McGee (75–94). Port Credit, Ont.: P. D. Meany, 1985.